COGNITIVE PSYCHOPHYSIOLOGY:

Event-Related Potentials and the Study of Cognition

The Carmel Conferences
Volume I

COGNITIVE PSYCHOPHYSIOLOGY:

Event-Related Potentials and the Study of Cognition

The Carmel Conferences
Volume I

Edited by

Emanuel Donchin
*University of Illinois
at Urbana-Champaign*

LEA LAWRENCE ERLBAUM ASSOCIATES, PUBLISHERS

1984   Hillsdale, New Jersey   London

Lawrence Erlbaum Associates, Inc., Publishers
365 Broadway
Hillsdale, New Jersey 07642

Library of Congress Cataloging in Publication Data
Main entry under title:

Cognitive psychophysiology.

   Consists of the rev. and updated proceedings of a
workshop entitled: Event-related brain potentials as
tools in the study of cognitive function, held in
Carmel, Calif., Jan 9-13, 1979, and sponsored by the
Alfred P. Sloan Foundation.
   Includes bibliographies and index.
   1. Cognition—Physiological aspects—Congresses.
2. Evoked potentials (Electrophysiology)—Congresses.
3. Neuropsychology—Congresses. I. Donchin, Emanuel.
II. Alfred P. Sloan Foundation. III. Title: Event-related
brain potentials as tools in the study of cognitive
function. [DNLM: 1. Attention—physiology—congresses.
2. Evoked Potentials—congresses. 3. Mental Processes—
physiology—congresses. WL 102 C676]
BF311.C55193   1984   153   84-8155
ISBN 0-89859-150-3

Printed in the United States of America
10 9 8 7 6 5 4 3 2 1

Contents

Preface

Carmel, as is well known, is a lovely community nestled along the stunning Pacific shore and offering the amenities of a very classy, but tasteful, resort. Yet it is sufficiently isolated to assure that conferees spend much time together. It was for these reasons that Carmel was selected in 1979 as the site for a series of conferences sponsored by the Alfred P. Sloan Foundation. The series was supported within the framework of Sloan's Cognitive Science program. The conferences were designed to examine in detail the assertion that the endogenous components of the Event-Related Brain Potential (ERP) can serve as a tool in the analysis of cognition.

To this effect six annual workshops were convened, five in Carmel and the sixth at the Rockefeller Foundation's Center in Bellagio. Each of the workshops brought together about a dozen Cognitive Psychophysiologists and a dozen investigators from another discipline. For a week the participants examined critically the concepts, methods, and findings of each other's discipline. All through the meetings, the analyses focused on the degree to which ERP data indeed augment the insights into Human Information Processing that can be gained by more traditional methods. The limits of the ERP techniques were explored and the theoretical implications of the work were examined critically.

The format remained the same throughout the series. The workshop began with a series of Tutorials designed to give the participants a quick overview of the state of the art as seen by practitioners of the other discipline. This was followed by two days in which the participants met in small groups. Each of these panels received a detailed charge addressing a specific segment of the workshop's topic. The panels conducted very intense discussions, leading in each case to an extended response to the charge. The response was given by the panel members during a session in which the panel reported to a plenary session of the workshop. The Charge to the Panels for the workshop whose proceedings are reported here follows this Preface (see p. xvii).

The Tutorials and the panel reports presented at the first Carmel meeting serve as the basis for this volume. The entire proceedings were recorded, transcribed, and subsequently edited and revised by the participants. For the first workshop, we convened with the Cognitive Psychophysiologists a diverse group of Cognitive Psychologists. The intent was to examine on a rather broad front the claims of Cognitive Psychophysiology to a niche in the domain of Cognitive Science. Subsequent meetings were more focused, taking on such topics as Psycholinguistics, Aging, Engineering Psychology, and the development of animal models that would allow a study of the neurophysiological bases of the ERP.

It has taken too long to bring this book to the press. In the years since the first Carmel Conference, Cognitive Psychophysiology has been a fast-moving discipline. I feel, nevertheless, that these proceedings remain of interest for two reasons. First, the material has undergone considerable revision since the original meeting. Many of the participants have added extensively to their remarks. More important, to my mind, is the special character of the record. It provides a reader with a unique opportunity to examine the interaction between investigators with different disciplinary backgrounds as they approach a common problem. The material presented in this volume may provide Cognitive Psychophysiologists with an understanding of the issues they must face if they wish to have their results accepted by students of Human Information Processing. It is also possible that traditional Experimental Psychologists will gain from this volume an understanding of the nature and purpose of Psychophysiology and its potential contribution to their discipline. This record derives additional value from the fact that it provides an interesting snapshot of the status of ERP research just as it was venturing assertively into Cognitive Science. I submit that even though much new data has been accumulated and considerably deeper understanding achieved over the last six years, issues with which we are still concerned received an early formulation in Carmel I. It is in this spirit that the present volume, and the succeeding volumes in this series, are offered.

The success of the Carmel Conferences owes much to many. Dr. Kenneth Klivington, who was the program manager for Cognitive Science at the Sloan Foundation, was a constant source of support and encouragement. The Foundation's very liberal provision for these workshops was critical to their success. Additional support came from the various grants and contracts that maintain the Cognitive Psychophysiology Laboratory at the

University of Illinois—especially the funding provided by AFOSR contract #F49620-79-C-0233, monitored by Dr. Al Fregley. While these contracts did not provide any direct support for the conferences, the viability of the CPL provided the crucial substrate for the organization of the workshops. My former secretary, Mrs. Diana Mitchell Gammon, was responsible for organizing the conference and recording the sessions. Kim Mitchell, and then Ruby Zimmerman, transcribed the material. It took long enough to get this book to print that Barbara Hartman, who took over from Diana, had a hand in this volume. Many thanks are also due to the staff at the La Playa Hotel in Carmel, and particularly to Christine Barrett, for being such impeccable hosts.

Emanuel Donchin
Cognitive Psychophysiology Laboratory
Department of Psychology
University of Illinois
*   at Urbana-Champaign*

Participants

Dr. Truett Allison, Neuropsychology Research Lab, Veterans Administration Hospital, West Haven, CT 06516

Dr. Enoch Callaway, Langley Porter Neuropsychiatric Institute, 401 Parnassus Avenue, San Francisco, CA 94123

Dr. William G. Chase*, Psychology Department, Carnegie-Mellon University, Pittsburgh, PA 15213

Dr. Lynn Cooper, University of Pittsburgh, LRDC, Pittsburgh, PA 15261

Dr. Judith M. Ford, Veterans Administration Hospital, 3801 Miranda Avenue, Palo Alto, CA 94304

Dr. M. Russell Harter, Department of Psychology, University of North Carolina, Greensboro, NC 27412

Dr. Steven Hillyard, Department of Neurosciences, University of California–San Diego, La Jolla, CA 92037

Dr. Daniel Kahneman, Psychology Department, University of British Columbia, Vancouver 8, BC, Canada

---

*deceased

Dr. J.A. Scott Kelso, Haskins Laboratories, 270 Crown Street, New Haven, CT 06511

Dr. Marta Kutas, Department of Neurosciences, University of California–San Diego, Scripps Institution of Oceanography, La Jolla, CA 92093

Dr. Gregory McCarthy, Neuropsychology Research Lab, Veterans Administration Hospital, West Haven, CT 06516

Dr. Donald A. Norman, Psychology Department, University of California–San Diego, La Jolla, CA 92093

Dr. Marlene Oscar-Berman, Psychiatry Service, Boston Veterans Administration Hospital, 150 S. Huntington Avenue, Boston, MA 02130

Dr. Stephen Palmer, Psychology Department, University of California, Berkeley, CA 94720

Dr. Terry Picton, Ottawa General Hospital, 501 Smythe, Ottawa, Ontario, Canada K1H 8L6

Dr. Michael Posner, Psychology Department, College of Arts & Sciences, University of Oregon, Eugene, OR 97403

Dr. David Martin Regan, Psychology Department, Dalhousie University, Halifax, NS, Canada

Dr. Walter Ritter, Department of Neuroscience, Albert Einstein College of Medicine, Bronx, NY 10468

Dr. Roger W. Schvaneveldt, Psychology Department, New Mexico State University, Las Cruces, NM 88003

Dr. Richard Shiffrin, Psychology Department, Indiana University, Bloomington, IN 47401

Dr. Kenneth Squires, Nicolet Instrument Corporation, Biomedical Division, 5225 Verona Road, Madison, WI 53711

Dr. Nancy Squires, Psychology Department, SUNY–Stony Brook, Stony Brook, NY 11790

Dr. Anne Treisman, Psychology Department, University of British Columbia, Vancouver 8, BC, Canada

Dr. Eran Zaidel, Psychology Department, University of California, Los Angeles, CA 90024

Event-Related Brain Potentials as Tools in the Study of Cognitive Function

La Playa Hotel, Carmel, California

CHARGE TO PANELS

To facilitate our ability to deal with the vast area we are taking on in this workshop, the participants will be divided into six panels. Each panel is assigned a topic. The topics represent different aspects of cognitive science to which ERP methods have been applied.

Each panel will be asked to prepare a report to be presented during the last two days of the workshop on the area it has been assigned. Three hours will be assigned to each panel during these last two days. This period should suffice for a presentation by the panel members of their principal findings as well as for a discussion of the area within the framework of the panel's report by the entire conference. One hopes, therefore, that the reports by the panels would be both constructive and provocative.

Each panel is free to choose the format it will use to present its findings to the group. A series of presentations by all members, a unified presentation by one member, or some other format are all acceptable (barring, I think, chanting the report in unison).

The panels will have one full day at the meeting to address their task. This is both ample and insufficient. It will be best if the panels begin working sooner. I have found on previous occasions that panels like this work best if the members have corresponded on the issues prior to the meeting. To get things underway, I have indicated a designated chairman for each panel. These chairmen will, I hope, initiate the correspondence as well as act, during the panel's discussions and presentations, in a chairmanly fashion.

The following is an attempt to identify the questions to which it seems the panels should respond. This is very tentatively proposed and the participants can, and should, take the discussion in any direction they find appropriate.

1. What are the specific empirical claims currently made concerning ERPs which appear relevant to the area under discussion?
2. Which experimental paradigms have been used by ERP researchers? What is the apparent quality of the data? Are there serious methodological problems? Which claims can be temporarily accepted and which are unconvincing?
3. Assuming a valid data base, which aspects of it are relevant to the cognitive problems in the panel's charge? Are there specific issues of importance to the cognitive scientist which are now unresolved and to the resolution of which the ERP data may contribute?
4. What further work would be necessary before such a contribution might be generally accepted? That is, for those issues for which ERP data may be relevant, what are the insufficiencies of the data and what additional work may be needed?

5. Are there any issues in cognitive science to which ERP data may be relevant but which are currently ignored? What implications does the answer to this question have for the direction of ERP research?

6. Are there any paradigms in cognitive science which are not in current use in ERP research which might be helpful in the attempts to understand the functional significance of the ERP? Are there any models, theories, concepts, etc. in cognitive science which may have a similar impact on ERP research?

7. Are there concepts, paradigms or prevailing opinions in cognitive science which are inconsistent with data or concepts developed on the basis of ERP studies?

8. What are the problems of greatest concern to the cognitive scientist to which the ERP investigator should attend? Conversely, what, if anything, have ERP investigators developed to which the cognitive scientist ought to attend?

Many similar topics can be raised but I think the above should provide the flavor of the panels' assignments. I would expect each panel to review the existing data, the current experimental techniques, and the underlying conceptual models. Its conclusions should be in the form of a critical analysis of the available data and the associated methodology, coupled with specific research recommendations.

The panels are as follows:

I. *Selective Attention*
   Harter, Hillyard, Posner, Treisman

II. *Decision and Memory Processes*
   Donchin, Ford, Kahneman, Norman, Picton

III. *Preparatory Processes*
   Kelso, Kutas, Ritter, Shiffrin

IV. *Mental Chronometry*
   Chase, McCarthy, Schvaneveldt, K. Squires

V. *Perceptual Processes*
   Allison, Cooper, Palmer, Regan

VI. *Individual Differences & Neuropsychology*
   Callaway, Oscar-Berman, N. Squires, Zaidel

COGNITIVE PSYCHOPHYSIOLOGY:

Event-Related Potentials and the Study of Cognition

The Carmel Conferences
Volume I

1 Recording and Interpreting Event-Related Potentials

Truett Allison
West Haven V.A. Hospital

1.1 PHRENOLOGY AND ELECTROPHRENOLOGY: IT TAKES A LOT OF GALL TO RECORD EVENT-RELATED POTENTIALS

I was asked to explain how one records brain electrical activity through the scalp and how one interprets the data.

To place things in historical perspective, I would point out that the recording of the electrical activity of the brain is similar in principle to the phrenologists' endeavor, "bumpologists," as they were called by the English caricaturists (Fig. 1.1). The bumpologists had a perfectly sound idea. They believed that there is localization of function in the brain. In the late 1700s and early 1800s this was a radical notion. Gall and his followers tried to convince everybody that there were mental faculties that could be studied objectively (Gall, 1810). The original bumpologists assumed that they could assess two features of mental faculties by these objective measures: the location of bumps and the height of the bumps. That is exactly what we do when we measure electrical bumps; we call it the *location* (or topography) and *amplitude* of the bump. We make the same assumptions that the phrenologists made: The bigger the bump, the more of this activity or function or mental faculty is occurring. Thus, in Fig. 1.2, the bumpologist on the right has concluded that bumps "No. 3 and 4 are very clear." (These are the very words an audiologist might use when discussing the Jewett bumps, as the records of brainstem activity are familiarly called.) For the phrenologist in Fig. 1.2, bumps No. 3 and 4 refer to influence and conceit and are slight parodies of the mental faculties that Gall and Spurtzheim worked out. Of course we don't use terms like those any more. We call Jewett's bumps 3 and 4 "activity in the superior olivary complex" and "activity in the

1

FIG. 1.1 "Bumpology." George Cruikshank, 1826. The legend reads, "Pores o'er the Cranial map with learned eyes/Eash rising hill and bumpy knoll descries/Here secret fires, and there deep mines of sense/His touch detects beneath each prominence." (Historical Library, Yale Medical Library.)

lateral lemniscus," respectively. For other bumps we use terms such as "activity in area 2 of somatosensory cortex," "association cortex responses," "readiness potentials," "expectancy waves," "readout from memory," and other equally rigorous and well-defined terms.

The original bumpologists were very interested in practical applications. These gentlemen in Fig. 1.2 are being considered for a job in the British Admiralty. The mental attribute that is desired in this case is bump No. 10, reflecting pride with ignorance. The candidate on the right will clearly win the contest. The bumpologists might have actually gotten somewhere with this scheme, because there was a grain of truth in their assumptions. But they should have stayed in the lab and tried to work out these correlations systematically. Instead they (Spurtzheim, in particular) went on the lecture circuit and discussed their ideas instead of working on them.

It is easy to poke fun at the original bumpologists, and one can therefore talk about ourselves as modern bumpologists in a rather deprecating fashion, but in fact I don't think we have to be embarrassed about it. Phrenology was based on the sound idea that there is localization of function in the brain that can be measured in some sort of objective manner: in their case by measuring physical bumps on the head; in our case by measuring electrical bumps. What, I hope, will give us a better future than the phrenologists is the commitment to data and to the scientific method that phrenology lacked.

1.2 ELECTROGENESIS: A BRIEF SUMMARY

1.2.1 Summation of Action Potentials

So now let's talk about measuring electrical bumps. The first question is, how many different kinds of electrical bumps can we record? The answer is, only two (excluding for the moment a possible third type of potential to be discussed later). We can record action potentials or we can record graded synaptic potentials. And the graded potentials come in only two flavors, so far as we know: hyperpolarizing postsynaptic potentials (called IPSPs), which tend to have an inhibitory effect on cell firing; and depolarizing potentials, which tend to have an excitatory effect and are called EPSPs. So, there are only a few kinds of bumps that we shall be recording, assuming of course that the bump is generated by neurons in the nervous system and not by muscles, eyes, or other structures that also generate electrical potentials.

First, consider action potentials. In Fig. 1.3 assume we have an isolated nerve trunk in a recording chamber. Stimulate the nerve at the left and record

FIG. 1.2 "Prenological illustrations, or the Science practically developed, dedicated to the Commander in Chief, as a sure guide to appropriation!!" Lewis Marks, 1824. (Historical Library, Yale Medical Library.)

the compound action potential as it moves down the axons. At the time when the volley reaches the first electrode, we see the local depolarization of the axons and we record that as a negative potential with respect to a reference electrode at a distance. Current is flowing into the cell at this point and is flowing out of the axons on either side of the depolarized region. Here we record a positive potential, usually called a "source potential," to the local depolarizing negative "sink" potential in the middle. As the nerve volley moves down the nerve, we record a positive- negative-positive sequence as the volley moves toward, across, and beyond the recording electrode. This is the classic triphasic, positive-negative-positive spike potential. What happens if we place an electrode at the end of the nerve? Now the local depolarization never passes by the electrode; it approaches it but never reaches it. Instead we see only the positive source potential. Bishop (1932) described this effect many years ago. He actually crushed the end of a nerve and recorded from the inactive portion; he called this the "killed-end" effect. Even if the nerve is intact and you move the electrode away from the end of the nerve, you record a monophasic positive wave (Landau, 1967; Schlag, 1973). The point is that even in this simple case the same phenomenon, the action potential, appears as a negativity or as a positivity depending on the location of the recording electrode with respect to the nerve.

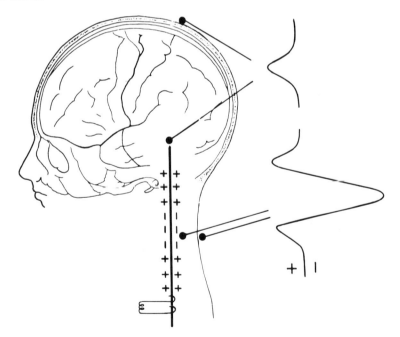

FIG. 1.3   Potentials recorded following stimulation of a peripheral nerve or fiber tract from electrodes at various locations.

Now let's put the nerve into the body in the manner shown in Fig. 1.3. In the neck we could call it the "dorsal column." A little further up, we call it the "medial lemniscus" in the case of the somatosensory system or the "lateral lemniscus" in the case of the auditory system. If we put an electrode on the neck and record the nerve volley moving up the spinal cord, we expect to see a triphasic potential, mainly negative, from a recording electrode placed at the back of the neck but a positivity from electrodes located rostral to the termination of that fiber tract, for example at the scalp. Schlag (1973) has discussed several examples of this effect. Thus, electrodes at the top of the head record ascending nerve volleys as positive potentials. This is exactly what is observed in actual recordings, seen in Fig. 1.4. We stimulate the median nerve and record from an electrode located on the collar bone, which overlies the nerve as it runs through the shoulder (top trace). We see a triphasic potential of the sort we discussed earlier. There is no doubt that it is a compound action potential in axons. You can track it up the arm, you can stimulate fast and it doesn't change, and so on. Now look at the middle trace. There is an upward deflection (preceding the deflection labelled P12) at approximately the same latency as the nerve volley shown in the top trace. This potential is the source positivity, recorded at the scalp, of the depolarizing nerve volley as recorded "locally" from the shoulder.

What happens once we reach the central nervous system? Let's put an electrode at the back of the neck and another one at the top of the head (middle trace). We see a sequence of three potentials that are labeled P12, P13, and P14. This nomenclature labels a bump by its polarity at the scalp (P meaning scalp positive; N meaning scalp negative) and the approximate peak latency in milliseconds (Donchin, Callaway, Cooper, Desmedt, Goff, Hillyard, & Sutton, 1977), so, for example, P12 will refer to a potential that in the normal young adult subject, under "typical" experimental conditions, has a latency of about 12 msec. The question arises, are these bumps compound action potentials that are generated in the spinal cord, or the medial lemniscus, or in any of the other fiber tracts that we know transmit somatosensory information into the brain? Well, they could be. One could assume that we have three different nerve volleys at slightly different latencies that all add together to produce what we see here—but not necessarily. We could be recording from cell bodies, as shown in Fig. 1.5. Forget for the moment that this is cerebral cortex and just consider that these are cell bodies anywhere, with a dendrite pointing upward. If we now depolarize the cell by excitatory synaptic action on the cell body, we record a negativity locally, and extracellular current will flow from the dendrite down into the cell body, just as it does into the depolarized region of a peripheral nerve. An electrode at or above the dendrite records a positive potential. The point here is that cell bodies and their processes act like axons. The way in which current flow is generated and the way in which it produces extracellular potentials is the same in both cases. In other words, we can make up a

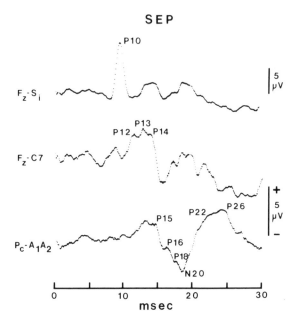

FIG. 1.4   Short-latency somatosensory evoked potentials recorded in human, to median nerve stimulation. Surface electrode derivations at left: Fz, midfrontal scalp; Si, shoulder ipsilateral to stimulated nerve; C7, spinous process of 7th cervical vertebra; Pc, parietal scalp contralateral to nerve stimulated; A1A2, linked ears. Scalp positivity (or non-scalp negativity) is displayed upward.

similar explanation for why we might be recording scalp positive potentials and local negative potentials if some of these early subcortical potentials that we can record are generated by cell bodies rather than by axons.

SHIFFRIN: I admit I don't know much about this, but I am lost already. I think I'd better get positive and negative straightened out. In the first figure, going down was negative. Positive went up, and now the polarities are reversed. Did I miss something?

ALLISON: No, you are very observant. Maybe we should take a minute with this. This will remain a problem, because some of us represent positivity by a downward deflection whereas others display positivity upward. That is one source of confusion. I have made relative positivity at the scalp upward in all of these figures. Now, in fact, potential P10 in Fig. 1.4 is partly a positivity at the scalp, for reasons we have already discussed, but it is mainly a negativity at the collar bone.

SHIFFRIN: What do you mean mainly? It is recorded in both places?

ALLISON: That's right, and that is the second source of confusion. We record between an electrode on the clavicle and a "reference" electrode, labeled Fz, that is placed on the forehead. The potential is scalp-positive and clavicle-negative, but mainly the latter.

I could just as easily say that a negativity at nonscalp leads is recorded upward, and I could call the nerve volley N10. But to be consistent across all channels of recording I say, for all of them, relative positivity at the scalp is recorded upward and is given a positive label. That doesn't necessarily mean the potential is seen primarily at Fz. In this case, it is seen primarily as a negativity at the clavicle. Most of these short-latency components are, in fact, recorded as positivities at the scalp *and* negativities from the neck. Now if I put the scalp and neck electrodes into a differential amplifier, the potentials will add. In none of these records is either electrode inactive. We are seeing these potentials at both of our recording electrodes, perhaps with greater amplitude at one than the other, but in none of these recordings do we have a so-called

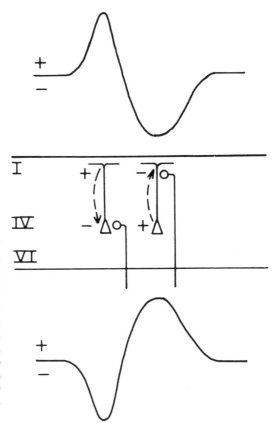

FIG. 1.5 A simplified model of electrogenesis of evoked potentials in cerebral cortex. Afferent fibers from the thalamus are shown terminating in layer IV on pyramidal cell bodies (left) and in more superficial layers on their dendrites (right). For illustrative purposes separate neurons are shown as generating the surface positive (left) and surface negative (right) potentials; most neurons probably generate both potentials sequentially.

"monopolar" or referential recording. So in this case it becomes a bit arbitrary as to whether we label the bump positive or negative.

To reiterate, the extracellular currents associated with activation of neurons produce simultaneously both negative and positive potentials, at different locations. Aside from the confusion this leads to in labeling a bump as N or P, this means that recording a bump as a positivity or negativity doesn't tell you anything unique about it, a point I perhaps didn't make explicit earlier.

SHIFFRIN: That N20 down in the bottom trace, is that a case where it is negative at the scalp?

ALLISON: That's right, that is a scalp negativity relative to a nonscalp lead, which in this case is the two ears linked together. This is confusing, no doubt about it. It is a matter of convention and different people use different conventions. It is just something you have to live with. Does that help?

SHIFFRIN: A little.

1.2.2 Summation of Synaptic Potentials

Dr. Shiffrin mentioned N20, and that brings us to somatosensory cortex, because N20 is the initial activation of cells in postcentral gyrus evoked by the afferent nerve volley. So now the question is, what are we seeing at the cortical level? Are we still seeing spike potentials generated either in axons or in cell bodies, or are we seeing that other variety of bump, the graded potential? Returning to Fig. 1.5, if we depolarize the cell body, we see a negativity in the lower part of the cortex and a positivity near or on the surface. The main generators of evoked potentials from cerebral cortex are the pyramidal cells, so called because the cell body has sort of a pyramidal shape. These cells send big dendrites up to layer I. So we have a vertical orientation of these cells, and if we depolarize the cell body, most of the extracellular current will be drawn from the big dendrite. So we record a negativity near the cell body and a positivity from an electrode placed on the surface of the cortex. Now, a little later there is a depolarization of the dendrite, either from direct synaptic activation of the dendrite, as illustrated in the right part of Fig. 1.5, or by electrotonic depolarization which moves up the dendrite from the cell body. Opinion differs as to which of these two mechanisms is more important, but for our purpose it doesn't matter. The point is that depolarization of the dendrite produces a surface negativity and a deep positivity, just the opposite of what happened when the cell body was depolarized. So far we have been talking about excitatory synaptic action on cells. If we reverse that and talk about inhibitory synaptic action—that is, *hyperpolarization* of the postsynaptic membrane—the situation is reversed, so that, for example, if we hyperpolarize the dendrite, we find a surface positivity and a deep negativity. Conversely, if we hyperpolarize the cell body, we obtain a deep positivity and a surface negativity.

So already we have a basic ambiguity; if we record a positivity from the scalp or cortical surface, we don't know whether we are dealing with a depolarization of cell bodies down in layers III and IV or a hyperpolarization of dendrites in the superficial layers of the cortex. The polarity of the bump gives no information whether you are recording neuronal excitation or inhibition.

We can be certain that we are dealing here with graded potentials and not with summated spike potentials. The evoked potential shown in Fig. 1.5 is the classical surface positive-negative response of primary sensory cortex that people have recorded for years. If you anesthetize an animal to the point where you eliminate spike potentials, the positive-negative potential is still present. So we know that in this case we are dealing primarily with graded potentials rather than with spike potentials. There are exceptions to this rule. For example, if I stimulate the thalamocortical fibers directly, I can record spikes generated by the cells. But if I stimulate peripherally, by the time the afferent volley reaches the cortex, the volley is asynchronous enough that what is recorded primarily is just graded potentials rather than summated spikes. Now if the earliest evoked potential in cortex is due to graded potential changes, certainly anything recorded later should also be due to graded potentials. So I think you can assume, in the absence of strong evidence to the contrary, that any medium- or long-latency evoked potential of the sort to be discussed in this meeting is due to graded potentials in the brain rather than summated spike potentials. Those of you who know the history of the EEG know that the same conclusion was reached for the EEG many years ago. If you recall, back in the early days of EEG recordings, Adrian and others suggested that perhaps the EEG represented summated spike potentials, but it became clear later that that was not the case; the EEG reflects graded potential changes (Brazier, 1964). The same generalization holds for evoked potentials, once you have reached the cortical level.

There is another point to be made from Fig. 1.5. In this example an electrode on the surface records a positive-negative sequence. If we now poke that electrode down through the cortex, we obtain a negative-positive sequence (Fig. 1.5, lower trace). We have what is called a *polarity inversion* from surface to depth. These cells are acting like a current dipole source, like a battery with positive and negative poles. So we see one polarity on one side of the battery and the other polarity on the other side. One implication of this is that if we find a polarity inversion between electrodes located at points A and B, we can infer that the potential is generated somewhere between A and B.

Furthermore, such a polarity inversion implies that the cell bodies whose activity we are recording are aligned in a fairly regular geometric fashion so that the extracellular current flow produced by each cell adds up to produce a measurable potential. The potential field we record is shown on the left side of

Fig. 1.6, which is redrawn from a paper by Lorente de No, who did some classical experimental and mathematical work on this problem some time ago (Lorente de No, 1947). Lorente de No called this an "open field" because, in principle, if you have a good enough preamplifier and the noise level is sufficiently low, you could record such dipole-like potentials any distance from the neurons as long as you stay in a conductive medium such as salt water or brain tissue. There are structures that produce a pretty good approximation to an open field. The cerebral cortex is one where the pyramidal cells are lined up. Their dendrites all point to the surface and they are all aligned similarly. Pyramidal cells in the hippocampus would be another example and the mitral cells in olfactory bulb still another. But, there are lots of places where that is not the case. Lorente de No asked, "What happens if we scramble up all these neurons and make their orientation random?" Well, it's very interesting. What happens is illustrated on the right side of Fig. 1.6. If we depolarize these cell bodies, all the source current flows inward from the periphery of this circle; there is no current flow and, therefore, no voltage outside this circle. So

NEURONAL ELECTROGENESIS

OPEN FIELD   CLOSED FIELD

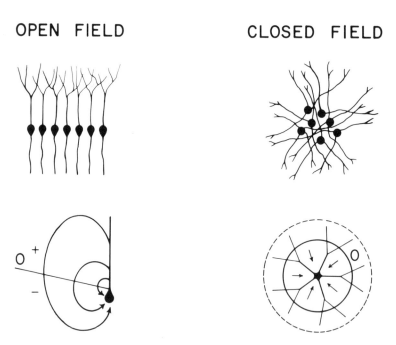

FIG. 1.6   Lorente de No's concept of potential fields produced by neurons aligned similarly, producing an "open" field; and aligned randomly, producing a "closed" field. Redrawn from Lorente de No (1947).

we have zero potential outside the circle and we only see a negative potential inside the circle. We no longer have a dipole field and no longer have a polarity inversion. This is a neurophysiological black hole, if you will, invisible from the outside, although we can study it if we place electrodes *inside* the field. Do closed fields really exist in the brain? Probably not. The orientation of neurons is never completely random, but there are situations that more or less approximate it. There are structures, for example in some of the cranial nerve nuclei studied by Lorente de No, in which we are not going to see a clearly defined open field, we are going to see something more complicated, something that may approximate a closed field. It is useful to bear this in mind, because it means that there may be structures in the brain that generate interesting activity that we shall never see in surface recordings because there is little current flow and hence an undetectably small potential field outside the structure.

1.2.3 Cephalic Seismology

The electrophysiologist's life is complicated. We have EPSPs and IPSPs and open and closed fields. Life is even more complicated when we record from humans, where we record these potentials from a volume conductor, the head, that is complex in shape. It is entertaining, perhaps even enlightening, to consider analogous problems in other scientific areas. So fantasize for a moment that you are a seismologist and your job is to locate earthquakes (Fig. 1.7). You place some electrodes at different locations on the surface of this sphere and record seismic activity. If you had electrodes in the right places, you could triangulate and localize the earthquake fairly accurately. For cephalic seismologists the task of localizing "brainquakes" is more difficult. First of all, the earth *is* a good approximation to a sphere. The head is a poor approximation to a sphere, but we usually assume, to facilitate analysis, that the top half of the head can be treated as a hemisphere.

In addition, if you are seeking the source of an earthquake, you are dealing with sound waves that travel at a finite rate of speed through the earth, so it is a fairly simple matter to determine the latency at different electrodes and locate the quake. Unfortunately, a brainquake will be recorded more or less simultaneously at all points on the surface, so it is not possible to use latencies to localize the disturbance.

There is still another problem. If the earth were a completely homogeneous sphere, that would make life a little simpler for seismologists because the sound waves would travel at a uniform rate of speed to any point on the earth. But that is not the case. As you know, the earth is built like an onion and when sound waves hit the different layers, they bounce off and are distorted in complicated ways (Fig. 1.7). Depending on the conductivity of the material, the waves can travel slower or faster, and so on. I don't know how much that

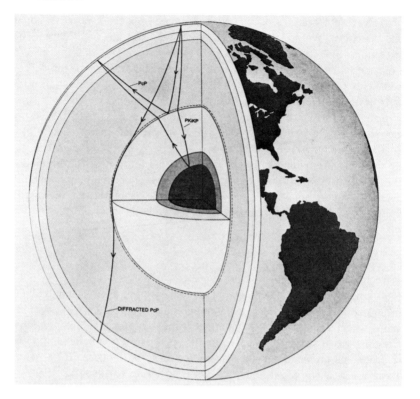

FIG. 1.7   Cross section of the earth and varieties of spontaneous seismic activity ("earth EEG"). (From "The Fine Structure of the Earth's Interior," B. Bolt. Copyright 1973 by Scientific American, Inc. All rights reserved.)

in fact complicates seismographic analyses, but the point is that we have the same problem in localizing brainquakes. The head is not homogenous. There is a layer of high-conductivity cerebrospinal fluid, then a layer of low conductivity, the skull; and finally another layer of high conductivity, the scalp. So, although earthquake localization may not be simple, I would argue that brainquake localization from surface recordings is even harder.

We can think of earthquakes as being analogous to the "spontaneous" EEG. (Of course, this is an egocentric way of looking at it. The EEG is not spontaneous, but we did not cause it ourselves or don't know what the cause is, so we say it is spontaneous.) One can also record evoked bumps (literally, since the unit of measurement is distance) from the earth (Fig. 1.8). In this case, stimulation in Nevada and recording in Montana produces physical bumps that are analogous to electrical bumps recorded from the head. Evoked earthquakes, like evoked brainquakes, are easier to interpret than their naturally occurring counterparts because they are elicited by a discrete stimulus at a known point in time and allow analysis of the fine detail of events occurring in the interior (cf. Bolt, 1973).

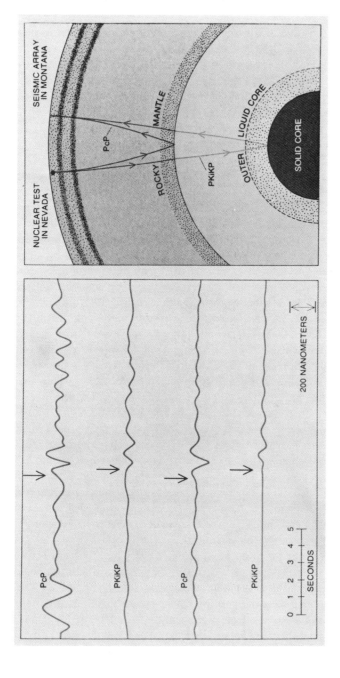

FIG. 1.8 Evoked seismic activity ("earth ERP") following an undergound nuclear explosion. (From "The Fine Structure of the Earth's Interior," B. Bolt. Copyright 1973 by Scientific American, Inc. All rights reserved.)

1.2.4 Comparison of Scalp and Intracranial Recordings

How can we assess the way in which these complicating layers get us into trouble when we try to analyze surface potentials? One way to get rid of the distortion introduced by these layers is to take them off and record directly from the interior. In our laboratory we have been doing this now for about six years (Allison, Goff, Williamson, & Vangilder, 1980), and others have done it also over the years. Figure 1.9 illustrates the recording situation. This is the pial surface of the right hemisphere of a patient who is severely epileptic. A localizable epileptic focus is being removed. We can record directly from the surface, without the overlying layers, and see how much difference it makes.

First let's assume that we are recording from the surface of a conductive medium. If we have a dipole source located a certain distance below that surface, we can, as shown in Fig. 1.10, calculate fairly readily what its potential distribution along the surface should be. The calculated value is the solid line. If we look at a real bump, does it look at all like what we might expect from theory? Well, in this particular case it does. This recording is from an array of electrodes on the postcentral gyrus (Fig. 1.9), and we're recording a particular somatosensory evoked potential that is scalp-negative and has a latency of about 80 msec. This is a locally generated potential of the hand area of somatosensory cortex. If we plot its amplitude distribution along the surface, the shape of the curve agrees pretty well with what we expect from theory. The region where the voltage drops off very rapidly as we move away from the maximum amplitude focus is called the "near field." This is a term introduced by Jewett and Williston (1971) and borrowed from electrical engineering terminology. It simply means that, close to a source, small differences in recording location make a great deal of difference in amplitude. But as we move away, we get out into a region in which the voltage is not dropping very fast; this region is called the "far field." This is a useful concept; where we are near a source, voltage is changing rapidly and away from the source it's not changing rapidly. So let's see what happens. If we record from C4, a scalp electrode that, if we could record simultaneously (we obviously can't; the scalp recording was made preoperatively), would overlie electrode 5 on the pial surface, we see a potential that is very similar in waveform but is smaller by a factor of about 40. In other words, as we move from the cortical surface up to the scalp, we are already out in the far field. Even going 15 to 17 mm from the cortical surface up to the scalp has put us way out in the far field where the potential is very small in relation to its maximum amplitude. So the point I want to make here is that although the concept of near field and far field is a very useful one, all the recordings we make from the scalp are, in effect, far field potentials. Here is a potential that is generated as close to the scalp as we are ever going to get; yet the potential is very small at the scalp compared to what it is at the surface. However, that's not a major problem. The more important question

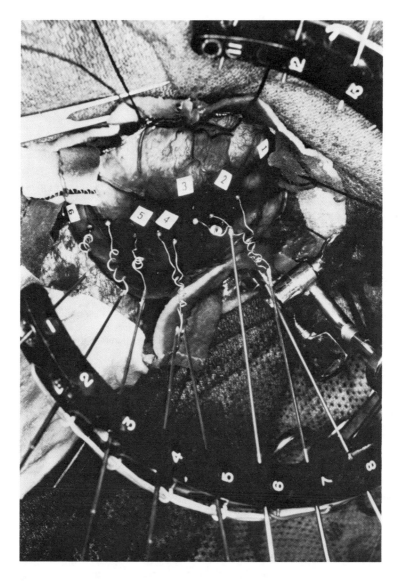

FIG. 1.9 Recording from the postcentral gyrus of a patient undergoing resection of epileptogenic tissue. Electrode 1 is near the midline of the right hemisphere, and electrode 8 is near the Sylvian fissure.

15

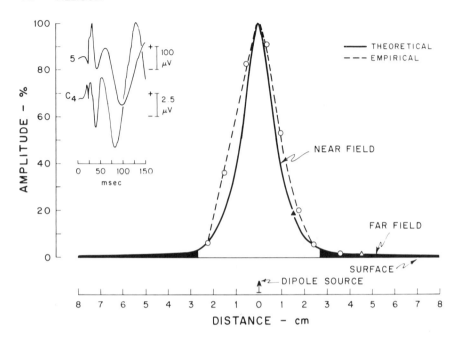

FIG. 1.10 Comparison of theoretical and empirical potential distributions along the surface of a plane under which a dipole current source is located. Location of cortical surface electrodes is shown in Fig. 9. Left median nerve stimuli.

is, "Do the scalp and the skull really distort the scalp-recorded-evoked potential compared to its intracranial counterpart?" People have often assumed that scalp recording is terrible because the skull and the scalp confuse things. That's not quite true. The waveforms here are very similar. The amplitude is much smaller in the scalp recording, but the waveform is quite similar, particularly if you allow me to assume that the latency increase in the cortical surface recording is due to the fact that the cortex has been exposed to the air for over an hour at this point and is a little cool. The patient is also sedated and that might also account for this latency shift. But the waveform is really quite similar. So we are doing a pretty good job at the scalp in recording potentials generated in cortex. Figure 1.11 gives another example. The scalp recording (P4) is a smaller version of the surface recording posterior to the central sulcus (location 2, surface), and anterior to the sulcus the scalp recording (Fz) is smaller in amplitude but similar to its cortical surface counterpart (location 1). So things aren't really distorted that much.

To digress for a moment, notice also that posterior to the central sulcus we record a negative-positive sequence, whereas anterior to the sulcus we record a positive-negative sequence. In other words, we have a polarity inversion across the central sulcus so we say: "ah ha, we have a dipole source." This is not necessarily so, but it is a reasonable assumption. In this case, we assume that because we have a polarity inversion from posterior to anterior, we have a tangential or "horizontal" dipole, and in this case it is reasonable to assume that it is located down in the posterior bank of the central sulcus, and is pointed anterior-posterior rather than up-down. Roger Broughton, who first discovered this effect, made that interpretation and I think he is essentially correct (Broughton, 1969). This means that we can place an array of electrodes on the central cortex, determine the polarity inversion, and thus locate motor cortex. The neurosurgeons can then avoid the motor area in making their excision.

Now let's look at another kind of evoked potential in which the concept of the near field and far field helps us understand what is going on. We have also been doing a lot of EEG recording from depth probes that are placed into the brain of epileptic patients to see whether they have a localizable, operable epileptogenic focus, and we take that opportunity to record evoked potentials. Let's look at the Jewett bumps at the scalp and at various locations along a depth probe; there is remarkably little difference (Fig. 1.12). The reason is

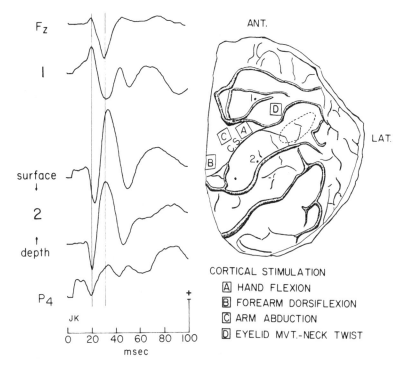

FIG. 1.11   Comparison of recordings from scalp and right hemisphere cortical surface. Extent of cortical excision shown by dashed line. Left median nerve stimuli. Isolatency lines at about 20 and 30 msec mark N20-P20 and P30-N30 polarity inversions. (From Allison et al., 1980).

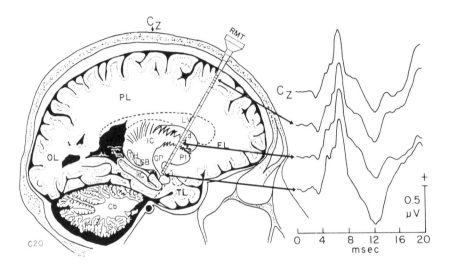

FIG. 1.12 Comparison of scalp (Cz) and intracranial recordings of brainstem auditory evoked potentials. Binaural click stimuli; reference electrode is linked ears.

that even though this probe is going down into the temporal lobe, it is still a fair distance away from the brainstem generators of these potentials. In other words, we are already out in the far field where differences in distance don't make much difference. So, in this case, we are no better off recording from inside the head than from the scalp. Of course, if we could place the recording electrode right into the brainstem and into the particular structures that generate these potentials, we could record very large evoked potentials. The point is that recording from inside the head, per se, doesn't necessarily help you. If you can get close to a focal source, then you will obtain an evoked potential that is much larger than what you can record from the scalp and is less noisy due to the absence of muscle activity. But to minimize the effect of this noise in scalp recordings all we have to do is a little more averaging to get our signal-to-noise ratio back to what it is in an intracranial recording. Archimedes said that, with a long enough lever and a place to stand, he could move the world. If you give me a long enough averaging time, I can record any time-locked activity generated anywhere in the brain. In other words the averaging technique is a temporal lever, and like Archimedes' spatial lever I can in principle make it as long as I want. When we do scalp recordings, we just have to average longer to get the desired signal-to-noise ratio.

What is more of a problem than amplitude attenuation in scalp recordings is the fact that scalp recordings are often said to "smear" the surface bump. That is true, as some straightforward calculations of the potential field generated by dipole sources show (Fig. 1.13). If we measure the potential along plane *a* of Fig. 1.13A (left), we obtain a nice sharp near field and a far field farther away

(Fig. 1.13A, right). If we now move the plane farther away from the source, to *b*, you see that we have a much broader amplitude distribution. (It is also much smaller; peak amplitudes are normalized). So we have smeared, or broadened, the topography of this potential by moving farther away from the source. Because the scalp always introduces an increased distance, we are always going to see this effect. In addition, the higher conductivity of the skull increases the smearing effect. So in scalp recordings we always find broader distributions, that is, poorer spatial resolution. But even that isn't too bad. In the case of a nice radial source that is oriented perpendicular to the cortical surface, we can still localize the source by the location of the peak amplitude. It is just that it is more broadly distributed around the peak. What is more of a problem is that if we now have two sources side by side, their potential fields become mixed up (Fig. 1.13B). If we record from plane *a* close to the sources, spatial resolution is quite good, and we can discriminate both sources. If we now move to plane *b*, we have pretty much lost our ability to discriminate the two spatially separate sources. So this is what people mean when they talk about spatial averaging of a scalp recording. It is simply that by getting your electrode away from the source of the potentials you will tend to see activities generated in different structures. This hurts when trying to localize sources, and it also hurts if functionally different neuronal activity is generated in nearby structures at about the same time. If the "pride" bump is too close to the

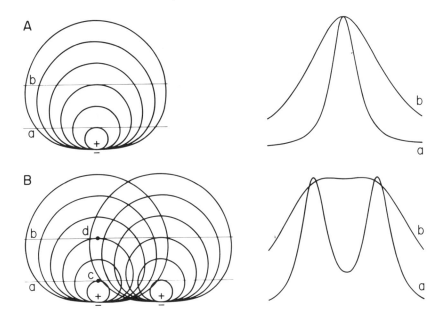

FIG. 1.13   Illustration of the effects of distance from dipole sources on spatial resolution (A) and spatial averaging (B). Negative sides of the potential fields are not shown.

"ignorance" bump, we are not able to separate the two by topographic record-ings. Some other method is required, for example varying pride while leaving ignorance constant.

To summarize, I hope I have convinced you, first, that the potentials gen-erated by neurons are, at the level of analysis we are concerned with, reason-ably well understood and, second, that scalp recordings—which nearly always are the only kind of recording available to the bumpologist interested in mental faculties—provide a reasonably good approximation to intracranial recordings, particularly if the bumps are not generated too close together in space or time. That is the end of the electrogenesis part of my sermon. I will now discuss the potentials we can record in this manner and see what kinds of conclusions have been reached about their origin.

1.3 THE ORIGINS OF ERP COMPONENTS

1.3.1 Somatosensory ERPs

Many bumps are raised when we deliver a sensory stimulus, so I necessarily have to oversimplify. I'll just give you a catalog of the bumps and the struc-tures that may generate them. When I say, "we," not only do I mean my par-ticular laboratory, but also what I take to be the consensus in the field. First the initial portion of the SEP (Fig. 1.14). P10 is the peripheral nerve volley. P12 is almost certainly generated in the cervical cord or perhaps in the dorsal roots. Bumps P13 and P14 may derive from the brainstem. It is not clear where P15 is coming from, but it may be generated at the level of either the medial lemniscus or the thalamus. P16 and P18 are probably generated in the thalamus, thalamocortical radiation fibers, or both. Vaughan and his group have obtained pretty recordings of these bumps in monkeys (Arezzo, Legatt, and Vaughan, 1979). They find that the potentials generated in the thalamus are quite small and are hard to pick up outside the thalamus, and so they use the standard explanation we reviewed, that cells in the thalamus are oriented more or less randomly and therefore generate more or less a closed field. And that may be true. It is difficult to see these bumps from the scalp or even in-side the head at any distance away from the thalamus. N20, P22, and P26 reflect initial activity in primary somatosensory cortex.

The next figure (Fig. 1.14) is out of date (the early subcortical bumps have become squashed together) but it doesn't matter. The point is that after the initial activation of somatosensory cortex numerous bumps appear on various parts of the head.

SHIFFRIN: Let me ask you a very simple question. If the afferent volley in the somatosensory system is recorded from the scalp as a positive potential, why don't you see a continuous positive potential because you have a potential

HUMAN SEP

RMN Stimulation

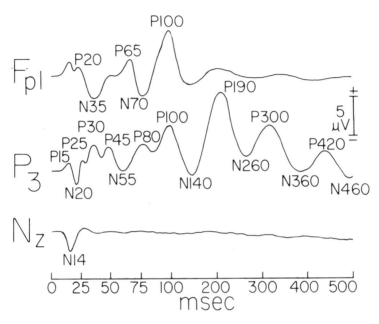

FIG. 1.14   Schematic summary of an SEP recorded from a young adult not performing a specific task. Components are not necessarily largest at the locations shown, and some are thought to be myogenic. Note nonlinear time base.

that is continuously moving from the peripheral nerve up to somatosensory cortex?

ALLISON: That's a very good question. I don't know. I have worried about that too. There has to be some sort of spatial discontinuity or temporal discontinuity in the conduction process. For example, when the peripheral nerve dives into the spinal cord at the level of the dorsal roots, the geometry must change in some way so that at that point we see a discrete bump. And at each synapse there is about a 1-msec gap that may produce a discontinuity and therefore a discrete bump. That is the best explanation I can offer, but in fact we see not a continuous slow potential but a series of discrete bumps.

NORMAN: Shiffrin's question makes sense only if you assume that the system is a wire that goes from the wrist up to the top of the scalp, therefore you wouldn't expect to see any peaks. However, I would assume that there is some sort of continual encoding or processing of the signal as it goes up. And in order to find some sort of transformation of the signal, you have to have other neurons that come into play. Each time you change the number of neurons, you are clearly going to change the distribution of activity.

ALLISON: That's fine. It is reasonable to expect a discontinuity everytime there is a synapse and whatever processing goes on, but it is a little harder to understand why, for example, in that long pathway from the median nerve up to the dorsal column nuclei there is no synapse, nevertheless we see discontinuous bumps.

DONCHIN: Well, you might have different latencies for different subpopulations of neurons.

ALLISON: Yes, you do. In the monkey the work of Vaughan's group indicates that two peaks are coming from the medial lemniscus (Arezzo et al., 1979), and there you could assume there are two populations of fibers with different conduction velocities. That presents no problem, but I am still not satisfied that I can give you an answer as to why things are seen as discretely as they seem to be.

All right, let me just go quickly through the sequence of longer-latency SEP components (Fig. 1.14). For N20, P25, P45, N55, P80, and the scalp-recorded portion of P100 the evidence suggests that all these potentials are generated in or near primary somatosensory cortex. Now we come to N140 and P190; these are the "vertex potentials." In the interests of time I don't want to talk about them. Suffice it to say that they continue to be very frustrating. This is now the fortieth anniversary of the discovery of vertex potentials by Pauline Davis (1939) and we still don't know where they are coming from. Vaughan and his colleagues think they are coming primarily from somatosensory cortex following a somatic stimulus; there is evidence pro and con. Picton and his associates think that they are coming from frontal association cortex following an auditory stimulus (Picton & Hillyard, 1974), and there is evidence pro and con there. In intracranial recordings we see activity in this latency range that sometimes seems to be a polarity-inverted version of the scalp-recorded potentials and sometimes not. If I had to guess at this point, I would say that the reason we can't localize the vertex potentials is because they are not localizable. I suspect there are several generators: partly in somatosensory cortex, partly subcortical, partly in association areas, and partly elsewhere. What we see at the top of the head, at the vertex where these things are largest, is some complex summation of all that activity. I suspect that about half the brain is lit up during the vertex potentials.

1.3.2 Auditory ERPs

Now let's talk about the auditory system (Fig. 1.15). In the first 10 msec after
an auditory stimulus there is the series of bumps discussed earlier, the *Jewett
bumps*. Here I am using the polarity/latency nomenclature; P2 through P9 are
the same as Jewett's waves I through VII. P2 is the auditory nerve volley, so
it is analogous to P10 in the somatosensory system; we are recording the peripheral nerve volley before it reaches the central nervous system. P3 is recorded from the cochlear nucleus, P4 from the superior olivary complex, P5 in or
near the lateral lemnisci (the plural because after the cochlear nucleus these
bumps tend to be generated bilaterally because of the decussation in the auditory system) and P6 in or near the inferior colliculi. After this we are on shaky
ground. The later bumps are not recorded well in cats, so we don't have the
data we have for the first five bumps. But what little clinical evidence there is
in man suggests—and it makes beautiful sense so I can't resist giving you the
story—that P7 reflects activity primarily from the medial geniculate nucleus and
P9 is the thalamocortical radiation volley. Now all this is probably too good to
be true. I don't think anybody wants to say that each of these waves, with the
exception of P2, is generated solely in the structure I named, but primarily it is
generated in or near those structures. These are all neurogenic components.

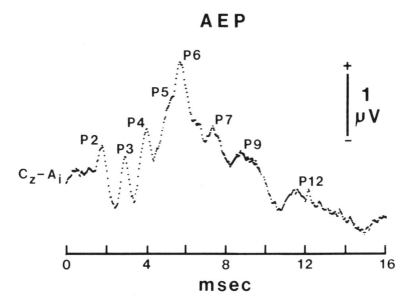

FIG. 1.15 Human brainstem auditory evoked potentials Ai, earlobe of stimulated ear.
Note submicrovolt amplitude of these potentials.

They are all generated by neurons inside the head. P12 may be myogenic, perhaps a recording of a muscle reflex of the middle ear.

Now, these are all scalp-positive potentials. In light of what we reviewed before, we may surmise they are scalp-positive source potentials of local depolarizing sinks. But are the sinks in fiber tracts or in cell bodies of nuclei in the auditory system? In light of the SEP results discussed earlier, one could assume they are primarily generated in the fiber tracts. Huang and Buchwald's (1977) single-unit data, on the other hand, suggest sources in cell bodies. I do not know how that is going to work out. One of the reasons I tend to favor the fiber tract notion is that the geometry of the fiber tracts is more coherent than for cell bodies. Take, for example, the case of the superior olivary complex, which really *is* a complex (Fig. 1.16). It is composed of several subnuclei whose morphology is very complicated. They receive input from the trapezoid

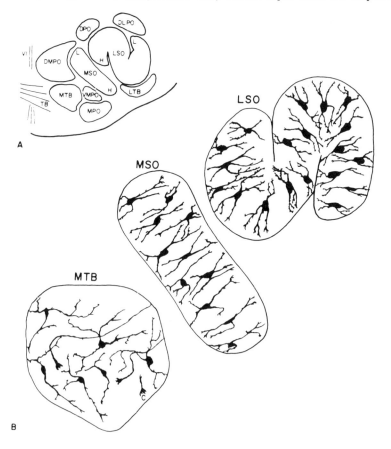

FIG. 1.16   Coronal schematic diagram of the superior olivary complex of the cat. Note complex orientation of neurons within and between the various cell groups. (From Harrison, 1978, with permission.)

body, which is a reasonably parallel set of fibers and might generate a good compound action potential. But once you reach the complex itself, who knows? How are you going to predict the potential field generated by these neurons? The medial nucleus (MSO) should produce an open field. The lateral nucleus (LSO) is complex in shape and might produce a complex potential field, while the nucleus at lower left (MTB) might produce a closed field. So I don't know how to predict whether we should expect P4 to be generated in cell bodies or in its afferent or efferent axons. We can't be dogmatic one way or the other. For clinical purposes it doesn't matter. Everybody is agreed that the source is in the lower pons and that is often a good enough localization for diagnostic purposes.

I'll quickly run through the later components of the auditory evoked potential (Fig. 1.17). Notice that time is on a log scale so we can spread apart the

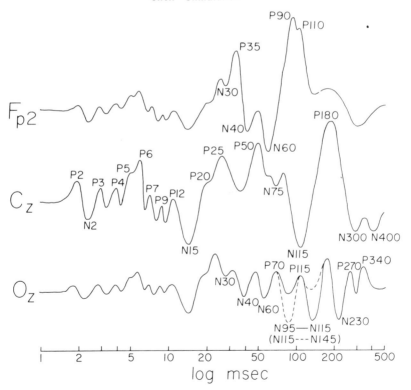

FIG. 1.17   Schematic summary of an AEP recorded from a young adult not performing a specific task. Components are not necessarily largest at the locations shown, and some are thought to be myogenic.

early components. N15 and P20 are myogenic potentials generated in the pos-tuaricular muscles behind the ear. We don't need to get into the problem of myogenic components. Suffice it to say that sensory stimuli can generate po-tentials in muscles around the head (the eye-blink reflex is the example you are probably most familiar with) that can combine with the neurogenic poten-tials in which we are interested. It is something one has to be aware of, but it is a manageable problem (Goff, Allison, & Vaughan, 1978). The P25, N40, and P80 components are probably generated in or around the auditory cortex in the temporal lobe. As far as the auditory vertex potentials are concerned, the same thing holds as for their somatosensory counterparts; various origins have been proposed. I suspect they are coming from a lot of different places and that is why we can't really localize them. But there is evidence that the auditory vertex potentials are generated at least partly in auditory cortex (Goff et al., 1978).

1.3.3 Visual Stimuli

The visual evoked potential generated by a flash is a complicated mess (Fig. 1.18). Suffice it to say that, of the neurogenic potentials that we can say any-thing about at all, most are probably generated primarily in striate or parastriate visual cortex. We can simplify this complex waveform a lot if, instead of blast-ing the retina with a flash of light, we move a pattern (say a checkerboard) across the retina. We now find a simpler waveform consisting primarily of a positivity (P100) at about 100 msec (Fig. 1.19). This potential is generated in visual cortex.

If you have been keeping score it will have struck you that, once we have reached the cortical level, all the potentials whose origin we can say much about are generated in or near the sensory cortex of the modality stimulated. For this conference, this is unfortunate. It would be helpful to say, "This bump is generated in parietal association cortex," because association cortex is presumably where some higher-level processing occurs and that is what we are interested in. Unfortunately, I don't think we can say that. That is not to say that those areas do not exist in man or that they don't generate evoked poten-tials. But if they do, for reasons unknown they don't generate large evoked potentials, or they are there and we just haven't been able to identify them properly. At any rate, there are no bumps that we can say definitely are gen-erated in some of the cortical areas in which a cognitive psychologist might be interested.

SHIFFRIN: By the way, are you defining components in the way Donchin, Ritter, and McCallum (1978) did in terms of controlled, observable variability? Especially for some of the smaller bumps, how do you define their presence? Do you use a different method?

HUMAN VEP
Flash Stimulation

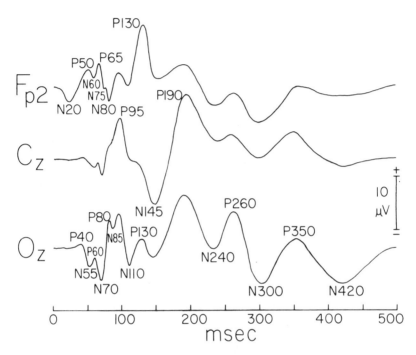

FIG. 1.18 Schematic summary of a typical VEP to unpatterned flashes recorded from a young adult subject not performing a specific task. Components are not necessarily largest at locations shown.

ALLISON: A bump by my definition is just a peak that is repeatable across averages and across subjects. That's all it is. This is the old-fashioned definition. I am not defining components in the way that Donchin et al. do. I mean they are real things in the sense that if you hook up anybody, you usually find them in that person. Whether the bump reflects a single neural event or mental faculty is an empirical question. Often it doesn't, and this is the issue Donchin et al. were addressing.

1.3.4 Endogenous Components

We now come to the potential of most interest to this group: P300, or the "stimulus evaluation" bump, to put it in terms of the phrenologists' mental faculties. This bump is located more or less over the parietal area or maybe

VEP

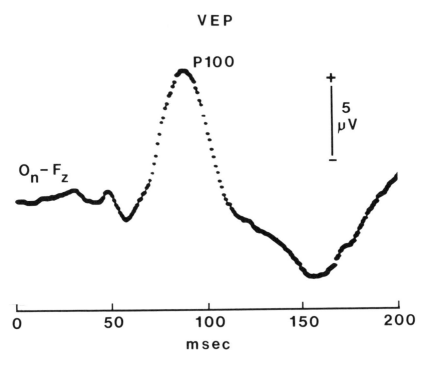

FIG. 1.19   Human visual evoked potential generated by 2/sec reversal of a checkerboard pattern in a normal adult fixating a point in the center of the pattern. On, occipital leads 01 and 02.

more frontally, depending on the task. Everybody has assumed, I think, that the location of these bumps means either that P300 is generated in the frontal or in the parietal association cortex. That may be true, but on the other hand it may not be. We have been doing a lot of intracranial recording of P300 using an oddball paradigm (Wood, Allison, Goff, Williamson, & Spencer, 1979). Figure 1.20 is an example. The solid tracings here are the responses to the frequent stimulus; the dotted lines are responses to the oddball stimulus. In scalp recordings, P300 is the late positive bump at about 400 msec. Looking down the central probes, beginning at locations in the frontal lobes and ending in the temporal lobes, we see very nice P300-like activity in the mid-probe area lateral to the thalamus. We never see a polarity inversion from surface to depth. What we see is a big positivity that certainly looks like P300 activity. The intracranial topography doesn't change whether auditory or somatosensory stimuli are used. Now, I don't want to argue that what we see at the scalp is all generated down in subcortical regions, although that may be. We can't say that on the basis of these data because of various limitations in the study. The point is that we cannot automatically assume that bumps related to mental activities—

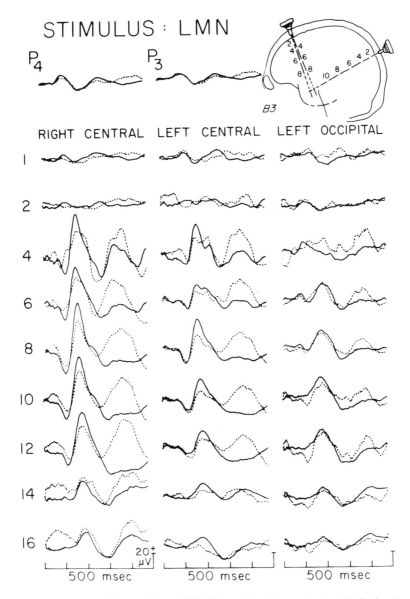

STIMULUS : LMN

FIG. 1.20   Intracranial recording of P300-like activity. Frequent and oddball stimuli are left median nerve shocks of slightly different intensity. (From Wood et al., 1979).

stimulus evaluation or task relevance or whatever label you want to put on it—
are generated in cerebral cortex. Maybe so; maybe not. There is no reason
why the thalamus, for example, can't generate these potentials.

Let me briefly discuss other slow potential shifts: CNVs, readiness potentials, and that sort of thing; these slow potentials that have interesting psychological correlates. In animal recordings (McSherry & Borda, 1973; Rowland &
Anderson, 1971), these slow potentials may show a polarity inversion from the
cortical surface to white matter. They may therefore be generated in cortex in
the way we have already discussed. In other studies, however, no polarity
inversion was seen as the electrode passed through the cortex (e.g. Ransom &
Goldring, 1973); a monophasic positive or negative potential was recorded,
usually in the deeper cortical layers. In this case, we have to invoke some kind
of closed field. Furthermore the situation is complicated by the fact that there
is now evidence that Somjen, Goldring, and others have summarized that
some of these slow potential shifts are actually generated in glial cells rather
than in neurons. One can make up an argument, as I have done here based on
Somjen (1973), to show why one can get polarity inversions from surface to
depth, even if these slow potentials are generated by glial cells (Fig. 1.21).
Furthermore, we don't know whether the slow potentials have anything to do
with information processing in the brain. Somjen, for example, thinks that the
glial cells are there to suck up excess extracellular potassium from nearby neurons that have fired a lot, and that is what glial depolarization reflects. If that
is the case, then there is no causal relationship between slow potential shifts
and anything we might be interested in. On the other hand, there might be a
good correlation; if glial depolarization is in effect a good measure of extracellular potassium, then we would have a measure of the integrated neuronal activity in that region, and if our electrode was in the right place, that activity
might be involved in the task that the subject was performing.

1.4 DISCUSSION

ZAIDEL: If I understand correctly what you have shown us here, you assume
that up to, say, 100 msec particular structures generate particular evoked potentials and we can tell where they are coming from. But after that there is
ambiguity. Is that correct?

ALLISON: Yes, 100 msec is a good place to draw the line; not that we are
certain where earlier components originate, but, such as it is, the evidence
points to generators in specific parts of afferent pathways and primary or para-
primary cortical areas.

ZAIDEL: You talked about a polarity inversion across the central sulcus.
Why was this?

GLIAL ELECTROGENESIS

OPEN FIELD   CLOSED FIELD

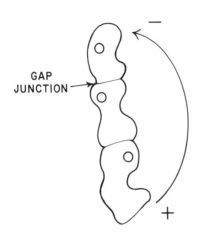

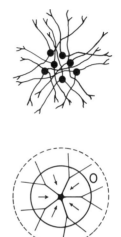

GAP
JUNCTION

FIG. 1.21   Schema of the manner in which depolarization of glial cells might generate slow potentials such as the CNV. Left. In model proposed by Somjen (1973), depolarization of glial cells in superficial cortical layers would produce a local depolarizing sink and associated negativity, while glia in deeper layers would serve as current sources recorded as a positivity; "intracellular" return current flow would be through low impedance gap junctions. Such a model would produce an open field dipole source and would account for polarity inversion of cortical slow potentials. (Adapted from Somjen, 1973.) Right. In cases where no polarity inversion is observed, it might be assumed that glial cells and their processes are oriented more or less randomly in which case cell body depolarization would produce a closed negative field in the same manner proposed for neurons. (Redrawn from Lorente de No, 1947.)

ALLISON: If we look at a sagittal section through somatosensory cortex, this is motor cortex anteriorly and somatosensory cortex posteriorly (Fig. 1.22). To explain evoked potentials like those shown in Fig. 1.11, we assume that the dipole is oriented horizontally down in the bank of the postcentral gyrus, in Brodmann's area 3b. We know from monkey studies that this area receives heavy input from the thalamus, much heavier in fact than the crown of the gyrus, in Brodmann's areas 1 and 2. Also, the area of cortex in the bank is large compared to the area on the crown. So a lot of somatosensory cortex is buried in the postcentral gyrus, and it seems reasonable to assume that when we see an anterior-posterior polarity inversion, we have a horizontally oriented dipole. That doesn't prove it, and not everybody believes it, but I believe it, and it is a reasonable hypothesis.

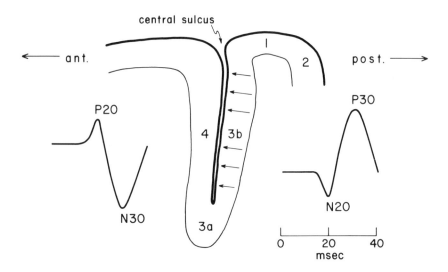

FIG. 1.22   Drawing of the somatomotor cortex of a human brain cut in the saggital plane 7 cm from the midline (corresponding to the hand representation); and proposed depole source in area 3b to account for polarity inversion of potentials across the central sulcus. The P20-N30 sequence recorded anterior to the central sulcus is assumed to correspond to the primary positive-negative sequence illustrated in Fig. 1.5. (Adapted from Sidman et al., 1978.)

ZAIDEL: Then you do always see the inversion?

ALLISON: Yes, we always see it. That is our criterion for localization of the central sulcus, where we see the polarity inversion.

ZAIDEL: Isn't the sulcus visible; I mean can't you see it?

ALLISON: No, we usually can't. Or to be accurate, we see several sulci and can't tell which is the central sulcus. That is why we need some method of localization. We can use the Penfield-Jasper method of cortical stimulation, but that doesn't always work, particularly if the patient is anesthetized. So it's useful to have another method. So far as we can tell, the evoked potential method always works.

PICTON: The probes that you have going into temporal lobe where you recorded a P300, where did they start?

ALLISON: The central probes enter the cortex a centimeter or two anterior to motor cortex; the posterior probes enter the posterior parietal region above the calcarine fissure.

PICTON: Are these probes anywhere near the parietal area?

ALLISON: That's a good point; no, they are not. If we had a probe that traversed parietal cortex and we still did not see a polarity inversion, I would think that would be stronger evidence that P300 is not generated cortically. So that is why I don't want to say much about the lack of polarity inversion from surface to depth, because we are not really in the right place, unless you believe that P300s are generated in frontal association cortex; the central electrodes are pretty close to that.

DONCHIN: Is there a possibility of finding a patient in whom it would be useful to put electrodes in the parietal area?

ALLISON: No, there is no reason for doing that, for starting in the parietal lobe and working your way down to the temporal lobe.

DONCHIN: These are interesting data, but they do not contradict any current concepts. I don't know of anybody who has really claimed explicitly that P300 is in the cortex.

ALLISON: I think that has been either the explicit or implicit assumption, don't you?

DONCHIN: I try to take great care to distinguish between the cortex and the brain. I am assuming P300 comes from the brain but I have no positive evidence that it is *cortical.*

ALLISON: Well, some workers have noted that the P300 scalp distribution is consistent with an origin in parietal association area. I assume that people have assumed that P300 is primarily cortical in origin. Maybe I'm wrong. I don't know anybody who has proposed a subcortical origin, although taken literally, the evidence from the depth probes is easier to square with a subcortical origin than with a cortical origin. I suspect that just as in the case of the vertex potentials, we are probably seeing activity in both places. What we see at the scalp may in fact be generated mainly in cortex and what we see in the depth probes may be generated mainly in deep structures. I don't know. But the neural operations involved in "task relevance" can be partly subcortical, I presume. That is the point I wanted to make. Do you accept the Hillyard-Picton contention that there are "frontal" versus "posterior" distributions of P300? Do you record a posterior or an anterior P300 or both?

DONCHIN: We have not seen an anterior P300. But we have never looked for it. We always record a posterior P300 and there is no way we can tell from our *scalp* recording whether we are recording cortical or subcortical potentials. There is nothing in our psychological interpretation of P300 that would make it necessary that it be in the cortex (Donchin, 1979).

ALLISON: True, but what I am getting at is maybe we would be more likely to see a polarity inversion if we look for a frontal P300. I mean, we can't change our electrode positions, the surgeons won't do it, so maybe we should change the task to fit the electrodes rather than the other way around. Maybe we should go to a "frontal" paradigm.

DONCHIN: Either that or find P300 in animals.

ALLISON: Sure. But nobody has yet recorded P300 in animals. Not that I am aware of. Why not? Animals can make complex decisions based on information contained in stimuli.

SHIFFRIN: Has somebody done the following? You stimulate at succesively more central locations along the somatosensory pathway. Does the pattern of evoked potentials remain the same?

ALLISON: The pattern is the same; we still record the same thalamic and cortical potentials, but with a corresponding decrease in latency (see Desmedt, Debecker, & Robertson, 1979).

SHIFFRIN: You don't lose components on the way up, as if there were parallel tracks?

ALLISON: I can't say that for sure. We seem to record the same potentials further centrally in that particular system. But of course that doesn't guarantee that we produce the same pattern in all other places. Maybe that is what you are getting at. For example, if we stimulate thalamocortical radiation fibers, obviously we do not reproduce all the input from peripheral nerve stimulation into the medial thalamus and the hypothalamus and other areas of the brain that receive somatosensory input, and we lose whatever patterning of activity that goes along with it that may eventually result in a sensation. In fact, Libet (Libet, Wright, Feinstein, & Pearl, 1979) suggests that is exactly what happens. If he stimulates the human thalamus, the patient doesn't report a sensation unless Libet gives a long train of impulses, suggesting that some sort of patterning has to occur before the stimulus enters the sensorium, to use a good phrenological phrase.

KUTAS: I was just wondering what sort of evidence there was that shows that P300 is neuronal?

ALLISON: Neuronal versus what?

KUTAS: Well, you seemed to suggest there is doubt about whether the readiness potential and the CNV and other slow potentials were neuronal in origin. So I was wondering what evidence there is that P300 is neuronal.

ALLISON: No direct evidence.

KUTAS: So, from a neurophysiological point of view, we don't know that P300 is neuronal. It is psychological manipulation that has resulted in our knowing more about the P300.

ALLISON: For a cognitive psychophysiologist, those are still perfectly good potentials with which to work. It is just that you can't say much about them beyond the fact that they can be recorded and that they are coming from the brain and are therefore worth recording. I didn't mean to say that the CNV is glial. It's just that we have to leave the possibility open that slow potential changes may be generated by glial cells as well as by neurons, and if so this would have implications for our interpretation of these potentials in relation to behavior.

KUTAS: But why do you think that possibility is stronger for slow potentials than for P300? The P300s can last for at least 200 msec.

ALLISON: I say that because depolarization of glial cells is a very slow process; it occurs over a period of *seconds*. So you don't find rapid changes of the sort you see with EPSPs and IPSPs, which have a duration similar to P300. But you are right, P300s might have a long duration if you opened up your filter. For all I know, everything after 200 msec is glial.

KELSO: Listening to what you are saying, one gets the viewpoint that there is a linear transformation of input as the information is flowing into the system. But neurophysiologists and psychologists would like to view the system not as one that promotes a dichotomy between afferents and efferents. In a behaving system it has been shown that there are descending influences on afferent systems. How do these affect these potentials?

ALLISON: I don't know.

KELSO: In a behaving system, we are typically moving at the same time we are processing information.

ALLISON: That is why we don't give those kinds of complicated stimuli, because the potential is going to be complicated. The vertex potential is an example. I don't think it reflects activity only in an ascending system. I think it is ascending and descending back to the thalamus, and it goes sideways, and at that point all hell breaks loose and things really do get complicated. So we can no longer talk about ascending or descending activities.

KELSO: Are there ways to delineate descending influences on afferent inputs?

ALLISON: Sure. Picton and Hillyard (1974), for example, had subjects attend or ignore clicks, and they looked for changes in the brainstem components, but there were no changes; those components just sat there. So Hernandez-Peon's idea that there is centrifugal control is beautiful. There are anatomical and single-unit data to suggest centrifugal control—but insofar as human evoked potentials are concerned, there is no evidence for it in afferent pathways.

CALLAWAY: Arnie Starr's recent recordings show that lesions above the area that is presumably giving rise to a Jewett bump may alter the Jewett bump. So this would be some evidence of the sort of thing you are talking about. He presented some of that at Konstanz (Starr & Achor, 1979). This would be even down at the level of the Jewett bumps. If you damage the medial geniculate, you can see an aberration in the response down in the brainstem.

ALLISON: That is interesting, but such results are difficult to interpret unless edema, trauma, and other extraneous factors can be ruled out.

2 Current Research in the Study of Selective Attention

Michael I. Posner
University of Oregon

2.1 INTRODUCTION

One way of viewing the problems of the conference is in terms of the subdisciplines of cognitive science. I take it that we are somewhere between psychology and neuroscience and that our task is to bring together concepts of neuroscience with those of cognitive psychology. These two fields ask somewhat different questions. Neuroscience concerns the most fundamental principles of how nervous systems are constructed. For that reason, there is a very strong emphasis on systems much simpler than the human being. On the other hand, cognitive science seems to be taking its lead from the study of language and artificial intelligence, and as such it tends to very complex problems such as a theory of how the human represents all real-world knowledge. Those of us who are studying very simple kinds of cognitive tasks feel on the fringe of cognitive science because the tasks we choose seem a bit trivial. Yet in another sense we deal with a most central question, the relationship between mind and brain. I think the most interesting topic currently dealing with the integration of mind (cognition) and brain (neuroscience) is the problem of attention.

I'd like to start by looking at a specific task as it might appear in neuroscience and as it might appear in cognitive science. I think it illustrates some of the differences in approach. It is the task of reading silently. First, we may view it by the measure of cerebral blood flow using, for example, the radioactive XENON technique (Lassen, Ingvar, & Skinhoje, 1978). The parts of the brain that are most active during the task of reading silently are visual areas, speech areas, and eye-movement areas. A neuroscientist looking at a complex task like reading silently can point to localization of the different brain processes that underlie the task.

The same task looks quite different to a cognitive psychologist who looks at the task of reading in terms of the time course of information flow (LaBerge & Samuels, 1974). The first method views reading silently in terms of localization of functions without concern for the fine temporal structure of the task. The emphasis in the second is on the fine temporal structure.

According to the cognitive view, the visual, phonetic, and semantic codes of a word build up automatically over a few hundred milliseconds. There are continuous outflow possibilities so that information from each code can have access to attention. Mechanisms that subserve selective attention are not found at a single processing stage but are independent of the automatic accrual of input codes. If the task demands it, one can devote attention to the visual representation of a stimulus, but this does not prevent the activation of habitual phonetic and semantic representations. While the subject's attention is occupied with visual analysis, one would expect overt responses to be based on the visual code. Attention can be directed or oriented toward different processes. Moreover, information flow may be either serial or parallel depending on whether there are habitual connections or not.

It is obviously very difficult to deal with a task as complex as silent reading. This is particularly true when one has as a goal illustrating the relationship between neuroscience and cognitive approaches. Reading is a task we do not share with other organisms and thus much animal work is excluded. However, we can try to study simpler model systems that capture aspects of the attentional mechanisms thought to be present in complex tasks like reading. Specifically there are three important issues about selective attention that come out of this particular view of silent reading.

2.2 SELECTIVE ATTENTION

The first is the independence of attention from the general stream of information processing. Even complex semantic processes may take place outside of attention. Like breathing, these same processes may also be performed under active attentional control.

A second problem of attention is the direction or "orienting" of attention. One can orient attention to the sensory surface. That is a simple way to study this aspect of attention. I want to consider orienting in visual space as a model system. I shall examine whether attention is separate from the structure of the visual system.

A third area is the role of attention in the formations of conjunctions of such visual dimensions as location, color, and form.

The reason I take these three questions is that they are the most active, current areas of investigation about selective attention. I don't believe they are exhaustive of all the questions one could ask about selective attention or that they necessarily form an overall theory of selective attention, but they do allow us to review much of the relevant literature.

2.2.1 Capacity

Let me start with one of the classical questions of attention, the idea of limited capacity. This way of viewing the problem separates the nervous system into two different capacities. One system, consisting of habitual pathways, is highly parallel so that many different pathways may be activated simultaneously. The attention system is of more limited capacity.

In one paradigm (shadowing), the subject's attention is directed toward information coming in one ear, by his having to repeat each word as it comes in. We look at what happens on the unattended ear. In these studies there is excellent evidence that the information on the unattended ear is heavily blocked from consciousness. It is almost as if information on the unattended ear is walled out. Not quite, however, because there is also evidence that some of the information to the unattended ear is getting through (Lewis, 1970; McKay, 1973). For example, a synonym on the unattended ear sometimes affects the reaction time on the attended ear, etc. (Lewis, 1970; Treisman, Squire, & Green, 1974).

When one goes from shadowing to a task like monitoring information coming on both ears, you obtain quite a different result (Ostry, Moray, & Marks, 1976; Kahneman, 1973). This has led cognitive psychologists to back away from a filter viewpoint. For example, it has been shown that subjects do about as well when they have to monitor information on both ears as when they confine attention to a single ear. They do badly when a target is detected on the attended ear. If one detects a target on the attended ear, the ability to obtain a target simultaneously on the other ear is very greatly reduced (Ostry, Moray, & Marks, 1976). We can presumably monitor sensory systems in parallel. Once attention is committed to one channel (e.g., when a target is detected); then there is real trouble on the other channel.

A second paradigm that has been used to study attention has been the psychological refractory period (Welford, 1952). If I present you with a stimulus to which you must respond and then before you emit your response I present a second stimulus, the classical observations suggest that the second stimulus "waits around" until the first stimulus is processed. It is as if the second signal is in a buffer and waits until things have been cleared. This result is very consistent with a peripheral block. But there have always been problems. For example, in some experiments, where the difficulty of the second signal is varied, there is evidence of more overlap between the first and second signal when the second signal is difficult than when it is easy (Karlin & Kestenbaum, 1968; Keele, 1973). It is this finding that made people doubt a strict single-channel view. In related work we studied a primary task of matching two visual letters and a secondary task, which was to press a key whenever a probe auditory tone occurred (Posner & Boies, 1971). We found a clear breakdown of the simple single-channel view. During the time when the subject is getting information from the first letter (e.g., first 300 msec), no delays to the probe auditory tone were found. As soon as the letter information was extracted (e.g., after 500 msec), there was interference with the auditory probe. It is as though the subject's nervous system can extract the information without interference, but as soon as one starts to think about the information, interference is found.

The most active domain in which this kind of two-state theory has been studied stems from experiments by Shiffrin and Gardner (1972). It has been thought to represent something of a puzzle for the two-state kind of view. In this kind of experiment four items are presented. In the simultaneous condition, they are presented at once. In the successive condition, one pair of items is presented and then, after subjects have had a chance to process that pair for the same time as in the simultaneous case, you present a second pair. In the simultaneous condition subjects are to process four things at once, whereas in the successive condition two things are processed at once. If the subjects are able to restrict attention to certain stimuli, they ought to do better in the successive than in the simultaneous condition. However, there is no advantage in the successive over the simultaneous case. Why is there no limited capacity system? What happened to attention? The whole system looks automatic.

Fairly minor changes in this experiment produce beautiful interference effects. John Duncan (1980) working in our laboratory modified the experiment just described. In his case the target was a digit and nontargets were letters. The subject received either the simultaneous or successive condition and had either one or two keys. The one-key condition requires subjects to report whenever there is a target present. The results are the same as just described. In the two-key experiment, subjects report separately when a target is present in each half of the display. In that case performance in response to successive stimuli becomes very much better than to simultaneous stimuli. You might think that this has something to do with the added task of localization of the target but it really doesn't. If you ask subjects to report in one condition zero versus one target and in the other condition one versus two targets, the results are the same as with localization. Whenever two targets are possible, there is strong interference. There are no speeded output demands in this task. Yet, when subjects have to observe two targets, you find strong interference between spatial positions. When only one target can occur, you don't find interference effects. The task of noticing a target apparently requires the attentive mechanism and changes the results from purely parallel to clearly increased interference as the number of spatial positions increases.

I would summarize all three of these paradigms, dichotic listening, refractory period, and visual search, as indicating support for the idea of two systems. One of them is highly parallel and can work automatically; the other is of limited capacity system and produces interference whenever it becomes involved.

The late positive wave (P300) of the event-related potential could be associated with the activity of this second limited capacity attentional system. The amplitude of P300 seems to be heavily influenced by surprise (Donchin, this volume) and that seems to make sense about the kinds of information that we would admit to conscious processing. The latency of P300 seems intimately connected to the degree of activation of the pathway for that stimulus (Duncan-Johnson, 1979; Posner, 1978). If a particular letter is presented and then followed by an identical letter, the latency of P300 is reduced. As a working hypothesis, I would like to think of P300 associated with the limited capacity attentional mechanism I have described.

One of the advantages of thinking about a two-state process is that one can divide many results obtained from reaction-time techniques into two parts. One part I call benefit, and it appears to be due to the activation of the parallel pathways described above. A second part I call cost, and it is due to the limited capacity system. When we say a person is set for a particular item, we usually mean he is set for something and set against something else. I am claiming that there are two fundamentally different kinds of set. One kind of set is when you have one of these pathways activated, but you are not attending to that pathway. You are then set only for something, not against anything. An unexpected item would be processed just as efficiently as if that pathway had not been activated. Once you attend to a pathway, then you also are set against other items so that if I now present an unexpected event, you process it inefficiently. There seem to be temporal asymmetries between benefit and cost of just the type you would expect (Posner & Snyder 1975). If I present an item, I receive benefit as quickly as I can measure after the occurrence of the item. Cost, however, takes time (Neely, 1977; Posner & Snyder, 1975). If we take the P300 as being related to the occurrence of cost due to the commitment of this central processor, we are left with N100 as something of a paradox. That is what I would like to deal with now.

2.2.2 Early Selection

Hillyard (this volume) has provided good evidence of early selection, that is, our ability to take in information from one area of the physical world, and to be unaware of information arising from another source. Some investigators have thought that evidence for late attentional selection by a mechanism such as I presented in the last section is evidence against early selection. If the nervous system can do things automatically, why should there also be early selection? To me these seem quite separate questions. Just as in respiration, one can perform without attentive control but one can also breathe under active attentional control if desired.

I have tried to develop a model system for studying our ability to commit attention to spatial positions (Posner, 1978; 1980). This seems to me to be the simplest example of selection. We already have a good example of overt selection of visual information in the orienting of head and eyes toward an object. If one can also orient with covert attention, we ought to be able to compare covert orienting to overt orienting. The ability to do so is one of the reasons that I think spatial attention is a particularly exciting model system to study.

A hundred years ago Wundt said we could easily keep our eyes straight ahead and move attention over the field. His evidence was introspective. However, recently objective evidence favoring our ability to attend independently of the line of sight has been reported (see Posner, 1978 for a review).

One of the reasons why orienting of this type is of interest is that it can also be studied with nonhuman animals. Goldberg and Wurtz (1972) have been studying orienting in alert monkeys by means of single-cell recording. Hillyard (this volume) has been studying the same process with event-related potentials in human beings. It is a task that has been studied with a variety of methods and seems to be a good one to try to find some sort of integration. Our method is a very simple one (Posner, Nissen, & Ogden, 1978). The subject is required to look straight ahead. We monitor EOG. They have a single key to press whenever a target occurs. The targets are bright squares of light that occur 7 degrees to the left or right of fixation. We provide either a neutral warning cue or an arrow that points to the left or the right. If the arrow points to the left, it is highly probable (.8) that the stimulus will occur on the left (valid trial), but sometimes it occurs on the right (.2) (invalid trial). The main result is that simple reaction time is about 35 msec faster on a valid trial than a neutral trial and about 35 msec slower on an invalid than on a neutral trial. So even in this austere situation of detecting a clear signal in a dark field a cue influences the efficiency with which they process that information.

What does that mean? I think it must index orienting of a covert attentional mechanism, not just our ability to set up different criteria for different positions in space. This conclusion arises because of several constraints on orienting we have explored.

Does attention depend on the fine structure of the visual system? For example, will there be different results when you are attending to the fovea and an event occurred in the periphery from when you are attending at the periphery and an event occurs in the fovea? Although reaction time is generally faster in the fovea than in the periphery, the cost induced by directing attention elsewhere is exactly the same. As far as the attention system goes, it doesn't matter whether the stimulus occurs in the periphery or in the fovea. However, the subjects behave as though the fovea really has more direct access to attention. If given a choice, they prepare for a peripheral stimulus rather than a foveal one presumably because they believe that the foveal stimulus has more direct access to attention. This is a rational strategy because in the real world, where acuity demands are present, we move our fovea to anything we are interested in. In the real world there is a correlation between the fovea and attention. However, when you disentangle these by experiment, you find that that is not a property of the attentional mechanism itself.

Another constraint is shown by Shulman, Remington, and McLean (1979). They presented subjects with a central cue as to where to move their attention. Eyes were fixed. They asked if attention moves from one position to another, does it move through the intermediate position? That is, does it move in an analog fashion? Now that is a pretty hard question to ask. If it does, they ought to be able to take a low-probability event that lies between the fixation point and the target and find RTs facilitated there at a period of time earlier than for the target. That is the result they obtained. So I think that there is some sense in which attention is moving across the field. The dynamics of this movement are clearer when we look at combination of attention movements and eye movements (Posner, 1980). Our most spectacular result is this one. Suppose you are looking straight ahead and you give the subject two tasks to do. One of them is to move their eyes to a peripheral target that occurs 10 degrees to the left or right of fixation. It takes about 250 msec to begin to move your eyes. During that time when the subject is still fixated straight ahead, you present them with stimuli to which they must respond. Stimuli can occur either at fixation or where the eyes are going to move. In this experiment they occur with a high probability at fixation and with a low probability at the target for the eye movement. We try to maintain attention at fixation, even though the eyes are to move. Before the eyes actually begin to move, we find that the most efficient detection occurs out at the target to a low-probability event rather than to a high-probability event at fixation. So something about the necessity of making the eye movement has shifted attention even against the probabilities.

There is also some independence between attention and eye movements. We did this experiment to show it. Subjects fixated at the left edge of a cathode-ray tube and had to make two eye movements. The critical time is when they were looking in the center but preparing to move the eyes to the right. We presented a high-probability detection stimulus at the original fixation point. We found the most efficient detection response is at the original fixation point, showing that there is a great deal of freedom between the programming of the eye-movement system and programming of the attentional system.

The general point I hope to have been making is that although I believe in late selection, I also believe we can set up model systems to study very early selection of the type that Hillyard is interested in. In such situations we obtain clear effects of attention on even the simplest sensory performance.

Our work on early selection can also be related to single-cell results. Goldberg and Wurtz (1972) have shown that in the superior colicullus there is selective enhancement of the activity of cells whose receptive field is the target for that eye movement, well before the eye movement begins. Originally Wurtz thought this had something to do with a general attentional system. But later he (Wurtz & Mohler, 1976) studied a paradigm in which the monkey had to maintain fixation but shift attention. Then you don't find selective enhancement in the superior colicullus. However, at the last neuroscience meeting it was reported (Bushnell, Robinson, & Goldberg, 1978) that at the level of parietal lobe you find this kind of selective enhancement.

The time courses of those selective enhancement effects are not unlike the time courses of the improvement in reaction time. So there is a certain amount of convergence between the single-cell work and our behavioral work.

There is still a problem with Hillyard's ERP work because the N100 effect seems to depend very heavily on maintaining set for one position in space. If you cue the subject trial by trial, at least in our primitive preliminary efforts, we haven't been able to obtain N100 effects. That represents the kind of difference between some of the results of the ERP and behavioral results that will require more work. Perhaps the N100 is telling us about our ability to erect some sort of a filter and that doesn't occur in a single trial but requires repeated information to develop. Perhaps only under maintained set you get blocking from consciousness and N100 effects, whereas if you do trial-by-trial cuing you obtain shifts of efficiency but not complete exclusion from awareness. These could be useful points to explore.

There is also some contact between studies of spatial attention and work on brain damage. Weiskrantz (1977) has argued that people with occipital scotoma are unable to bring to consciousness events that occur within that scotoma but can still orient to them if forced to do so. That argues that there can be orienting without detecting in the sense of conscious report. A kind of opposite is the parietal lobe syndrome (Heilman & Watson, 1977) where subjects can detect stimuli that occur in the field opposite the lesion, but they have very great difficulty orienting toward the stimuli spontaneously or when there are competing stimuli in the field. That is the kind of dissociation under pathological conditions that fit with the separation of orienting and detecting as cognitive operations.

2.2.3 Conjunctions

Time allows only a brief treatment of one of the most active areas in the field of attention. I have been arguing as if there is a very primitive knowledge of spatial location of visual stimuli. This makes spatial orienting an excellent means of selection. But there is also evidence of dissociations between a stimulus event and its location.

The most dramatic results of these are the results that have been obtained by Treisman (1979). She argues that, under some conditions, we have attributes of an object represented in the nervous system but we don't know where those attributes are coming from. If we look at a visual field for a single attribute (e.g., red), we first know there is a red object and only later know where it is coming from. If orienting is a very primitive process, then it seems strange that we would obtain dissociations between the attributes of a stimulus and their location in physical space.

One solution to this paradox might be that we use one word for several different things. Luminance detection in an empty field may involve a very primitive kind of orienting—what A.O. Dick (1978) called egocentric orienting. This simple form of orienting may arise when we are stimulated with an imbalance of energy. The kind of tasks that Treisman (1979) studies involve complex visual fields and relate to the construction of objects. This may reflect what Dick calls retinotopic orienting. Treisman's idea that attention is necessary to paste together the activated attributes of objects is an important one. It suggests that although automatic activation may occur, we may not always have the object automatically assembled for us.

This dissociation between an object and its constituent attributes is reminiscent of some results with language tasks. We argue that there are isolable systems activated by a letter or word. These include physical, phonetic, and semantic representations. Somehow they have to be brought together. That may not always be a trivial process. In a recent review article Keele and Neill (1978) relate the difficulty that one can have in pasting together isolable codes with the neurological syndrome of deep dyslexia (Marshall & Newcombe, 1973). Here the subject cannot find the proper phonetic code to a visual word but produces semantic associates instead. It is as though the various codes of the input cannot be related. This is a dramatic demonstration of isolable code of a single visual stimulus that we infer from chronometric studies in normal subjects (Posner, 1978).

2.3 CONCLUSION AND DISCUSSION

Attention is a very complicated field. It is a field that I think represents the current cutting edge of the relationship between brain and mind and thus is at the center of neuroscience and cognitive science. Some results suggest that we are starting to be able to relate studies of electrical activity both with performance and subjective experience. This argues for the importance of sustained contact between users of these various methods.

KELSO: I'd like to know why you think the field of attention is the crux to understanding the mind-brain problem as opposed to some other set of processes. Secondly, I'd like to . . .

POSNER: That is something you cannot document except by opinion.

KELSO: I am not questioning your data, which are very interesting indeed. I am trying to understand why you feel attention is the main interface.

POSNER: I think because it deals with the question of consciousness. However we want to hide it and, however embarrassing it is, the study of mind involves consciousness, I think it is central. We have made progress. For example, we now have psychological techniques so that we can study the activation pattern of an ambiguous word. We can show experimentally, even though the person is only aware of one meaning, that both are active. I think that is important because it really does say something about what comes to consciousness and what doesn't. I think the brain-mind problem is largely a problem of coming to understand the nature of consciousness and problems over which we have control and over which we don't. Attention is the name for that field.

KELSO: I would also submit that the problem for the neurophysiologist is not, as you say, localizing structures but rather understanding the temporal coordination among those structures just as it is for psychologists to understand the temporal relationship among the so-called codes.

POSNER: If you listen to people in neurophysiology talk in general, the problem of localization seems to be the one they are working on. I don't think that is an uninteresting problem. It just isn't the only problem and I agree temporal coordination is as important. If someone takes as the basic question the organization of nervous systems, unless they are able to localize, they cannot find what is happening in the membrane potential, etc. For them, localization is critical. It is not as important a question for people whose main interest is the physical basis of the mind.

ALLISON: But that is precisely the point at which the neurophysiology gets difficult. If you have a nice sequential model, whether you call it a sensory afferent system or a model of the type Hillyard (this volume) showed, then localization is a fairly tractable problem. It is when things start happening in parallel that they are hard to pick apart. But that is where things start getting interesting, interesting for you.

POSNER: Some new techniques, like cerebral blood flow, might be useful in the study of localization of different cognitive tasks. Unfortunately, the XE-NON scan technique is somewhat invasive.

KAHNEMAN: There seems to be at least a minor apparent inconsistency with two parts of your talk, the one where you emphasize automatic activation and the last one. I have always understood automatic activation to be as good as possible.

POSNER: As good as possible?

KAHNEMAN: In the sense that you can't improve things by paying attention to them. This was certainly the way in which LaBerge (1975) defined automatic processing. In fact, he defined automaticity by the absence of facilitation, that is, by the absence of benefits. If attending to a particular location in space speeds you up in detecting things in that location, for example, attention must be doing something. Could you clear that up?

POSNER: That clearly has to be wrong, it is not that attention doesn't do anything, at least for early selection. You might think of it as kind of a shunting of processing to an output mechanism.

KAHNEMAN: Oh, no. In that case, there is no debate, because there is no such thing as purely automatic processing. There is processing that occurs outside the focus of attention and is distinctly slower than attentive processing—if we are agreed on that.

POSNER: The output is slower. That is what you mean. The difference in RT between physical and name codes is the same under high- and low-attention conditions even though the output is slower under low-attention conditions.

NORMAN: I think that you said there is no change in accuracy.

KAHNEMAN: There is no such speed/accuracy tradeoff as Posner indeed pointed out. Thus, if you obtain a benefit in one dimension, you could presumably cash it in for a benefit in the other.

POSNER: You can get output faster and maybe more accurately too. It is hard to judge by this paradigm. Insofar as that is inconsistent—there is a paradox. It is inconsistent with certain senses of automatic, but not with others.

DONCHIN: It is a little hard to pin down what you are saying, all of you, because you are talking about attention as if it is a known active entity that sits somewhere and pays out things. Yet, it is only a metaphor. It is a term that has really not been defined sufficiently but that is used to label a very complex set of processes. I don't quite see the difference between saying "attention is not paid" and saying "automatic processes operate." These are descriptions of different aspects of the same process by which we interact with stimuli. There is no agent that pays out resources! I think at some point we have to understand what we mean when we use the word *attention* as the subject of a sentence.

KAHNEMAN: I think that we mean to describe the results of a particular paradigm, typically an interference paradigm where we study the effect of presenting more than one stimulus. Alternatively, we study the effect of instructing the subject ahead of time about the location in which the stimulus will occur, or about the stimulus that will require more processing than others. We use *attention* as shorthand to refer to those paradigms.

DONCHIN: But "automatic activation" and "attention" are both names for a mechanism. They are not just descriptions of paradigms. You are posing a choice between two mechanisms as if either one or the other is exclusively appropriate although in actuality, for different paradigms, different strategies are adopted by the system to produce the output in response to the input.

POSNER: Well, yes, that might be what you have to mean in the end but you would like to push it a little harder than that. I don't want to spend my life working on a metaphor. I would like to work on a mechanism. If you want to reach mechanisms, you must take a specific situation. That is why I stress the model system approach. You have to talk within a particular context. If attention is moving across the visual field, that means it is tightly time locked, just as are the eyes. Now, no one calls eye movements a metaphor. Suppose we could do with attention movements everything you can do with eye movements. Why isn't that an operational definition of a mechanism?

DONCHIN: But what you are saying, Mike, is that there is an improved performance not at two extremes of a dimension but all across the dimension.

POSNER: No, not at the same time. The performance changes over the course of time and is improved maximally at the probe at an intermediate time interval, just as though there were a physical process moving. Cooper has shown in mental rotation studies that you can find the rate of rotation and present the probe where you think it ought to be and, sure enough, it is fast. If it were physically rotating, you couldn't do any better than her data, so I think it is getting close to mechanism.

SHIFFRIN: Posner's response to Kahneman's question is worth emphasizing. It is not necessarily the case that automatic processing is as good as possible.

KAHNEMAN: Well, I just wanted to correct the impression given by LaBerge that attention does not matter for information traveling along the solid lines. And as it turns out, the data suggest that the direction of attention matters regardless of where you are looking.

POSNER: Information travels along those solid lines but perhaps not so well along the other lines.

KAHNEMAN: That's right, and I think that is what you said.

POSNER: Remember that the data I presented on early selection are obtained in quite a different paradigm than physical and phonetic codes. I do have data that suggest that the distance between physical and phonetic codes is the same even though the reaction time, the output, is changing very dramatically (Posner, 1978). There are, thus, some paradoxes.

KAHNEMAN: You might want to consider what attention is directed to. Here again, I think, the LaBerge diagram is misleading. The impression it gives is that attention is necessarily directed to a particular code. In effect, the analysis of attention is identified with the analysis of expectations. But the basic results of the filtering paradigm simply cannot be explained by a mechanism of expectation. It simply won't work. In early filtering paradigms, for example in the shadowing experiments, any word in the language was equally likely to be presented to either ear. Yet, advantages to that attended ear appeared even though no specific expectancy could be built up for any code. The same occurs when subjects are shadowing random words and there are no linguistic and context effects. Posner's hybrid theory may be an exception, but it does appear to be the case that there has been a major swing to late-selection and to expectation-based models of attention in recent years. This change is associated with a loss of interest in the filtering paradigm. As a result, we have beautiful models to study search and priming, but these models may no longer explain the data base that was available to Broadbent when he wrote *Perception and Communication* (1958). This is somewhat bewildering.

POSNER: If you believe that there is early selection, the LaBerge model suggests that the attention mechanism can be pointed at a modality or a location or a frequency and, therefore, picks up the stimulus earlier.

NORMAN: Absolutely. LaBerge is using the same model we discussed earlier, where sensory attributes govern selection at the early stages of processing.

KAHNEMAN: That seems to me to be very puzzling. I can understand how LaBerge can suggest that we have two sources of activation for the same code —an expectation and a sensory input. But it seems difficult to apply the same idea to the activation of a modality or a location in space.

NORMAN: Why is that?

KAHNEMAN: I mean how is that represented? Units in memory are activated, logogens, or other codes that were set up in advance. How do you activate a code if it is not represented in memory?

NORMAN: Well, this depends on your notion of what gets into memory. But the data from selective attention studies suggest that you can select a male versus a female voice or a particular spatial region. I believe that a hierarchical selection mechanism is an important one. The ERP data have to be able to account for that. I think LaBerge's diagram didn't show how this could be done, but only because it does not extend far enough. But that is, I believe, because LaBerge's model is concerned mainly with the process of reading. It is not difficult to expand the model. To activate a region of space it is necessary to activate the neurological circuits that deal with that region. You can't orient to (or activate) an unknown thing, but you certainly can orient to a location, or a modality, or to a specific, known, object or even a word.

POSNER: The process can be handled by directing the attention mechanism toward a modality or a position in space. Any diagram does violence to reality in some ways, yet, I do not think that attention works by activating all the things that could be represented in that modality. This is basic to the notion of orienting. You can orient toward a position in space. That doesn't mean that you have activated everything that could be represented at that position in space.

KAHNEMAN: That is essentially different.

POSNER: Different from what?

TREISMAN: . . . from activating a particular word.

POSNER: Yes, certainly. But the point is that this model didn't deal with orienting toward a position in space or modalities or anything like that. LaBerge does not address the manner in which the system obtains facilitation of a particular code. Whether that is done by pointing the attention mechanism in that way or by preactivation of that particular item.

3 Event-Related Potentials and Selective Attention

Steven A. Hillyard
University of California, San Diego

3.1 THE ERP, ITS STRUCTURE AND USE

With many others at this conference, I share the optimistic outlook that the event-related electric fields we record on the scalp are related to important aspects of information processing in the brain. Yet, the question recurs as to whether or not the ERP is an appropriate level to study the encoding and transmission of neural information. It seems to me there is no a priori reason for believing that studies of single-unit activities will provide more immediate insight into complex brain functions than investigations of the field properties of large neural populations. Because we know so little about the codes used by the brain, it may well be the case that measures of ensemble activity such as the ERPs will reveal critical parameters of brain function. My optimism is fueled by the increasing numbers of interesting correlations that are being revealed between the scalp-recorded ERPs and cognitive functions in man.

Figure 3.1 expresses the optimism that some of us feel. These are data from a mouse experiment. The ERPs are being recorded from two church mice as they spy their friend Samson the cat looking in at them. At the precise moment they notice the cat, the ERP has a specific configuration that is related to each mouse's perceptual experience. However, even this elegant experiment has some ambiguity, because the poor mice also "cheered up a bit" when they saw Samson. Thus, we really can't be sure whether this ERP reflects their perception of Samson or their delight at meeting him. Such ambiguities are often encountered in ERP research.

Figure 3.2 may present a slightly more realistic view, though I'm told it's a little outdated. Actually, it is a perversion of a figure from Lindsay and

The poor mice were having a terrible time. They cheered
up a bit when they saw Sampson . . .

FIG. 3.1   ERPs recorded from two church mice who are being trained as astronauts.
Graham Oakley, *The Church Mice and the Moon*. Copyright (c) 1974 by Graham
Oakley (New York: Atheneum, 1974). Reprinted with the permission of Atheneum
Publishers.

Norman's book on human information processing (1972). In the lower part,
we have a linear, neo-Broadbentian flow diagram of information processing of
the sort that used to be in vogue. Whatever the merits of this type of model, I
want to use this diagram to illustrate some of the conceptual issues involved in
relating an ERP triggered by a stimulus to concurrent sensory processing.

The ERP elicited by an auditory signal consists of some 16 oscillations that
can be reliably recorded from the scalp (Hillyard, Picton, & Regan, 1978). The
solid line represents the exogenous components of the ERP that are always
evoked by the signal no matter how it is being processed. The dotted lines
represent the "late," endogenous waves that vary according to the manner in

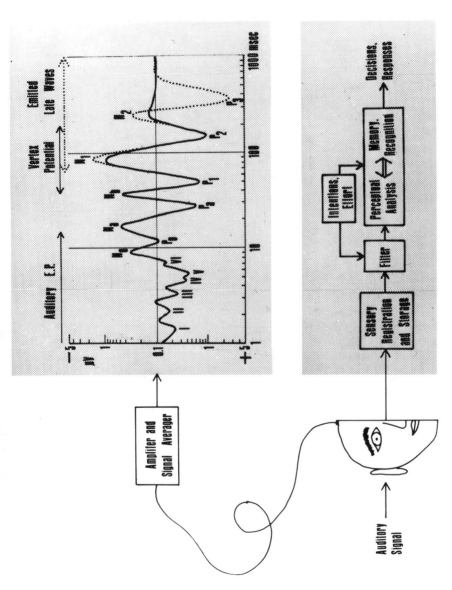

FIG. 3.2   The two domains of inquiry that are coordinated by cognitive psychophysiologists. In the upper panel is the sequence of exogenous and endogenous ERPs that are elicited by an auditory signal. The lower panel shows some hypothetical "stages" of processing that might be inferred from the subject's behavioral performance. To specify relationships between these physiological and psychological events is a major experimental goal.

53

which the information is processed. These components are affected by the direction of attention, the decision strategy being used, and so forth. Our task as cognitive psychophysiologists is to establish the nature of the relationships between these endogenous ERP components and the psychological constructs we infer from behavorial evidence. In this framework, the search for psychophysiological correlations not only makes sense but is the major goal. We typically set up an experimental paradigm and obtain behavioral data, from which we infer that certain processes of memory, attention, or whatever are operative. We also notice which ERP components covary as a function of the same experimental variables. Such correlations imply that the ERP components in question and the behavioral observations may be converging measures of the inferred process or construct under investigation. In some cases, there are good correlations between inferred processes and the behavior of ERPs; both measures may respond similarly to stimulus parameters and may be affected similarly by manipulation of other task variables. On other occasions, there may be gross dissociations between the pattern of behavioral and electrophysiological results. In that case, we have to consider whether it is necessary to redefine the psychological constructs that once appeared to be appropriate. In some situations, it might even be the case that the ERP in question is not related to the behavioral variables or constructs of interest. By examining the correlational evidence and identifying ERPs as markers of behaviorally defined intervening processes, we can, I think, help to clarify the structure of these information-processing sequences. For example, if an ERP correlate of an attentional "filtering" operation (Broadbent, 1971) could be identified, one could then see more clearly how the filtering process fits in other types of stimulus selections (e.g., whether they have a serial or parallel relationship).

Another useful function of ERPs is to help create a proper taxonomy of psychological processes. To get at the question of how many different varieties of memory, attention, expectancy, or whatever can be distinguished, we can look for patterns of communalities and differences in the ERPs, under the assumption that differentiated ERP configurations imply different psychological events. This strategy has been used, for example, to investigate whether decisions about relevant stimuli invoke the same brain processes for auditory, visual, and somatosensory cues. The answer appears to be that modality-specific processes are engaged initially in the course of the decision (indexed by the N2 or N200 component), followed by a modality-nonspecific process (associated with the P3 or P300 wave) (Simson, Vaughan, & Ritter, 1977; Snyder, Hillyard, & Galambos, 1980).

ERP measures may also permit inferences about the allocation of processing resources to different stimuli and tasks. If we have an ERP measure of an attentional process, for instance, we can look at its amplitude in response to a wide array of concurrent stimuli and thereby obtain an indication of where attention is being directed, without the need for any behavioral responses from the subject. Thus, ERP measures do not necessarily suffer from behavioral response limitations. It may be possible to assay how a person is distributing his attention more sensitively through the ERP than through the responses of his fingers on a set of buttons, once the ERP measure has been validated.

ERPs may be especially useful for determining how much, or to what depth, processing is carried out upon irrevelant stimuli. It is difficult to ascertain whether or not a person is paying attention to something he is not supposed to. Yet, such determinations are often needed in the study of attention and have been achieved most effectively by the use of interference paradigms (Lewis, 1970). By recording ERPs to an unattended stimulus, however, it may be possible to find out the extent to which it is being processed without assigning that stimulus any direct or indirect behavioral relevance. Experiments by N. Squires et al. (Squires, N.K., Donchin, Squires, K.C., & Grossberg, 1977), for instance, show that an irrelevant stimulus in an unattended modality may be processed to a significant degree under certain circumstances.

3.2 THE COCKTAIL PARTY EFFECT AND THE N1

With these generalities out of the way, I'd like to describe one of the shorter-latency endogenous ERPs, which has been related to a particular kind of selective attention. The data I shall discuss are recorded in variants of the so-called "cocktail party" situation wherein multiple channels of auditory stimuli are presented to the subject at rapid rates. In the experiment described in Fig. 3.3, three channels of clicks are presented—to the left ear, to the midline (binaural), and to the right ear, respectively. Clicks occur at a rate of several per second, delivered in random order to the different channels. Order of presentation must be unpredictable, or else nonselective preparatory variables cannot be dissociated from attentional variables (Naatanen, 1975). The task here is to attend to one channel at a time and press a button after every tenth click in that channel. In Fig. 3.3, the solid-line ERPs were elicited by clicks presented in the attended channel, and the dotted-line ERPs were elicited by clicks presented in the same channel when attention was directed to one of the other channels. The difference between the solid and dotted ERPs includes a broad negativity that overlaps the N1 peak. We have frequently referred to this attention effect as the "N1 enhancement" (Hillyard, Hink, Schwent, & Picton, 1973), because the amplitude of the N1 peak (measured from baseline or the preceding P1 peak) is larger in response to attended-channel stimuli. In reality, however, this so-called "N1 effect" is at least partly composed of a broad endogenous negativity that begins as early as 50 msec poststimulus and lasts for as long as several hundred msec (Naatanen & Michie, 1979; Hansen & Hillyard, 1980). The early, exogenous click-evoked potentials (Na, Pa) remain stable.

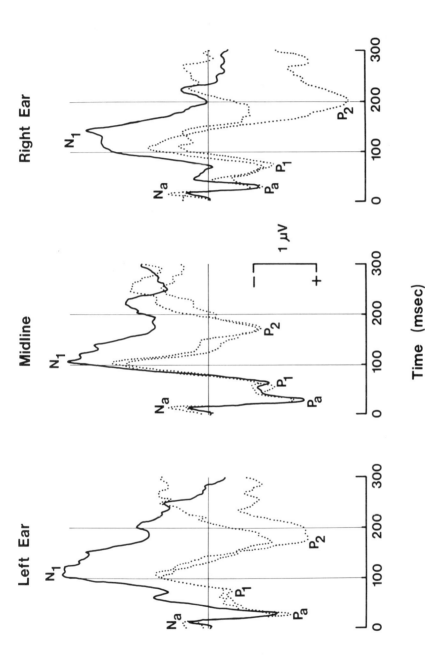

Left Ear

Midline

Right Ear

Time (msec)

FIG. 3.3   ERPs triggered by three channels of 60-dB SL clicks, delivered in random order to the left ear, midline (binaural), and right ear at intervals of 200–400 msec. The subject counted the clicks in one channel at a time and pressed a button after every tenth click. Solid tracings are ERPs to the clicks in the channel being attended and the dotted tracings are ERPs to the same stimuli when attention was focused on another channel. ERPs are averaged over 512 clicks. Subject R.N. Unpublished data from a study by Van Voorhis, Hillyard, and Naatanen.

The N1 effect has been examined in a series of experiments. It seems that the difference in N1 amplitude between attended and unattended channels develops best under conditions of rapid stimulation, when a high-information load is placed on the subject. At a rate of one tone per second or less, for instance, the difference between N1 amplitudes to attended and unattended channels in not significant (Schwent, Hillyard, & Galambos, 1976). Parasuraman (1978) also reported a comparison of this attention effect obtained with fast and slow rates of stimulation. At the slow rate (ISIs of 700-1400 msec), no ERP changes with attention were observed in the N1 latency zone. At the faster rate of stimulation (ISIs of 350-800 msec), performance fell off as attention was divided among the three channels, and an enlarged negativity was elicited by attended-channel sounds.

Another property of this N1 effect is that the channels may be specified either by locational cues or by pitch cues. In another experiment, the three stimulus channels were not three locations in space but rather three different tone frequencies. All three tones appeared to come from one location; yet the usual attention effects were obtained (Schwent, Snyder, & Hillyard, 1976). Relating this effect to the psychological literature on attention, we recalled that Broadbent (1970; 1971) had proposed a type of selective attention that he called a "filter" or "stimulus set." This hypothesized selection process appears to have the same functional properties as the negative ERP effect; that is, a simple physical cue must distinguish the competing channels of stimuli, and selection is more effective at higher loads. This early attention effect on N1 thus appears to be a neural sign of the preferential processing of stimuli that have been selected by a stimulus set mechanism.

Whether or not this particular hypothesis turns out to be correct, the N1 effect can be exploited to test certain theoretical proposals, such as Moray's (1975) hypothesis that dichotic sequences of tones are not processed selectively when attention is focused on one ear. According to this model of attention, all channels are processed in parallel until a deviant event (target) occurs, whereupon attention is switched to the channel containing the target for a brief period. There is no selection of inputs prior to target presentations.

This hypothesis of Moray's is difficult to reconcile, however, with a reanalysis of the ERP data from the study of Schwent (Schwent, Snyder, & Hillyard, 1976) made by J. Hansen in our laboratory. He found that the N1 to attended-channel tones was indeed much larger than to unattended tones, even when target and immediately post-target tones were excluded from the averaged ERP. It seems unlikely, therefore, that stimuli are processed in parallel in the different channels, because of the ERP difference between them. Physiologically, the different channels were certainly not being processed in parallel.

Another experiment was designed to see how the amplitude of this attention-related ERP varies with the distribution of the subject's attention

(Hink, Van Voorhis, Hillyard, & Smith, 1977). We used a focused versus divided attention paradigm, where the stimuli in one ear were syllables, /da/, /ba/, /ja/, and /ga/, and in the other ear environmental sounds. These stimuli could just as well have been clicks and tones, but for other reasons they happened to be more complex. There were three experimental conditions: attend to the ear with syllables and count a target syllable, attend to the environmental sounds and count a target sound, and divide attention between the ears and count targets in both. We found that the amplitude of the negativity at 100 msec evoked by the syllables was largest when the syllables were attended and smallest when attention was focused on the other ear. When attention was divided between the ears, the N1 amplitude was intermediate. This suggests that the *total* amount of attention-related negativity that was being generated per unit time was constant and could be allocated either to one channel primarily or to both ears at once. This constancy of total N1 amplitude over time is in line with a resource-limited type of attentional process.

All of these experiments might well be challenged on the grounds of being artificial, because people don't ordinarily listen much to sequences of clicks and tones or da's and ba's in real life. I think that's a valid criticism. Listening to one voice amidst the chatter of a cocktail party would seem to be a more realistic kind of situation with which our attentional systems are better designed to deal. These considerations led to a study in which subjects listened to a female voice reading from a novel in the left ear and a male voice reading from a different novel in the right ear (Hink & Hillyard, 1976). In this case, the ERPs were elicited by superimposed "probe" stimuli (the vowel sound "ah") that had the same pitch characteristics as the speaker's voice in each ear. For both male and female voices, it was found that the probe in the attended ear elicited a larger N1 (and P2 as well in this case) than the probe in the unattended ear. This result illustrates another property of this N1 effect—it is elicited not as a function of the *meaning* of the stimulus but only as a function of whether or not it belongs to an attended channel. The "ah" probes were generated by an artificial resonance machine and were easily recognizable as nonwords, yet because they had roughly similar physical cue characteristics as the voices on the attended channels, they elicited a larger N1-P2 complex. This further supports the idea that this ERP is a sign of the channel selection or stimulus set variety of selective attention.

In more recent experiments we looked at this negative ERP when elicited by the words themselves in a selective listening situation. It seems that this attention-related ERP to natural speech is asymmetrically distributed on the scalp (Fig. 3.4), being larger over the left cerebral hemisphere than over the right (Hillyard & Woods, 1979). The history of ERP research on cerebral specialization is a long and tragic story (see Donchin, Kutas, & McCarthy, 1977, for a review), but this seems to be one experiment where the lateral asymmetry did come out the way one "knows" it ought to be. This effect was seen

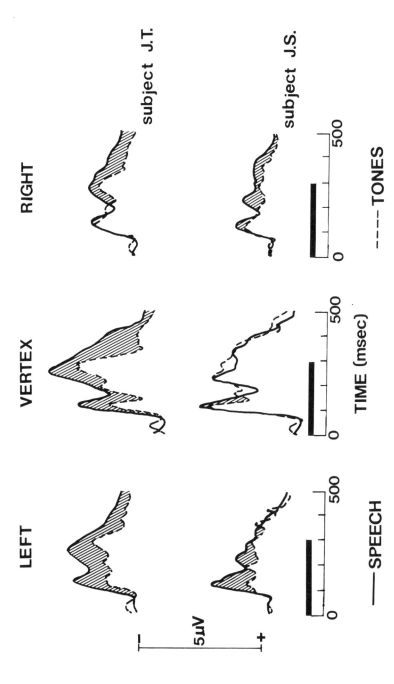

FIG. 3.4 ERPs from two subjects averaged over all single-syllable words in a spoken passage and to tone bursts matched for loudness and interstimulus intervals. Subjects were required to answer difficult questions on the content of the speech but listened passively to tones (Hillyard & Woods, 1979).

over 12 subjects at the p < .001 level, but, like all lateral asymmetry effects, ought to be replicated before believing it. If this result is correct, however, it suggests that the negativity that follows attended-channel stimuli might be distributed over the brain region that is most actively engaged in scrutinizing the signals.

This idea is supported by some elegant experiments in the somatosensory modality, where attention was directed to shocks to one hand as opposed to shocks to the other hand (Desmedt & Robertson, 1977). Comparing the ERP to shocks in the attended hand versus shocks to that hand when it was not attended, the attention effect is again a broad negativity overlapping the N1 wave, beginning at around 100 msec and peaking at 140 msec. The late somatosensory evoked components are a little later than those in the auditory system, but focusing attention on a somatosensory "channel" seems to produce the same kind of negativity as auditory attention, except that the wave is asymmetrical, being largest over the contralateral scalp. This negativity then seems to reflect the extra processing that is given to a stimulus that has been selected by a stimulus set process, and it may be distributed in the brain according to where this extra processing takes place.

In the visual system, Harter and Previc (1978) have also reported broad negativities localized to the occipital area when a person is attending to spatial frequency cues. The visual attention story seems to be more complicated, however, with many different components being affected. Eason et al. (Eason, Harter, & White, 1969) and later Van Voorhis and Hillyard (1977) reported a visual attention experiment that is analogous to the auditory experiments I have discussed. Two spots of light were flashing in the left and right visual fields in a random sequence. The subject attends to one visual field at a time or to both simultaneously. The task is to detect a slightly brighter flash that occurs occasionally in one of the channels. The first component at the vertex that is clearly sensitive to the direction of attention is again a negativity in the N1 range (about 150-170 msec latency). The flash in the attended field elicits the largest N1, and dividing attention between the two sources of light again results in an intermediate N1 amplitude elicited to both. Visual-spatial attention differs from most of the auditory attention experiments, however, in that the P2 wave at 220 msec or so is also consistently larger to the attended flashes. Moreover, at the occipital electrode, a number of components change systematically with attention to these light sources; it appears that in the occipital areas some of the exogenous waves are actually enhanced to the attended flashes. Eason and Ritchie (1976) have interpreted these ERP changes as reflecting a filtering operation at the level of the occipital lobe or lateral geniculate nucleus.

In a more recent experiment, we wanted to investigate whether spatial attention is a modality-specific process or facilitates processing in different modalities at the same time. This experiment was based on the idea that our sensory systems should be designed to perceive *objects* rather than isolated modalities in space. There are a number of behavioral experiments suggesting that auditory events are actually transformed onto a visual mapping of external space and that vision serves as a common frame of reference for spatial attention in all modalities. We recorded ERPs to two lights flashing in the right and left visual fields and to tones coming from speakers directly behind each light. Flashes and tones were given in a random sequence at right and left locations. The question was, would paying attention to the lights on one side influence the auditory-evoked potentials to tones on that same side, even though the tones were irrelevant? That is, does focusing attention upon a visual source also enhance auditory processing of sounds at that location? Such a result would suggest that attention to spatial location is, at least in part, a modality-nonspecific process.

The results came out along these lines, or I wouldn't have built up the story in this way. Figure 3.5 shows the ERPs to visual stimuli. When the lights were attended (lower tracings), the vertex N1 and P2 were enhanced to attended-field flashes, as noted previously. At the top are shown the visual-evoked potentials, while the tones were being attended. It turned out that the same N1 and P2 components were affected. When the subject attended to the auditory signals on the left, the visual N1-P2 was larger to the left flashes. When attention was shifted to the sounds on the right, the visual ERPs to right flashes became larger.

Similar effects were seen with the auditory ERPs. Paying attention to the visual stimuli on one side resulted in an enhancement of the auditory N1 wave to tones on that side and vice versa. It seems, however, that spatial attention affects different components in the two modalities, the N1-P2 in vision and the broad negativity in audition. Nonetheless, the results seem consistent with the idea that localizing an object in space does occur within a common-modality framework.

DONCHIN: How do you know the subject is not using stimuli in the irrelevant modality to aid in the task?

HILLYARD: To check on that possibility, we're doing control experiments in which we take away the irrelevant stimuli and put them back again, to see if that influences performance. This paradigm is actually an irrelevant-probe type of design. The subject is attending to one thing, and we measure to what extent another stimulus gets in.

3.3 STIMULUS SET AND RESPONSE SET

So far I've been talking about a kind of experiment where a person focuses attention on one channel of stimuli that is spatially or otherwise distinguished by a simple cue. There are at least half a dozen experiments in the literature now

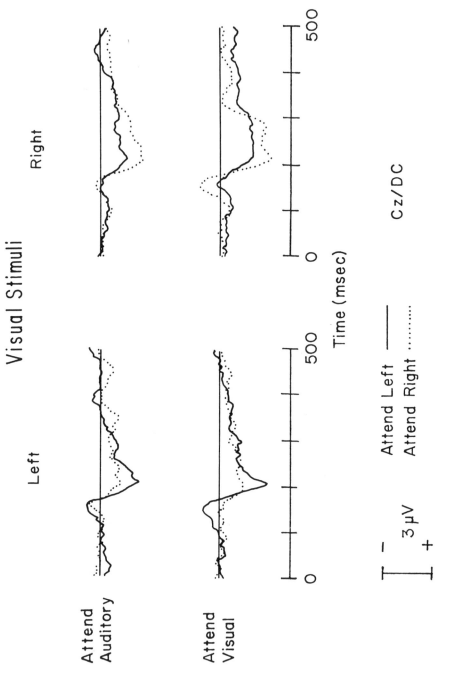

FIG. 3.5 ERPs to brief flashes in a cross-modal attention experiment. Flashes and tones were presented in random order from locations 30 degrees to the right and left of the midline. In successive conditions subjects attended to left tones, right tones, left flashes, and right flashes. Note that both auditory and visual attention affect these visual ERPs. Grand averages over eight subjects, vertex recordings. Unpublished data of Hillyard, Van Voorhis, and Simpson.

suggesting that this so-called stimulus set variety of attention is associated with a different ERP configuration than is a second type of attention, which might be called response set, again following Broadbent (1970; 1971). This second type of attention comes into play when a subject is presented with a sequence of events, some of which are labeled as task-relevant and/or require one type of response, whereas other stimuli require a different type of response. The standard "oddball" experiment in which the P300 is produced is of this type: In a repetitive sequence of events there is an occasional deviant stimulus that requires a different response from that made to the ongoing stimuli. As far as P300 production is concerned, it doesn't matter very much what kinds of stimuli are used or which responses are made to the two categories of events. The critical feature is that one class of stimulus is plugged into one response "vocabulary" (Broadbent, 1971) in the subject's category scheme as opposed to another. This is contrasted with stimulus set attention where stimulus relevance is defined solely by a peripheral physical cue instead of the subject's response classes. It remains to be seen, however, whether stimulus/response set constitutes a hard dichotomy rather than two ends of a conceptual continuum (Keren, 1976).

Both types of attention are operating in many of the experiments we have done, because the subject was required to focus attention on a channel that was defined by a peripheral cue and to make a particular response to occasional target events within that channel. Figure 3.6 shows the ERP to target stimuli in an experiment where the subject attends to syllables (ba, da, ga, ja) in one ear at a time and counts one of the syllables as a target (Hink, Hillyard, & Benson, 1978). In other conditions, the subject pushes a button to report the targets, with the same result. The data pattern indicates that all the stimuli in the attended ear (targets and nontargets) are processed equivalently insofar as the N1 index is concerned. In the nonattended ear, targets and nontargets also elicit N1 waves of equal amplitude, but they are much smaller than to attended-ear syllables. This is the same negativity associated with selection of channels that we've been seeing all along. The differentiation between the targets and the nontarget in the attended ear, however, comes in the P300 complex of components, which begins usually with an N2 wave at about 200 msec. The P300 accompanying the detection of the targets is completely dissociable from the N1 effect and has a hierarchical relationship with it. Whereas all stimuli in the attended ear (i.e., those with proper pitch and localization attributes) initiate the negativity at N1, only the targets in that ear elicited the P300 complex. This hierarchical relationship parallels Treisman's (1969) notion of a series of attentional modes or stages, the first of which selects stimuli for their peripheral sensory attributes (stimulus set) and the second stage matches those stimuli that pass the first test against an internal response vocabulary and allows the appropriate response to be made. I would say that the evidence from many experiments is consistent with the idea that the P300 wave is dependent

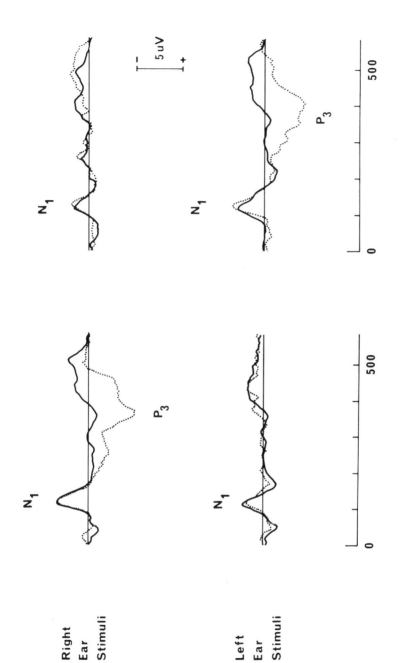

FIG. 3.6   ERPs to random sequence of four syllables presented to left and right ears on a 50/50 random basis. Dotted tracings are ERPs to the "target" syllable (one per run) that was counted in one ear at a time. Solid tracings are ERPs to the other three syllables (non-targets). ERPs are averaged across 16 runs in which different syllables in either ear served as targets. Vertex-mastoid recordings, from Hink et al., 1978.

(among other things) on a subject's adopting a response set mode of attention. Thus, the effects of attention on N1 and the P300 components seem to follow the functional specifications that are called for by Broadbent's distinction between stimulus and response set attention.

The P300 amplitude also depends very much, however, on the likelihoods or expectancies for the different classes of stimuli and responses that may be required. The less frequent response or the less expected stimulus-response pairing produces the larger P300 waves (Karlin & Martz, 1973). The N1 phenomenon is not probability-sensitive in the same way.

If the P300 has to do with classification of a stimulus as relevant and making a decision about it, as many of us here presume, then it ought to obey different principles of temporal dynamics than those ERPs that are not so closely coupled with endogenous processes. Specifically, it is known that people can make rapid sequential decisions at intervals of about half a second, with performance decrementing at shorter ISIs (the psychological refractory period). If the P300 is a correlate of stimulus classification and decision, it ought to follow rapid sequential decisions at this rate without decrementing. This would make the P300 very different from other long-latency ERPs (N1, P2, etc.), which are enormously decremented (i.e., they have long refractory periods) when stimuli are repeated at short intervals.

The experiment illustrated in Fig. 3.7 was designed to generate P300 waves in rapid sequence to see whether they would be regenerated fully at short ISIs. This experiment, done by David Woods in our laboratory (Woods, Hillyard, Courchesne, & Galambos, 1980), elicited P300 waves in a threshold-detection paradigm. As K. Squires et al. showed some time ago (Squires, K.C., Hillyard, & Lindsay, 1973; Squires, K.C., Squires, N.K., & Hillyard, 1975), when a subject correctly detects a threshold-level stimulus, there is a large P300 wave elicited in proportion to the confidence of his detection. The new paradigm called for the presentation of between zero and three threshold-level tones in a rapid sequence, as illustrated on the abscissa. After a warning light there are five positions at which the tone might occur: The first is termed Sa, followed by three Sb positions that occur at 300, 600, 900 msec after Sa. The Sc position is 1200 msec after Sa. Tones were delivered at Sa, Sb, or Sc according to a random sequence, with each position having a 50-50 chance of containing a stimulus. Hence, on one-eighth of the trials, there were three beeps in a row and on one-eighth there were no beeps at all. Following the other binomial probabilities, one tone occurred on 37.5% and two tones on another 37.5% of the trials. Looking at the ERPs to the different stimulus combinations, on those trials where there were no signals presented, what you see is the EP to the warning flash followed by the CNV, which is the slow negative potential shift that arises in anticipation of practically anything in life. The CNV stays up until a second flash asks the subject to report how many tones were heard. When only one threshold-level stimulus was presented (second through fourth

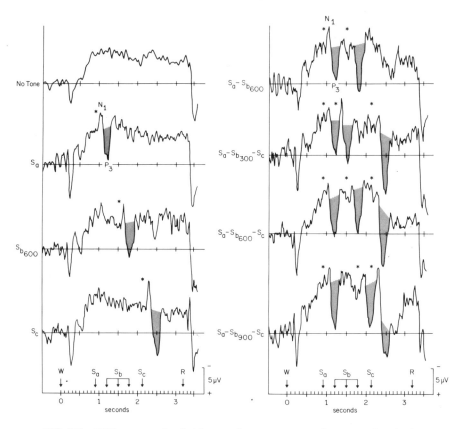

FIG. 3.7 ERPs to near-threshold tones that were presented on a random basis at specific times after a warning flash (W). On each trial there could be either zero (upper left tracing), one (lower left tracings), two (upper right), or three (lower right) tones presented at the times indicated by arrows on the abscissa. The subject reported the number of tones perceived after a response cue (R) came on. Grand averaged vertex recordings over five subjects. Based on data from Woods et al., 1980.

trac-ings), there is a large P300 at that position. The interesting trials were when two or three tones were presented in rapid sequence. What happened was that the P300 waves to the latter stimuli were not at all decremented in relation to the initial P300 and were even slightly enlarged. The P300 to the final tone in a triplet was very difficult to measure, as evoked potential buffs will appreciate, because it overlaps with the positive-going resolution of the CNV. To combat this problem, four different measures of P300 amplitude were taken, and it was clear from all of them that P300 was actually larger to the last stimulus than to the first two. This indicates that the P300 wave is rather unique among its ERP brethren in having very fast recovery properties to rapid sequences of stimuli.

By way of contrast, the exogenous N1-P2 wave recorded in a passive condition was greatly decremented upon repetition at the same ISIs. The P300 amplitude, no matter how it was measured, actually increased with repetition, which parallels a phenomenon in the psychological refractory period literature: If paired stimuli are presented at ISIs of 1/2 to 1 sec, there is sometimes a facilitation of the second decision. When stimuli are presented at intervals shorter than 1/2 sec, however, refractory effects are incurred and the decisions aren't made as promptly. Thus, the P300 amplitude seems to parallel the refractoriness of the decision process in these rapid sequential conditions.

There is a final aspect of this experiment that is interesting to contemplate. The results are very different from those of an important P300 experiment by Squires et al. (Squires, K.C., Wickens, Squires, N.K., & Donchin, 1976) that Donchin has described (this volume). In their experiment, the P300 wave became progressively smaller when the same stimulus was repeated in the oddball paradigm. This effect was attributed to the raising of the subject's expectancy for successive stimulus repetitions. In the present experiment, however, when three threshold stimuli in a row were detected at very short intervals, the P300 did not become progressively smaller. Now that has some interesting implications, I think, concerning the psychological correlates of the P300 wave; if the P300 is not reduced here with repetition, that would suggest that the subject is not recalculating his expectancies after each stimulus as in the oddball paradigm. But, if there is no moment-to-moment readjustment of expectancies here, then this type of "context updating" would not seem to be a likely correlate of the P300s that occurred. No doubt, this point can be disputed and alternative schemes proposed to account for this "nonrefractory" behavior of P300.

The final experiment I want to talk about also examines ERPs to unexpected stimuli and might be entitled "the P300 experiment that wasn't." This is an experiment that Marta Kutas and I have been carrying out for the past year or so. We tried to develop a task in which P300s would be elicited by unexpected stimuli in a situation more naturalistic than in most of our ERP endeavors. There must be more to the human mind, after all, than its ability to process beeps, boops, and clicks. One type of expectancy that the human brain is well-suited to compute is that which occurs when natural language is being analyzed. According to many theories, expectancies are established from moment to moment about the words that are likely to come next in a sentence, based on the ongoing semantic and syntactic contexts; that is, people process sentences in terms of a continual updating of the semantic context or schema of the message being received.

In these studies (Kutas & Hillyard, 1980) we set up a semantic context by presenting meaningful seven-word sentences visually, one word at a time. We wanted to examine in particular the properties of the P300 wave that would be elicited when an unexpected, semantically absurd word is inserted at the end of a sentence. The subjects were shown 160 sentences, three-quarters of which make sense and one-quarter of which had semantically inappropriate endings. Figure 3.8 shows ERPs averaged over the entire seven-word epoch. This is not your most natural reading situation, of course, but one has to do what one has to do to obtain good ERPs.

During a sentence like "roses are red and violets are blue," there is a shift in the baseline negativity, the CNV, which lasts throughout the entire sentence. After the last word in the sentence, there is a tapering off of the CNV back to baseline. Then there are other sentences like "a female chicken is called a hen" and "he returned the book to the library." No problem, the CNV also goes down afterward. But, look what happens when you read something like "I take coffee with cream and dog." "Dog" is not at all what you expected to see at the end of this sentence. The ERP that we expected to see at the end of such a sentence, of course, was a P300 wave accompanying the person's linguistic surprise. However, if you look at the dotted line in Fig. 3.8, there is no P300 wave at all to the anamalous word but rather a monophasic *negativity*. To our surprise, a long-latency negative wave followed the words that were semantically incongruous with the given context. Figure 3.9 shows the superaveraged ERP over 12 subjects in this experiment to the terminal words in the 40 sentences that were semantically absurd. The other three tracings are ERPs to the words that did make sense. All words elicited the N1-P2 of the visual-evoked potential, but the absurd words alone were followed by this late negativity that begins at about 200 msec, peaks at 400 msec, and goes out to maybe 600 msec. This "N400" component was seen consistently in each of the 12 subjects tested. Our first guess is that N400 may be a correlate of the "second-look" process,

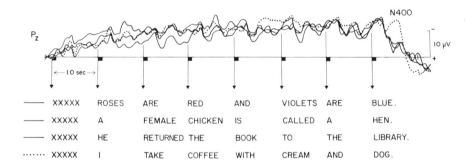

——	XXXXX	ROSES	ARE	RED	AND	VIOLETS	ARE	BLUE.
——	XXXXX	A	FEMALE	CHICKEN	IS	CALLED	A	HEN.
——	XXXXX	HE	RETURNED	THE	BOOK	TO	THE	LIBRARY.
······	XXXXX	I	TAKE	COFFEE	WITH	CREAM	AND	DOG.

FIG. 3.8 ERPs recorded throughout the presentation of complete seven-word sentences, with the words flashed at one per second. Each tracing is the averaged ERP across 40 sentences in which the last word was either appropriate for the context (solid lines) or semantically inappropriate (dotted line). Samples of the 160 different sentences that were presented to this subject are shown below. The "semantic mismatches" occurred on 40 of the 160 sentences and elicited a prominent N400 component. D.C. recordings from the Pz electrode. Kutas and Hillyard, unpublished data.

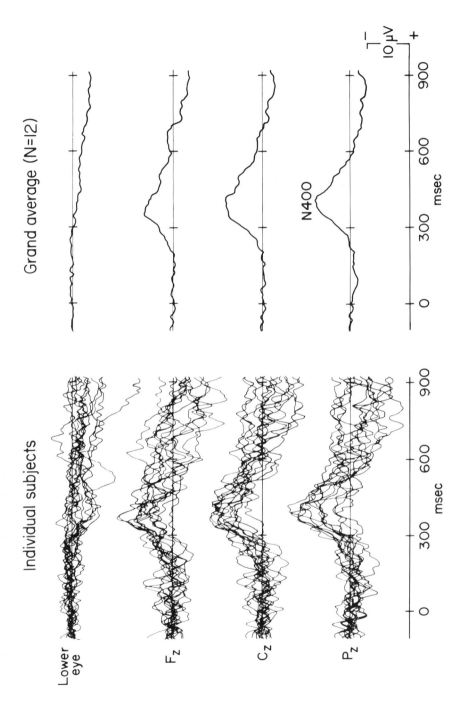

FIG. 3.9 These difference waveforms were obtained by subtracting the averaged ERPs to the semantically congruous from the ERPs to the semantically incongruous seventh words. Each superimposed tracing (A) represents the difference wave from one subject. The ERPs in (B) are the corresponding grand average waveforms over all 12 subjects. From Kutas and Hillyard, 1980.

69

whereby subjects reexamine their schema of the sentence's meaning in an attempt to make sense of it. This would be similar to a context-updating type of process.

This experiment also suggests that ERP evidence may be used to classify different varieties of surprise and expectancy. It appears that disconfirmation of semantic expectancies, if you want to call them that, are associated with a very different ERP complex than are the other kinds of disconfirmations that have been more extensively studied in oddball paradigms. To verify this in a language setting, we did a control experiment where 25% of the last words in the sentences were semantically congruent but were physically different from the rest of the words in the sentence. The first six words were presented in small typeface and the last word in giant, bold typeface. The unexpected, bold-face words elicited a series of late positive waves of the parietal-central, P300 variety. The waveform is a bit more complicated than your run-of-the-mill P300 complex and contains several definite lobes, but it's definitely a positive series of waves akin to P300.

It seems reasonable to suppose that very different processing systems would underlie wholly negative and mostly positive waves. We don't know exactly what kinds of concepts to invoke to account for this apparent dichotomy, but we are thinking that possibly any unexpected event in a natural, meaningful context, linguistic or not, might elicit an N400. Maybe the violation of natural, overlearned, regularities is associated with the late negativity, whereas artificial, laboratory-bred irregularities like odd tones in a sequence are associated with a late positivity. So we're trying to come up with some kind of psychological classification scheme that parallels the apparent physiological dichotomy.

3.4 DISCUSSION

KAHNEMAN: Steve, a question about divided attention in the context of the Broadbent theory. Do you have any indication as to whether the responses during divided attention are associated with a greater variance than during focused attention? This would occur if subjects were switching attention back and forth between the channels, spending half the time doing one and half the time the other rather than sustaining attention at an intermediate level to both channels. This is critical to the whole of the post-Broadbent analysis of early selection. Now, there is the question of whether in the Broadbent scheme you are selecting one channel at a time and switching, or, in fact, you are dividing. Do you have any evidence on that?

HILLYARD: No, unfortunately.

KAHNEMAN: All it would take really would be to look at the variance of the data.

HILLYARD: These N1-type responses are so small and the noise level of the recording is so great that this would not be easy.

KAHNEMAN: I think it ought to be possible to examine the variance over trials at the critical times for the focused attention condition and compare that to the divided attention condition. When the mean amplitude is intermediate during divided attention, the variance should be a great deal larger if you are focusing on one channel at a time. If the variance is about the same magnitude in the two conditions, then indeed you are dividing, and that would make a crucial difference in the interpretation of these data. And as it happens, this has been a big issue in the theory of attention. You can nail that one down.

HILLYARD: O.K. Maybe we could take a crack at that. This particular experiment was not optimally designed for it because the stimuli were too loud and they weren't presented rapidly enough, but I think we could design one where the attention effect was very large and then look at the variance changes, if the signal-to-noise ratios would allow it.

HARTER: Was the scalp distribution of that negative component like that of the CNV and, if so, could that odd word at the end of the sentence be triggering an expectation? You know, like the subject says "I must have missed something" and the subject is waiting for some more information.

HILLYARD: Yes, I think that is a possible interpretation. The scalp distribution of the negativity to the absurd words is a bit more posterior than the distribution of the CNV in this task, but this is not a sharp difference.

KUTAS: There is a general tendency to think of the CNV as having a fronto-central distribution. However, there are a number of reports demonstrating that the distribution of the CNV is influenced by the nature of the stimuli and the task. Thus, it is difficult for me to tell whether the N400 has the same distribution as that of the "classical CNV," because that concept has been revised over the past several years.

HILLYARD: So you should only consider the distribution of the CNV in this particular situation in comparison with the N400?

KUTAS: That's true. Unfortunately, for a variety of reasons it has been a difficult measurement to take. The distribution of the CNV varied considerably from subject to subject. On the whole, however, it was equally large at the midline locations. The N400, on the other hand, had a slightly more centroparietal distribution.

CALLAWAY: Steve, there are two things. Your negative wave looks exactly like Timsit-Berthier's postimperative negative variation (Timsit-Berthier, Dehaunoy, & Gerono, 1978).

HILLYARD: I don't think so. Her component lasts much longer.

CALLAWAY: As I remember, . . . she did one experiment with a CNV paradigm and omitted some of the trials, so as to establish a kind of uncertainty in normal persons. Some of these people then developed this postimperative negative variation that looked to me like some of the late negative waves she showed in psychotic patients.

HILLYARD: I guess the N400 could conceivably be an abbreviated version of that wave; right now we're not sure what the N400 is related to.

CALLAWAY: There have been some more recent studies that seem to bear on your data by Timsit-Berthier et al. (1978). The question I wanted to ask while you have your slides in there is about the experiment where subjects listen to male and female voices in the two ears. In one case you find a P2 increase that goes with the N1 and in the other you have a P2 that goes in exactly the opposite direction from the N1. I just wanted to know what you think P2 is related to.

HILLYARD: Yes, you're right. I was hoping you wouldn't notice that. You're referring to the experiment where there is a voice in one ear and a voice in the other and we're recording ERPs to the probes. This is the only case we've seen where the P2 is getting larger as well as the N1 during auditory selective attention. If you look at the evoked potential to the speech sounds themselves, you don't find that kind of enhancement of P2 (Hillyard & Woods, 1979). In the probe experiment, the probes came at long intervals and maybe this is what brings in the P2 enlargement. I don't have an interpretation, really, but it seems to be unique to that situation.

CALLAWAY: The visual P2 tends to go with the N1, whereas the auditory P2 does not go with N1.

HILLYARD: That's right. So there is some kind of selectivity to P2 that occurs in the speech probe situation and during visual-spatial attention (Van Voorhis & Hillyard, 1977).

CALLAWAY: Would it be possible to postulate that P2 represents a somewhat later type of selection, if you are going to *postulate* a series of attentive processes (Halliday, Callaway, Rosenthal, & Naylor, 1979)? Maybe P2 represents a later selection, and in your rapid-delivery situation where P2 doesn't respond you're not using this later process. At your slower rates of presentation, you might bring in this later process.

4 Report of Panel I: Selective Attention

Panel chair: M. Posner

Panel members: R. Harter
                   S. Hillyard
                   A. Treisman

POSNER: During the discussions of the panel on selective attention we were struck by some of the similarities between the concepts of early and late selection, as defined by cognitive psychologists, and the distinction made in psychophysiology between the N100 and the P300 components. Given this parallelism, we sought ways in which important problems of cognitive psychology could be approached using joint behavioral and ERP methodology. We discussed seven related topics. These topics were: (1) the definition of a channel; (2) attention: facilitation or suppression? (3) the time course of selection; (4) the processing of features and conjunctions; (5) category selection; (6) discrete versus continuous processes; and (7) arousal and selection. In this session we shall deal with a subset of these issues.

In general, we shall describe psychological issues whose resolution may be advanced by the joint application of behavioral and psychophysiological methods. We shall review the relevant data and we shall suggest experiments, sometimes in fairly great detail, some rather more sketchily.

As "selective attention" is often defined as a process that selects among input "channels", it is natural to begin with the difficulties encountered when trying to define the term *channel*. Russ Harter will begin the review of this topic.

HARTER: Because attention, by definition, is selective, one of the first questions our panel considered was "what is being selected?" The answer often given to this question is that "a channel" is selected. This leads to the next question, "what is a channel?" Regardless of how a channel is defined, its definition, to avoid circularity, should be independent of the definition of attention; that is, it is inadequate to define *attention* as the process that allows selection between channels and then to define *channel* as that which is selected by attention. I prefer to adopt the definition of channel that is used by investigators of sensory processes. A "channel consists of those neurons that are selectively responsive to some aspect of a stimulus, the selectivity of the neurons presumably being due to their receptive field organization" (Blakemore & Campbell, 1969; Campbell, Cooper, & Enroth-Cugell, 1969). I would like to present an example of how we have used ERPs to describe spatial frequency or "size" channels, using this operational definition, and how the bandwidth of such channels can predict the selectivity of the effects of attention to a particular check size on ERPs.

We begin by identifying the "size" channels by using an interocular suppression paradigm with the ERPs serving as the dependent variable (Harter, Towle, & Musso, 1976). We assume that intense, continuous, stimulation of one eye with a checkerboard of a given check size will saturate the binocular "size" channel over which the checks of this size are processed. If a checkerboard with the same check size is presented briefly to the other eye, an ERP with a reduced amplitude will be elicited, because fewer elements in the shared central channel would be free to respond to the additional input. As shown in Fig. 4.1, the bandwidth of the binocular size channel is defined as the range of check sizes that when continuously presented to the right eye would suppress interocularly the amplitude of ERPs to a check size flashed to the left eye. The results of our experiments indicate that interocular suppression of ERPs was: (1) greatest when both eyes viewed the same check size (either 12 or 35 min); and (2) most evident 160 msec after the flash. The degree of the suppression decreased as the check sizes viewed by the two eyes were made progressively more different. The half-amplitude, half-bandwidth, of the size-amplitude tuning functions at 160-msec poststimulus was about 1 octave. We, therefore, concluded that for these stimuli, cortical size channels are maximally activated about 160 msec after stimulus. The channels appear to have a bandwidth of about 1 octave.

We then tested the hypothesis that attending selectively to a particular check size influences the processing of information within the channel tuned to that check size (Harter & Previc, 1978). This hypothesis leads to the prediction that ERPs elicited by checkerboards of check sizes that are within a ± 1 octave bandwidth about the attended check size or channel should be enhanced. The degree of enhancement should depend on the similarity of the evoking check size to the size associated with the center of the attended channel. In addition, we predicted that selective attention should have the greatest effect on ERP measures of processing at about 160-msec poststimulus.

The subjects were instructed to attend selectively either to diffuse light or to a checkerboard (12- or 35-min check size). Attention was assured by requiring the subject to respond to the stimulus, or to count stimuli. One of eight checkerboards was illuminated according to a random schedule. A stimulus

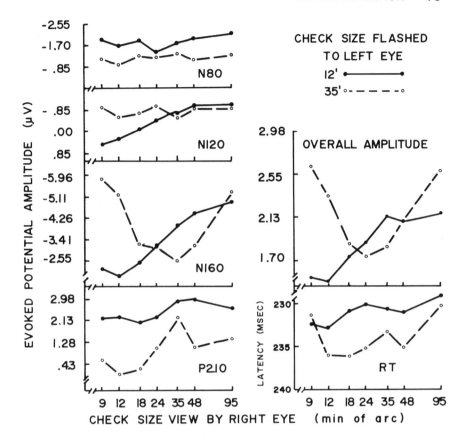

FIG. 4.1 Size-specific channels indicated by interocular suppression of ERPs. Changes in monocular ERPs to checkerboard flashed to the left eye (12' and 35' check size indicated by solid and dashed lines) as a function of the check size (9–95') continuously viewed by the opposite (right) eye. N80, N120, N160, and P210 refer to the average polarity and latency at which the amplitude measures were taken. RT refers to behavioral reaction time. Note that the N160 measure indicated the greatest reduction in amplitude when the flashed and continuously stimulated eye viewed the same size check, the reduction decreasing as these two check sizes became more different. From Harter, Towle, and Musso (1976).

was triggered once every 555 to 999 msec. The subjects' central visual field was stimulated. The stimuli were either diffuse light or checkerboards with check sizes ranging from 9 to 95 min.

The effects of attending to a particular check size on the amplitude of the ERP elicited by the various check sizes is shown in Fig. 4.2. The amplitude of the ERP between 120 and 270 msec after the stimulus was most negative when the evoking and attended stimuli were of the same check size. The extent to which attending to a given check size enhanced VEPs elicited by similar check sizes varied across the epoch. As we predicted, the enhancement was evident 160 msec after the stimulus and had a bandwidth of about ± 1 octave (second and fourth rows of Fig. 4.2). Thus, our data support the hypothesis that the processing in spatial frequency (i.e., size) channels may be influenced by attentional mechanisms and that the characteristics of such channels may determine the characteristics of attentional effects. Unexpectedly, the changes in the effects of attention on ERP amplitude from about 160 to 260 msec indicated a progression of the selection process. The magnitude, and selectivity, of the differential processing of relevant and irrelevant stimuli increased, as reflected by the increased difference in ERP amplitude to relevant and irrelevant stimuli and decreased bandwidth of the selective attention effects (about 1 to 0.5 octaves). Thus, changes in ERPs may provide an electrophysiological measure of the time course of the sequence of information processing between the reception of the stimulus and the initiation of the response.

Note that this progression is not consistent with the suggestion that components of ERP reflect discrete stages of information processing that occur at specific points in time, such as the model proposed by Hillyard (Hillyard, Picton, & Regan, 1978) that assumes that N1 and P3 represent the activity of different selection stages. In our experiment, selection appeared to take place progressively over a 200-msec period, starting at about 100 msec and ending at about 260 msec just prior to the initiation of the motor response. The selection process, furthermore, was complete well before the occurrence of the P300 component. The narrowing of the selective attention-tuning functions, as reflected by the changes in ERP negativity measured at progressively later points in time after stimulation, further suggests a sequence of many underlying processes, each associated with a greater degree of selectivity rather than a few underlying processes.

KAHNEMAN: Is that attention or discrimination?

HARTER: I'm not sure I can answer this question without knowing how you define *discrimination*. Discrimination is typically defined as the differential response to different stimuli. The ERP component that appears 100 msec after the stimulus has a different amplitude in response to each of the eight different stimuli. I would say this early component indicates the eight stimuli were discriminated. Selective attention was indicated by the different ERP amplitude associated with the same stimulus, as a function of its task relevance. This effect was not reflected by the early 100-msec component but was reflected by ERP amplitudes from about 120- to 260-msec stimulus. I would say the early 100-msec and late 235-msec components tend to reflect neural discrimination and attention processes, respectively.

DONCHIN: Suppose you ran this experiment and failed to get these results? Would you have concluded that, according to your definition of channel, there are no "size" channels? You are arguing from a *sensory* analysis that there are such channels. You predict that the channel that was identified in one set of studies will be a channel for the attention mechanism. But if the prediction is not fulfilled, will you reject the hypothesis? Will you then decide that there are no "size" channels?

HARTER: No! If I had not obtained the predicted results, I would assume that the sensory size channels were perhaps not involved in attentional processes.

DONCHIN: Well, but you define channel in terms of selectivity of the response and then show that you get a selective response. What would you say if you would not get the selective response? Would you say that this is a channel for some purposes but not for others? What's the point of making a prediction that, should it be rejected, would not affect your thinking? I am puzzled because you said that you're going to define channel without reference to the concept of attention. Attention in turn is defined in terms of selection. If you define channel by the existence of a selective response you have, I think, defined the concept in terms of attention. I want to be able to know what will be a channel without running an attention experiment to find out if it is a channel; otherwise, the definition is somewhat circular.

HARTER: If I understand your argument correctly, it is based on the assumption that the selectivity in the attention study was, in part, used to define the nature of size channels. That assumption is not correct, at least from my point of view. The previous study on size-specific interocular suppression provided the definition and description of channels. In this interocular suppression experiment, selectivity was due to the interaction between the stimuli presented to the left and right eye and presumably reflects the organization of receptive fields of aggregates of neurons or size detectors. This type of selectivity was demonstrated independently of attention. In the context of the second experiment, selectivity was due to the interaction between the nature of stimuli and the cognitive representation of the relevant and/or irrelevant information and presumably reflects the descending influence of such cognitive representations on the activity of sensory channels processing the stimuli.

The nature of channels suggested by the data from the interocular suppression study, in conjunction with the assumption that attention might influence the processing of information in such channels, was used to predict the outcome of the subsequent attention study. If this prediction had not been supported, I would have simply concluded that selective attention to size doesn't appear to influence the processing of information in the sensory size channels described in the interocular suppression study. One cannot really say too much about negative results. However, the results of the attention study were positive and can be interpreted as supporting the prediction. I think these two stud-

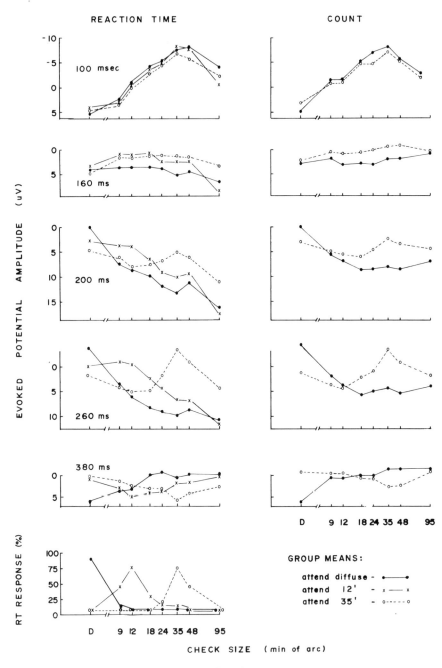

CONDITION

FIG. 4.2

78

ies provide an example of how this definition of channel can predict the effects of selective attention on information processing.

TREISMAN: I think the term *channel* is used rather differently in the context of behavioral studies of human selective attention (Broadbent, 1958).

KAHNEMAN: It's not even remotely similar. The use of channel in the attention literature is quite different from Harter's.

TREISMAN: There are two main differences between Harter's concept of channel and the definition of channel in experimental studies of attention in humans. One is that, for those attention theorists who use the term, channel is not usually defined a priori. It is not defined independently of attention. Second, a logically different experimental paradigm has typically been used in the study of human attention. In the early studies of attention, reviewed by Broadbent in 'Perception and Communication,' the term *channel* was used in two different ways: First, in operational terms, channel was simply a label for one of several, physically different, ways of presenting a message. For example, a spoken message could be presented to the left ear or the right, in a man's voice or in a woman's, at a high or low intensity and so on. The second use of the term was theoretical within the framework of the filter theory of attention. In this context the term *channel* labeled any class of stimuli to which attention could be selectively directed. In this sense, the definition was probably circular, because any basis for classification that was shown empirically to support selective attention would thereby be said to differentiate two or more attention channels. Classes of words, such as names of food, were included as potential channels in this sense.

Many experiments were run to discover which classes of stimuli could function as channels in this attentional sense. It was found that attention could be focused quite efficiently on one of two messages whenever these differed in some simple physical characteristic such as location, pitch, intensity, or color. Thus, although no a priori definition, independent of attention, was proposed, an inductive generalization was made as follows: Because every clearly discriminable physical difference between messages (so far tested) has allowed atten-

---

FIG. 4.2 *(Opposite page)* Effects of selective attention on size-specific channels. ERP amplitude measured 100, 160, 200, 260 and 380 msec after the stimulus flash (top to bottom). Changes in amplitude within each figure are due to check size of the stimulus flashed (horizontal axis) and attended (diffuse, 12' or 35'). Attention was controlled by having subjects give a RT response (left) or count (right) the relevant stimuli. Note that at about 260 msec poststimulus, attending the stimuli resulted in enhanced ERP amplitude, the degree of enhancement increasing with the similarity between the attended and flashed stimuli. Bottom, left: percentage of RT responses to each flash (median latency = 322 msec). From Harter and Previc (1978).

tion to operate selectively, it is likely that any new physical distinction that is as easily discriminable will also allow the functional separation of attention channels. Harter's experiments are very interesting in this context, because they offer a different empirical criterion for distinguishing classes of stimuli, a criterion that is physiologically defined. It would be valuable to see whether the properties for which Harter obtains physiological selectivity correlate with those that empirically define a channel for human selective attention.

However, before pursuing this possibility, it is essential to note the second important difference between Harter's use of channel and its use in filter theories of attention. This is a logical difference in the tasks used to study attention. In the study Harter described, the subject was both attending to a particular channel (for example, a red item or a vertical grating), and also responding to the feature that defined that channel, namely that it was red or vertical or whatever the physical property happened to be. In Broadbent's paradigm, subjects would attend to a channel, for example, red items, but respond to some other property of these red items. For example, their shape, their orientation, or their meaning. The channel-defining feature determined the direction of attention but not the response that was demanded of the subject. In other words, a two-stage process was built into the paradigm. Subjects were required to use one discrimination to select items for a further discrimination. This has implications for the models one can propose. In Harter's paradigm, one can think of attention as priming nodes, which is a currently popular way of conceptualizing selection. Attention is seen as providing some kind of priming that operates on an internal representation. I think that in the Broadbentian paradigm such an account will not work. The more attention primes the nodes that respond to red, the more evidence it will produce that the items are red, and the more ready the subject will be to believe that they are red, but that won't tell the subject what else they are. It won't tell him that they are uppercase letters, that they spell the word *cat*, and so on.

POSNER: You could perhaps combine the two paradigms and predict that if a subject was attending to a 35-min check, he should be better at recognizing the color of a 40-min check than of a 5-min check. That would be an a priori definition of a channel but would use Broadbent's method of assessing whether attention selected not only the check size but also all the other properties of the 35-min check when it was selectively tuned to that particular spatial frequency.

HILLYARD: In a similar vein, let's consider a sensory dimension such as position in space. You attend to one position on that dimension. For stimuli presented at that location there is some measure of improved processing. You can then define stimuli outside that channel as those that are not affected by attention--their processing is not affected, or it may be actually suppressed.

This is the definition Shiffrin et al. used in their "49 positions in space" paper (Shiffrin, McKay, & Shaffer, 1976).

DONCHIN: But suppose the word *channel* was banned. You could describe the same experiment without losing anything.

HILLYARD: It doesn't matter what term one uses to define the phenomenon. The concept of channel is based on the observation that specific sets of inputs are facilitated by selective attention. That these sets have certain boundaries, tuning curves, etc., is a real phenomenon, which is described by the term *channel*.

KAHNEMAN: It is a basis on which you can select.

DONCHIN: It does not allow you to predict what will be selected. Unless you do the experiment and find out, you cannot know.

KAHNEMAN: There are by now enough experiments to show that you can select by certain physical attributes and that you find it a great deal more difficult to select by others.

DONCHIN: Look, you can determine what can be selected, but that doesn't clarify the concept of a channel. In theorizing channels have acquired a reality that is not justified by conceptual and theoretical considerations.

NORMAN: That's because we keep waiting for you to define the physiological bases for channels that we have discovered.

KAHNEMAN: Maybe the whole thing is a bad metaphor. Saying that we are selecting channels is a bad metaphor because we don't select channels. I don't think there is any such thing in the context of attention. I think we select objects, locations in space, by the fact that they have a particular property. Traditionally, if we can select by a property, we call that property a channel. I agree with Donchin that it doesn't add anything, but it doesn't detract anything either.

DONCHIN: It is the same to me if you prefer to call it a bad metaphor rather than a meaningless term.

TREISMAN: People use it simply as a label.

NORMAN: I think it's important to know what the basic phenomenon is. We can cause enhanced processing over a certain region of a sensory domain and this is apparently accompanied by diminished processing, or neutral processing, on the rest of the domain. The point is that by willful application of something that we do not understand, one can indeed decide to process one kind of signal. For the moment I'm not going to worry about whether that signal is defined by the observer as something that corresponds to physical dimensions. There are certain restrictions, though, on the sorts of things to which we can apply our attention. Moreover, there is a certain width to that application of attention. The phenomenon is not fully understood. The definition of restricted range is indeed circular at the moment, but the concept is correct.

DONCHIN: It can be argued that one should use terms from information theory only in their precise application in information theory. *Channel* is a technical term; it is defined by an origin and a terminus and by the information transmitted over the channel between the origin and the terminus. One can measure the transmission rate and many other attributes of the channel. One can therefore objectively assess the extent to which any particular mechanism does, or does not, behave like a communication channel. I have no objection to the use of labels or metaphors as long as we don't carry the metaphor too far.

HARTER: Are you objecting to the use of the term channel like a sensory psychophysicist and neurophysiologist would use it? For them, a channel is an aggregate of neurons that all have similar receptive field organization and, therefore, that are most sensitive to the same type of stimuli. Activation of a channel is a means of coding information. When the channel is active, it indicates a particular type of stimulus is present in the environment.

KAHNEMAN: That's not the way the term *channel* is used in the theory of selective attention. Historically the word channel may have been used by attention theorists because of the fact that most of the early studies used auditory stimuli. There are two channels on tape recorders, and there are two ears to which messages can be separately delivered. I am convinced that had the early experimenters used visual stimuli, we wouldn't have used the channel metaphor.

CALLAWAY: Russ, how did you call your subjects' attention to the checks?

HARTER: We showed the check size to the subjects and either required them to count the checks of a given size or instructed them to respond rapidly to the stimuli.

CALLAWAY: This is different than Hillyard's experiments. When Hillyard tells subjects to attend to a point in space, that point contains either a high tone or a low tone.

HARTER: That was Dr. Treisman's point.

KAHNEMAN: But in selective attention we do not select a channel in that sense. You select information that arrives on a channel.

POSNER: We look at the consequences of selecting a channel by what happens with respect to information arriving on that channel versus some other channel. This brings us to our second topic that is also an old one that we hope to clarify similarly: Does attention produce suppression or facilitation?

HILLYARD: The selectivity of attention is illustrated very well in an experiment by Greenberg and Larkin (1968) in which a series of near-threshold tone pips of different frequencies was presented and the subject attended to a tone pip of a particular pitch. The subjects were very good at detecting tones of that frequency and were progressively less accurate at detecting tones of adjacent frequencies. One could determine the breadth of the "frequency space" within which there was facilitation of signal detections, and if one wants to label this empirical phenomenon, the term channel seems as good as any.

I would like to discuss the following question. When one attends to a given locus on a sensory dimension, is attention more a facilitation of information coming from that locus or more a suppression of inputs from adjacent loci? Or do both mechanisms operate? To address this question with ERP techniques we must define the truly "neutral" condition of attention where information is neither accentuated nor suppressed. In a recent study by J. Hansen in our laboratory (unpublished) the subject attended to 700-Hz tones while ignoring 400 Hz tones presented in a random sequence. The ERP to the attended tones contained a broad negativity between 100-300 msec, overlapping the N1 component, which was absent or even positive-going, to the unattended tones. We wondered whether this lower level of negativity seen to unattended-channel tones actually represented a suppression of input, so Hansen ran some supposedly neutral conditions where the subject was either reading, that is, attending to a different modality, or just sitting with no instructions. Both of those conditions produced an ERP with an intermediate level of the late negativity, suggesting that attention involved both a facilitation of one channel and a suppression of the other. The problem, however, is that we have no way of knowing how neutral our control conditions were *vis a vis* auditory attention. Further, it is not clear whether the reduced N1 negativity would occur to all unattended stimuli or only those that are repeated and need to be ignored.

One can imagine evoked potential paradigms that would test these ideas in a more rigorous fashion. Russ Harter described one possiblity. One could present a range of stimuli across an entire sensory dimension (e.g., of pitch or space) and focus attention on one point in that dimension. ERPs would be recorded to stimuli at the focus of attention, at loci adjacent to the focus of attention, and to stimuli greatly distant from the locus of attention. Possibly, the suppression of the ERPs to adjacent stimuli would disappear for the more distant stimuli. This would be a nice result that would be interpretable in terms of suppression/facilitation acting together. If ERP amplitudes were reduced to all nonattended loci, however, it wouldn't be clear how much active suppression was involved because you wouldn't know what the "null level" of the ERP was. One could also use a "probe paradigm" with two channels of competing stimuli, one attended and one ignored (Hink & Hillyard, 1976) with probes given over a range of values around the channel. Measuring the amplitudes of the different probe ERPs might give an interpretable result.

Experiments like this may, however, confound attention and refractory effects on the ERPs. Refractory effects would probably produce a depression of the exogenous portions of the ERP for stimuli that were adjacent to one another (Picton, Hillyard, & Galambos, 1976). However, by subtracting the refractory effects I think one might be able to find out whether there is an actual accentuation or suppression of ERPs at the points of attention and at the points of inattention, respectively, and thus get at the basic question of whether attention involves both the commitment of "resources" to one channel and their withdrawal from others.

NORMAN: A technical question, is that interaction temporal?

HILLYARD: Yes, if you present one stimulus immediately after another, the response to the second stimulus will be depressed to the extent that it resembles the first stimulus.

NORMAN: For what duration?

HILLYARD: For the waves we're talking about, many seconds. Does anyone consider this sort of experiment worth doing?

NORMAN: Yes, I think it's worth doing, but I do have a question. The picture you drew shows that the unattended waveform actually goes positive and that is information too, I would presume. So it isn't quite clear why you consider that to be a suppression?

HILLYARD: Well, the net effect of attention is seen in the difference waveform between the attended condition and the unattended condition, which is the broad negative component. The difference between those conditions can be construed as arising from more negativity in one or more positivity in the other. It isn't clear what the true "neutral" baseline is. Further, the fact that the unattended ERP goes below the baseline (positive) may be due to exogenous components added on to it. So I don't really know whether it is important that the unattended ERP is actually positive at this point.

SHIFFRIN: Are you saying that departure from some baseline in either direction is carrying information? Then, why call a departure in one direction a suppression and the other one facilitation? Why not call them both facilitation?

HILLYARD: There is a large negativity that distinguishes the attended from the unattended channel waveforms, and there appears to be a smaller amount of that negativity separating the control ERP from the unattended-channel ERP. There appears to be a continuum of more or less negativity, with the neutral reading condition somewhere in the middle.

SHIFFRIN: But if the subject has reference to some kind of neutral level that is in between the possibility [presence] of a lower level of this negativity or a higher level of this positivity, could not both be taken as an indication of the presence of processing?

HILLYARD: Yes, I suppose that could be another interpretation. There is some ambiguity in my argument because when I suggest that more negativity indicates attention and a minimal negativity reflects inattention, while a medium value is the null point, another interpretation could be that there is another, overlapping positive process that is being added. It is difficult to know, in general, whether the component you think you are measuring is changing or whether another component is lurking underneath.

KUTAS: Despite our lack of sophistication in determining the extent to which a short segment of an ERP such as a large negative wave represents a single negative component or a combination of a large negative component and a smaller positive component, the waveforms obtained in these types of selective attention experiments are consistent and reliable enough to enable us to use the difference between the ERPs elicited by attended and nonattended stimuli, that is, the difference wave as an indication of whether the subject was paying attention to the channel as instructed or whether he was attending to a different stimulus or channel that he had been instructed to ignore.

HILLYARD: In addition, we have some behavioral data suggesting that when a lot of this negativity is present, one is better at detecting events in the attended channel. There are behavioral measures that relate to this.

DONCHIN: Let's consider the definition of the effects of the attention on the component you call N100. Suppose you eliminate the top trace from this figure, leaving the traces obtained during the "neutral" and the "nonattention" conditions. By the definition you gave for the effects of attention, would you have to say that there is an effect of attention because you have a selective response, and one ERP is more negative than the other?

HILLYARD: No, not necessarily. This comparison wouldn't fulfill the behavioral criterion for a good selective attention experiment (Hillyard & Picton, 1979).

NORMAN: But the difference between the two traces *is* the result of attention.

HILLYARD: Maybe not. You can't simply compare a neutral condition with an active attention condition, because the general state of the observer might be different in other ways between the conditions.

DONCHIN: That's the point I'm trying to make. The fact that you see a difference between two waveforms in two conditions does not, in and of itself, define attention.

HILLYARD: True, I could insert a couple of high tones in between the two experimental conditions and that would change your responses in a way that would not necessarily reflect selective attention.

DONCHIN: That is important, because very frequently the argument is made that if you see a difference in the response to the stimulus, there must be an act of selection. We infer the act of selection from the difference between the waveforms.

TREISMAN: There is also the fact that the subject has been told to attend.

DONCHIN: Yet, it is important to agree that one cannot infer the existence of a selection mechanism simply because there is a difference between two ERPs, even when the subject had received different instructions. The operation of a selector is inferred from what the subject was doing, how he was performing, what the instructions to the subject were, how you want to interpret the data. The selectivity of electrophysiological response does not demonstrate the existence of selective attention.

TREISMAN: But when you tell him to attend, he in fact shows the expected difference in his behavioral, as well as his electrophysiological, response to the attended and the unattended items.

DONCHIN: Are we agreeing that it is not enough for two waveforms to differ to say that there has been selective attention?

KAHNEMAN: There is plenty of evidence that those instructions have effects.

DONCHIN: I'm not denying the effects of attention. I'm just trying to agree on a criterion and to establish that ERPs, by themselves, do not establish "selection."

CALLAWAY: Let me give you an example that might clarify what Donchin is saying. I can ask a person to press a switch that will trigger a click. This click will elicit an ERP with a greatly reduced N100. If the same click is presented to the subject under the computer's control, the click elicits an N100. The reduction of N100 in the ERP elicited by the subject-triggered click does not imply that the subject is paying less attention to the click. So there you have a dissociation between N100 and attention.

HARTER: Well, you have to assume that all stimulus parameters are held constant and you have to study ERPs elicited by at least two stimuli, one attended and the other not, and show that the effect appears in response to one of those stimuli and not to the other. If these criteria are met, you can infer "attention" from the ERPs.

HILLYARD: I agree with that. Picton and I made a similar argument in the Brussels symposium (Hillyard & Picton, 1979). That's a physiological criterion for selective attention. I think a behavioral definition of attention using measures of facilitated processing could follow the same guidelines.

SHIFFRIN: To what extent does the ERP tell you more about the direction of attention than the subject can tell you with his overt responses?

HILLYARD: That's one of the main issues facing the conference. Why did you have to bring it up so baldly?

HARTER: One thing indicated by ERPs is the time course of the selection process. If you look at the changes in the evoked potential at different points in time after stimulation, you can get a hint as to the progression of events starting with the stimulus up to the time the response is given.

DONCHIN: But here again you infer the course of selection from the difference between two waveforms. That is what bothers me. There may well be a continually ongoing selection process that manifests itself *in the ERP* at specific points.

KUTAS: There are in fact experimental situations in which a change in an ERP parameter can tell the investigator something more about a person's processing than the subject's overt response. For example, Hillyard and associates ran an experiment in which stimuli were presented in two different locations in space. The stimuli at either location could be auditory or visual. On any given run, the subjects' task was to respond to a target in *one* modality at *one* location in space. What the subject did not know at the time of the testing (and was unable to report later) was that a small percentage of the stimuli were bimodal (i.e., the auditory and visual stimuli occurred simultaneously at the same location in space). And yet, even a cursory inspection of the ERPs shows that the bimodal stimuli were "noticed." Not only did the bimodal ERP differ from the unimodal ERP, but in addition ERPs elicited by the bimodal stimuli were different depending on whether they were presented in the same or different location than the to-be-attended unimodal targets.

HILLYARD: Yes, that's a good example of a more general point. Once you've established that an ERP component is a valid measure of attention, you can use that component to determine which events in the environment are attended at any given moment. The distribution of a subject's attention can be evaluated with ERPs, even though he/she can't possibly make overt responses to that many stimuli.

SHIFFRIN: Suppose the ERP is, as someone said, an indication of what a subject consciously perceived after the fact. That kind of model would imply that the ERP gives some representation such as surprise, the appreciation of a signal, or something. Further, the response may be prior to the conscious awareness of the presence or absence of signal. Now, is the evoked response a more critical indicator of the presence or absence of signal than overt responses, or is the order of events the other way around?

HILLYARD: I'd like to give a general answer to Shiffrin's point. I think that, in the long run, studies of event-related potentials are unlikely to yield additional information about cognitive processes over and above what can be derived from behavioral data alone. In some cases, fluctuations in ERP components may turn out not to have any behavioral correlates, no matter how many experiments one does. Some ERP components may well be epiphenomena, physiological artifacts that don't have anything to do with information processing. However, I think that in our day-to-day experimental bootstrapping, an ERP differentiation between two experimental conditions should be a cause to poke up one's ears and consider whether different kinds of psychological processes are operating. Then, one can aim a behavioral experiment at those processes. The ERP can be used in this way as a converging measure, helping in the identification of psychological processes. So, I think that in the short run ERPs can be used to guide for behavioral research.

SCHVANEVELDT: Steve, you talked about the difficulty of finding a neutral condition. I think Mike Posner and his associates have been performing attention experiments for some time, where a neutral condition is defined by a warning stimulus that carries no information about the next event. Thus, if you selectively try to focus subjects' attention on each trial on different events, you may be able to have a neutral condition.

KAHNEMAN: There is a difference between the two paradigms. Posner's involves priming rather than filtering. The whole idea of filtering is that you have to reset the subject to select, say, the red stimuli and not the blue ones or the high-pitched voice and not the low-pitched voice. Mike's strategy will not work for filtering.

TREISMAN: Perhaps a divided attention situation would be equivalent to Posner's neutral condition. Why do you think that is not the correct comparison?

HILLYARD: Well, if you divide attention between two kinds of stimuli only, there are still many other stimuli in the world that may be suppressed or that receive varying amounts of attention.

TREISMAN: But would they not also be present in the focused attention condition?

HILLYARD: I don't know. In the neutral, or 50-50 prime, condition studied by Posner, the subject could be directing attention to both stimuli. The overall "amount" of attention may be different if the subject is certain where the stimulus will occur. But both of these conditions may require more attention than the "null" condition.

SCHVANEVELDT: One can run the same experiment with a very wide range of stimuli. I don't know whether it would work with these very early components. It probably will not, but Neely (1977), for example, studied word recognition where the priming stimulus indicated a class of stimuli that might occur next. Neely obtained very orderly behavioral data when comparing a neutral condition with a properly primed condition and with a falsely primed condition.

POSNER: I worry about what Hillyard said because you never know when you have a truly neutral condition. In the last year or so people have been looking at the patterns of costs and benefits and comparing the neutral conditions where they obtain different patterns of costs and benefits. The neutral condition seems to be stable (Becker, 1980).

TREISMAN: It seems to me to be logically equivalent. If there are problems with divided attention, there are also with the 50-50 arrangement of stimuli in the priming experiment.

POSNER: I think the only hope is to obtain a body of empirical data that would persuade you that it works; otherwise I don't think, a priori, you can decide what's the right thing to do.

TREISMAN: On this question of whether we actively suppress or actively enhance, I want to mention one point that occurred to me. We do, behaviorally anyway, detect a change of stimulus along almost any physical dimension. This seems to suggest, doesn't it, that we are tuned around the unattended stimulus. So we may selectively suppress, for example, just the tones to the left ear, because if their location or frequency is changed, we register the difference at once.

HILLYARD: You could record ERPs to probes that were fairly similar to the irrelevant stimuli, and these may be smaller than ERPs to probes that are more deviant. I think you could design a clean evoked-potential experiment that would get at this.

POSNER: I think we should move on to the next topic. We want to discuss the time course of selection and three different experiments that emerged from the discussions of our panel on this set of issues. Let me try to outline the issue from the point of view of a cognitive psychologist. I can illustrate my point by referring to an experiment that Anne Treisman reported a number of years ago. Her subjects were supposed to attend to the information in one ear (Treisman, Squire, & Green, 1974). Occasionally a synonym occurs in the other ear. You determine whether a synonym, of the word you are shadowing, influences the shadowing of the material on the attended ear. Lewis (1970) first conducted an experiment of this type and presented evidence that seems to indicate that the unattended information was getting in because it affected the rate at which a person could shadow, even though he never reported anything about it. Subjects never seemed aware of the information in the unattended ear. Nonetheless, some kind of semantic analysis of the unattended information must have been going on. When Treisman repeated the study, she replicated Lewis' results, but only for the first few words in a list. After a few words, it seemed that the subjects were blocking the unattended information quite thoroughly and one did not get the effect. Perhaps it takes a while to set up a filter that causes the exclusion from consciousness of the unattended information. Our own results are somewhat different. If a subject is instructed to attend to a given location in space, the selective effect develops in about 200 msec. So it appears that it is possible to set up, whatever you're setting up, very quickly (Posner, 1978; 1980). On the other hand, you do not exclude the unattended events from consciousness. If an event happens on the unattended location, it's not that the subject misses it, but they are slow. So it is possible that in our experiments we are not obtaining real filtering. Certainly, I'm not getting the kind of filtering that produces a phenomenological exclusion from consciousness the way it occurs in shadowing. The paradigm Hillyard uses seems to require quite a bit of information on the channel before you can set up the kinds of selection that produces the N100 effect. But we really don't know how much. In Hillyard's experiments, there are a lot of data in both channels and, if you reduce the presentation rate by too much, you lose the N100 effect. It appears that some information is required on the channel before we can exclude inputs and produce an N100 difference. Both Hillyard and I have tried to obtain that N100 effect trial by trial by cuing the subject where to attend. We did not find an N100 effect. The question is, how long does it take to set up the kind of exclusion device that produces the N100 effect? This would be a nice way of trying to use the ERP. I don't know what the best experiment might be, but a possibility is to have the subject shift attention many times during the session. You average separately the first trial in the sequences, then the second trial, etc. Do we find the full N100 exclusion on the first trial? What is the time course with which we develop the filter? It seemed to me that might be a way of bridging between the paradigms I talked about yesterday and those Steve Hillyard uses. This may be a way of answering the question that Treisman's work raised about whether exclusion doesn't require getting into the task on the attended ear.

TREISMAN: One reason why it might take time to focus attention exclusively on one channel is that the filter may be selectively tuned to exclude the properties of the unattended channel rather than to select those of the attended one. If so, it might take a while before a representation of the stimuli to be rejected is built up. It is also important, when we are trying to develop empirical tests that would allow a choice between early and late selection theories, to remember that it takes time for attention to narrow down effectively. Many of the experiments that found no limits to attention on the perceptual side have used few stimuli or few presentations. Perhaps the attention filter simply takes time to set up.

DONCHIN: What would be the conclusion if you do not get the effect?

POSNER: If you never get it?

DONCHIN: If it turns out that it doesn't develop over time? Would one conclude that the filter develops instantaneously or would you conclude that the ERP is not sensitive?

POSNER: I'm sorry, but either it has to be there on the first trial or it has to develop over time. One or the other! Because we know that after a while you get the effect. If the effect appears on the first trial, it means you can switch in the selection immediately. If it takes time, then we find out how long it takes. This is not an experiment where one outcome is interpretable and the other is not.

CALLAWAY: The technical problem when you are doing the experiment is that you've got to take some time to show the person what you want.

POSNER: This isn't a problem because you could use the first day's data as just practice and because you can keep switching back from channel to channel for any number of sessions so you can develop a very practiced subject and still study the dynamics of the switching.

CALLAWAY: But with a very practiced subject, would you still take time to develop?

POSNER: Well, yes. In most of the shadowing studies, one uses practiced subjects.

CALLAWAY: I can tell you that with children, using Hillyard's paradigm, there is almost no shift. Once you train the child to attend to the high tones in the right ear, for example, you can get him to attend to the low tone in the left ear, but you can't get him to attend to the low tone in the right ear or a high tone in the left ear.

HILLYARD: Using an evoked potential criterion for attention?

CALLAWAY: By any criterion. They burst into tears. They say, "I can't do it. I'm still listening to the low tone in my right ear, I can listen to the high tone in my left ear but not the low tone in my left ear."

NORMAN: In doing that experiment, take note of Anne's warning. You may have to set the parameters by listening for a while until you can do it both with clear tones and with something more complex like Steve's waveforms.

OSCAR-BERMAN: There are a lot of dimensions in a shadowing experiment and the loss of a lot of dimensions will take probably a lot more time than a single dimension.

HILLYARD: The ERP effect is present to probes superimposed onto speech channels so you should be able to look at this. You start out listening to speech alone and then present the probe a varying amount of time after the speech begins. If Posner's proposed experiment were to demonstrate that subjects can indeed build up an N100 effect instantaneously, then I would be tempted to conclude that his experiment where the arrow cues you to the right or the left involves a different kind of attention than is employed for attending to a continuous, ongoing channel and ignoring another ongoing channel.

KAHNEMAN: I think orientation is really specialized that way. The flexibility is built right into the orientation system.

SCHVANEVELDT: Don't you have to worry about the loading effect? I mean, you're saying that even in standard situations like dichotic listening if you slow down the rate of stimulation, you don't get the difference.

HILLYARD: That's right. One interpretation of the loading effect is that the long ISIs may not allow the subject to "build up" or focus attention effectively.

TREISMAN: We suggest that another interpretation of the loading effect is that the subject needs to be reminded of what is being excluded.

SCHVANEVELDT: The load has to be heavy enough for that exclusion to be necessary.

TREISMAN: Those are the two alternatives.

MCCARTHY: I have a question about the switching of attention between the attended and unattended channels. I was wondering if it would be interesting perhaps to do an experiment whereon we present a signal to an unattended channel and require the subject to pay attention momentarily to that channel and then look at the standards on that unattended channel following the target that appeared on that channel to see if attention had switched back and how long it would take to switch back to the attended channel. Is that worthwhile?

POSNER: It better be because that's my next experiment. At least *I* think it's worthwhile.

MCCARTHY: Then let's do it.

POSNER: I have a little story about this experiment. We argued, yesterday after my tutorial, about the way nodes in memory are primed. When an A, for example, is expected, the the A node is supposedly primed. If you then turn attention to B, the A node remains active for awhile and then decays away. McLean and Shulman (1978) traced the time course of the decay process. If directing attention to a locus in space is similar to the priming of a node in memory, then it should be possible to trace the time course of decay of facilitation following a switch in the direction of attention. If attention is more like a pointer, then as soon as attention is directed away from a locus, the initial locus loses whatever advantage it had. Thus, by examining the time course of facilitation it may be possible to determine if channel selection could be described by the same model that accounts for node activation.

PALMER: One thing you suggested yesterday was that when you are changing your attention in space from one point to another, then there is a trajectory and at intermediate points attention is located between the two points. If there is any spread to your attentional focus, you could have a pointing mechanism that would give you what would look like a decay over time by virtue of the fact that it slides across. It seems to me that that's a possible interpretation of data that you would take to look like a time decay of a node in memory.

POSNER: This could be a problem. It is really a beautiful explanation, but if the time course for this was at all like the time course for decay of a node in memory, it would require a longer duration than anything one gets from moving attention (Shulman, Remington, & McLean, 1979). So it may work, or it may not.

SHIFFRIN: Well, wouldn't you think it would be a lot faster than that?

POSNER: I think you'd never get any facilitation. I think it's due to a pointer mechanism. On the other hand, I thought that was true of memory too, until I was shown otherwise (McLean & Shulman, 1978). Our next topic may require more time. We shall consider processing features and conjunctions of features and Treisman will introduce the problem.

TREISMAN: In some tasks there appear to be no limits to attention. The early stages of perceptual processing can occur in parallel; we can register physical features across the whole visual field; we can detect texture boundaries; in visual search we find no effect of display size on simple nonconfusable targets and distractors. If we look at the physiology, we find evidence that features like spatial orientation, frequency, and color are initially registered by separate populations of neurons, which have specialized tuning functions. Harter also showed evidence of independence of feature channels in the sense that one can be selectively enhanced and others suppressed. If it is the case that we have relatively independent feature detectors that operate in parallel across the visual field, and produce separate maps for color, orientation, movement and so on, the question arises as to how these features are recombined to make the objects that form our normal visual experience. It occurred to me that this might be the stage at which attention limits first appear. We might put together features to form objects (e.g., deciding that it is the 0 that is red and the X that is green) by attempting to process each item sequentially, attending to one location and then to another. We could then put together as parts of the same object any features that received simultaneous attention, which occurred concurrently in the same central fixation of attention.

In order to test this idea, we have run a number of experiments, using different paradigms to try to obtain converging evidence for the hypothesis (Treisman, Sykes, & Gelade, 1977; Treisman, 1979; Treisman & Gelade, 1980). We compared performance in a visual search task in which subjects were looking for a target defined by a single feature (such as the color red) to performance in a search task in which the target was defined by a conjunction of features (such as both red and O). We used displays in which there were always two kinds of distractors, red X's and green O's. In one condition, subjects were looking for a target defined by either of two single features, an H or a blue letter; in another condition, they were looking for a target that was defined only by the way in which its two features were put together, a red 0. We presented differing numbers of distractors in the display. We chose targets that were of equal difficulty when just a single item was presented and attention need not be divided. So there was no difference in the difficulty of discrimination. We wanted to know what happens as we increase the number of items in the display, in other words, when we start loading the subject. Do subjects have to scan the items serially, paying attention to each in turn before they can decide if an item is the target? Does this occur only if they must decide how the features are put together, as in the case of conjunction targets and not in the case of single-feature targets? What we found was a linear increase in search time for conjunction targets, as display size increased from 1 to 5 to 15 to 30 distractors. The ratio of negative to positive slopes was approximately 2 to 1. The results strongly suggest a serial, self-terminating scan. On the other hand, the targets defined by a single feature (blue or H), were apparently detected in parallel. Positive search times were almost unaffected by display size. The results support the idea that attention limits for these search tasks depend on whether the subject has to specify how features are put together to form compound objects or whether they can respond just on the basis of a single feature.

I shall briefly mention a few other findings. If feature integration depends on attention, it should be interesting to manipulate attention explicitly by giving subjects an advance cue. In another experiment, we used displays of 12 items arranged in circular array. The subject's task was again to detect a target item defined either by a feature (red or O) or by a conjunction of features (red and O). One condition required divided attention, because no advance cue was given to the target's location. Subjects were to press a key as soon as they decided whether a target was present anywhere in the display. In the other condition, 100 msec in advance of the display, they were given a cue (a pointer) indicating the one relevant location to be checked. The task was to decide whether the target was in the cued location or not and to ignore it if it was elsewhere in the display (which it was on half the negative trials). In this condition, they were therefore forced to focus attention on the cued location and they were given 100-msec advance warning to do so. If attention limits are restricted to the conjunction level where features are put together, we expect the precue to help when subjects are looking for a conjunction target, because it tells them in advance where to focus attention. In the feature condition, however, it might actually be harder to specify a particular location for the target than to detect it by checking the whole display in parallel. The results confirmed our predictions: Subjects were much quicker at detecting a conjunction target in a specific location than at finding it in the display as a whole, whereas with the single-feature color and shape targets, subjects were, if anything, worse in the precued condition. They gained no advantage from knowing where to attend (presumably because attention is not needed to detect the target).

Another paradigm we used was detection of texture boundaries. If features are registered in parallel across a display, a boundary between spatial groups of different items should be salient and easy to find when it is formed by feature differences like color (red X's and O's on one side; blue X's and O's on the other) or shape (red and blue X's on one side; red and blue O's on the other). However, it should no longer be immediately salient or available when it depends on a conjunction of features (blue X's and red O's on one side; red X's and blue O's on the other). The results again confirmed the prediction: Subjects were extremely slow to decide whether the boundary was horizontal or vertical when it was defined only by conjunctions of features and very fast with single features, whether color or shape. It seems that differences in conjunctions of features cannot mediate texture segregation or figure-ground differences.

The last experiment tested the dependency of identification on prior spatial localization for conjunctions and for features. For a conjunction, the hypothesis is that localization must precede identification, because attention must be focused on the relevant location in order to define what the conjunction is. In this experiment we used a forced-choice task. Subjects were to say which of two targets was present in the display. In one case, the two differed from the distractors in a single feature. The task was to decide whether the display of pink O's and blue X's also contained an H or an orange letter. In the conjunction condition, the distractors were again pink O's and blue X's and the targets to be discriminated were a blue O or a pink X. In addition to deciding which of the two targets was present in each display, subjects were to say where in the display of eight items the target was located. We then looked to see if there was any interdependence in the accuracy of localization and of identification. We predicted a high degree of dependency in the case of conjunctions and much less with the features, because attention need not be directed to the target location in order to identify which single feature is present. The conditional probabilities, corrected for chance guessing, were in fact very high, averaging about 0.9 for the conjunctions, and low, only 0.4 for the features. With the features, subjects were, on a large proportion of trials, correctly saying it's an H rather than an orange target, or vice versa, without knowing where it was in the display.

That was a brief summary of some of the evidence I have collected, which, I think, suggests that at least one kind of attention limit arises at the stage where features are combined to form coherent, complex objects. One can apply the same ideas to selective listening and auditory attention. Words are conjunctions of properties, and attention appears to be quite limited when we are required to identify the verbal content of two messages at once. Single features, such as differences of pitch or location, can, on the other hand, be identified on the unattended as well as the attended channel.

The panel tried to design experiments for exploring this hypothesis that utilize ERPs. We found it rather complicated. I shall briefly outline one suggestion. We define, as two channels (in Broadbent's sense), two visual locations, one of which is attended and one of which is unattended. Let us say the items on the left will be attended and the items on the right will be unattended. We also define four kinds of stimuli that can be presented: red vertical, red horizontal, blue vertical, and blue horizontal bars. Pairs of these stimuli will be presented in a random sequence at short ISI's, one of each pair on the left channel and the other on the right. The subjects' task is to detect a target on the attended channel only and to ignore the unattended channel. The target will be defined either by color (red) or by orientation (vertical), both of which are single features, or by a conjunction of features (red vertical or blue horizontal). We would measure ERPs to both targets and distractors on both the attended and the unattended channel. If the evoked responses reflect the conjunction limit on attention, we can make some predictions about what should happen. First, we would expect a much bigger asymmetry between the evoked responses on the two channels in the conjunction condition, because that is the condition in which attention is loaded. If my hypothesis is correct, we cannot attend to both conjunctions at the same time. Second, if features are registered automatically and in parallel, without requiring attention, we would expect a bigger difference between responses to the targets and responses to the distractors on the unattended channel when the targets are defined by features than when they are defined by conjunctions. If we cannot discriminate conjunctions of features without attending to them, and if attention is directed elsewhere, we should in fact find no difference between targets and distractors on the unattended channel in the conjunction condition. What would be interesting, of course, would be to see which component of the ERP is affected, if any, and whether it is the same component that is affected for the feature target/distractor difference on the unattended channel and for the attended versus the unattended channel in the conjunction condition.

POSNER: This paradigm takes advantage of one of the properties of ERPs that we mentioned earlier, namely that you can obtain data on the response to something that is occurring in the unattended channel even though the subject doesn't respond to it.

DONCHIN: What is the purpose of this experiment?

TREISMAN: To see whether the type of selection that occurs when you load the subject by presenting simultaneous conjunctions is reflected in the N100 component or in the P300 component. We are also interested in whether the ERP to the unattended items reflects any differentiation between conjunctions in a task in which subjects are not responding overtly to the unattended channel. This is similar to Hillyard's study of ERPs elicited by targets on the attended and on the unattended channels. He recorded an N100 difference between the attended and unattended ear and a P300 difference between targets and distractors on the attended ear only and not between targets and distractors on the unattended ear. His stimuli were syllables and therefore conjunctions in my terms, and he obtained the results I would expect. This proposal is a replication, in which we specifically vary whether the targets are conjunctions or features.

HILLYARD: Another way to put it is like this: If you are attending to one simple attribute as opposed to another, there ought to be a differentiation of ERPs between those attributes at both the attended and unattended locations in space, because simple attributes can be identified or discriminated without having a spatial localization. In contrast, having a spatial focus should greatly improve the identification of conjunctions. In a recent experiment of this type (see Fig. 3.5), we presented stimuli in both auditory and visual modalities at one position in space and the same stimuli in another position, all in a random sequence. The result was that attending to the visual stimuli at one point in space produced an auditory-visual differentiation of ERPs to stimuli at that point in space, and also an auditory-visual differentiation at the unattended point in space. Thus, the ERPs showed that modality was being discriminated outside the spatial focus of attention.

POSNER: It is certainly counter-intuitive to think that you have an object in an unattended channel that really isn't an object because you're not attending to it. That is the psychological issue. If you are not attending to the channel, that thing is just two features coming from a common position in space; it isn't an object.

TREISMAN: It would be nice if evoked potential studies could help define up to what point in time the features are separate and at what point they are combined. Harter's data suggest that they are initially registered separately.

HARTER: The data Dr. Treisman is referring to were distributed in the pre-circulated material and were published in the proceedings of the Konstanz meeting (Harter, Previc, & Towle, 1979). In this study, the subjects were instructed to attend the conjunction of features. The time course of the changes in ERPs following relevant and irrelevant stimuli, however, indicated the individual features were selected prior to the conjunction of features. It would be easier to describe these data if I could show you a slide (Fig. 4.3) of the data taken from our experiment. The features were the size and orientation of black-and-white bar-grating patterns. There were four such gratings consisting of 9- or 36-min bar widths oriented vertically or horizontally. These four patterns are referred to as 9V, 9H, 36V, and 36H, respectively, across the bottom of the figure. They were flashed in random order at a rate of about 1/780 msec. The subjects attention was directed to each of these four gratings during the course of the experiment by making that grating relevant to a RT task. Only ERP amplitude to the 9V and 36H flashed gratings are shown in this figure. ERP amplitude was measured at 75-, 125-, 175-, 200-, 250-, and 375-msec poststimulus in order to assess the time-course of the attention effects.

ERP amplitude at 225-msec poststimuli (second graph on the right in Fig. 4.3) indicated selective attention caused enhanced processing of the features of the attended grating even though the target stimulus was a conjunction of these features. For example, take the ERP amplitude to the 36H flashed grating (open bars). Amplitude was increased (shifted more negative) when the 36H grating was relevant as compared to when it was irrelevant (the 9V grating was relevant). Note that this negative shift is riding on top of a positive potential and appears as a decrease in the amplitude of the positive potential. This total shift in amplitude approximates the summation of the effects of changing the individual features of the relevant gratings--that is, the effects of changing orientation (9V to 9H) plus the effects of changing size (9V to 36V) approximately equal the total effects of changing both size and orientation (9V to 36H). This indicates the features were selected fairly independently and in parallel. This "early" (225-msec) effect appears to support Anne's suggestion that features were processed in parallel. The selection process, however, had clearly started at this point in time, although it was not specific to the conjunction of features in the target grating.

The changes in ERP amplitude from 225 to 250 msec and 375 msec reflect a trend toward the selection of the conjunction of features in the target rating rather than the features per se. Again, take ERP amplitude to the 36H flashed gratings (open bars). At 250-msec poststimulus, changing the orientation (9V to 9H) or the size (9V to 36V) of the relevant stimulus so as to match the evoking flash had relatively little effect on VEP amplitude to the 36H flashed

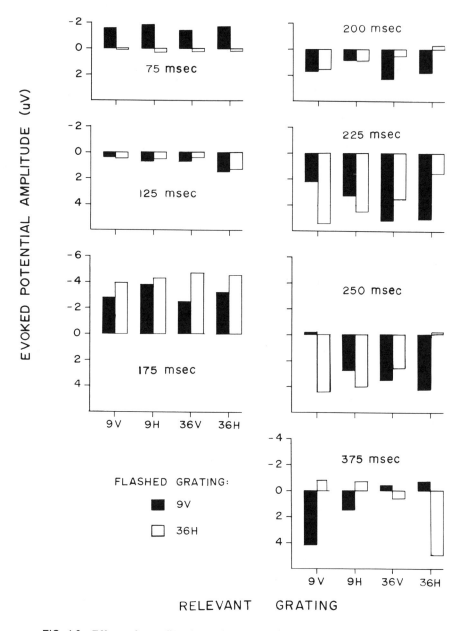

EVOKED POTENTIAL AMPLITUDE (uV)

FLASHED GRATING:
■ 9V
□ 36H

RELEVANT   GRATING

FIG. 4.3 Effects of attending the conjunction of features (size and orientation) on
ERPs to grating patterns of either verticle (V) or horizontal (H) orientation and 9' or 36'
bar widths. ERPs to the 9V (solid bars) and 36H (open bars) grating (9V, 9H, 36V,
36H). The different graphs indicate ERP amplitude measured at different latencies (75,
125, 175, 200, 225, 250, and 375 msec). Note at 225–250 msec, ERPs to the gratings
were sensitive to both features of the relevant grating; whereas at 375 msec, they were
sensitive primarily to the conjunction of features. From Harter, Previc, and Towle
(1979).

grating. The negative shift was primarily associated with the flashed stimulus containing the conjunction of both the size and orientation of the target grating. This "conjunction-specific" effect was even more apparent on ERP amplitude measured at 375-msec poststimulus. These data, therefore, suggest the selection process progressively shifts from being feature-specific to conjunction-specific from early to late in processing time.

DONCHIN: What do you mean by later in time? Do you mean later in the session or in the epoch?

HARTER: By early I mean starting at about 120-225 msec after the evoking flash, whereas by late I mean ending at about 375 msec. I did not mean to infer a dichotomy in the effects but a continuum in the nature of the effects.

DONCHIN: Are you saying that different components of the evoked response respond differentially to different attributes of the stimulus so that if a target is defined in terms of a conjunction of properties or attributes then you get a late component--that the late components are in fact responsive to what defines the target?

HARTER: That's right, but the early components are not sensitive to the conjunction of features which define the target.

DONCHIN: But what's surprising about that?

HARTER: There is nothing very surprising about the fact that the late components are related to what was defined as the target. What is interesting is that the early components are not directly related: (1) to the target but to the features of the target; and (2) to the behavioral response. The progressive change in the nature of the negativity between about 120- and 260-msec poststimulus suggests a progression in the selection process that leads to the selection of the target and the initiation of the motor response.

DONCHIN: It seems to me that what you are saying is that exogenous components of the ERP are sensitive to the physical features of the stimuli and the late components are sensitive to the logical attributes of stimuli.

HARTER: No! That is not what I'm saying. All the changes in evoked potentials I have been discussing are endogenous according to your definition. These changes were obtained under conditions when stimulus parameters were held constant. The changes were due to what the subjects were instructed to attend. In this sense, both feature-specific and conjunction-specific changes reflected endogenous processes.

POSNER: Are there more comments from people here about this question of conjunctions? If not, let Anne proceed with our last topic.

TREISMAN: The issue of automatization and attention is currently much debated. As I showed earlier, simple features appear to be processed in parallel spatially. People can pick out red letters in a black background with no effect of display size and so on. On the other hand, semantic content appears to require serial processing. For example, if subjects look for an 8 in a background of digits, they seem to scan them serially. The distinction initially seemed quite clear-cut. However, some puzzling and apparently conflicting results began to appear. For example, Brand (1971) discovered what is now called a *category effect*. If instead of looking for an 8 in digits, subjects look for a letter in digits, any letter in digits, they seem to be able to do that in parallel as well. There is no effect of the number of digits presented. The letter seems to "jump out" perceptually in the same way as a red item "jumps out" of a black background. That was one finding, which has been replicated by many other studies. The second finding was made by Shiffrin and Schneider (1977). They showed that if you give subjects a great deal of practice with a consistent mapping of targets and distractors, they show an apparent change to parallel processing with any arbitrarily selected set of targets and distractors. This now raises the question whether the whole dichotomy between early selection of physical features and late selection of meaningful categories can be eliminated by practice. Do highly practiced categories come to behave like channels or features? This is perhaps a problem on which the ERP could throw light. There does seem to be a clear distinction between the component of the evoked response that selects on the basis of physical features and the component that reflects detection of complex targets, like syllables, when they are not highly practiced.

I should also mention that there are some doubts about the nature of the letter-digit category effect, even in the behavioral data, that suggest that it may not be exactly equivalent to feature-based selection. For example, Francolini and Egeth (1979) asked subjects to count how many targets were present in a display rather than responding simply to their presence or absence. They found that subjects could easily and in parallel count targets defined by their color but that they could no longer process letters and digits in parallel when asked to count them. So there is some behavioral evidence suggesting that the category effect is not identical to the feature-detection effect. We perhaps have a dichotomy, but its nature is not quite what was thought originally.

One possible experiment that the panel considered would present sequences of visual digits in a fixed location and ask the subject to detect differently defined targets as follows: In the first control condition the target would be a digit in a background of other digits. Here we would expect serial processing and we know that the evoked response would show a P300 effect (Hillyard &

Picton, 1979). In the second control condition, we could ask subjects to detect a shift in location, and we would expect an N100 effect. These two extremes of target search should look clearly different in their associated ERPs. We can then see what ERP changes correspond to category targets, like a letter in digits. One possibility is that the P300 effect occurs simply when processing takes a longer time. It may be that distinguishing one digit from another digit is simply slower than detecting a change in location, and therefore it affects a late component rather than an early component of the ERP. Another, more interesting possibility is that the difference is one of level or depth processing. We could try to dissociate processing time and processing depth by using two types of targets that differ in the level at which they are defined but are matched in detection latency, that is, they are equally difficult but for different reasons. For example, we could vary the difficulty of detecting a shift in spatial location by moving the target and distractor locations closer and closer together. In this way, we could calibrate the difficulty of the physical targets until they are as slow to detect as a letter in digits. We could then look at the evoked potentials to see whether the same component is affected when the behavioral response times are equated or whether the difference in level of processing is still reflected in a difference in the ERP component that is affected. I think this might be informative.

KAHNEMAN: It might be interesting to compare consistent mapping (keeping the same target from trial to trial) with varied mapping, interchanging target and distractors across trials. From the research of Shiffrin and Schneider, you would certainly expect very different results to occur with consistent mapping. Could the suggestion be that you should eventually have an N100 effect with consistent mapping, when the detection becomes automatized? Does the level of processing shift with consistent practice?

TREISMAN: One possibility is that automatization has the effect of moving the relevant discrimination back to an earlier stage of processing, so that even a complex distinction becomes featurelike.

DONCHIN: I'm bothered by something that is not to the point we are discussing. The label the "N1" effect has a certain meaning in the evoked potential literature. You're talking about an exogenous component that, though it is somewhat slow to appear, has been attributed by some investigators to activity in primary sensory areas. This, therefore, leads to a certain set of interpretations of the effect. However, there is evidence now that the selective attention does not operate on N100; rather, it's a novel component that has not been described before. I think we should avoid referring to the N100 effect.

KAHNEMAN: What is important is that it is an *early* effect.

DONCHIN: Well, I think it is an important distinction. I realize that for those interested in selective attention the crucial aspect is that the ERP differences are "early." The ERPs are indeed different. But, as we agreed earlier, the differences in the waveforms must be interpreted in the framework of electrophysiology and the subject's task. Now, N1 (or N100) is a well-studied component. It is extremely sensitive to stimulus features. There has been a tendency, therefore, to interpret the selective attention effect as if it reflects feature-sensitive selection. This is implied, for example, by Hillyard's interpretation of the N100 effect as reflecting stimulus set. But, if we are dealing with a new (endogenous) component, we cannot make the same inferences about the underlying process. It is also important to note that recent data suggest that there *are* differences in this new "negative displacement" between the ERPs elicited by the "standard" and by the "target" stimuli (Hansen & Hillyard, 1980; Naatanen & Michie, 1979; Chesney, Michie, & Donchin, 1980).

KUTAS: Such a standard/target differentiation for the N100 is not always obtained. For example, several papers of Hillyard's group show waveforms demonstrating no difference between the standards and the targets in the region of the N1 effect (e.g., Hink, Hillyard, & Benson, 1978).

DONCHIN: You cannot really argue from negative results. If you don't see the difference, then for some reason your technique may not be sensitive enough to differentiate the standards and targets. If you show strong positive results in any situation, then the negative results are irrelevant.

KAHNEMAN: I don't see that there is a difference between a target effect and a selective attention effect. Why should there be? I mean operationally they are really the same. You get a target effect when you are confounding the dimension of selection and the dimension that controls the response and in the selective attention paradigm you are separating them. Now in principle it really is the same. You have to make a distinction that in one case controls the response directly and in the other case controls the property that will control the response. It's not at all surprising that you would find a target effect fairly early if you can find a selective attention effect.

DONCHIN: Well, but then you can't say that the early effect is purely a stimulus-specific feature-detection process.

KAHNEMAN: It is quite possible that you find your target in a similar situation by invoking the selective attention mechanism, so that you are actually more sensitized to targets than you are to nontargets in the same way that you are sensitized to a channel in the classic selective attention paradigm.

DONCHIN: But that wouldn't bother me. It just isn't consistent with the Broadbentian dichotomy between stimulus set and response set.

HILLYARD: I might add that I don't think there are any convincing data to support that position that there is a larger N1 to targets.

DONCHIN: I can show you the data.

HILLYARD: Yes, but the data has another interpretation. The difference may be due to refractory periods of the exogenous components, but this is an esoteric ERP point, and I don't think it's worth belaboring.

5 Dissociation Between Electrophysiology and Behavior—A Disaster or a Challenge?

Emanuel Donchin
University of Illinois at Urbana-Champaign

5.1 INTRODUCTION: IN PRAISE OF DISSOCIATION

It is the point of this chapter that some of the more interesting results in cognitive psychophysiology derive from instances in which the "behavioral" and the "physiological" observations appear to conflict. My thesis is that to seek interesting physiological "correlates" of *psychological* processes we should concentrate our effort on the search for physiological "dissociates" of behavioral processes. To illustrate this thesis I shall describe studies of the latency of the P300 component of the event-related brain potential (ERP). I shall also try to fulfill, in part, the tutorial mission of this discussion by highlighting some of the methodological problems encountered during the acquisition, and analysis, of ERPs. Due to time limitations, many of the details needed to support the various assertions are ignored.

An assertion that electrophysiological data need not correlate with behavioral data is not self-evident. On the contrary, much has been made of such dissociations. Most commonly, when a dissociation is found, the investigators conclude, with sorrow or with glee, that the data indicate that the electrophysiological signals are not *meaningful*, or valid, or interesting. A pithy, if not entirely original, statement of this conclusion by Clark, Butler, and Rosner (1969) was that evoked potentials are "full of sound and fury, signifying nothing." They supported this conclusion by purporting to show that stimuli of which the subject was still cognizant failed to elicit an ERP. Clark et al. believed that their data show that "perceptual response was obtained at levels of stimulation at which no AEP could be recorded." From this "dissociation of sensation and evoked responses" they inferred that "evoked activity . . . may play no essential or important role in determining perceptual reactions to (stimulus) parameters." This, of course, is a far-reaching typical inference from "dissociations."

If one analyzes Clark et al.'s study with care, as Sutton and I were annoyed into doing (Donchin & Sutton, 1970), one does find a dissociation, but it is between the study Clark et al. ran and the study they wished to run. Their procedure was not unusual. As a measure of sensation, Clark et al. used the subject's "threshold," as measured by the method of limits. They used as an electrophysiological measure the gross amplitude of the evoked potential. These are, of course, only two of a multitude of possible measures, each having its own attributes. The choice of the measures is quite arbitrary, and the fact that the conclusions are always limited by the choice of the measures must be borne in mind. Furthermore, Clark et al. made the two measurements on separate occasions; that is, the ERPs they analyzed were not elicited by the same stimuli that were used in measuring the thresholds. Their subjects were anesthetized in both instances, but when they recorded the ERPs, the subjects were left alone in a room "detached from their environment . . . experiencing a sensation of while the subjects were at a nadir of attention. The psychophysical thresholds, on the other hand, were measured while an experimenter was prodding the subject to be as attentive as possible under the circumstances. In other words, the "behavioral" and the electrophysiological measures were obtained under conditions that were not comparable. The conclusions were, therefore, ill-founded.

This sorry affair is discussed here in some detail because it demonstrates some of the preconditions to the study of the electrophysiological manifestations of psychological processes. First, if at all possible, the physiological and the behavioral data must be obtained concurrently. Comparisons between ERPs and behavioral measures that were not taken simultaneously are suspect. At the least, the onus must be on the experimenter to show that the data were obtained under comparable conditions. Second, the measures of the ERPs cannot be cavalierly chosen. One must be aware that there are different ERP components and that these components have different interpretations. Studies not sensitive to the distinction between components are best ignored.

In short, before a dissociation is claimed, it should be very clear that one in fact exists. Often the dissociations will turn out to be merely consequences of shoddy technique. For a while, especially when studies like that of Clark et al. were used as an excuse to withdraw support from ERP research, I was driven to argue that there are no such dissociations. However, as time went on, we began to observe dissociations in our own lab, where we were convinced the methodology was not shoddy. Almost invariably we were able to account for these discrepancies by a reevaluation of our assumptions about the study. We eventually recognized that the electrophysiological data were frequently a better indicator of the state of affairs in the experiment than were our presumptions concerning the experiment. It slowly penetrated our consciousness that the

ERPs are giving us data that *complements* rather than *supplants* the behavioral data and that, when treated with the requisite respect, the ERPs may provide data on human information processing that are not otherwise readily available.

5.2 THE ERPS ELICITED BY RHYMING WORDS

I shall illustrate the point by describing a dissociaton obtained in a study by Polich, McCarthy, Wang, and Donchin (1983). We were concerned with the manner in which individuals process words for their phonological representation. The study attempts to determine whether the orthographic and the phonological processing stages are as separable and serial as some theorists imply. The subjects were shown pairs of words on a computer terminal. They were told to indicate, by pressing one of two buttons, whether the two words rhyme or not. The word pairs were selected from one of four lists, two lists of rhyming pairs and two lists of nonrhyming pairs. The rhyming pairs may appear to rhyme, as in CAKE—BAKE, and this list is labeled RO, or they may not appear to rhyme, as in WAY—WEIGH (labeled R). The nonrhyming pairs will either look as if they rhyme (as in COUGH—DOUGH), and this list is labeled WO, or they will clearly appear not to rhyme, as in TABLE—CHAIR. This last list we labeled W. In each condition the subject received an equal number of rhyming and nonrhyming pairs. In condition I, these came from the RO and W lists in equal proportions. In condition II, half of the nonrhymes came from the WO list. In condition III, half of the rhyming words came from the RP list. In condition IV, all the rhymes came from the RO list and all the nonrhymes came from the WO list. The subjects are thoroughly informed about the nature of the stimuli and about their respective probabilities.

Consider the design then. In conditions I and IV the orthography alone provides sufficient data for subjects to perform the task accurately. If they see that the two final syllables match, they ought to know that they should respond "rhyme" in condition I, and "no rhyme" in condition IV. In the other two conditions they must, of course, supplement the orthographic analysis by a phonological analysis. So the simple prediction is that in conditions I and IV the reaction times will be quite similar. In conditions II and III the RTs will reflect the time consummed by the additional level of phonological analysis. The results shown in Fig. 10.16 were in some interesting ways strikingly different from the predictions (see Donchin & McCarthy, 1980). The shortest RTs were recorded in condition I. There was no difference between the RTs to RO and W pairs. In condition II, there was a 100-msec increase in RTs to RO and W. This increase can be attributed to the additional time required for phonological processing. Clearly this increment must be sufficient to allow the subjects to complete the phonological analysis; otherwise they could not give correct responses to the W and the RO pairs. This time should also be adequate for processing and responding to the WO items. However, it turned out that the RT to the WO items exceeded by at least 300 msec the RT to W and RO items. Similarly, the RT to R items in condition III exceeded the RT to W and RO. Even more striking—in condition IV, where the orthographic information should have sufficed—the RTs to both R and WO are considerably longer than are the RTs in condition I. These data can be summarized by stating that whenever there is a conflict between the orthographic and phonological cues, there is a substantial increase in RT. It is, we think, a Stroop-like affect, that strongly indicates that, at least when dealing with words, the orthographic and the phonological processes are not "isolable" processing components in Posner's sense (1978). Subsequent studies, in which we controlled for a number of difficulties presented by the design of the study I just described, yielded the same pattern of results (see Polich et al., in press; Kramer & Donchin, in press).

Is there a value to an examination of the ERPs elicited by these complex stimuli? Part of the electrophysiological data are shown in Fig. 5.1. The word pair to be evaluated was presented at the point indicated by the second vertical line. We show superimposed the ERPs elicited by the WO and W pairs and the ERPs elicited by the RP and RO pairs. The large, positive-going, component that appears in all these ERPs is the P300. Of interest here is the latency of this component. Note that there is no difference between the latencies of the P300 elicited by the WO and W pairs, despite a 300-msec difference in the corresponding RT. So these data illustrate a *dissociation* between the ERPs and the "behavioral" data. The second pair of waveforms demonstrates an "association." The latencies of the P300 elicited by the R and RO pairs are different as are the RTs associated with these two stimuli. Thus, the dissociation between RT and P300 shown for the W/WO pairs cannot be attributed to an inability of P300 latency to change. It is apparently the case that the overt response to WO stimuli requires an additional 300 msec, relative to W stimuli, but the P300 shows no such effect. Do we conclude then that the ERPs fail to show a behavioral significance? Do we conclude that they are not as sensitive a measure of processing as is RT? I think not. I tend to believe that this dissociation tells us something fundamental and important about the way in which individuals process stimuli, and it thus augments the RT data. (It should be noted in subsequent experiments in which all 4 pair classes were used in the same sequence the Wo, did elicit a P300 with an increased latency, see Kramer & Donchin, 1982).

5.3 THE AMPLITUDE OF P300

To support this assertion I now lead you through a detour that will attempt to establish why we think that the latency of P300 is of value in mental chronometry. This requires a discussion of the process that P300 manifests, and how it leads to an interpretation of latency. I shall describe how latency can be

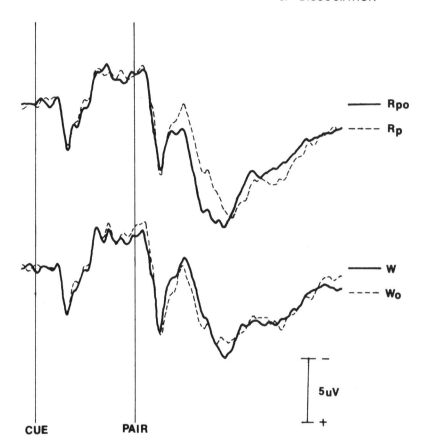

FIG. 5.1   Grand-averaged (across 8 subjects) ERP waveforms for the four list types averaged cross conditions. Waveforms elicited by the Rpo (Rhymes, phonologically and orthographically similar) and Rp (Rhymes, phonological only) are overlapped in the top graph while waveforms elicited by the Wo (Words, orthographically similar but phonologically dissimilar) and W (Words, orthographically and phonologically dissimilar) word pairs are overlapped in the bottom graph. The vertical lines represent the onset of the cue and word pairs and are 800 msec apart. The total duration of the waveform is 2560 msec. (Note: Rpo = Ro, Rp = R)

measured and then present evidence that changes in P300 latency can be interpreted in a very specific manner. This interpretation will then be used to support conclusions concerning the locus of the Stroop effect we observed in the "rhyme" data.

The following discussion, then, is concerned with one component of the ERP. The ERP waveform should not, of course, be considered a unitary waveform, a damped oscillation, whose different peaks and troughs are merely the subsiding perturbations of an oscillator. The waveforms that normally span epochs with durations of several hundred milliseconds are manifestations at the scalp of the activation of several different neuronal populations. The specific pattern with which these are activated and the resultant wave pattern depend on many factors. In an ERP elicited by a mild tone, it is possible to detect activity within the first few milliseconds after the stimulus. The activity continues well into the epoch for a few hundred msec. Allison (this volume) surveys some of what we know of the origin of these potentials (Goff, Allison, & Vaughan, 1978). He dwells, of course, mostly in the early segment of the epoch where one can make reasonable hypotheses about the source of the potentials and then try to test these hypotheses. This becomes rather difficult when we move into the later segments of the epoch. We do, however, adopt as a working hypothesis a series of postualtes, namely that each distinct component of the ERP is observed, when it is observed, because the elements of a distinct population of neurons, which happen to have a geometry that allows their electrical fields to summate, are synchronously activated in the course of the informational transactions of the brain. Thus, a potential appearing between two electrodes placed on the scalp is interpreted as an indication that some specific neural process has been activated, either endogenously or exogenously, inside the cranium (Donchin, Ritter, & McCallum, 1978).

How do we know that we are observing a distinct component? Only a brief treatment to this problem is given, even though it is central to ERP work. For more detail, see the volume edited by Callaway, Tueting, and Koslow (1978). As it is becoming clearer that the analysis of ERPs must be made in terms of components, the elucidation of the number of components and the development of effective tehcniques for the isolation and measurement of the components becomes a serious problem. It has been customary in the field to measure peak-to-peak, or base-to-peak, amplitudes of selected features of the waveform. This presents serious problems (Donchin, 1979; Donchin & Heffley, 1979). One, inescapable, difficulty is that of component overlap. An attempt to measure the amplitude of a given component reached by using a base-to-peak measure, will be affected by the value of the preceding or succeeding components at the same. Measuring peak-to-peak amplitude may also be insufficient because the two peaks may well represent distinct components.

The approach we have taken assumes that components should be defined in relation to the effects of experimental manipulations on the waveform of the ERP. Thus, if the voltages recorded in two segments of the epoch can be shown to vary independently with respect to, say, the recording site or the modality of the stimulation or the task the subject is performing, the two subepochs will be considered as having defined two distinct components. One method that has proved very powerful for isolating, measuring, and analyzing the ERPs is principal component analysis (PCA). In the past few years PCA has been yielding very consistent results. There is a remarkable similarity between the structure of the experimental variance teased out of a number of quite different studies (see Donchin & Heffley, 1979, for a review). Each of the humps identifies the existence of a distinct component that underlies the experimental variance. The "component scores" for each of the components can be used to measure the magnitude of the component, and these are related to the experimental variables. So that, for example, to say that some manipulation, such as task difficulty, affects component X, we must show that the component scores associated with X are reliably different at different levels of task difficulty.

The P300 emerges from such analyses as a component with a characteristic scalp distribution and a typical response to several interesting experimental manipulations. Consider, for example, the data of Squires, Donchin, Herning, and McCarthy (1977) obtained in the "oddball" paradigm. In this paradigm a Bernoulli sequence of tones is presented, and the probabilities of the two tones are highly unbalanced. The subject either counts one of the tones or performs some other task. The results were quite similar to those obtained in numerous other studies (Donchin, 1979). A large P300 is elicited by the rare events when tones are counted. A PCA of these data reveals the structure we have observed so often. A study of the factor scores revealed the picture that is very well-supported by a host of other studies (Donchin, Ritter, & McCallum, 1978). The P300 is elicited by rare, task-relevant stimuli (but see Donchin, 1981, for some caveats).

In general, the P300 component is largest at the parietal electrodes and is quite small in frontal electrodes. Finally, and this we have found is its most interesting feature, its amplitude appears to reflect the subjective probabilty that has been assigned to the eliciting event. That the relative frequency of the eliciting stimulus affects P300 amplitude has been known for quite some time (Tueting, Sutton, & Zubin, 1971). Duncan-Johnson and Donchin have shown that this relation is very systematic as prior probability is changed over the entire range from .10 to .90. In the last few years we have also presented extensive evidence that the effect of prior probability can be modulated by a host of subjective factors that modulate prior probability to determine subjective probability. One of the clearest demonstrations of the effect has been the finding that the amplitude of P300 of stimuli presented in a Bernoulli series depends on the specific sequence of preceding stimuli. Squires, Wickens, Squires, and Donchin (1976) showed that the waveforms can be arranged in a tree displaying the sequential structure of the preceding series of stimuli. Clearly, the amplitudes vary as the number of unlike events presented prior to the eliciting event increases. We have been able to establish that the effect is not due to receptor adaptation or some other perceptual factor but rather that it depends on the subject's knowledge concerning the probabilities of events. Furthermore, the evidence is strong that the probability in question is not associated with specific physical stimuli but rather with the categories into which stimuli must be classified according to the subject's task.

5.4 THE LATENCY OF P300

This conclusion leads, quite directly, to our interpretation of the latency of P300. The reasoning is straightforward. If P300 is elicited by the occurrence of an event that has been classified into the "rare" category, then the categorization of the stimulus must be complete before the P300 can be elicited. The more difficult and time consuming the categorization, the longer the latency of P300. As Kutas, McCarthy, and Donchin (1976) put it, if P300 amplitude reflects the degree to which a stimulus is "surprising," the stimulus must first be recognized as surprising before it can, in fact, surprise. From this logic flows an obvious prediction, namely that the latency of P300 would be positively correlated with reaction time; the longer the latency of P300, the longer the reaction time. By and large, this prediction has been confirmed, most convincingly in a study by Ritter, Simson, and Vaughan (1972). These investigators have, valiantly, proceeded to measure the latency of P300 in the raw, paper, records of EEG, these they compared to the reaction times on the corresponding trials, and the correlation between these variables was convincingly positive. A more recent reanalysis of these data (Ritter, Simson, Vaughan, & Friedman, 1979) confirmed the conclusion. Yet, despite this apparently clear demonstration, the water remained muddy, this because several other investigators reported low correlations between P300 latency and RT (see Donchin, Ritter, & McCallum, 1978, for a review). How can two variables sometimes correlate and sometimes not? How can one support a claim that P300 reflects categorization time when its relation to RT is so tenuous? These questions presented to some a grave obstacle to the idea that P300 is strongly related to human information processing. This difficulty was exacerbated by the observation that the latency of P300 sometimes exceeded and sometimes lagged behind reaction time. It appears unlikely, to some, that P300 is related to stimulus processing, when it occurs after processing has been "completed." This question implies that processing culminates in the button-press and, therefore, any measure whose latency exceeds RT must be unrelated to processing. The model implied by such a question views an experimental trial as a series of successive processing stages, each leading to a consequent stage. Ultimately, the response emerges, and the trial is then concluded. The components of the ERP, in this view, must be shown to correspond to distinct intertrial stages. This framework cannot accommodate an ERP component whose latency exceeds RT, but this model is not plausible. It fails, I think, to capture the complexity of the human information-processing activities. I tend to favor (Donchin, 1979) a more "cognitive" model. This model postulates the existence of multiple, parallel, interacting processors, continually active. Stimuli impinge on this stream of processing and modulate and activate in different ways this complex matrix. Multiple responses are evoked by a given stimulus, some with immediate consequences, others will not be manifested for some time, exercising their effect through changes in the subjects' strategies rather than through effects on their immediate responses. If P300 is associated with processes that are more related to strategic rather than to tactical information processing, then the degree to which it correlates with RT will depend on the strategies the subjects tend to adopt. A dissociation between RT and P300 latency becomes, in this context, far more interesting than associations between these variables.

Evidence that the correlation between P300 latency and RT depends on the subjects' strategies has been presented by Kutas et al. (1977). In this experiment we again used the oddball paradigm, except that this time, the stimuli consisted of words presented on a computer terminal. The words could be classified, at each of three experimental conditions, into one of two categories, one occurring 20% of the time and the other 80% of the time. For example, in one condition 20% of the words were female names and 80% were male names. Or, in another condition, 20% were synonyms of "PROD" and 80% were randomly chosen words. Events from the rare category indeed elicited a large P300. But this is routine. What is more to the point is that the latency of the average ERP appeared to vary with the difficulty of the categorization. The latency when counting synonyms was longer than the latency when counting names. The picture became quite complex, however, when the study was run as a choice RT study; that is, the subjects were instructed to press one of two buttons in response to the words. Again we encountered a dissociation, the P300s no longer followed the RTs as precisely as one would hope. This dissociation was clarified, however, when we examined the data in more detail. The key to the analysis was an adaptive filter (Woody, 1967) that allows the measurement of P300 on individual trials. Consider, for example, the individual EEG records shown in Fig. 10.6, each associated with the presentation of one "rare" stimulus. It is obvious that fairly large P300s can be seen in these records. One might follow Ritter et al. (1972) and identify peak latencies in the individual trials. This has two drawbacks. First, it is excruciatingly laborious. In each of our recent studies we have thousands of single trials. Perusing each for its latency is prohibitively tedious and disproportionately time consuming. Second, I tend to distrust any procedure that makes the primary data so thoroughly dependent on the judgment of the individual investigator exercised over a long series of evaluations. We preferred to automate the process and are therefore using the Woody filter. The version we use has been programmed by Heffley and McCarthy, who made use of routines written by Ruchkin. The lines that appear below each trace in Fig. 10.6 define the peak of P300 identified by the Woody filter. The algorithm involves an interactive process that assumes that the peak of P300 in any trial is at the point at which the trial's record is maximally correlated with a template of P300. The problem is, of course, that we do not have a ready-made template. This is circumvented by using the average ERP as an approximate template. The latency of every trial is estimated by the cross-correlation with this template. These data are, however, treated with suspicion. An attempt is made, therefore, to improve the template by aligning all trials by their estimated latency and computing a new average ERP over these shifted trials. The cross-correlations between the trials and the new template is computed and a test is available to determine if this new step improved our estimate of the latencies. If it did not, the process is terminated. If it did, the process is repeated, yielding yet another estimate of the template, a new reshuffling of the data, and a new test for the value of the new step. This interactive bootstrapping continues until it seems wise to stop. The lag at which the trial best correlates with the final template is the estimate of the latency of P300. A useful preliminary step filters the data to eliminate potentially misleading high-frequency components. The details of this procedure are described by McCarthy in Chapter 10.

Now that we have an estimate of P300 latency on each trial, we can correlate it with the value of RT on corresponding trials. The pattern that emerges is fascinating. As Kutas et al. (1977) have shown the scattergrams obtained in the two conditions are quite different. The instructions to be as fast or as accurate as possible have a clear effect on the scattergrams. When the subjects are instructed to be fast, there is a low correlation between P300 latency and RT. Also, the response tends to precede P300. It is striking that for error trials, the RT is much shorter than P300 latency. When the subjects are striving to be accurate, there is a substantial increase in the correlation between the two variables. Furthermore, the RT now appears to follow P300 latency. At the risk of oversimplification, we conclude that when the subjects are trying to be accurate, they couple the response elicitation quite tightly to the processes associated with P300 elicitation. They think, if you will, before they act. This is not so when they try to be fast. There they release the reaction long before they complete the full processing of the stimulus. They act without necessarily thinking.

This decoupling of response execution processes from the categorization process, one of whose consequences is the appearance of P300 between scalp electrodes, is even more convincingly demonstrated by a study reported by McCarthy, Kutas, and Donchin (1978). Again the subjects had to discriminate male from female names, male names appearing with a probability equal to .20. Matters, however, were so arranged that this time subjects made many more errors. The latency of the ERPs on error trials turned out to be much longer than on trials on which the subject was correct. Error trials are thus characterized by an exceedingly short reaction time and an exceedingly long latency P300. In fact, this pattern has proved so typical of error trials that we were able to develop an algorithm that permits on-line identification of the subjects' errors (for more details, see Donchin & McCarthy, 1980).

Note the implications. If we consider reaction-time measures alone, we conclude merely that for some reason (perhaps due to response bias) the subjects respond to some of the rare items too fast and invariably press the wrong button. What, however, happens after they press the button? Do they continue to process the stimuli? Is there a consequence to an error? As you know, there has been much controversy on this matter. Rabbitt (1979) and Welford (1952) were among the disputants. It turns out to be somewhat difficult to establish, on the basis of response times, if such a process does or does not exist. The P300, on the other hand, allows a direct demonstration that the subject continues to process the stimulus sufficiently to recognize it as a rare stimulus. Moreover, it turns out that the commission of an error leads to a substantial delay in the emission of P300. We have apparently discovered a new stage of processing invoked by a discrepancy between the stimulus presented and the response given.

Thus, evidence is accumulating for the proposition put forth in Kutas et al. (1977). We start from the often articulated notion that the presentation of a stimulus initiates multiple processes, some involved in response selection and execution and the others being purely perceptual in nature. We suggested that P300 latency, as a reflection of the later process, provides a pure measure of processing time that is uncontaminated by response-related processes. We have much circumstantial evidence for this assertion, but we no longer need to rely solely on circumstantial and logical arguements. More direct evidence has been obtained in a study by McCarthy and Donchin (1979).

The subjects saw, on every trial, either the word "right" or the word "left" on the screen of a computer terminal. If the words were in uppercase, the word indicates the hand with which the subject is to respond. If the words are in lowercase, an incompatible response is called for. The left hand is invoked by the word "right," the right hand by the word "left." In addition, on half the trials the words, no matter what their case is, appear surrounded by a frame of other characters. On half the trials, these "noise" characters are absent. Thus, there are two experimental manipulations, both of which are known to affect reaction time. One, however, should have its effect on response selection processes and the other, on stimulus decoding processes.

Ten subjects have been run. The data indicate that the effect of response incompatibility and of stimulus degradation are completely additive. These data provide an excellent framework for testing our hypothesis concerning P300. Our hypothesis leads to the straightforward prediction that the degradation of the stimulus will have an effect on P300 latency but that the response incompatibility will have no effect on P300 latency. This is precisely what we find.

I must emphasize that these are early data from an ongoing experiment; for a more powerful version of the same study, see the detailed report by McCarthy (1980) and the brief report by McCarthy & Donchin (1981). There are some interesting complications that require additional work but, despite these caveats, the principal conclusion holds. The RTs are shown subject to the additive effect of two factors, and only one of these factors, that related to stimulus encoding, affects P300 latency! So it seems reasonable to adopt as a working hypothesis that P300 latency can serve as a measure of encoding and that is uncontaminated by response processes.

It is here that I finally return to the rhyme experiment. Consider again the data. Recall that we showed that when there is a conflict between the phonological and the orthographic cues, there is a 300-msec increase in RT but no increase in P300 latency. I am lead to conclude from this that the locus of the process that delays the RT is invoked *after* encoding the stimulus. By the time the P300 process in invoked the stimulus has been categorized as rhyming or not rhyming. The overt response is, however, withheld for yet another 300 msec, and the reason must be anchored in "criterion-," not in "sensitivity"-related processes. The conflict, the data about the conflict, are retained long after the "processing" stages have been completed and somehow retard the response.

The picture that I hope emerges then is well in accord with the conceptual scheme labeled as "cognitive." Information processing is not simply a matter of choosing responses. Information processing does not "culminate in behavior" in the sense that some arbitrarily selected overt response is emitted as the sole and unique consequence of processing. Rather, multiple, interacting, concurrent processes are continually active. To assay this matrix with a single response, as is done when one depends exclusively on the RT, may lead to a rather limited, perhaps distorted view of the process. It is my thesis that if we examine carefully those instances in which the picture yielded by ERPs is distinct from the picture revealed by such "behavioral" measures as reaction time, the true dimensions of human information processing might be thrown into sharper relief.

6 Theories and Models in Cognitive Psychology

Donald A. Norman
University of California, San Diego

6.1 INTRODUCTION

As I learn more, I know less. If I had been invited to write this chapter 10 or even 5 years ago, I would have had a lot to write. Then I knew the answers. I could have told you what the cognitive mechanism was. The problem is that the more the field progresses, the less I know. Today I will simply give a short commentary of my view of evoked potentials, which is bound to be controversial, along with a commentary on my view of cognitive mechanisms, which is also bound to be controversial.

The main point to those who study evoked potentials is: "Welcome to Cognitive Psychology." I'm impressed by how much all of you are like all of us. I have been following the evoked potential literature for a number of years for several different reasons. For one, I find it interesting. It is obvious that there is a relationship between what goes on in the brain and what goes on in the mind. ERPs give direct measurements of ongoing events that we cannot get by behavioral measurements. By combining electrical recording with the behavioral measurement and with observations of introspections and beliefs, we obtain a more complete picture. In fact I don't think that we ought to be in two fields. We are all interested in related issues: We should be one field.

The thing that bothers me, though, is that those who study ERPs have awfully simple notions about the mechanisms of the brain. This is very surprising to me. I thought that anybody who knew anything about neurological circuits would be more sophisticated, not more simple. Look at the brain. It is quite clear that there is not a simple, sequential, linear stage of operation. You have all those millions and billions of neurons, billions of neuronal connections, and

119

parallel processing. There are many, many different kinds of mechanisms, many kinds of electrical transmissions and chemical transmissions. There are systems that appear to be independent of each other at some points, related to each other at other points. Yet ERP theories tend to be simple, linear stage theories, templates, even: These notions are just too simple.

Another point of difference: When psychologists do an experiment, we present the signal of interest 90% of the time. We throw in another 10% of the signals to keep the subject honest, to make sure where the decision criterion is, and to make it so the person can't cheat. We really care about those 90% of the signals. ERP experiments are the complement: ERP people only care about those 10%. The other 90% of the trials are there only to make sure that the 10% of trials yield good responses.

And—one more point; one that Donchin has also made. For a while, the ERP literature seemed to say: "Hey look, we must be doing something right because look at the high correlation between our responses and your responses." But if there really was perfect correlation, then nobody would care. ERPs would convey no information. The important findings are the differences. It is different responses and different measures that give us information. The more correlations we find, the less I become interested.

Finally, my last comment before I start talking about theories: I don't think we've learned anything from the ERP studies, not yet. My views of information processing have changed very radically over the past years, in fact even over the past months. Yet these major changes have not been affected one bit by anything that I've learned from the evoked potential literature. That is not the way it ought to be.

6.2 SOME SIMPLE PSYCHOLOGICAL THEORIES

Let me now quickly review some of the mechanisms that cognitive psychologists have looked at. It's going to be quick because, as I noted, a few years ago I could have presented a fairly complete picture, but not today. The story then was very pretty. Today I don't understand what is happening.

6.2.1 Stage Models

We began with rather straightforward theories. They looked very much like the theory labeled by Donchin (1979) as "cognitive." Of course in those days we called his S-R model the "cognitive" model, and it made a good deal of sense. We said, look, the stimulus has to arrive at the sensory organs and eventually it has to be understood. We have the two ends of the continuum: what happens in between? Well, the sensory system extracts features, so we have a stage of feature analysis. There must be a short-term memory that is probably pretty early in the system. And then the issues such as making decisions and comparisons and extracting the deep underlying meaning of the signals would come next in nice logical progression. Then, there were attentional limits. The human is incapable of analyzing all the information that is arriving at the sensory organs. We are incapable of thinking about the implications of what someone has said while we listen to what they are saying next. There is a limit on the amount of mental work we can do. And we debated about where the restriction occurs.

The simple model from those days was that there were stimulus feature analyzers, a short-term memory mechanism, further processing, and then finally a decision and a response. That's not a bad theory. It characterizes a large amount of data. But I think that the real system is much more complex. It may not be possible to draw a single, simple analysis of that system. We might need to have different analyses for different tasks. If you have a complex system, it might look like a linear stage model for a particular class of tasks of this sort. When it does a different task, it might look like a very different kind of model.

The current view says: "Look, it's a fairly complex system with a large number of mechanisms operating simultaneously. Which operations get done first depends on the nature of the task, the nature of the general information available to the person, the purpose for which the person is doing the task, and a lot of other variables."

Let me show you what I mean. In Fig. 6.1 I present a version of the stage model. Physical signals undergo sensory transduction, some sort of sensory information storage, and then enter a short-term memory. The information in short-term memory appears to be already recognized and identified, which therefore means that there should be pattern recognition stages prior to short-term memory. All this appears to be relatively automatic. The first time there is much conscious control in short-term memory where one can evoke strategies to interpret and attend to material.

This story is not the "truth." It is a simple model of what is happening. Although this model is wrong, it is a good approximation for much of what happens. This basic model has been around for a number of years. One problem is that recognition requires the use of information experienced in the past: The pattern recognition stage simply can't be located as simply as shown here. We need some more arrows to interconnect stages. One of the problems is that as the field went on and on and on, analyzing different experiments and conditions, we all had to add arrows. We added a connection from here to there, and maybe from there to over there, and then here to across there, and there to there, and before we were finished, it wasn't a nice simple model anymore.

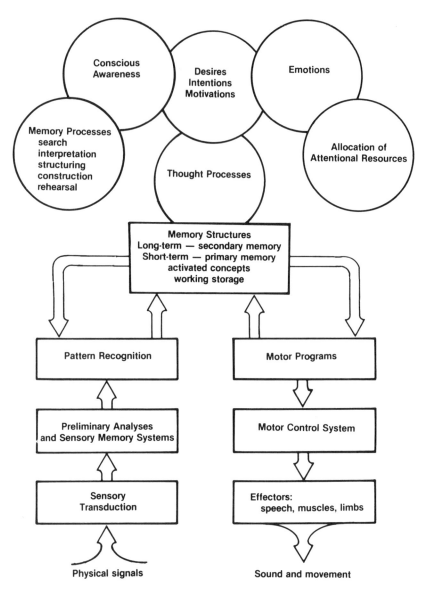

FIG. 6.1   A version of stage model of human information processing. This model has served a useful function, but has now probably outlived its usefulness. [From Norman, D. A. Twelve issues for cognitive science. In D. A. Norman, *Perspectives in Cognitive Science*. Published jointly by Erlbaum and Ablex. Norwood, N.J.: Ablex, 1981. Hillsdale, N.J.: Erlbaum, 1981.]

6.2.2 A Schema Model

Let me show you another kind of model. Here is an example, adapted from the work of Steve Palmer (1975). I am going to put the parts of Fig. 6.2a together into a recognizable image. I want to show you that to recognize a figure it doesn't suffice to recognize the parts. First, you have to know what the figure is. Then you can recognize the parts. From Fig. 6.2a alone you can't tell what image I'm going to make. If I rearrange Fig. 6.2a into the face of Fig. 6.2b, you can recognize the parts. You recognize the parts because you see the face. But you see the face because you recognize the parts. The two go hand in hand. A simple stage model will not explain this. We need a model that simultaneously recognizes components and recognizes the whole.

An alternative information-processing structure is for physical signals to pass through sensory transduction and then sit in a data pool (Fig. 6.3). Various kinds of structures—schemas or demons—continually examine the data pool, looking for relevant information. Essentially, each schema looks for the configuration of data relevant to it, and to others. There is continual communication among schemas, and there might be other communications and

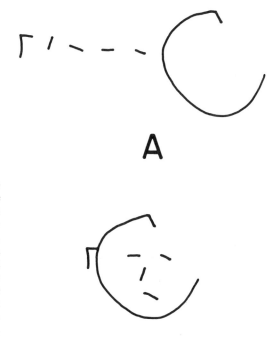

A

FIG. 6.2   The parts of A make no sense until put together into the face shown in B. The face is recognizable because it has the correct parts; two eyes, a nose, mouth, and ear. But the parts in A are not recognizable until put together in B as a face. To recognize both the face and the parts requires continual interaction among the possible interpretations of the parts and the whole. [From Norman and Bobrow (1976), after a suggestion by Palmer (1975).]

B

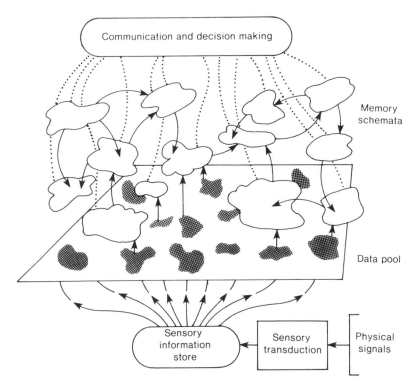

FIG. 6.3 Active schemas examine a data pool, being triggered when data relevant to the schema are present. Schemas activate and inhibit one another, forming a cooperative, competitive data processing structure. [From Norman and Bobrow (1976).]

decision-making structures. Note that this is not the only possible alternative model. There are a wide variety of models that can be considered.

The model shown in Fig. 6.3 contains a number of elements that seem necessary according to our contemporary views of processing. When you recognize a face, according to this model, the sensory features of the face get placed in the data pool. Then, schemas for perceptual objects such as the schemas for a milk jug or a water jug shown in the figure recognize components relevant to themselves and determine how strongly the data support their existence. In the example shown in the figure, there appears to be a spout and a handle, providing evidence that the perceptual object is a jug. But there is also weak evidence for an eye, a nose, and a mouth: evidence that is appropriate for the existence of a face. Indeed, the evidence for the face schema is much stronger than the evidence for the jug schema. By a selection process—perhaps a lateral inhibitory process—the stronger schema wins out over the weaker one. In this situation, the head schema will be most likely to be selected. The important thing about this model is that information flows in all directions.

6.2.3 An Interactive Model

Here is another illustration: In Fig. 6.4a the word *hospital* is shown covered with noise. Just below *hospital* I have arranged the same letters in random order. It is easier to see the word in noise than it is to see the random letters. Now this particular figure is obviously not well controlled, but this is a very well-known, robust, experimental result.

DONCHIN: Is it easier to see or easier to read?

NORMAN: It is easier to *perceive*. Perceiving is the result of a combination of your prior knowledge, of expectations, and of the information that is arriving. Thus, the word is actually easier to "read" more than it is easier to "see." But I would rather not say either read or see. I would rather use the word *perceive*.

One major concern of cognitive psychologists is the interaction of data-driven and conceptually driven processes. One direction of processing is that which derives from the data: Data-driven or bottom-up processing, processing in which the signal arrives, is analyzed into features, then perhaps letters, words, or items.

Note: Almost all evoked potential studies consider only data-driven analysis. Indeed, earlier work in cognitive psychology, including many of the first models, were based almost entirely on data-driven analysis. Data-driven analysis is necessary. Data-driven models are necessary. *But data-driven models are not sufficient.* If the task is to recognize a sequence of letters, I P T A O S L H, data-driven analysis is about all you can do. It does make sense to start the analysis with the arriving signals and push it as far as possible. But there are limits on how far you can go this way.

In everyday life there is almost always a tremendous amount of context. The signals are noisy, but with very noisy signals most of the information must come from that context. This is what we call *conceptually driven* or *top-down* analysis. In my figure, semantic information suggests possible syntactic classes, which suggests possible words, which suggests possible letters. And that meshes with the sensory analysis of the signals—the bottom-up analysis—to try to put together what the word might be. Top-down, conceptually guided analysis is necessary. *But conceptually guided models are not sufficient.* Both data-driven and conceptually guided analyses are necessary: Neither alone is sufficient. We need an interactive model. Information from the sensory analysis goes up, towards memory schemas. Conceptual information comes

126

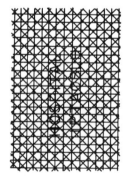

A

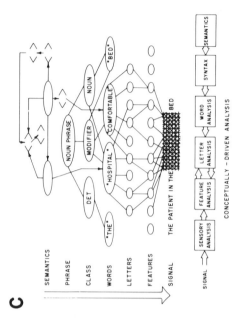

C

SEMANTICS

PHRASE

CLASS

WORDS

LETTERS

FEATURES

SIGNAL

THE PATIENT IN THE BED

SIGNAL → SENSORY ANALYSIS ⟷ FEATURE ANALYSIS ⟷ LETTER ANALYSIS ⟷ WORD ANALYSIS ⟷ SYNTAX ⟷ SEMANTICS

CONCEPTUALLY - DRIVEN ANALYSIS

"THE" "HOSPITAL" "COMFORTABLE" "BED"

DET MODIFIER NOUN

NOUN PHRASE

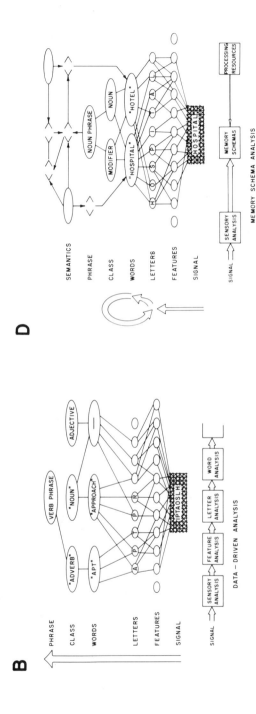

FIG. 6.4   The letters that form the word "HOSPITAL" are easier to read in noise when they form the word than when they do not, as shown in part A. This is because, as shown in B, data driven processing alone will not suffice. But the conceptually driven processing of C will not suffice either: there must be a combination of information from the data and conceptual information from above if words in noise are to be deciphered. As shown in D, words in noise are easier to read than random letters because both data driven and conceptually driven processing can supplement one another, cooperatively interacting to yield the final perception. [From Norman, D. A. Perception, memory, and mental processes. In L.-G. Nilsson (Ed.), *Perspectives on Memory Research*. Hilsdale, N.J.: Erlbaum, 1979.]

127

down, exciting memory schemas, altering the semantics. The system tries to find the best match, some place in the middle. The interactive model is quite different from those normally examined in the literature of evoked potentials. It is reasonably common in the general cognitive psychology-cognitive science literature (Norman & Bobrow, 1976b; McClelland & Rumelhart, 1981). I think this model is quite consistent with some of those shown to us by Donchin.

The interactive model says several things. First, different kinds of experiments are necessary to tap different parts of the model. If you do one experiment, it might appear to result from a linear set of stages. But if you do another experiment, you might get a different linear set of stages. Which linear set of stages are being tested are determined by the particular task the subject does. Linear stages are only approximations for the particular task under study.

6.2.4 Summary and Principles

Let me summarize some key concepts in general cognitive models. First, I've shown you a stage model. In the basic stage model, information goes from one stage, is transformed, and then is shipped over to the next stage. Well, that makes some sense, but there is a hidden assumption in this model. The hidden assumption is that information stays within a stage until all the stage processes are completed, when it is shifted over to the next stage. This is a conveyor belt model; things are neatly packaged. When the processing is complete, you ship the data out.

A very important analysis in cognitive psychology is that provided by Sternberg's additive factors method. This method, although powerful, makes the assumption that each stage completes its operation before it sends information on to the next stage. This strikes me as a very unnatural assumption.

I believe information processing is a continuous operation: Bobrow and I (Norman & Bobrow, 1976b) have called this the *principle of continually available output*. As analysis starts, each stage continually makes available the preliminary parts of its analysis to other stages. In perception, this allows us to note the existence of objects and stop processing at that point. Or, if the system wishes, it can continue processing to find out just what that object is (e.g., a person). We might continue the process even further to identify the details. But the processes do not have to go to completion. The important point is that the partial analysis is always available, always usable.

Jay McClelland, at UC San Diego (McClelland, 1979), has shown one way to analyze this system, a method he calls *cascade stages*. This makes a considerable amount of difference in the kinds of interpretations we draw from data. Many experiments analyzed with Sternberg's additive factors analysis yield different interpretations with McClelland's cascade analysis. The difference results from the simple, basic assumption that outputs are continually passing through the stages, that each stage always has available the partial results from the preceding stage. In the computer science literature, this is called a "pipeline" process.

6.3 ATTENTIONAL LIMITATIONS

It seems clear that the human has limited attentional abilities (the data are overwhelming). The question is, what is the nature of the limit? What is the nature of the system? How is that limit imposed?

One mechanism that yields a processing limitation is for there to be a single processor that can only operate on one task at a time. If this were so, then this processor could not start a second task until it had completely finished the first. In this case, each new task has to wait its turn. A single processor can actually appear to do many tasks simultaneously by a process called round-robin switching: The processor can do a little bit of this task, then switch to a little bit of that one, and then a little bit of yet another. Then it goes back and does the next bit of the first, and so on. This is the method used by most time-shared computers. One central processor gives the illusion of doing many tasks simultaneously by rapidly switching among them. Round-robin switching systems have the penalty of a high overhead, because when each task is stopped, the place where processing is going on must be saved so that when the processor comes back, it can resume as if it had not stopped. Extra memory is required.

Another mechanism that allows several tasks to be done together is to have truly parallel systems. There could be a whole set of visual processors and auditory processors, processors for information coming from here, processors for information coming from there. There could be separate processors for each of the separately localizable places in the three-dimensional world about us. But there must be some limits. We cannot have parallel mechanisms for each possible task.

Behavioral data indicate that similar tasks interfere with each other. There are several possible mechanisms that could explain this. One is round-robin switching. Another is to assume that similar tasks draw processing from some limited set of resources. Each time one more task is added (or each time a task requires more processing resources), more resources are used. When the limit of available resources is reached, each of the tasks have to slow up. So it is possible to do many things at the same time, but the more tasks being done, the slower each one gets (this is the model of Norman & Bobrow, 1976a; Navon & Gopher, 1979).

When performance on a task is less than perfect, it could be because the resources are the limiting factor (the *resource-limited* situation) or it could be because the quality of the data being analyzed is the limiting factor (the *data-limited* factor).

Remember that other principle, the principle of continually available output. This means that a processor is continually making available partial outputs, partial results. This allows for graceful degradation of function when there is overload. Contemporary digital computers have a property that if they don't have sufficient resources, they go dead. You don't receive any output. Contemporary human beings have the property that when they don't have sufficient output, well, they make a few more errors, or they take longer, or they don't do quite so well. But, in fact, we humans are very robust. We manage to keep going. Very seldom do we have a calamitous failure of our processing. This assumption of continually available output—and its corollary, graceful degradation—implies a kind of processing model with which we have very little experience. Most of our experience about processing comes from our knowledge of physically available processors, mostly electronic. Some human operations simply cannot be mapped onto contemporary electronic models with ease.

6.4 SOME COMMENTS ON MEMORY STRUCTURE

One set of studies (Chapman, McCrary, & Chapman, 1978) seems to suggest that if only we do the right analysis of evoked potentials, say a principal components analysis, that we can find those trials on which the subject stores away something in memory. This implies a strange model of memory. It says whenever you encounter something of interest, you activate a special signal saying "now store." This strikes me as an incredibly unlikely model of the human memory process.

The analytical technique used by Chapman is called a "principal components analysis." I know I'm going to step on people's toes here, but that is what I was told to do. The principal components analysis uses classical multidimensional scaling or factor analysis to find independent orthogonal components of the evoked potential wave. But what does it mean for components to be orthogonal? What psychological or physiological sense does it mean to try to extract orthogonal independent components? The brain is presumably an integrated system. Tukey (1978) has perhaps said this best. Tukey points out that the power of orthogonal systems is far overrated and that they may do more harm than good. You run the risk that the statistics begin to guide your intuitions.

Consider the memory system and the rationale for a "now store" signal. The difficulty with memory does not lie in the storage. The difficulty appears to be in retrieving what has been stored: The difficulties of retrieval far outweigh all the other problems of memory. Retrieval requires that there be organization of the information that is stored and later retrieved. Organization is critical, because if you are able to find something in a memory in which millions (billions) of items are stored, you have to be able to know where to look and, then, how to recognize that the information that is found is the information that was sought.

Information can be processed in many different ways, with many different aims. Our ability to retrieve information later depends, to a large extent, on *what*, *why*, and *how* it was processed immediately upon presentation. It is not that some information receives a signal to be stored, rather that information can be processed differently, processed for different purposes. And our ability to retrieve requires that we are able to find the way in which it was processed and stored. Different kinds of initial processing will yield different evoked potentials. This is not the same as a "now store" signal.

Cognitive psychology has not made much progress on one of the more difficult and more important aspects of information processing: the differences between conscious and subconscious processing. It is clear that a lot of processing does go on consciously, with awareness of what is happening. This is a slow (mostly) serial mode of processing. But it is probably the case that even more goes on subconsciously. I don't mean simple, regulatory control. I mean fairly complex, information processing that goes on without awareness. When I talk, there is not much awareness. I am often not aware of the words I am going to say until I say them. Yet language is one of the most cognitive operations we do, and most of language processing is subconscious. We know very little about the difference between conscious and subconscious processing, but it is sensible that we should know little. The problems are extremely complex. Don't be deluded into thinking that cognitive psychologists have powerful theories. We do, but we are missing a tremendous amount that goes on.

6.5 SUMMARY AND DISCUSSION

In the early days of cognitive psychology, we analyzed how incoming sensory information was processed, how simple language and memory got done. Now we realize that there is a lot more to do. We realize that information must flow in many directions. Two principal directions are those of data-driven and conceptually driven processing. Consideration of even these two directions of processing requires novel kinds of models. They cannot be simple stage models. (But simple stage models can still be used as approximations for particular tasks.) The individual stages of processing are cascades or pipelines, not discrete stages. There are limitations on our ability to do things that might be best described as some kind of resource models. There are control processes and conscious processes that we know little about. And a large amount of our skilled performance of a task is done subconsciously without conscious awareness, fairly rapidly and efficiently and apparently without drawing from the limited pool of resources that seem to be so important for attentional analyses. With extreme practice, the kinds of interference that we obtain with tasks that are so important for the study of attention no longer seem to be so apparent. Whether this means that no resources at all are required or some different mechanism is being used is not known.

Finally, I want to point out one other difference among the kinds of studies used by those who study evoked potentials and those used by cognitive psychologists: the fact that the P300 wave occurs after the response, at least for some kinds of tasks.

There clearly are ongoing changes over the course of the experiment. It is clear that the subject is using the results of one trial of an experiment to help prepare and adjust to continuing signals. It is quite clear that there are strong response dependencies, so that the kind of response made on one trial severely affects what is made next. These kinds of dependencies are heavily affected by the rare signal. Well, this is exactly what appears to be visible in the evoked potential studies. It seems to me that evoked potentials give us the possibility of seeing things that we could not see otherwise. They can tell us about the events that occur after the response, as well as about events that occur prior to the response. Usually, we are only able to obtain a single behavioral response on a trial, but obviously a lot goes on both before and after that response. I believe we can make the best progress only if we try to understand the mechanism of cognition by using all the possible measures that we have available—using both behavioral measures and using electrophysiological measures.

HILLYARD: I was struck by a couple of points that you made: first, that your thinking hasn't been influenced at all by evoked potential research and, second, that you know a lot less about selective attention than you used to. I wonder if you consider the evoked potential literature to be in the same category as the cognitive and perceptual literature in that it has produced confusion and disruption of your previous certainties? Or is the electrophysiological approach at too early a stage to have any interaction with cognitive psychology?

NORMAN: I think it is a good thing that I don't understand attention. There have been a lot of experiments. The problem is to piece the results together into one cohesive model. It would be wrong to have a set of models that describes selective attention, another set that describes perception, and another one for pattern recognition and memory. What I want is the single viewpoint that will handle all of these phenomena.

The reason I claim to be unaffected by the evoked potential literature is that there has been little that was unusual or new, little that was not already in the other literature. The EP results are confirmatory, but, as you pointed out continually throughout your talk, not very new. You didn't show new puzzles. In fact, you argued that your results were consistent with Broadbent's early models or Treisman's early selection models. That is actually a bit disturbing because I don't think either Broadbent or Treisman believe those models anymore.

KUTAS: It would seem that only electrophysiological data could influence you to choose between what seem to be two equally plausible models of information processing, attention, etc. In your research you assume that the brain operates according to some model, but you have no structural or physiological basis for that model whatever it may be. However, if you had some data (for example, event-related potentials) showing you that changes in the activity of certain parts of the brain occur with the relative timing you predicted on the basis of your cognitive theory, would it not, in your estimation, bolster your position?

NORMAN: Yes, if ERPs could show the relative timing, that could be important evidence. But evidence about *where* the brain processes take place is not important to cognitive theory. But, I believe that the assumption that mental processes are carried out by the brain is a reasonable assumption.

AUDIENCE: That's a working hypothesis.

NORMAN: I am interested in the psychological mechanisms. I want to describe the way that psychological mechanisms interpret the data that are arriving at the sensory organs. Psychological explanation is at a different level of description than physiological evidence. Psychological explanation is deliberately chosen to be at a higher level. The exact locations of the brain mechanisms are of no consequence for psychological theorizing.

Physiological psychologists have other interests. They are interested in exactly how neural components do their task. They should be very concerned about where these tasks are performed. Those who study evoked potentials are sort of in the middle. You often cannot localize exactly where your components come from. It may be impossible to do so. In fact, it is a basic problem in studying the physiological system that there are so many cells, that one cannot study all of it, that you must chose between studying a few cells in great detail—single-cell analyses—or many cells together, in gross responses. If you do the latter, you study overall systems.

I believe that the only way to understand the brain is to understand it at many different levels, each with different descriptions, different models. We need to understand the brain at the biochemical level. There, we are going to have to understand the chemical transmissions that take place. We are going to have to understand the operation of the individual neurons. We are going to have to understand groups of neurons, systems. We are going to have to understand how the various systems are put together. We are going to have to understand the brain at the psychological level, which is yet a different level, the level of mind.

I believe that we can collect many different types of data to tell us about the nature of attention: neurological, physiological, behavioral, phenomenological. We must have EP data. But I think it is completely wrong to say that without these electrophysiological data we are just making wild inferences and that we have no idea at all what is going on.

As far as I am concerned, the brain could be in the big toe. It wouldn't change my theories.

DONCHIN: You said it was unlikely that there is a "now print" signal that might have an electrophysiological manifestation. For example, I find very remarkable the similarity between the kinds of concepts that we are developing about P300 and the Wagner/Rescorla models of reinforcement. On reading contemporary studies of animal learning, one finds that a "surprise" mechanism plays a crucial role in the models proposed to account for "learning and memory." The animal will learn, it seems, only if "surprised." We might be studying the electrophysiological manifestation of the surprise process that is so crucial to learning. I think in fact that Chapman's et al. (1978) experiment had more to do with surprise than with memory. I tend to agree with your critique of Chapman's experiment; yet I think the conceptual point you make in conjunction with that critique, namely that it is very unlikely that there will be a "now print" signal, is not well-founded.

NORMAN: People can learn without being surprised. I am always learning, but I am not in a constant state of surprise. It is clear that a mismatch to our expectations is a very important event, and it is used in informative ways. We often do remember better those events that mismatch than those that match. But consider this story that I heard from Dick Solomon about how the wild rat discovers its food. Consider the wild rat who lives, say, in the alleys of Baltimore. It has a route it follows everyday. First it goes over the complete route. When it is all finished, it simply goes back to those places where the food was. (Actually, I do the same thing when I find a parking spot). Now what kind of surprise factor is involved with this kind of learning? This is the normal, typical kind of learning, not the sort of learning that we do in the laboratory, very constrained and very artificial, where maybe you must have some unique event in order to distinguish it or care about it.

DONCHIN: I would rephrase your description by saying that the animal was exploring a route and it somehow recalled places where it found food. This is not different from what you just said. There is a tendency to remember better things that were mismatched. I postulate that somewhere, inside the nervous system exists a processor that was activated as a consequence of that mismatch.

The interaction between that processor and the memory system increases the strength of memory in some way. And it is possible (I don't know that we have any evidence for that, but it is not inconceivable) that the activation of that processor is reflected on the head by a potential that appears 300 msec after the eliciting stimulus. So there is no a priori reason why one would say that the system is so complicated that it will never be possible to detect a scalp manifestation of a signal indicating that something has happened, that there was a mismatch.

NORMAN: I certainly did not say that. But here is an interpretation that I think will reconcile our points of view.

Consider that in memory we have various schemas for the various events that go on around us: schemas for rooms, schemas for people, and schemas for much of our experiences. There is a reasonable amount of evidence that when there is an experience that matches an existing schema well, little attention is paid to it. In fact one need not even look at those parts of a room that are already known. The more one knows about a situation, the less processing needs to be done about it. That's a very important part about our processing abilities. When there is a mismatch, there may have to be a fair amount of processing. It may turn out that the schema is inappropriate or that it must be modified considerably. Therefore, I expect that under periods of mismatch that there is considerble processing going on. And of course the more processing that takes place, the more likely it is to lead to a measureable EP.

REGAN: I was very puzzled by two things, but maybe I have it wrong. First of all, you queried why one would want orthogonal functions to describe a system. Second, you criticized the so-called linear model. I would look at it this way, and tell me if I have the picture wrong. When you have a very simple system like a TV set, there are not too many people who could look at the physical elements and tell you at once what its function is. It is much easier to understand a block diagram that sets out function. As far as I can understand it, the reason for using a block diagram of function is because the way the system performs its function is too difficult to handle, at least in the first instance, and if you want to make quantitative predictions, it is easier to use orthogonal differential equations because, if they are not orthogonal, the mathematics are more difficult. So the reason one draws it out in linear stages with orthogonal variables is as a crutch, because of the weakness of one's own mind.

NORMAN: But the only way that people are capable of describing television sets as a simple set of boxes, or aircraft as simple discrete functional components is first to understand thoroughly how the aircraft or the television set works and then know how to divide it up appropriately; that is, simplification follows complete knowledge. What I am complaining about is for an EP scientist to start as if there were no idea at all about what is going on and then to take the waveforms from a bunch of experiments and throw them into the mathematical hopper, turn the handle, and hope that from independent defined-to-be-orthogonal things, out will come meaningful components. Then the scientists look at the data and say, "My analysis shows this to be independent from all the others, so it must have some independent meaning. Now what could it be?"

DONCHIN: But that is a distortion of what is being done.

NORMAN: Of course it is a distortion. But tell me what all the years of factor analysis have taught us? Absolutely nothing! I claim the principal components method is just the same.

DONCHIN: You're missing the point, Don. The reason that factor analysts didn't get very far (and this view is not universally accepted) was because the factor analysts were interested in the structure. We are not performing PCAs of ERP data because we are interested in the *structure* that comes out. The PCA is only a tool for developing measurements so I can handle them statistically (Donchin & Heffley, 1979). I don't think the components that emerge during principal components analysis are inherently important. They are interesting because the "factor scores" may be related to the independent variables of the experiment. Seven components may be extracted, yet only one of these may be related to such independent variables as task difficulty or to motivation or to right-left comparisons or to capability. It is only *that* component that is meaningful. All other components are not interpretable. We use the principal components analysis simply as a way for developing dependent variables that can be related to the independent variables and, to the extent that this happens, we have something here that when it doesn't happen, we have nothing. The structure itself is really not interesting.

NORMAN: I hope so. Look, let me be positive and supportive for a change. I was impressed with Regan's work. He said, "look, here is a wave. I am interested in this little bump. I have reason to believe it has importance. How on earth am I going to get the bump out so I can measure it?" And then, by using Fourier analysis techniques, he was able to extract that bump out and then . . .

DONCHIN: Spectral analysis and principal component analysis are identical in this sense. They represent two kinds of linear decomposition of data.

REGAN: There are an indefinite number of such decompositions.

NORMAN: Even were the mathematics identical, it would not matter. I am not complaining about the mathematics. The mathematics are exquisite: pure and proper. I complain about *why* the analyses are being done. *Why?* What do you hope to do with them?

DONCHIN: Regan has a complex waveform to which he applies a linear decomposition technique. He then relates the results to the independent variables and shows that the scores that come out of the linear decomposition are meaningfully related to that independent variable. As he is manipulating stimuli in the frequency domain, it is natural that he looks for frequency components. The "transient" evoked response is primarily a time-domain phenomenon. The independent variables cannot be translated into 18 Hz and 9 Hz and 9.2 Hz. Regan has this additional constraint on his data that they are defined in terms of frequency so he can use a more powerful linear decomposition technique. With a PCA you do a similar linear decomposition, but it makes no presumptions about what is in the data. Whatever comes out you test against your independent variables. And if it comes out straight, it comes out meaningful, that's something. If not, not.

KAHNEMAN: Don, I think you might have gone a bit far from the simplistic origins of cognitive psychology. It is not true, I think, that we have gone from a linear Sternberg-like stage model to a bushy tree where everything is interconnected with everything else. Our models are still sufficiently simple to make a fair amount of sense. We both agree that useful theories are generally much more complicated than the diagrams that were in the vogue 8 or 10 years ago. But we would probably still say that there is some structure in the arrangement of mechanisms or of processing stages, such that not everything is connected with everything else. The objective of description today is perhaps not to find stages that fit in a nonrecursive linear sequence, but processing devices that Mike Posner calls isolable subsystems can still be studied.

There is another point I would like to raise. We generally agree, I think, that in our capacity as cognitive psychologists we haven't learned anything from evoked potentials. A serious question to which we ought to address ourselves is whether, in our capacity as cognitive psychologists, we are capable of learning anything from techniques other than our own. The history is disheartening, when one considers other attempts to import other methods into cognitive psychology. I have had my bits of experience with the study of pupillary dilation and heart rate, and there have been other techniques, such as eye-movement recordings. The net input into cognitive psychology, to an excellent first approximation, has been zero. It appears that some kinds of evidence are simply not acceptable, because they use tools and techniques that do not fit elegantly into particular paradigms with which cognitive psychologists are concerned. I would like to raise as a hypothesis the possibility that study of evoked potentials will meet with the same fate. I am not yet convinced that there will be much to be learned. But a serious question for this conference to face is whether we would recognize a genuinely significant contribution from the study of evoked potentials. Would we be able to learn from it? I am doubtful.

NORMAN: Let me comment on both. I'll try to do it briefly. I believe that the system for processing that we have in our heads has evolved over the years. It is apt to be quite complex. But for any given task, it may very well be that there is a nice simple model that describes well how it is operating. That is what I tried to do. For any given task, we might be able to take out a subpart. Each task gives a special view of the system, each view is from a different perspective. Each view might even make it look like a different system. But that is only because we don't yet know the whole picture. Sometimes the temptation is to throw up your hands in disgust and to say, "ah well, the results of task A contradict the results of task B." This need not be the case. They supplement each other.

The second point is this: On the one hand, I agree with Danny; on the other hand, I hope he is wrong. I think that we haven't been able to use data from other disciplines because we haven't been ready. The best case I can talk about is Danny Kahneman's use of pupillary size response. I have known of his work for many, many years. Danny made sure I was aware of it. He kept wondering why I wasn't doing those studies myself. The reason is that I didn't know what I would do with the results. It wasn't that I rejected them because they came from different techniques. I just didn't know what to do with them. Psychology did not reject the findings from studies of pupillary response. Rather, our knowledge was too primitive and so we were not yet ready to use them. This is a fundamental phenomenon of all science. Results alone are not sufficient. There must be a framework within which to interpret them. There must be a theoretical paradigm.

7 Report of Panel II: The ERP and Decision and Memory Processes

Panel chair: T. Picton

Panel members: E. Donchin
                  J. Ford
                  D. Kahneman
                  D. Norman

7.1 THE DATA BASE ON P300

PICTON: I shall begin with an apology. Our presentation may not correspond to your expectations because our panel failed to identify a clear interface between cognitive psychology and the event-related potentials. We shall not propose crucial experiments to determine the psychophysiological mechanisms of human memory and decision. Rather, we shall concentrate on the "P300" wave and its possible psychological meaning. I shall begin by presenting a "classical data base." These data place constraints on any theory of P300 that might be suggested. I shall identify four major aspects of the available data.

The first important attribute of the late positive component is its *timing*. This is usually measured as the latency to the peak of the component. It is crucial to note that the P300 may occur before, during, or after the point in time when a decision is possible. This relation of the P300 latency to the timing of mental events is discussed in greater detail in Chapter 10.

A second important fact is that P300 is very much related to *attention*. P300 is not elicited by an unattended stimulus. There are two significant corollaries of the statement that events must be attended if they are to elicit a P300. First, attention is intimately related to "conscious awareness." I feel strongly that the P300 is elicited only if the subject is aware of the signal that elicited it. Of course, the subject may be conscious of stimuli that do not elicit a measurable P300. Nevertheless, if a P300 did appear, the subject must have been aware of the eliciting event. Second, attention has an intensity—subjects may be more or less attentive to particular stimuli. The P300 process seems to be related to the "relevance" (importance, significance, salience, or utility) of the eliciting signal to the subject. Relevance can interact with the other variables that affect the P300. An experiment (Picton, Campbell, Baribeau-Braun, & Proulx, 1978) that supports this statement presents a sequence of two different stimuli to a subject in two different experimental conditions. In one condition the stimuli provide the subject with feedback information about his performance on a concurrent task. In another condition the stimuli are merely counted. The stimulus probabilities are the same in both conditions, but the "relevance" of the stimuli is quite different. P300 components are elicited in both conditions and in each the amplitude depends on the probability of the eliciting stimulus. However, when the stimuli carry feedback information, the P300 is much bigger than when the stimuli are merely counted. It is not clear whether this difference is due to the amount of attention paid to the stimuli, to the effort invested in their processing, or to the actual amount of processing performed. It is clear that the more relevant the stimuli are considered, the larger the P300 they evoke.

A third variable that is important in determining P300 is *probability*. The more improbable an attended stimulus, the larger the P300 it elicits. This variable can control most of the P300 variance. Three refinements to this general rule might be mentioned. One derives from the data of Squires, Donchin, and their colleagues concerning the effect of sequencing (Squires, K.C., Wickens, Squires, N.K., & Donchin, 1976). The strong effect of global probability of the stimulus is modulated by the immediately preceding sequence of stimuli. This applies to attended Bernoulli series and may be affected by the interval between events. In other conditions this sequential effect may not appear. A second refinement involves considering different kinds of probability. In a feedback task a subject makes a response and then receives feedback informing him whether his response was right or wrong. The amplitude of the P300 to the feedback stimulus is not simply determined by the "stimulus probability," nor is it determined by the "outcome probability"—the combined probability of response that is given and the feedback that follows. It is determined by the "contingent probability" of a particular feedback stimulus occurring given a particular response by the subject (Campbell, Courchesne, Picton, & Squires, K.C., 1979). Probability and information are closely related and thus the P300 might be associated with the processing of relevant information. A third refinement to the general probability rule concerns "confidence." When stimulus discrimination becomes difficult and the subject more uncertain, the P300 becomes smaller in amplitude. Ruchkin and Sutton (1978) have interpreted these results using the concept of "equivocation." The P300 amplitude is related to the amount of relevant information available less the equivocation in its processing.

A final set of data that we should consider concerns the *physiological features* of the late positive component. First, it has a place. It is recorded with largest amplitude in central and parietal electrodes. Second, it appears to be stimulus-independent. A visual signal, an auditory signal, and a somatosensory signal all elicit very similar P300s provided they have the same logical character in the task (Simson, Vaughan, & Ritter, 1977). Third, at the time the P300 is elicited, other physiological processes appear to be active. If we seek an interpretation of the function of P300, we must remember that there are many other processes—P165, N2, P3a, P4, N400, and "slow wave"—occurring at about the same time. If we propose that the P300 occurs in association with a particular cognitive process, we must also assess the relationship of other concurrent ERP phenomena to that psychological process.

Our panel presentation is very loosely organized. Judy Ford will review some ideas concerning the relationship between P300 and stimulus evaluation processes. This will be followed by a consideration of one aspect of stimulus evaluation—subjective probability. Manny Donchin will lead with a statement of his ideas on the topic, and Dan Kahneman will follow with a critique. Finally, Don Norman will review the concept of "world models" and how they are built, changed, and structured. The relationship of these concepts to the P300 and other ERP components will then be generally discussed.

7.2 STIMULUS EVALUATION TIME AND P300

FORD: I shall consider the degree to which we can assume that P300 reflects the evaluation of a stimulus. Although there is controversy regarding the specific relation between P300 *amplitude* and the task relevance or improbability of the eliciting stimulus, a consistent picture does emerge from the literature regarding the relation between P300 *latency* and the duration of stimulus evaluation. The theory that P300 latency depends on the duration of stimulus evaluation has been proposed by Donchin and his co-workers (Squires, N.K., Donchin, & Squires, K.C., 1977; Kutas, McCarthy, & Donchin, 1977; Duncan-Johnson, 1978). I find this theory useful in interpreting my own data. The theory is specifically related to the latency of P300 and asserts that certain stimulus evaluation activities must be completed before the process reflected by P300 can be invoked. Therefore, the duration of these stimulus evaluation processes can be indexed by the latency of P300. Any attempt to interpret the latency of P300 has always been confronted by the inconsistency of the relation between the latency of P300 and reaction time. Some investigators report a dissociation between the latency of P300 and reaction time, others report a positive correlation. Furthermore, P300 latency is sometimes shorter and sometimes longer than RT. Donchin and his colleagues (Kutas et al., 1977;

Duncan-Johnson, 1978) presented a theory that attempts to reconcile these conflicts by noting that RT is multiply determined. Although RT represents the effects of many factors such as stimulus evaluation, response processing, and response execution, P300 latency is determined essentially by the duration of stimulus evaluation. If this is true, there is no reason to expect the correlation between P300 latency and reaction time to always be the same. To the extent that most of the variance in RT is contributed by stimulus evaluation time, then P300 latency and RT will be correlated. Detailed consideration of the evidence for this view will be undertaken by the mental chronometry panel. I have found this view very useful in interpreting the data we have been recording from young and elderly subjects.

KELSO: Could you clarify the stimulus evaluation and response processes distinction for me? Are they parallel?

FORD: Stimulus evaluation is an imprecise term, and you can certainly make it fit whatever you want. For me, stimulus evaluation processes include those activities that involve the encoding and proper categorization of the stimulus, whereas response processes include those activities that pertain to the selection and execution of the response. In the task I have assigned my subjects, I assume that the subject must evaluate the stimulus to some extent before deciding how to respond. It is important to realize that the response can be initiated prior to complete evaluation of the stimulus (i.e., the stimulus evaluation and response processes can occur in parallel, at least partially).

CHASE: Why should reaction time not be dependent on stimulus evaluation?

FORD: Sometimes the subject does not evaluate the stimulus fully before responding, in which case RT may precede P300, and errors are more likely to occur (Kutas et al., 1977). For me, the problem is just the opposite. I am having difficulty dealing with the fact that P300 precedes the RT by about 300 msec. You have to assume that several time-consuming processes occur after the stimulus has been evaluated. Subjects must decide which button to press; they may hesitate over the decision; etc. Some of my experiments require more difficult decisions of the subject than the tasks Donchin described in his tutorial. It is in these experiments that I observe a very long interval elapsing between P300 and reaction time.

TREISMAN: Can you describe the task you use?

FORD: I have been using a variant of Sternberg's memory-search paradigms (Sternberg, 1966). The subject is presented with a set of items to memorize and then asked if a certain item was or was not a member of that set. In my studies the P300s have a latency of 300 to 400 msec. The reaction times are on the order of 600 to 800 msec.

OSCAR-BERMAN: Do you find any other significant components after the P300?

FORD: I have not formally analyzed those data for additional components after P300. There is a recent report (Adam & Collins, 1978) also using Sternberg's paradigm in which components occurring after P300 are described. They are believed to be additional P300 components and may be related to such activities as *deciding* that the probe stimulus is a positive or negative instance of the set; *deciding* whether to press right or press left; *deciding* to rescan memory or recheck your answers. I have not analyzed the data to that extent yet, but it seems that there are about three positive peaks in the P300 range. These are even seen in the single trials and do not appear to be the alpha frequency of the EEG. I do not know yet if they are consistent or correlated to any of my manipulations. (See Ford, Mohs, Pfefferbaum, & Kopell, 1980, for a preliminary report of these data.)

TREISMAN: You said the slope of P300 latency when plotted against size of set is smaller than the slope of the RT when plotted against the same variable. This is interesting because it suggests that the RT slope reflects two components, one of which is early and is also seen in the P300 latency. The other component must reflect another serial operation that is included in the response latency but not in the P300.

FORD: That's right.

RITTER: Terry Picton has mentioned a complex of components, N2, P300, slow wave, P4, etc. Some of us think that these waves are involved in one way or another with different kinds of stimulus evaluation.

FORD: Well, as you have shown, N2 is correlated with reaction time (Ritter, Simson, Vaughan, & Friedman, 1979).

RITTER: It is important to note that in experiments where reaction time occurs before P300, then the kind of stimulus evaluation that P300 reflects is associated not with the discrimination that determines the response on that trial but with actions that will be taken on subsequent trials. This interpretation of P300, which I think is appropriate, would then equally well apply to P4 or to slow waves.

MCCARTHY: It must be realized that to say that P300 is related to stimulus evaluation time is not to say that P300 reflects a stimulus evaluation process.

All we mean is that whatever stimulus evaluation processes take place they must be completed before the P300. This is discussed in Chapter 10.

PICTON: P300 latency reflects only that part of stimulus evaluation that is necessary for its generation. You can obviously further evaluate the stimulus after the P300 has been elicited.

McCARTHY: I'm simply saying that if the stimulus is going to be evaluated, it is evaluated before P300 occurs. And if you manipulate stimulus evaluation, you're going to manipulate P300 latency because it is dependent on that process. I am saying that P300 latency is just a metric for stimulus evaluation time. Certainly reaction time is a metric for temporal variations in other processes. But no one assumes that the movement of the button *is* the mental process being measured.

PICTON: But there is a lot more stimulus evaluation that can go on after the P300. So why are you saying that P300 reflects stimulus evaluation?

DONCHIN: This is precisely the issue that has been addressed by the mental chronometry panel, so we should not go into too much detail at this session. At that panel we agonized over the development of a precise definition of the distinction we made between stimulus evaluation and response selection. We do not have a very clear rule. A good statement of the issue is presented by Lappin (1978). He says—in effect—there is a gross distinction between perceptual and motor processes and it's very difficult to define a cut point that clearly distinguishes the two. Yet, we all understand that there are some processes that are involved in encoding the stimulus, evaluating and categorizing it, etc. There is also a class of processes that are involved in selecting the response and executing it. We know clearly which are the extremes on this dimension, and that's what we're talking about. We can do this usefully even though we may not know how to make all the fine distinctions implied by this dichotomy. Now, I think P300 is sensitive to processes that are involved in stimulus evaluation in Lappin's sense of the term. Reaction times are affected by stimulus evaluation as well as by the processes that are on the other side of the dimension. By using P300 latency we can obtain an aide to the conventional analysis of reaction times by having an additional independent measure of timing.

KAHNEMAN: I am puzzled by some aspects of these data. The statement that the latency of P300 is insensitive to response selection implies that P300 represents one side of the information-processing stream. Then Judy casually mentions a finding that the memory load affects the latency of P300 in the Sternberg paradigm. I find this very odd.

DONCHIN: Why? This seems to me perfectly consistent with my view of P300 latency.

FORD: I do, in fact, use Donchin's interpretation to explain my data.

DONCHIN: We have presented data that show that full categorization of the stimulus is necessary before the P300 can be elicited. Memory search and indentification of the stimulus is clearly required for categorization.

PICTON: It will clearly be very difficult to discuss chronometry without knowledge of the process reflected by P300. It's also very difficult for us to know what the P300 reflects unless we know its temporal relationship to decision processes. Thus this panel and the one on mental chronometry necessarily overlap. Perhaps we can move on and review a topic that is latency-independent. Donchin will present a theory of P300 suggesting that it reflects subjective probability.

7.3 SUBJECTIVE PROBABILITY AND P300

DONCHIN: I'm not presenting a theory. I'm stating an argument and presenting some data to bolster the argument. I shall state the argument more strongly than it merits so that the issues raised during this panel's discussions are presented. I shall present data only as required to illustrate the argument. Our first premise is that when all else is held constant and task relevance increases, P300 amplitude increases. Furthermore, when everything is held constant, across experimental conditions, then the lower the prior probability (i.e., the relative frequency) of stimuli, the larger the P300 they elicit. Provided that they are task-relevant. I conclude that P300 amplitude depends on some combination of task relevance and prior probability. Yet, it is clearly the case that even when task relevance and probability are held constant, at least as far as the experimenter is concerned, P300 amplitude still varies. We can use the same generating rule to create stimulus sequences. We can give identical instructions to the subject and still P300 amplitude will vary from trial to trial. It is not possible to observe this variance when only the averaged ERPs are examined. But an analysis of trial-to-trial variations in P300 amplitude reveals the differences. This variance may be caused by variations in the task relevance of the stimuli from trial to trial (because the subject's perceptions, say, of the task varies). It is also possible that the probability varies from trial to trial. In this argument I assume that task relevance remains constant and therefore that some aspect of the probability does vary across trials. Subjective probability varies, I assume, as do other psychological quantities that are determined by external events. External events are always filtered by the subject's perceptual and information-processing mechanisms. Thus, to describe a psychological quantity it is not sufficient to consider only the physical description of the external events. What is important is how the external data are manipulated by internal factors to determine *subjective* probability. This subjective probability does vary across trials, and this variation is reflected in changes in P300 amplitude. The evidence for this assertion is based in part on our studies of sequential effect in P300 amplitude; on the importance of categorization of the stimuli in determining P300 effect, the probability effects on P300, the effects of prior knowledge that the subjects had on the behavior of the P300 probability relationship, and various resource limitation arguments. I shall present data to illustrate each of these points.

I shall first, however, state a proposition with which Kahneman disagrees. A convenient approach to the analysis of the reactions to stimuli, that is to the overt output of the system, derives from signal detection theory. This theory asserts that the overt output (i.e., the subject's descriptions of his perceptions) is determined by the combined effects of the internal representation of the data and some action rules. The internal representation can be reduced to some numerical value. This representation is not necessarily a linear metric; it may be derived from the external events by a very complex computational process. Yet, it can always be reduced to a magnitude that ultimately can be represented by a number (perhaps a vector quantity). This internal representation combines with a set of factors that in signal detection theory are called "criteria" to determine the subject's response to a stimulus. It is generally agreed that whether a subject says "stimulus present" or "stimulus absent" depends, according to signal detection theory, on the representation of stimulus data, called "sensory magnitude" and on the subject's response criterion. Similarly, for expectations data that can be the external stimulus-based data as well as data about the past history combined with general knowledge about events determine a representation, or an internal magnitude, that can be called subjective probability. For simplicity, I would say that this probability is represented by some number that can be between 0 and 1 and follows the rules of probability. But, this is not crucial to the argument. This subjective probability, when combined with what I take Kahneman and Tversky to call heuristics, determines the subjects' response to specific questions about their expectations. Different questions will call forth different heuristics and different mixtures. So, a distinction can be made between the internal representation of probability and its overt manifestation.

My assertion is that P300 allows us a direct look at the internal magnitude independent of heuristics. If I am right, P300 measures can supplement the work that relies entirely on the overt decisions. In P300 we have a probe that looks inside the box and provides, in certain circumstances, a direct measure of subjective probability. I'm presuming to say, and I know this is a very controversial point, but I'm presuming to say, that our position is similar to that of a psychophysicist who found a way to measure "sensory magnitude" independently of the subject's responses on a trial. This will make it unnecessary to infer d' and beta. Sensory magnitude could be measured directly. That will surely allow you to make strong inferences about data. I propose that P300 allows such a direct examination of the value of an internal representation.

For support of these claims I shall review some data directly related to the argument. I want to be sure that it is clear that although it is true that subjective probability has a major controlling effect on P300, the amplitude of P300 is controlled considerably more dramatically by the manipulation of task relevance. One can find enormous differences in P300 amplitude by manipulating task relevance. These are far larger in amplitude than the differences obtained by manipulating probability. In Fig. 7.1 are data from an experiment by Heffley, Wickens, & Donchin (1978). The subject is looking at targets that are moving across a screen. There are two kinds of targets: triangles and squares. Occasionally, every 4 to 8 sec, one of the targets intensifies for 50 msec. The intensification is clearly detectable. The subject must monitor triangle flashes and ignore square flashes or vice versa. The relevant stimuli elicit a P300 that is much larger in amplitude than the P300 we find from the tones that we used in the sequential effect studies. It reaches some 20 μV (microvolts) in amplitude. Incidentally, note that as we increase the number of targets on the screen, the amplitude of P300 does not change though its latency does change.

Now, consider the task-relevant stimuli as their probability is varied. As prior probability of the stimulus (i.e., its relative frequency) is varied, amplitude of P300 is also changing. This is generally well-accepted, and supporting data were obtained in many different laboratories. It is crucial to my argument that not all the rare events elicit the same P300, some do and some do not. If one examines the ERPs elicited by the frequent events, some elicit a P300 and some do not. So there is trial-to-trial variability in P300 amplitude even though the task relevance and the prior probabilities are presumably constant. The sequence generating rule does not change; yet, something does seem to change from trial to trial. It is possible that this trial-to-trial variation is due to inevitable noise and that the amplitude varies for some boring reason. It is also possible that there is some logic to this variability and that some rule may be found that explains this variability. Such a rule emerges if we perform a sequential analysis of the data obtained in the oddball experiment. The amplitude of P300 from trial to trial is shown to depend on the exact sequence of stimuli that just preceded the eliciting stimulus (Squires, K.C., et al., 1976). It turns out that even though all the ERPs are elicited by the same high tone, which appeared with a .50 probability. If all the high tones are averaged together, no P300 can be seen. But, when trials are sorted according to the preceding sequence, a P300 appears whenever the high tone is preceded by low

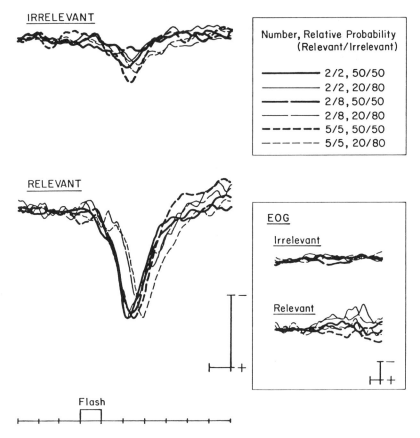

GRAND AVERAGE   ERPs — Pz
6 SUBJECTS

IRRELEVANT

Number, Relative Probability (Relevant/Irrelevant)
——————— 2/2, 50/50
——————— 2/2, 20/80
—— —— 2/8, 50/50
—— —— 2/8, 20/80
- - - - - 5/5, 50/50
– – – – 5/5, 20/80

RELEVANT

EOG

Irrelevant

Relevant

Flash

FIG. 7.1   The ERPs elicited by the intensifications of triangular and square targets moving on a screen in random trajectories from left to right. The insert indicates the number of targets on the screen for each trace (targets/nontargets) and the probability (x100) that the stimulus will intensify. Note that relevant stimuli elicit a large P300. The amplitude of the P300 is not affected by the probability that the events will occur. However, the latency is clearly affected by the number of items on the screen and by the probability. (After Heffley et al., 1978.)

tones. We proposed on the basis of these data that the amplitude of the P300 elicited on any given trial, given fixed task relevance, is a function of the expectancy of the stimulus. I consider expectancy, in this context, to be a function of subjective probability. The lower the subjective probability of the stimulus, the lower the expectancy and the larger the P300 it will elicit. In Bernoulli series, when the subject has no information about the probability of events (other than the prior probability), estimates of subjective probability are derived from the past history of the sequence. Three different factors determine the expectancy according to our model: the prior probability of the stimulus; the structure of the sequence, and the effects of alternation runs.

To make sure that it is clear that the effect of surprising events is not limited to boring, random, Bernoulli sequences but may be obtained in fairly complex situations, I'll describe, again very, very briefly, a study in which Horst, Johnson, and Donchin (1980) presented subjects with a paired-associates learning task. A syllable was presented, and the subject typed what he believed to be the correct response, specified a confidence level indicating whether he believed he was sure that this was the correct answer, and then saw the answer. If the answer matched what he typed, then the subject was correct. If the answer did not match what was typed, the subject was incorrect (see Fig. 7.2). We analyzed the ERPs for different confidence levels for different outcomes. Figure 7.2 shows the amplitude of the P300 elicited in response to the syllables that tell the subject if he was correct or incorrect. The ERPs drawn with a dashed line were obtained when the subject was incorrect; the solid line was obtained when the subject was correct. These are plotted against the confidence judgment specified on a 4-point scale. The data show that if the subject is correct, a big P300 is elicited if he was not confident. If the subject was incorrect, a bigger P300 is elicited when he was confident. This pattern is consistent with the statement that a surprising outcome produces the large P300. If the subject thought he didn't know the answer and it turned out he knew the answer, he was surprised. If he thought that he knew the answer and it turned out he didn't, he was also surprised.

Thus far, I have argued that task relevance is important, but if you keep it constant, prior probability is important. If you keep probability constant, P300 still varies because the subjective probability does vary from trial to trial. I'm also suggesting that the estimate of subjective probability is somewhat independent of what the subject actually says on a trial; that is, P300 reflects subjective probabilities in a way that is somewhat different from the indication one finds by asking people to predict what will happen or asking them to place bets or to move levers. Experiments Greg Chesney ran in my laboratory illustrate this point. We used the same Bernoulli series with visual stimuli. This time, the subject guessed before each trial which stimulus will be presented on that trial. It turns out that the same results emerge if the subject is guessing or if the subject is counting. In the guessing condition, each stimulus confirms or disconfirms a subject's guess. We find, as others do, that it does not matter if the stimulus confirmed or disconfirmed the subject's prediction and the amplitude of P300.

This seems to contradict the idea that P300 measures surprise, because the subject should presumably be surprised by a disconfirmation. If the fact that the subject predicts A indicates that he expects an A, he should be more surprised by a B then by an A. But the P300 data contradict this interpretation.

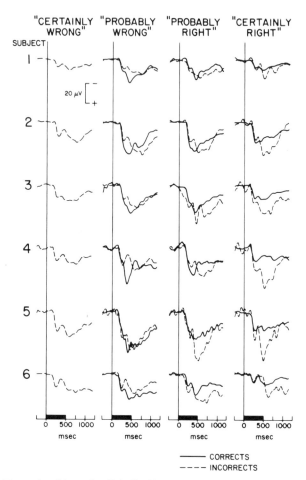

FIG. 7.2   For each subject, the digitally filtered averaged ERPs from Cz that were elicited by the "response" CVC. ERPs from correct and incorrect trials are superimposed for ratings in each of the four confidence ranges. There was an insufficient number of trials in the "certainly wrong"/correct category to consider. (From Horst et al., 1980.)

A logical pattern does emerge if we consider the logic of the predictions. If the subject predicts repetition, confirmations elicit a small P300. If they predict alternations, disconfirmations produce a bigger P300.

We ran another experiment in which we controlled the probability of alternations. The data, very briefly summarized, show that if the subject predicts a low-probability event, no matter if it's an alternation or repetition, the following stimulus elicits a large P300, whether or not it confirms the subject's prediction. So what matters is not the specific relationship between the prediction and the event but whether the prediction was of an unlikely event. If the subject commits himself to an unlikely event, a large P300 is elicited by the following stimulus. We also have strong evidence that the subject's data base, his knowledge about the situation, makes a difference to the variation in P300 amplitude. Support for this assertion comes from the dissertations of Connie Duncan-Johnson and Skip Johnson. In both cases we used essentially the same stimulus series but varied what the subjects *knew* about the series.

Duncan-Johnson (1978) has shown that if the subject obtains, on a trial-by-trial basis, information about the probability of events, he no longer utilizes the past history of the sequence. He uses rather the information on hand. So we are not viewing here an automatic, bottom-up process. You can provide input at the top and it will have "downward" effects. In Johnson's (1979) study the probabilities reversed unpredictably, so that every 40-80 trials the probabilities switched. The subjects, in the beginning of the experiment, did not know that at all; then in the second part of the experiment they knew that and were looking for the point at which the probability changes. By and large we find that it doesn't really matter if the subject knows or does not know that the probabilities change. Even though they are told that they are presented with a 50-50 Bernoulli sequence, the sequential effects are determined by the changing probabilities. Nevertheless, there is an effect of knowledge in various critical places, so that knowledge does interact with the amplitude of P300. (For details see Johnson & Donchin, 1982). Again, we cannot consider this a bottom-up process by which a series of stimuli are automatically processed. There is a very detailed interaction among what you know about events, what the past history is, what the task is, and how you have to categorize the stimuli.

Finally, I'd like to point out that the process we're dealing with is, I think, resource-limited in the sense that Don Norman has been using this word. If the subject performs an oddball task in conjunction with another task, there will be a strong effect on the amplitude of P300 and on the sequential effects. To summarize briefly, if the subject counts tones in a random series in conjunction with a tracking task, then it turns out that the P300 is greatly diminished, as soon as the subject begins to track. As you increase the difficulty of the tracking, no further effect on P300 is seen. On the other hand, if the subject is counting tones while monitoring a complex visual display, then the different levels of difficulty of the monitoring task affect the amplitude of the P300 elicited. So if the task is perceptual and requires monitoring, then increasing the task difficulty of the perceptual task eats into the rescources that are available for performing the oddball task. In summary, then, the argument can be viewed as a series of assertions, some of which are more controversial than others. Of course, the more tied we are to the data, the less controversial the assertion. There is no question, I think, that the probability of the stimulus, as filtered by numerous cognitive factors, determines the amplitude of P300. Whether this is indeed an independent measure of pure probability or of the output of the pure probability evaluator or can be viewed in a different way is a matter that we now discuss.

KUTAS: On one point you seem to disagree with Picton's presentation of the data base. You appear to think that task relevance has a larger effect on P300 amplitude than does probability. But in evidence you show Heffley's data and say "look at this big P300" (Heffley et al., 1978). But really how does that relate to task relevance? I don't understand. I agree with you at a gut level but I don't think you presented any relevant data.

DONCHIN: The triangles are task-relevant; the squares are not. Therefore we find this enormous difference in amplitude even though the probabilities are constant. I wanted to be sure that we keep in mind that *you can keep probability constant* and yet obtain enormous differences in the amplitude of P300. I think Heffley's data very clearly depend on the task relevance of the stimulus. I don't see how else you could interpret that.

KUTAS: Aren't there situations where you keep the probability constant with regular tones and you find this amplitude enhancement as well?

DONCHIN: This is true at the single-trial level. With single-trial analysis you can pull out the sequential effects. But as you know, 80% of the single trials in Heffley's experiment are detectable as having large P300s. I was reacting to Picton's statement that probability is the largest, and major, effect. I just wanted to be sure that we don't forget that task relevance is enormously important. Task relevance, as it turned out, is very difficult to deal with because we don't know how to measure it. That's a point Posner and I debated in the preconference correspondence. I said that one of our biggest problems is that we cannot quantify task relevance. And Posner said "What's the problem? Everybody knows how to design experiments to make the stimuli relevant." This, of course, is true.

POSNER: And you provided good evidence for that I think. I mean the triangles *are* relevant there.

DONCHIN: Yes, but I would like to measure the amount of task relevance. It is very easy to design experiments where something is relevant and something else is not. But suppose I want to modulate the *amounts* of relevance, what do I do? Even in Heffley's data we encounter a serious problem. If you tell the subject to monitor course changes in the trajectories of the triangles, the flashes fail to elicit a P300. Yet, the triangles are what I think will be called a channel. It is a clearly relevant channel. The flash is an attribute of the stimuli that is clearly there and can't be missed, yet there is absolutely no P300. Now it is simple to say is that the flashes are no longer task-relevant. But this happens to be circular. I want to be able to design experiments that will allow me ahead of time to predict if the triangles will, or will not be, task-relevant. I would like the cognitive psychologist to provide some algorithms for defining, measuring, and predicting when a stimulus will be task-relevant.

TREISMAN: That's very strange, Manny, because task relevance isn't the problem. You defined it properly. What you are saying is that you want to be able to predict what the subject will attend to on a given trial. Subjects may not attend to the thing that is task-relevant. One way around that is to make the task difficult enough for you to be able to see if they are attending because if they don't attend, they fail.

DONCHIN: Well, there are several problems here. I don't think that what *I* define as the task to the subject is all that crucial. What is important is how *the subject* perceives my instructions and the extent to which the subject is following the instructions. You can always set up something that makes sure the subject attends to the stimuli and they are relevant. What I seek is a measure that will tell me if the subject is attending half as much as he did in another condition, and then a quarter as much or maybe three-quarters as much in yet other conditions. I would like to use an abscissa that task relevance is plotted

TREISMAN: One way is to vary task relevance so that the subject can't exercise any options.

DONCHIN: But that turns out also to be very difficult, because on the basis of the human factors literature one would predict that when increasing tracking bandwidth in a tracking task, one increased difficulty. It turns out not to affect P300.

TREISMAN: Vary your tasks, and see which tasks subjects can combine and which they can't combine. You can't know that a priori. It is an empirical question.

DONCHIN: But how do you design an experiment? In order to calibrate this you have to know that you vary difficulty so that it pulls resources in a reasonable way.

TREISMAN: Yes, but if you don't have an a priori assumption that every task draws on the same resources, that isn't possible. You are forced actually to investigate which tasks can be combined and which cannot. Once you have that information, you can then vary the difficulty of the tasks that you know compete. I think you have to measure the competition for resources behaviorally, and then you can look at the evoked responses to see how the competition affects P300.

DONCHIN: What you're saying is correct. But you're saying, are you not, that task relevance cannot be defined objectively and a priori. It only can be inferred from the consequences of the experiment.

TREISMAN: Right, but you do have behavior as well as P300 to manipulate.

DONCHIN: But I can manipulate stimulus intensity very nicely and I don't need to see how the subject responds to manipulate stimulus intensity.

TREISMAN AND KAHNEMAN: This is because nobody has a metric for task relevance.

DONCHIN: Yes, that's exactly what I'm saying. I would like somebody to come up with a measure of task relevance that would be equivalent to stimulus intensity. We don't have this and that is our problem.

NORMAN: Let me point out that intensity is not the relevant variable. The relevant variable is the *psychological* variable of brightness, and brightness is not a monotonic function of intensity.

DONCHIN: It doesn't have to be monotonic as long as you know the function.

TREISMAN: You have to find out what rule determines task relevance. The same problem arises with attention. With task relevance it may be more difficult, but it's the same problem.

RITTER: I have a question. There's something that puzzles me. Manny mentioned the Chesney experiment. A similar experiment was conducted in several labs by Campbell, Courchesne, Picton, and Squires (1979). These data suggest that P300 could be related to consciousness and the limited capacity process that has conscious attributes. Manny has remarked elsewhere that the P300 does not reflect the gamblers' fallacy. What struck me is that the P300 reflects another kind of fallacy. If there are two stimuli with a 50-50 probability and eight of one of them come in a row, it's just as fallacious to expect that the same stimulus will occur on the next trial as to expect a change. We have here two kinds of fallacies. We have the so-called gamblers' fallacy, which we are all familiar with, and now we have the P300 fallacy, which is a different kind of fallacy. Now, furthermore, when we talk about subjective probability, it seems to me that when the subject operates on the gamblers' fallacy that in his subjective experience he indeed expects a change after a long run of the same stimulus. And what the data seem to show is that the P300 does not reflect that kind of subjective probability, or what the subject expects *phenomenologically*. The amplitude of P300 does not seem to be related to the kind of experience the subject has in the gamblers' fallacy, but it is related to this other kind of fallacy. I don't understand how it is known which is the subjective probability here. Is it the phenomenological experience of the gambler who has the fallacy of consciously thinking that it will go one way, or this other fallaccy which is reflected in the amplitude of P300?

DONCHIN: In response to this question I would ask how you would know that the subject expects the B after a run of four A's? Why do you think his response is veridical anymore that you are willing to accept, in a signal-detection experiment, the response to the question "do you see a light?" Do you really believe that the subjects saw a light when they said "yes"? No, you don't. You will say that on some of the trials on which the subjects said "I saw the light" they were actually responding so on a "noise" trial because the sensory magnitude invoked by the noise led them to a "false alarm."

NORMAN: They said they did see it, but it really wasn't there.

DONCHIN: Even though it really wasn't there! It is the interaction of sensory magnitude and the criterion that led the subject to say "yes." It's not novel to assert that subjects' verbal report is not a veridical image of their internal representation of the data. There is always an interaction between response tendencies and perceptual outcomes.

There is much complexity here. Consider the study reported by Messick and Rapoport (1965). They varied the payoff and drove the subjects to make the gamblers' fallacy. At the same time, the subjects give a perfectly correct indication of the relative frequency of events; that is, their reports are dissociated from their perceptions of the probabilities. And this is achieved by varying the payoffs. If I had to bet at a $1000 a throw, I would probably be much more inclined to consider what I *know* about probability than if it costs me one cent a throw.

KAHNEMAN: If you're betting on your P300, you won't do much better. I mean, look at your P300 and bet a quarter—it's not a good guide.

SHIFFRIN: I don't know if Danny Kahneman would agree, but one could argue that the evidence for gamblers' fallacy is not relevant here. An anti-gamblers' fallacy in regard to repetition could very well be a useful strategy. One always wants to predict that what's been happening is going to continue to happen. Life tends to work that way.

DONCHIN: I should point out that the gambler's fallacy does appear in our data. If you have very unbalanced probability, then the bottom branch of the tree tends to curve upward so that after very long runs the subject does seem to reflect gamblers' fallacy even for P300. It is a relatively small effect.

7.4 DECISION THEORY AND ERPS

KAHNEMAN: The remarks I have to make are an extension of the other responses of Manny's presentation. I was fascinated by the probability effects on P300, and this leads me to speculate about the kinds of ERP findings that cognitive psychologists are going to find captivating. This question, of course, has implications for the interfacing of the two disciplines. It turns out that I resonate strongly to evoked potential findings only when they confirm some behavioral hypotheses for which I have independent evidence or when I can link the ERP data with a schema that has already been built from behavorial evidence. Thus, I am excited by the Hillyard findings on N1 because I happen to believe in early selection. I found the Squires, Donchin set of findings on expectation and probabilities very interesting, not because they relate to my work on subjective probability, but because they reminded me of two older findings that appear to make the same point. The first is from a study by Epstein and Rock (1960). They constructed a reversible figure with two double profiles and showed subjects the two profiles in alternation on successive trials. Finally, after a long series of alternations they showed the double profile. The question was whether, after being exposed to profile A on the preceding trial, subjects would perceive profile A or B on the next trial. The experiment neatly contrasts a cognitive expectation of alternation with a priming effect. The results were unequivocal, and they indicated that priming, rather than conscious expectation, controlled perception in this situation: Subjects who had just been shown profile A saw profile A in the ambiguous figure. Here we see something that seems to behave much like P300. Because I knew that result and had been impressed by it, I was more than usually responsive to the evoked potential evidence that seems to make the same point. The evidence suggests a discrepancy between a cognitive expectation and a state of priming or perceptual readiness. It appears that you may be primed or prepared for something else than that which you consciously believe will happen. Similar findings have been reported in the orienting-response literature. Furedy and Scull (1971) exposed subjects to Bernoulli sequences of two possible events, and they noted that repetitions caused smaller orienting responses than alternations, contrary to the normal pattern of negative recency effects in conscious expectations. A more dramatic result was reported by Maltzman, Harris, Ingram, and Wolff (1971). They exposed subjects to a constant level of illumination for 10 min. The illumination was then changed, then restored, in a series of regular alternations. Although the subjects surely realized the repetitive pattern of events, they continued to show larger OR's when the illumination was changed from the initial adapting level than when it was restored to that level. The initial adaptation period had apparently established a neuronal model that defined some changes of illumination as deviations from the standard and others as restorations of standard conditions.

Here again we seem to have a discrepancy between two types of expectations: a conscious, or cognitive, expectation (I have no doubt that the subject knows what is going on) and a more primitive expectation that controls the orienting response. There must be a mechanism that somehow distinguishes the standard state of the room, in which there is little or no novelty from a new state that is treated as novel. When we find such a discrepancy between two types of expectation, I really see no need to label one of them as more fundamental than the other. The fact that they differ is fascinating, but I am not prepared to agree that the expectation that triggers P300, the orienting response, and the percept in the Epstein-Rock study represents *the* subjective probability, whereas the expectation that is measured by asking people what they think, or by making them bet, reflects subsequent distortion by biases, heuristics, lies, and criterion effects. There may exist a multiplicity of representations of a situation, each associated with its own set of expectations, and we may be able to measure responses of violations of these diverse expectations in several ways, by P300 or by behavior. But I see no adequate reason to say that one of the expectations is primary and that the others are transformations of it.

We can certainly agree that P300 is somehow hooked to the violation of an expectation, but I wouldn't want to say that the magnitude of P300 indicates the value of *the* subjective probability of an event, because I don't believe that such a thing exists. It may be useful to pursue further the notion that expectations are multidimensional in several ways. One distinction, which can be studied by evoked potential methodology, is between top-down and bottom-up induction of expectations. This distinction relates to the speed with which we acquire control over expectations. If I tell you something about what is going to happen next, and you believe me, does that control your expectations? By telling you, I'm feeding information through the cognitive system. It's very much like training the subject to expect an alternation in the Epstein-Rock paradigm, but in that paradigm such cognitive manipulations did not fully control expectations. So there seems to be another way in which we build expectations, which is much more like learning a skill—where we need reinforced repetition and where merely telling the subject what's going to happen isn't enough. We might combine the two ways of inducing expectations to find out whether constructing expectations top-down or building them through exposure to sequences can substitute for one another. There is a great deal to be done here, which I think is valuable to our understanding of how expectations are set up and to the separation of skill learning from cognitive control aspects in the generation of expectancies.

SHIFFRIN: You describe these two kinds of expectations, top-down versus bottom-up. Is it possible that instead of that distinction there is a line along a different dimension? For example, repetition might be one level and alternations another . . .

KAHNEMAN: No, because you could tell the subject that things are going to alternate. You could tell the subject what to expect at any level of detail, and you could also let the subject discover that there is an alternation.

SHIFFRIN: Yes, but I'm saying that if the subject tends to expect repetition, the system will simply give you responses indicating, as Manny would say, that he expects repetition all the time.

KAHNEMAN: Well, it could be the repetitions of alternations. If you're exposing the subject to a sequence of alternations, then the subject is going to learn to expect an alternation.

PALMER: I have the feeling that I may have the same thoughts or similar thoughts to Shiffrin's. This thing that your're calling bottom-up, this P300, is sensitive to stimulus probabilities and repetitions. This may be the same as saying that it is the mechanism of generating stimulus probability or subjective probabilities. I guess I'm arguing more with Manny. To say that P300 reflects expectations doesn't mean that it is the mechanism for generating them. It may be just a repetition effect that is just consistent with the notion of a greased analysis pathway. That might be what's going on. P300 might reflect a mechanism due to facilitation of a pathway by repetitions and not have anything to do with subjective probability.

DONCHIN: Can I say two things about this? First, I agree with you. What we're seeing is not necessarily the probability evaluation itself but rather its consequences. It just happens to be related monotonically to probability and, therefore, is a useful index response of subjective probability. As far as a greased pathway, I think we have the evidence that if it *is* a greased pathway, it takes an awful lot of cognition to grease the pathway; that is, it's not simply a repetition effect where stimulus adaptation or receptor fatigue is important. You can vary the effects on P300 by just telling the subject different things and exactly the same physical sequence will elicit a different P300 pattern. Also you can have very different stimuli physically that fall in different categories. The sequential effects are between categories. They are not between physical stimuli, so that, for example, you could have three stimuli instead of two, two of which are uncounted and one of which is counted. The two uncounted stimuli behave, as far as P300 is concerned, indistinguishably. It's not the physcial stimulus that is important.

PALMER: Well, that may just be a matter of which pathways you're talking about: the ones that go to the place categorized or the ones from the physical stimulus.

DONCHIN: O.K. I agree with that.

PALMER: You say you can change radically the way the subject responds to a stimulus by telling him different things?

DONCHIN: The only way to respond is to show more data. Let me just say simply if you use a cued S1-S2 experiment as Connie Duncan-Johnson did (see Duncan-Johnson & Donchin, 1982), where the S2s were a Bernoulli series of two events, the S1s either informed the subjects of the probability of the S2 or they did not give them any information at all. In the experiment in which the S1 gives no information about the S2, the P300 elicited by the S2 shows the sequential dependencies, just in the way you predict. If you use essentially the same stimulus series, but now the S1 indicates to the subjects the probability of the S2, the sequential effect disappears. The amplitude of P300 is determined entirely by what the S1 tells the subjects about the probability of S2. That's one example. Another example is when the subjects are hunting for the point at which the probability changes. If they know that it changes, you obtain very different effects around the time at which they make a decision from what you find from exactly the same stimulus series when they don't know the probabilities are changing, even though they actually track the probability changes. In one case, however, they track it gradually and slowly, but when they know it's about to change and then suddenly it boops, then an upshot of P300 amplitude that sort of slowly and gradually rises to the point where the subjects report the change. Then it goes down. So that the same physical stimuli in both of these experiments elicit different P3s and the same sequences produce different P300 amplitudes depending on when the subjects know about the situation.

TREISMAN: I wonder if anything has been done with animals. Maybe you'll find it easier to separate the more primitive kind of probability evaluation from the conscious hypotheses.

DONCHIN: I think the answer is no, at least at this time.

TREISMAN: It would be interesting to see if you obtain the same P300 effects as in humans.

DONCHIN: Work searching for P300 in animals has begun in the last few months in several laboratories. I don't think anybody has sufficient data yet.

KAHNEMAN: I'm grateful to Manny, and to the present conference, for forcing me to think about expectations in a different way and probably more deeply than I had in the past. Can we represent expectations by probabilities? In a psychological analysis, my impression is that we cannot. Let me try to present a preliminary hypothesis about what is happening in the expectation system. We are accustomed to use this term: The subjects expect stimuli. There is a set of possible stimuli and the subjects expect those stimuli, and the degree to which they expect each of these stimuli is indexed by a subjective probability. It is quite possible, however, that this is not the way in which expectations are distributed. It is certainly not a proper account of the surprise that occurs when an expectation is violated. Let me give an example to make this point. Suppose we present stimuli that vary in the dimensions of color and shape. Suppose we have three values of color and three values of shape. Now, imagine that the color red is most frequent and the square is most frequent; so that 50% of the stimuli are red and 50% are square; but there never are any red squares. The question is this; when presented with an object that has a relatively rare color and a relatively rare shape, are the subjects going to be surprised that it is not red and that it is not a square? It is quite possible, in my view, that expectations are in fact arranged by properties and not by stimuli and that the expectation is inherently multidimensional, in a way that would have serious implications for an analysis of surprise. Let's look at another example. Suppose a coin is tossed 40 times. What number of heads do you expect? There are actually two different expectations that conflict. In one sense, you know that the coin is fair, so you expect 20. But if 20-20 actually occurs, there will be a large P300, because you don't really expect 20-20. You know that there is randomness in the series and so you somehow expect the result of the sample to be one standard deviation away from the mean. So you expect the outcome to represent the central tendency and also to be one standard deviation away from the mean to reflect the randomness of the series. You will be surprised if either of these is violated. In particular, you will be surprised to observe a result that is precisely at the mean and, therefore, fails to reflect the anticipated variability. This may be the case even in Bernoulli series, where I suggest that we expect each stimulus to do things that no single Bernoulli stimulus can do. We expect it to be the most frequent stimuli, but we also expect some degree of alternation because the series as a whole has to look like a

Bernoulli series with a particular probability. We might have some expectations of runs. We might have some expectations of repetitions, etc., and no single stimulus will completely fail to surprise us. So that the notion that we expect or predict a particular stimulus may be rather simpleminded, because there may be no stimulus that will not surprise us and because the pattern of our surprises may suggest that we expect something that cannot in fact happen: a red square, for example, where red squares have a probability of zero but red is very frequent and squares are very frequent. The rules of expectancies are, I think, a wide-open problem, and the notion that these rules will fall in any simple way from the calculus of probability is unlikely indeed. I am not inclined to believe that the rules of expectancies that we observe in an analysis of P300 will follow the calculus of probabilities, because I know that even the more cognitively controlled expectancies don't follow that calculus. However, it is clear that some important questions concerning the nature of expectancies could be studied with P300 as a measure.

SHIFFRIN: Can you make a prediction about the P300 of red squares in that case? Is it going to increase, decrease, or remain stable?

KAHNEMAN: Well this is very curious because the question, of course, is whether you'd get a large P300 the first time a red square appears. You might obtain a large P300 to anything that is not a square because it's not a square; to anything that's not red because it's not red; to a red square because it's never happened before. There is no need for the set of our expectancies to be totally consistent or to converge in the manner that is described by the probability calculus.

DONCHIN: What you are saying, I think, is that the set of objects over which the probabilities are defined is not the set simpleminded stimuli. One has to be careful in deciding what is the set and which probabilities are defined and there may be multiple sets.

KAHNEMAN: There may be multiple sets and then we are not dealing with probability calculus anymore, because if we can't define a set over which probabilities add up to 1, then, you know, we're in a different world. And I think we probably should be in a different world and in a different calculus when we study expectancies and surprises, because the calculus of probabilities may well not be the most appropriate one. The standard calculus is not the only one. In the field of statistics, Glen Shafer (1976) has recently advanced the claim that the familiar notion that probabilities necessarily add up to 1 needs to be revised. Psychologists should be watching for such alternative conceptualizations of probability and expectations. Specifically, we might want to consider the possibility that a proper measure of our expectations should not add up to 1, that it is a mistake to normalize the degree to which we expect various things to happen, as if the sum of our expectations for various possibilities is bound to add up to anything in particular. Perhaps when I'm intensely involved in something, then I'm expecting many things with great intensity and then, whichever of those happens, I'll be surprised that the others didn't because I was expecting them as well. And perhaps when I'm not very involved in a situation, I'm just not generating very much by way of expectancies and will therefore not be very suprised, regardless of what happens. Indeed, the effects of task relevance could be related to the active generation of expectancy: The fewer expectancies that are generated, the fewer the surprise responses that are likely to occur later. To summarize, I don't really know what subjective probability is, but if I had to choose a measure for it, it wouldn't be P300. I'm not sure that the calculus of probabilities is the most useful calculus in thinking about expectancies. And I believe that if we free ourselves of the conceptual straightjacket of probability theory, many results should become more interesting, and the study of P300 would make a substantial contribution to the analysis of expectancies.

SHIFFRIN: It sounds like you're really saying that there's about four or five different measures that we have to consider—surprise, expectancy, probability, etc. Could these all be different and could they pick evoked potentials and components and relate to aspects of these expectancies?

KAHNEMAN: I suppose so. Naturally what we have in P300 is an event that occurs after the stimulus. This event provides us with no direct evidence for any process that occurred before the stimulus. In general, P300 reflects the properties of some sort of surprise response rather more than it reflects the properties of a probability. We don't observe the probability estimation as such; we only observe the graded response to a violation of expectations. This is the nature of the evidence that is available to us.

DONCHIN: I think that the point about P300 following the stimulus is not very germane. You can develop a model about how people develop probability estimates and then validate it with a measure that we take after the stimulus. You make predictions based on what the model tells about the development of expectation. I did not claim that the values I call subjective probability add up to a constant that is equal to 1.0. I don't think that the amplitude of P300 has to somehow be related to the calculus of probabilities. I view matters in this way—we plot a function; there is some variable on the abcissa and P300 amplitude on the ordinate. That variable on the abcissa is a measurement of what Danny calls a violation of expectation. For me this is synonymous with "subjective" probability. I don't think our views are all that different.

KAHNEMAN: Just leave out the word *probability*, because many other people have a claim on it.

DONCHIN: The important point, though, and I think that is what you miss if you become too involved in the calculus of probability, is that it is not the *objective* determinants of expectations that determine the amplitude of P300. It's the way they are filtered by the cognitive factors. The adjective *subjective* is required to explain why the same relative frequency yields different P300s. This is why, in the context of this work, the notion of subjective probability was introduced, because it was quite clear that you can keep the *objective* determinants of probability constant and yet find large variance in the P300. You can call it expectancy, or you can call it subjective probability. That's just a choice of terms.

KAHNEMAN: Well, then, I think the debate merely concerns a tactical issue of whether your audience will find your treatment most useful if you refer to subjective probabilities as the object of your measurement. Paradoxically, I would argue that if you want to communicate with people who are really interested in the psychology of subjective probability, you should not claim that P300 measures probability, because this term is loaded with conflicting associations. Your potential audience will find your analysis more helpful if you do not use a term in a manner that violates common usage.

DONCHIN: The distinction between expectancy and output is a valid distinction. I think the output is the result of the conjunction of the interaction of heuristics with expectancy.

KAHNEMAN: I object to the idea that the gamblers' fallacy is somehow less fundamental than other properties of expectations. This is the kind of thing that happens when we use loaded terms. For me, certainly, the gamblers' fallacy is one of the most salient findings about subjective probability, and I'm going to resist somebody who offers a novel measure of subjective probability, which suggests that the subjective probability of repetitions is higher that that of alternations. Why become involved in such debates about words?

DONCHIN: I don't see the point of all this worry about what is fundamental.

KAHNEMAN: You assume a subjective probability processor that is not subject to the gamblers' fallacy and a set of heuristics that biases the responses. It seems to me that you have been claiming that P300 measures a more fundamental subjective probability . . .

DONCHIN: No, there are two very distinct things, two distinct processes at work here. I don't know that one is more or less fundamental than the other. But I think subjects have data, and they operate on the data with their heurisitcs and then they generate an output and the heuristics are as fundamental as the probabilities. Norman will call this, in a minute, a discrepancy in world model. What you do depends on your world model and on your strategies.

NORMAN: The problem is a very simple problem, which is really trivial. Whenever you say subjective probability, I'm reminded of the words of Ward Edwards and Amos Tversky and a variety of other people, all of whom have spoken about subjective probability. They have worried a lot about what it means in decision contexts and have developed theories about the way that subjective probability is developed and the way they add within the decision process. More recently, they have rejected that entire notion. So, in fact, the minute you say that key word, it brings to mind all of these relevant studies that lead me to say, "ah hah, you see, that's no longer appropriate." And therefore I dismiss all your results too.

DONCHIN: But they do not deal with the same thing. I use the concept of "subjective probability" in the same way that you claimed the right to use the term "channel." "Channel" has been defined in a different context and yet you claimed the right to use it according to the convenience of your work. I don't see how you can support such terminological imperialism.

KUTAS: One of the problems you have with this model is that it is fairly limited because you don't know what happens if you are presenting these stimuli at random intervals coming anywhere from 200 to 700 msec. You don't know that they are still expecting the stimuli to repeat. Nobody has done that. At this point, you know, it can be shown for 1-sec intervals and 1 1/2 sec, and some people have used 3 sec. But you have no idea what would happen if we really start playing around with interstimulus intervals. I'm saying that behaviorally there are situations in which people are shown to follow the gamblers' fallacy and there are behavioral situations in which they do not. With the P300 we only have one side so far. There may be stimulus situations that have just not been tested because we've had a tendency to use the same intervals because that's what gave us good results in the first place.

REGAN: Can I interrupt with what is probably a quite naive point. There must be between these different views a very firm path. It is useful to think about probability and subjective probability from the subject's point. For example, people who climb mountains have found there is a very objective danger that a rock will fall on your head. The only way of operating is to take a subjective probability of zero. It will never happen to you. When you cross the road, there is a certain objective chance you're going to get hit, but you have to look to the subjective probability of zero. So a naive subject will have very strongly built-in complete tendency to take absolutely little notice of what the statistical probabilities are in making this choice.

DONCHIN: You *know* the probability here. Your heuristic is such that it pays you to cross the street, even though you realize that you might be hit. I know perfectly well, every time I board a plane, how often planes fall. Nevertheless the payoff is such that I do get on a plane. If things will get worse, my payoff will change and then I will decide not to get on a plane. The fact is that I do know the probability that something will happen to the plane just as I know what will happen if I get on the Bay Shore freeway. But the payoff structure forces me to do so, and my heuristics lead me to drive carefully in the right lane.

KELSO: I don't think so. It seems to me that there are many occasions in real life that you have to have a broader viewpoint about what expectancy might mean. I doubt that when we are moving around in our environment that we are computing probabilities of events. "Expectancy" in this sense can be dispensed with. For example, would we say about an animal that's about to jump from one branch of a tree to another that that animal is expecting something? Or, if I "pull" (by electrical stimulation) the animal's eyes in an upward direction and show that the animal is prepared to jump, is the animal computing a subjective probability that he is about to move? Or if I throw you a ball, just to follow on Regan's point, do you compute a subjective probability that that ball is going to hit or miss you? I think there are many cases in the real world that we don't actually generate or compute subjective probabilities.

KAHNEMAN: You get a huge surprise response here. Now if you throw a ball at some animal and somehow make it vanish in mid-air or change trajectories, you will get a huge response, probably in an animal, certainly in a human. So you are expecting the ball to follow a trajectory and you can be very surprised indeed and you are generating those expectancies.

KELSO: But are you computing subjective probabilities, in that case, or are you sensitive to the perceptual information that guides activity?

DONCHIN: Well, the question is, who is doing the computing? The idea is not that you are actually doing some multiplications consciously and with awareness. I think the process is unconscious.

SHIFFRIN: There is something that I can't get straight about these kinds of primitive processes that we measure with P300. On one hand, you show evidence that if given a sign of total probability and told that the next trial is going to be something special, then the subject operates, not on the basis of the past history of the sequence but on the basis of what the sign has told him. That is a consciously controlled process, and it is not primitive at all. Isn't there some inconsistency or some sort of problem here that isn't being addressed, even in your own thinking?

DONCHIN: If you force the information on him, he uses it. In a Bernoulli series, if you have no other source of information, then you compute from the past history of the sequence. As soon as you give them other information, then that past history becomes nonsalient and irrelevant and they don't use it anymore.

SHIFFRIN: In these studies, do you ask the subjects on those trials to predict those kinds of things?

DONCHIN: We had an experiment like that, yes. And they predicted what the next trial would be.

SHIFFRIN: And then you compared the P300 versus predictions for a dissociation?

DONCHIN: That's what I said. This is the study I mentioned of the disconfirmation of stimuli. This is work that other people have done as well. If surprise affects P300, then you may say—if a person predicts an A, that person obviously "expects" an A. Well, if P300 is related to surprise, then if the person gets a B, it should elicit a large P300. So disconfirmations should give you large P300s and confirmations should give you small P300s, if peoples' predictions truly reflected expectations. But, that just doesn't work out. There is no direct relationship between confirmation and disconfirmation and the amplitude of P300. There are two possibilities. Either this is so because surprise does not affect P300 or what people predict is not necessarily what they expect. If subjects predicted a low probability event, then the next stimulus elicits a large P300 whether or not it confirms their prediction. So whatever they predicted, they were evidently aware of the probabilities of the events. What I'm saying is that there is a dissociation between the overt prediction and knowledge of probabilities. And that's why I'm forced to this dissociation between the internal magnitude, which I like to call subjective probability but am willing to call channel capacity or channel content or whatever, and the strategic considerations the subject uses to determine his overt responses.

7.5 WORLD MODELS, SCHEMAS, AND ERPS

NORMAN: I take a different point of view. The human is not designed to count flashes, or even to make predictions of the next events in a Bernoulli sequence. I worry about the general functioning of mental processes. What happens within the rest of the brain when you get past the sensory system and the sensory cortex? I must therefore speculate about things for which there is very little evidence, except the fact that we exist, that we think and we create, and that if one sits down and tries to develop an artificial intelligence, then one is forced to confront the problems of the use of information and the ways in which information from various sources is integrated. The attempt to develop an artificial intelligence is a very useful pursuit because it forces one to think about the general relevance of the information that a human might see. It's not a way of finding out how a human works. It's a way of speculating about the way that intelligence is put together. What I want to do is talk above the data, talk about the things we do not have any data about, except to state there is a logical necessity for some kinds of operations of a sort that I shall talk about. Presumably, over the next decade or two or three, we shall obtain more and more data about these kinds of issues. And it may very well be that we must find data of the sort that has been talked about today. The basic notion that I want to argue for is that normal processing is fairly complex and that it exists to do at least two separate things. One is developing a world model, updating our general knowledge about the location of objects in the world and the events that are occurring all about us. Two is separation from or interaction with that world. In fact, Kelso will tell you that the preparation and maybe even the orientation is probably oriented toward coordinates based in the world, not based around the person. So that, for example, when I pick up this cup, my intention is "pick up this cup"—not "move my hand from my body in this direction and then do a grasping motion." The specification of my act is in terms of the real world. When I listen to sounds, I listen not to particular intensity or phase ratios between the two ears but rather to a spatial localization in space. I must coordinate my impression of spatial location from all the different sensory information that arrives. If this information contains inconsistencies, it is the apparent visual location in space that drives much of the other sensory analyses. There can be a large discrepancy between the direction I would think the sound would come from, if it were in isolation, and the direction that I see a visual object. To make the two correspond I move the apparent location of the sound to the location that I see. The point is that I believe that the function of our system is to put together a world model, an internal model of the world that allows us to operate in the world. That removes the interpretation from the analysis of particular sensory events and puts it into the interpretation of things that happen in the world.

It would be interesting if Steve Hillyard could do his experiment that shows that you get increased sensitivity to an auditory signal when you are attending to the correct spatial location to see if that was increased sensitivity to the *apparent* location of the source or the *real* location of the source. Because you can get visual capture of the localization of the sound, I think it is a fairly straightforward experiment to do. The visual location could be one place, the real sound could be another place. It's the same thing you get with your television set. The speaker is one place but you hear the voices come from the mouths of the speaking people. There is a nice experiment on masking in which a masking flash is presented to the eye while the eye is moving. The question is, does the mask affect the apparent location of the object or the retinal location? And the answer is both. If you ask the person where the mask appeared to be, it's at the apparent location. If you do the psychophysical experiment on where the mask is detected, it's the retinal location. Presumably, therefore, obviously the information comes from the sensory system, but among the jobs of the brain is to interpret that information in terms of the world coordinates.

When we do an experiment, I believe that the information that is arriving at the person is being used to update the world model. The world model contains information about the environment and about the events that are occurring in the environment. Along the way, the person is asked to make a response to a particular aspect of that environment, to pick an item that the experimenter is interested in. Some of the information that is being used for the internal model is relevant to the kinds of responses the person will make. For example, a person is making an estimate of the relative frequency of certain kinds of events. The fact that a particular signal has arrived on this trial is important information about the environment. It is used to ready the person for the next signal. P300 appears to be related to the evaluation of the signal. If I were asked to speculate upon the functional role of P300, I might suggest that P300 is involved in the continual updating of the internal model, which involves, of course, such things as assessing the signal and assessing its place. But it is not directly involved in the decision to respond to that signal. Now if you take a point of view like this, then you begin to see that there will be correlations between response times and latency of P300, but only because the signal is being used for two different processes; when there are properties of the signal that take longer to be analyzed, it will affect both stages. But it is perfectly sensible to expect that sometimes this process will finish before a decision and sometimes it will finish long after a decision. There need not be a direct relationship between the two. An increment in the amount of time it takes to get the P300 may not always correlate with an equal increment in reaction time. The basic notion is consistent with: (1) thinking about the general function of our human cognitive system; (2) a reasonable amount of study within cognitive psychology; and (3) a larger view developing in the field of cognitive science or artificial intelligence and the attempt to understand how an organism perceives. Basically we're constructing some kind of internal model, using schemas for a framework or, whatever. The internal model will create expectations at many different levels. As Danny Kahneman has suggested, some of those levels may in fact be contradictory, such that I may expect the sequence of trials or an event to follow a certain pattern but this may contradict the actual expectations for a particular trial. Within the framework of say a Bernoulli detection task, I may very well have a general notion of the task that is happening and ideas about the sequence of signals that are occurring. I also shall have expectations about the next signal that might occur. There is an important datum that has to be accounted for, the fact that you get a large P300 only with the unexpected signal. Yet the unexpected signal is not really unexpected. After all, the unexpected signal occurs 20% of the time. I should expect it to occur 20% of the time and it's a puzzle, perhaps, why I should be surprised when 20% of the time that signal occurs.

I think the answer is that even if you have a good model, what counts is the part you are attending to at the moment. For example, I want you to think of a fly sitting on the ear of an elephant. Now, when you do this, I claim that although you may have a lot of information about the elephant available, you cannot now immediately tell me what is the shape of the tail of the elephant. The reason is that as you try to see the fly on the ear, that occupies your conscious attention. In order to get to the tail of the elephant, you must now switch from one part of the general global model of the elephant to the other part. Steve Kosslyn at Harvard has shown that you must switch your attention to the tail. Now let's go back to the experiment. If you concentrate on a particular form for the next signal, you may very well lose some of the information about the general statistical properties of the overall sequence.

One other aspect about this model is that even if you have a world view, you only exert processing effort when information arrives that causes you to modify the world view. In fact, there have been a number of memory experiments that demonstrate that people fail to remember the information that is consistent with the model (schema). What they do seem to remember and exert effort with is information that is discrepant or novel or that has to be specified. So, if I tell you that fire engines in Del Mar are green, it is not consistent with the general color of fire engines in the United States, red. So, you'll have to update your schema of information about fire engines in Del Mar to say, yes, they're green. You use processing effort in doing that. O.K. The other thing is that occasionally the schemas that we are modifying are so inappropriate that either they must be modified substantially or a new set of expectations, a new schema, a new model, has to be created. I think that we shall find this in a number of experiments that have been discussed.

Suppose that I give subjects two different conditions: condition A and condition B. In condition A, they are asked to do some particular task—maybe it's a

Bernoulli task with certain probabilities, and for condition B, maybe it's a similar Bernoulli task with a different set of probabilities. Maybe a different response is required, maybe the opposite response. At the transition from A to B, the subjects have to develop a new model, a new representation for what is happening. And therefore I would expect to find considerable processing effort exerted at the transition from one condition to the next, despite the fact that the subject's subjective probability and maybe even the real probabilities of the events when you start condition B are known almost immediately. You could tell the subjects. There doesn't have to be any doubt about what is happening on the new condition. Yet the subject must build up a new internal model of this condition. I believe this will exert considerable processing effort over the first couple of trials which should result in fairly large P300s at the beginning of any new kind of condition. This will be a situation, therefore, where you get P300s despite the fact that probabilities actually may not have changed.

In the development of these expectations it is quite possible that we develop prototypes and that we are surprised by the discrepancy between the real events and the prototype we have developed. There have been a number of different experiments about prototypes. One of the earliest was done by Mike Posner. I was reminded of this because the experiment that Danny Kahneman talked about could very well be the experiment developing prototypes. That is to say, if I am shown various sensory images with different properties, I can build up a prototype of an image that has never itself been presented but rather combines, if you will, the average features of things that have been shown. And therefore when this new item that matches the prototype is shown, I won't be surprised at all. I should give no P300, despite the fact that it is a novel item and has never been seen. So I would predict, in this case, that if I have seen a lot of red objects (half the objects are red) and a lot of squares (half the objects are squares) but never a red square, nonetheless my prototypical object is likely to be a red square. If a red square is now presented to me, I will not be surprised.

KUTAS: Well, if I understand your models correctly, the model you suggest is, in fact, one of the models that has been proposed for what the P300 represents. It was called, I think, "context updating." The problem with that model has been and remains that even though it sounds like a nice model, it is not clear how it can be tested. What sort of predictions does this model make about amplitude and latency of P300?

NORMAN: I think it might make some predictions. I think, in particular, it might make you design experiments a little bit differently; that is, if you believe the person is building up a particular expectation, then you design the experiment so that you deliberately lead the person to expect, to develop, a certain kind of model of what is happening, and then you violate that expectation. I think you may not even have to change the probabilities much, as in the experiment that Manny presented, in which the subject was counting flashing triangles and ignoring flashing squares or counting changes in direction of triangles and ignoring whether they flashed or not. I think it is possible to make a person use different aspects of the situation to build up a model and then test whether this is indeed what has happened by appropriate presentations. It was argued recently (during a panel discussion) that if we dropped the term "subjective probability" and replaced it with "expectation," there will be no effect on our work. On the other hand, such a change in concept might lead you, by the very choice of words, to think of some different types of experiments.

TREISMAN: You're suggesting that P300 is reflecting some kind of learning as opposed to some kind of a decision relevant to the task. A possible test occurred to me when you reminded us of Manny's experiment. Supposing you tell subjects that in this condition the triangles are relevant, but that in the next condition the squares will become relevant. I wonder if you would get much bigger P300s to the squares even while they are responding to the triangles, as they are trying to build up some representation of the probabilities of the squares that are going to be relevant next.

DONCHIN: We repeatedly change the "relevant" target during the session, and it doesn't seem to make a difference; that is, after a while the subject knows that he will count both targets.

TREISMAN: Yes, but you have two conditions, one in which the squares are irrelevant and the subject does not think the squares are ever going to be relevant.

DONCHIN: Yes, but quite soon the squares are relevant, then the triangles, then again the squares.

TREISMAN: So the subject does seem to be ignoring the "other" target.

NORMAN: But Anne, I think you used the word *learning*, which I didn't. I used the word *updating*. It is a fine distinction but one distinction is that, in this case, if you were working on triangles and you know the next thing is going to be squares, attending to the squares a little bit on the side now doesn't help. I mean there is nothing for you to learn about squares now that is going to help you later on.

TREISMAN: I know, but you might be learning that . . .

NORMAN: Well, I think if you arranged the situation so that you could get a later advantage by paying attention now, you might very well find that.

TREISMAN: Yes, that's what I had in mind.

NORMAN: But I don't think the experiment that has now been done does that.

TREISMAN: No, I guess not. I'm suggesting one possible way of discriminating learning for the future, whether you call it updating or whatever.

HILLYARD: I think the experiment that Marta Kutas and I have been running suggests that there are at least two qualitively different kinds of models that you build up. In fact, we have done an experiment very much like the one you proposed about the fire engines in Del Mar being green. When the subject sees the word *green*, there is not a big P300 wave. In fact, there is a large negative wave peaking at around 400 msec (Fig. 3.8, 3.9). When you set up a model of the meaning of a sentence in natural language, a disconfirmation of such a semantic model produces this N400 wave. If you set up a model of the world that says expect this physical cue with this probability and that cue with that probability, then the low-probability event produces a P300 wave. How different can two brain events be than negative and positive? This suggests that there really are different brain systems involved in building up and testing these two different kinds of world models, but we certainly don't know how to conceptualize the difference yet.

KAHNEMAN: I was struck by your example "I have coffee with cream and dog." I really repeated that sentence to myself several times and I was working at resolving the conflict between semantic ambiguities and incongruities. But if I have been processing a series of stimuli in lowercase, and then a word comes in uppercase, well I shall be surprised and have P300s, but there is precious little that I can do with such a situation. This could suggest a distinction between the more active type of model building, where one tries to make sense of an incongruity, and passive sort of updating in which it is registered quite passively that relatively rare stimulus has occurred. The negativity that you mentioned seems to be correlated in many other settings with other indices of heightened arousal or mental effort. The P300 does not seem to be primarily an index of mental effort. I have the impression that where you find our negativity, you would also observe large pupillary dilatations, associated with the effort of resolving the incongruity.

HILLYARD: It turns out that the pupil also dilates in conjunction with P300 waves in response to simple surprising events (Friedman, Hakerem, Sutton, & Fleiss, 1973).

KAHNEMAN: It does? Even on trivial surprises like . . .

HILLYARD: Yes, as trivial as flash versus click, but I think that's a good thought you have that the ERP varies with the amount of active updating you have to do. If it's simply a couple of simple physical stimuli such as A versus B, you shove the stimulus in the appropriate slot and be done with it; but if it's a complicated disconfirmation, you have to mull it over more thoroughly.

POSNER: Is it clear that the subject knows that that's the last word in that sentence? Could he be expecting more?

KUTAS: No, there is a period after the last word.

HILLYARD: There's a period but it doesn't always grab you that that's the end of the sentence.

DONCHIN: Didn't you always have seven words in the sentence?

KUTAS: Yes, on the whole, they know that that's the end of the sentence.

DONCHIN: I think you have to have the "case" surprise and the "semantic" surprise factorially varied in an experiment and see what happens when the two vary in the same condition, because it is possible that this negative wave obscures the occurrence of a positivity because it's such a powerful effect. There might still be a positivity in the semantic condition that is obscured. I would like to see an experiment in which you have semantic incongruities presented in the same case and in different cases and see what happens.

7.6 CONTROLLED PROCESSING AND P300

PICTON: We have been discussing what the P300 is. One possibility is that the P300 represents context-updating or model revision. I would like to mention a few problems I have with this interpretation. First, there are many times when a large P300 occurs without any necessary revision of a world model. It is not clear why, when you get the 10% stimulus in the Bernoulli series to which you have been listening for the last half hour, you should have to revise your world model. Surely your world model would already include the 10% probability of the "oddball" stimulus. Second, if you were going to revise your model, you should base this revision upon full and complete stimulus-response evaluation. This should occur after a reaction time. Why should you revise your world model before you even have the confidence to make a reaction? Although model revision is very important, I do not think that it is necessarily associated with the P300 process. I think the P300 process represents something earlier than context updating.

When we first did the studies of selective attention, Hillyard and I proposed (1979) that the N100 process represented selection by "stimulus set" and the P300 component selection by "response set." We proposed that P300 represented the activation of the responses that were necessary once a particular target had been recognized. That is a very diffuse and almost untestable suggestion, because whatever can be said about the P300 can be attributed to the response set. It could perhaps be refined a little. My present thinking is that in the processing of information your strategy (or response set) sometimes requires the use of "controlled" ("conscious" or "aware") processing. Access to that kind of processing is reflected by the P300 process.

I shall consider some aspects of the data base in this light. One is timing. A fast and simple reaction can occur prior to the P300 process being activated. Such simple reactions can be made prior to becoming aware of either the stimulus or the response. Paradigms with longer reaction times require controlled processing. The initial evaluation of a stimulus activates the controlled processing necessary to select an appropriate response. P300 latency can then occur before reaction time. What I am suggesting is that the P300 represents an "activation" rather than an "activity." Physiologically we can detect phasic neural processes more easily than ongoing processes. The P300 represents the beginning of controlled processing.

At the end of controlled processing it may become necessary to re-evaluate your world model, but I think this will occur in a variety of ways and be associated with a variety of different physiological processes. Don Stuss and I (1978) have reported a "P4" wave that occurs after the usual P300. This is evoked by negative feedback in a paradigm where the subject's task is to determine by trial and error a sorting criterion for a set of visual stimuli. Eric Courchesne and his colleagues (Courchesne, Hillyard, & Galambos, 1975) have described a frontal positive wave in association with novel (i.e., outside the world model) stimuli. Marta and Steve are finding a late negative wave to semantically incongruent words. I think after about 300 msec a lot of different processes can occur physiologically in relation to different ways of revising the world model. Before that happens, however, controlled processing must have considered the world model, assessed how the stimulus information did or did not fit into the model, and evaluated the necessity for changing the model. The first step is to get into controlled processing—I think this is what the P300 represents.

SHIFFRIN: My understanding was that, in the Sternberg search paradigm, P300 latency depends on the set size that is searched.

PICTON: Controlled processing must be provided with both stimulus information and context. This provision will take an amount of time that might be reflected by P300 peak latency. With a greater amount of context (a greater set size) the peak latency may be a little longer but not necessarily as much longer as the final reaction time.

NORMAN: There is a control condition that has to be added here as well. The result may simply be a fact of short-term memory loading, not of a search process. I would like to see Judy Ford do an experiment in which the person has to keep constant the Sternberg search size value. But the subject also has to remember, say, a group of people's names, for example, increasing memory load. I would like to see if memory load by itself will change P300 latency.

POSNER: There is a concise explanation for this. The literature would lead you to expect that you'd find reduced changes in the P300 slope. Kirsner (1972) has shown that even when you don't search memory but simply name the probe reaction time is a function of the set size of the prior positive set so that the time to reach any information about the probe seems to be decreased when some pathway has been previously activated. It has been shown for repetitions of the same item, P300 latency is reduced. This would predict, in the Sternberg paradigm, that latency of P300 would be a function of positive set size.

DONCHIN: I want to make a point that is related to what you said. I think we have a problem. I don't have a solution though I think one is necessary if we are ever going to be able to identify the process manifested by P300. Think of all the experiments that have been described here. They all have a basic structure. They all attempt to identify the *antecedent* conditions for eliciting a P300. We all try to find out what it takes to assure that P300 will be elicited and to determine what controls its amplitude, its latency. What we need, and I don't know yet how to accomplish that, are experiments that allow us to measure the *consequences* of the P300 in addition to its antecedent conditions. The question is, what difference does it make to the subject that a P300 has been elicited? The design is simple in principle. Clearly, we need a study in which everything is exactly the same, except sometimes you do and somethimes you do not have a P300, and you use some independent variable and see what happens to it. Unfortunately, you can't have everything exactly the same.

KAHNEMAN: A possibility that was mentioned during the panel's discussions was something that I've tried with autonomic measures of arousal and completely failed to obtain. The idea is to use operant conditioning techniques on the P300 or on some aspect of P300, whether the latency or the amplitude, with the ultimate objective of getting control of P300 and checking which behavorial correlates (say reaction time) might covary with P300 once you have obtained control of it. People will probably raise many questions about such an experiment because, necessarily, when you reinforce P300, you are reinforcing things that are correlated with it, so it is not quite clear what is cause and what is effect. Yet I have the feeling that this experiment could be instructive in various ways. The idea is that when you are reinforcing P300, the underlying processes that are most directly associated with it get reinforced more systematically that anything else. And a change of underlying process should have other observable effects. It seems to be worth a try. Unfortunately, as I mentioned earlier, I have failed in some attempts to obtain operant conditioning of heart rate in a situation of mental effort.

RITTER: First of all, I find your suggestions interesting. The question, however, that I have concerns those conditions where reaction time precedes P300 and where also, as Terry pointed out, the subject really does not need to change his model because the infrequent stimuli come 10% of the time in that kind of condition. What is the control process that is being activated by the P300 in your thinking?

PICTON: Well, in the typical oddball the subject is asked to keep a running mental count of one of the stimuli.

RITTER: What happens in reaction time tasks when you're not counting?

PICTON: The reaction time might be faster. When you "re-alert" a subject performing fairly automatic tasks by asking him to pay particular attention to the task, the reaction time becomes slower. I think subjects can use unnecessary controlled processing in very simple tasks—trying to supervise performance as much as possible. One characteristic of simple attention experiments is that the subject becomes very "bored." The boredom perhaps comes from the fact that the subject is so much aware that he is activating (P300) controlled processes unnecessarily. They are being used in an experiment for which somebody is paying, but it's going against any strategic organization of mental function and the subject feels bored.

DONCHIN: People perform, most of the time, boring tasks that they are paid to do.

PICTON: These people are not happy. On the other hand, if you make a very "engaging" task, then there are huge P300s.

DONCHIN: I don't disagree with what you said.

PICTON: But I think I disagree with what you said.

DONCHIN: No, I don't think so. I never said that I think that P300 manifests the *process* of context updating. I think that P300 is invoked in association with the call for context updating. It is related to the conflict between what was expected and what happened. Now, the call for context updating may begin with a call for control processes. The fact is that this occurs when a discrepancy is discovered. In this circumstance something is activated that I think has to do with *the need* for context updating. The fact that people do it when they are bored is a puzzle, but there are many things that puzzle me about P300. But I don't think that we should try to decide intuitively just because it doesn't seem to have any purpose that it does not. I don't think we have real disagreement here.

PICTON: Yes we do. I am saying that P300 can occur without context updating.

DONCHIN: Well, I think that until we measure the consequences of context updating and determine how they are affected by P300, we shall not resolve the issue.

8   Report of Panel III:
Preparatory Processes

Panel chair: W. Ritter

Panel members: S. Kelso
                        M. Kutas
                        R. Shiffrin

8.1 SURVEY OF EVENT PRECEDING NEGATIVITIES

RITTER: After a brief survey of ERP components such as the CNV and the readiness potential, I shall outline recent changes in thinking about these potentials. Marta Kutas will then comment on the view that there are several subcomponents to the CNV. Then Scott Kelso will present an analysis of the process of movement control.

The CNV is usually studied while subjects are assigned a warned reaction-time task, in which two stimuli, S1 and S2, are presented and the interval between S1 and S2 is constant. The S1 is the "warning" stimulus, and S2 is a target or "imperative" stimulus to which the subject must somehow respond. Figure 8.1 illustrates the ERPs that are recorded in this situation (note that in my figures, negative is "down"). These data were reported by Simson, Vaughan, and Ritter (1977). The interval between S1 and S2 was 1 sec, and the interval between successive presentations of the pair (trials) was 8 sec. S1 was identical on all trials of a given condition and served only as a warning cue. On the other hand, one of two stimuli, chosen randomly, were presented as S2. The subject was instructed to respond to one of these stimuli and to ignore the other (this is often called a "Go-No-Go" task). The two ERPs in the left column of the figure were recorded in a condition in which S1 and S2 were auditory. The waveforms in the right column were elicited by a visual S1 and S2. All these ERPs are recorded at a vertex electrode. The S1 elicited an ERP with a sequence of components. It is clear that auditory and visual stimuli elicit

180

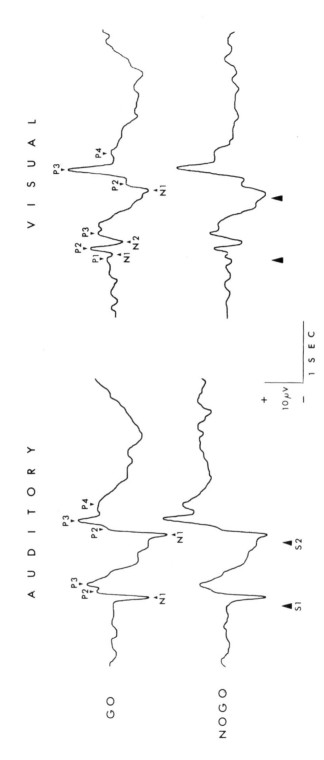

FIG. 8.1   Averaged event-related potentials at the vertex for one subject in the auditory and visual conditions. Reproduced from Simson et al. (1977).

ERPs that differ in morphology. These early components are followed by a prominent negative shift that continues until S2 is presented. This negative shift was called by Grey Walter (1964) the "contingent negative variation" (CNV). Unlike the early components, whose shapes vary with the modality of the stimuli, similar shaped CNVs were elicited by the auditory and the visual stimuli. It has been commonly assumed that the CNV's waveform is independent of the modality of the eliciting stimuli. This conventional view needs to be qualified in light of new data I shall discuss in the following.

The CNV was first discovered by Walter, Cooper, Aldridge, McCallum, and Winter (1964). They assumed that this negative variation (the term the English sometimes use for "potential") can be recorded only when a contingency is established between two stimuli. It was suggested, in the early reports, that the CNV reflected brain activity related to anticipation, preparation, or attention to the task.

At about the same time, in other laboratories, a different experimental procedure was being employed. The subjects were instructed to make a repetitive movement. They were told, for example, to lift a hand repeatedly. No stimuli were presented and the subjects were instructed to respond at their own pace. The averaging computer was triggered by the myographic activity at the responding muscles. Note that in this case we are averaging the EEG recorded before and after the myographic trigger. A slow negativity that begins 500 to 1000 msec prior to the movement can be observed. Slightly before the actual response the slope of the wave increases and a new negative component appears. This later negativity has been shown in studies of monkeys to reflect pyramidal tract discharge from precentral gyrus (Arezzo, Vaughan, & Koss, 1977). Figure 8.2 illustrates these potentials. The ERPs in this figure from Vaughan, Costa, and Ritter (1968) were recorded from the scalp of a human subject, and the brain outline in the figure shows the estimated location of the electrodes with respect to the precentral gyrus. The arrows indicate the triggering point.

The slow negative shifts obtained in these two different ways were assumed to reflect different functions and anatomical substrates. One was labeled the *Bereitschaft* potential, or the readiness potential, by Kornhuber and Deecke (1964). Vaughan et al. (1968) referred to it as the N1 because it is the first negative wave that is observed in the "motor" potential. The other was called the CNV.

The readiness potential is asymmetric over the two cerebral hemispheres. If the subject makes a movement with a right limb, then the potential is larger over the left hemisphere and vice versa (Kutas & Donchin, 1974). In our laboratory, subjects were instructed to move their feet, hands, tongue, etc., on different runs (Vaughan et al., 1968). As different muscles were moved, the maximal amplitude of the readiness potential varied in a way that is consistent with the known distribution of motor control along the precentral gyrus. In

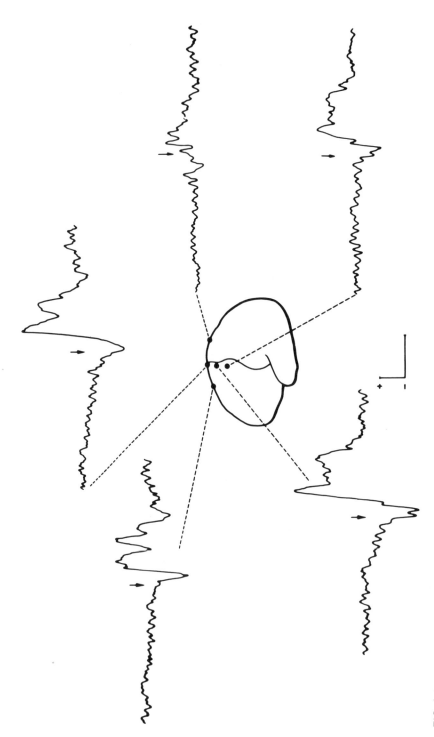

FIG. 8.2   Event-related potentials associated with dorsiflexion of the right foot. Calibration 500 msec, 2.5 l.c.GK mu. Reproduced from Vaughan et al. (1968).

Fig. 8.2, for example, the ERPs were recorded while the subject flexed his right foot backward. The readiness potential was largest in the vicinity of the most dorsal portion of the left precentral gyrus, that is, the area from where the leg is "controlled." By contrast, according to most reports, the CNV is symmetric over the two sides of the head. So these two different experimental paradigms apparently yield two different types of slow negative activity; yet, both seem to have something to do with preparation. In the case of the readiness potential, it is preparation to perform a skeletal movement, whereas the CNV is associated with preparation of a more psychological nature related to the task assigned to the subject. Furthermore, the CNV is called forth by an external warning stimulus whereas the readiness potential appears to be elicited by the internal pacing of the subject's responses.

OSCAR-BERMAN: What's the response required in the warned reaction-time tasks that causes a CNV to appear?

RITTER: You mean what responses were required at S2?

OSCAR-BERMAN: Yes. You said that the CNV is contingent on some kind of task given to the subject. Is it motor or covert? Must the subject speak? Press a key?

RITTER: Often a key press is required, but a purely perceptual task requiring no immediate motor response on each trial can also be used. For example, a signal detection task in which S2 is near-threshold and occurs on only 50% of the trials can be employed, and the subject's task is subsequently to report verbally if S2 was presented.

Recently, this neat and simple view of the preparatory potentials has been challenged (see Gaillard, 1978, for review). Impetus for the challenge was provided by experiments in which the interval between S1 and S2 was longer than usual. When S1 and S2 are separated, for example, by a 3-sec interval instead of the 1-sec interval used in the classical CNV paradigms, the S1 elicits the usual ERP that is followed by a negativity that reaches a peak somewhere between 600 and 800 msec. But unlike the "classical" CNV, the negativity is not sustained until S2. Rather the voltage may return to the baseline some 1200 or 1500 msec after S1. About a second or so prior to S2, a *second* negativity appears and is maintained until S2. If a motor response is required following S2, this "late" slow wave is asymmetric across the head as is the readiness potential. If the EEG is triggered from the key press, or from the EMG burst, then the late negativity is larger in amplitude; this implies that it is time-locked to the motor response rather than to S2. Furthermore, the late negativity becomes more asymmetric when averaged with respect to the motor response. The earlier slow wave, however, is *not* asymmetric. These results led to the suggestion that the original, "classical" CNV consists of at least two kinds of slow negativity: the early slow negative wave that appears in the vicinity of S1 and a later slow negativity, which is "nothing but" a readiness potential. It may be that the early negativity continues well beyond the traditional 1000-msec interval between S1 and S2; therefore, it persists into the period immediately prior to S2, and as it is not asymmetric, it obscures the asymmetry of the readiness potential. The failure in the past to observe an asymmetry of the CNV with a 1-sec interval between S1 and S2, even for warned, simple reaction-time tasks, could be accounted for by a combination of two factors: first, an overlap in time between the early and late slow negativities; second, triggering the EEG only from the stimuli rather than also triggering the EEG from the motor response.

Let us return now to the experiment from which the waveforms of Fig. 8.1 were obtained. In that study there were two conditions, one in which S1 and S2 were auditory and a second in which S1 and S2 were visual. Both conditions used a 1-sec interval between S1 and S2, and S2 in each condition was one of two possible stimuli that provided the basis for a go-no-go task. Although the slow negative shifts in Fig. 8.1 appear similar for the auditory and visual conditions, this similarity is somewhat deceptive. We recorded ERPs at 13 recording sites in order to examine the scalp distribution of different ERP components. In Fig. 8.3, the two columns of waveforms in the center are grand averages pooled across all subjects. The numbers to the left of the waveforms designate the recording sites indicated on the outline of the head in the upper right-hand corner. Immediately below the 13 waveforms are arrows that specify the occurrence of S1 and S2. The waveforms stop shortly after S2, so the ERP components elicited by S2 are not seen in this figure. Notice that after the sharp deflections which follow S1, there is a slow negativity that is most prominent for electrode 3 (the vertex) at the time of S2. The isopotential maps of the far left and far right columns are to be read in the following manner. The line with the 90 on it means that the particular component depicted was 90% or more of maximum voltage within its confines. The lines with 70 and 50 on them mean that the voltage of that component within their confines were 70% and 50% of maximum, respectively.

Until the S2 appears, the slow negativity has a similar scalp distribution on the go and the no-go trials within the auditory condition, and within the visual condition. That makes sense because the subject did not know which S2 would be presented on any trial. The go and no-go trials for each condition were averaged together in Fig. 8.3. The ERPs associated with the two S2s differed, of course, as the stimuli called forth different responses.

The three lower isopotential maps in the left column of Fig. 8.3 depict the scalp distribution of the slow negativity 500, 700, and 900 msec after S1 in the auditory condition. The three corresponding maps of the right column depict similar data for the visual condition. It can be seen that in response to the auditory condition there is a progressive shift in the slow negative wave from a more frontal to a more central distribution from the 500- to 700- to 900-msec latency measurements. By contrast, in the visual condition there is a double focus 500 msec after S1, one frontocentral and another in the vicinity of the occipital area. The visual maps at 700- and 900-msec latency exhibit a decrease in the amplitude of the posterior focus and a change in the frontocentral focus to a more central focus. These results suggested to us that an early portion of the CNV (the "early slow negative wave") is modality-specific. There is also a later portion of the CNV whose attributes do not depend on the modality of the stimulus. This later negativity appears to be mainly a readiness potential, as discussed previously. Figure 8.1 provides support for this interpretation. The subjects were instructed to withhold their responses to the "go" stimuli for about a second. Note that in the upper two waveforms (go trials) the negative shift persists well beyond the instant at which S2 is presented, whereas in the other two waveforms (no-go trials) the negative shift returns to baseline shortly after S2. The readiness potential appears to be maintained until the response is executed.

Unfortunately, this study did not provide data needed to determine whether the modality specificity of the early negativity was in response to S1 or in anticipation of S2. Both stimuli were always of the same modality. We therefore ran another study (Ritter, Rotkin, & Vaughan, 1980) in which the interval between S1 and S2 was 3000 msec. We could thus examine the early negativity in more detail. There were four conditions. In one condition, S1 and S2 were both auditory. In another condition, S1 was auditory and S2 was visual. In a third condition S1 and S2 were both visual. And in a fourth condition, S1 was visual and S2 was auditory. In all cases, the subject was instructed to respond to S2 by pressing a button.

Grand averages from the four conditions are shown in Fig. 8.4. The modality of the stimulus is indicated by Vis (for visual) and Aud (for auditory). The small triangles at the bottom of the figure indicate the time of occurrence of the stimuli. When S1 was auditory (the upper panels), the sharp deflections associated with S1 are followed by the early slow negative wave that peaks roughly 600 to 800 msec after S1 and is largest at the vertex (Cz) and next largest at the frontal recording site (Fz). There is little or no negativity in this latency range at the temporal (T5) or occipital (Oz) recording sites, whether the sensory modality of S2 was auditory or visual. About 1 sec prior to S2 a late slow negativity appears. Its amplitude gradually increases until the presentation of S2. The maximum amplitude of this component is recorded at the vertex. When S1 was visual (the lower two panels), the sharp deflections associated with S1 are again followed by an early slow negativity, also largest in amplitude at the vertex and with a peak latency about 600 to 800 msec after S1, except that in these conditions a negative process can be seen at T5 and Oz (compare the upper and lower panels at these recording sites). As with the

A U D I T O R Y

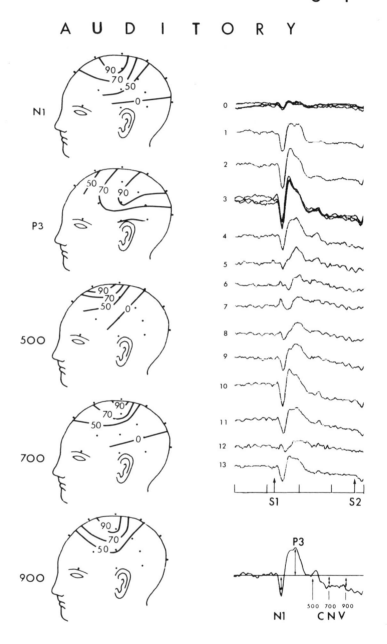

FIG. 8.3 Event-related potential average over eight subjects to all S1 stimuli in the auditory and visual conditions. Supraorbital (0) and vertex (3) waveforms superimposed

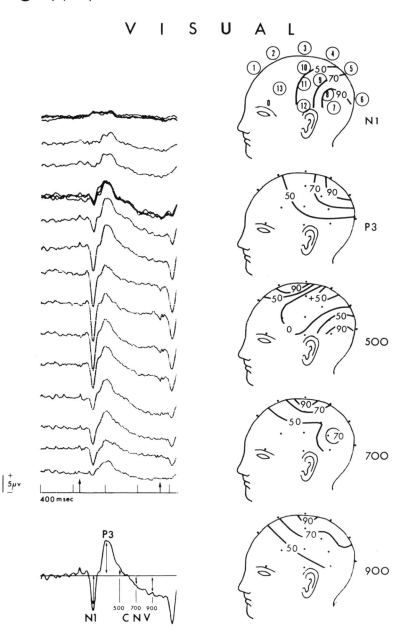

for three runs. See text for explanation of the isopotential maps. Reproduced from Simson et al. (1977).

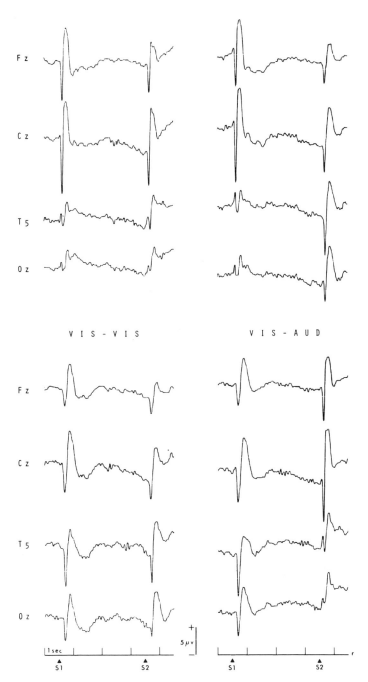

FIG. 8.4 Grand mean waveforms from eight subjects for four conditions. See text for an explanation of the experimental conditions. Reproduced from Ritter et al. (in press).

data displayed in the upper panels, the scalp distribution of the early slow nega-tivity is essentially unaffected by the sensory modality of S2. Finally, a late slow negativity begins about 1 sec prior to S2, increases until S2 occurs, and is largest in amplitude at the vertex.

The left two panels of Fig. 8.4 replicate the results depicted in the isopoten-tial maps of Fig. 8.3 with respect to the early and late portions of the slow negativity when S1 and S2 are of the same modality. When S1 is auditory, there is a single frontocentral focus of the early slow negativity, but when S1 is visual, there is a frontocentral and a posterior focus. In Fig. 8.3 the scalp dis-tributions of the slow negativities for the two sensory modalities had pretty much merged by 900 msec after S1, whereas in Fig. 8.4 this was not the case. The reason for the merging in Fig. 8.3 by 900 msec was probably because of overlap with the late negativity, which in Fig. 8.4 is delayed until 2 sec after S1. In both Fig. 8.3 and 8.4 the negativity prior to S2 has mainly a single, central focus, consistent with its being a readiness potential.

When the left and right panels of Fig. 8.4 are compared, it is clear that the modality-specific distribution of the early negativity is related to the modality of S1 and not S2. Thus the early negativity is not an event-preceding negativity (in the original sense of the CNV reflecting preparation for perception of or response to S2) but rather is a response to S1.

The late negativity has been sometimes labeled the terminal CNV, as it is measured in the last 100 to 200 msec immediately before S2. It has struck me that the use of that word *terminal* here may be appropriate. Perhaps the CNV is a terminal case. Several investigators (Gaillard, 1978) have suggested that the "classical" CNV is a combination of a slow negative wave that occurs as part of the ERP elicited by S1 and the readiness potential that occurs immedi-ately prior to S2. The CNV recorded when the interval between S1 and S2 is 1 sec is a combination of these two potentials. There is, according to this view, no CNV. It is merely a combination of two other phenomena. I do not be-lieve, however, that the issue is closed. Marta Kutas will review data that sug-gest that there are yet other negative waves associated with preparation that cannot be accounted for by the two negativities that I have just described.

POSNER: Are you suggesting that the early slow negative wave is exogenous?

RITTER: That is an excellent question. Our data cannot answer that question. I guess at this point I am undecided. John Rohrbaugh and colleagues (Rohrbaugh, Syndulko, & Lindsley, 1978) have reported a slow negative wave, in the general latency range of the early negativity we have been discussing, in response to unpaired stimuli in a "passive" condition. It is not clear, however, that the slow negative wave reported by Rohrbaugh et al. is the same as the early negativity obtained for paired stimuli.

POSNER: Was that to an auditory warning signal?

RITTER: There was no warning signal. They just presented tones about once every 6 sec.

POSNER: It was an auditory transient event. For how long was the wave sustained?

KUTAS: The first of two waves they describe peaked 500 to 600 msec after the stimulus. Rohrbaugh (Rohrbaugh et al., 1978) reports that the negativity in a totally passive situation peaks around 550 msec.

RITTER: I see. And when does the second component begin?

KUTAS: The onset of the second component is difficult to determine as the two components overlap; it seems to start around 500 to 700 msec post-S1. Rohrbaugh has found that the entire negativity lasts for a second.

RITTER: Or more. The second negativity persisted beyond 1500 msec.

DONCHIN: There is no such thing as a totally passive situation.

RITTER: The subjects were asked to "listen attentively" to the tones, so they were not totally passive.

ALLISON: I'm still confused by the answers to Posner's question. There is a difference between these two situations. You don't obtain a slow negative wave if no information is carried by the stimulus and the subject doesn't have to perform any task. If the component is exogenous, why don't you see a slow negative wave in passive conditions?

RITTER: If the negativity peaking at 550 msec reported by Rohrbaugh is the same as the early slow negativity I have been discussing, then you do.

DONCHIN: Well, I am not ready to accept Rohrbaugh's claim that he can record this slow wave in a passive, "no-task" situation. I take issue with the no-task concept. Their study is very similar to the oddball experiments, and we know a slow wave is elicited in these conditions (Squires, N.K., Donchin, Squires, K.C., & Grossberg, 1977).

RITTER: But they used a passive condition and neither a P300 nor a slow wave were observed.

DONCHIN: There is no such thing as a "passive" condition! All the phrase means is that the experimenter had no information about the subject's reaction to stimuli.

PICTON: Walter, why do you think there are two foci in the early slow negativity when S1 is visual in Fig. 8.3 and 8.4?

RITTER: We think the scalp distributions of the modality-specific early negativities are consistent with the notion that they are generated in their respective primary and secondary cortical areas (Simson et al., 1977, pp. 869-871). As with the P2 component of auditory and visual stimuli, the early slow negative wave has a single fronto-central focus for auditory stimuli and two foci, one in the parieto-occipital region and one in the central region, for visual stimuli. There is an interesting implication of this interpretation, because of the long peak latency (600-800 msec) of these slow negativities. Note in Fig. 8.1 that a small P300 was elicited by S1 (and was mapped in Fig. 8.3). As is well-known, P300 is considered to be modality-nonspecific. What this suggests is that a stimulus can elicit the exogenous components up to P2, which are modality-specific, followed by P3, and that the latter is followed by further activity in primary- and secondary-specific cortex. It is analogous to the overlapping, parallel activity that occurs in occipital and inferotemporal cortex to visual stimulation.

8.2 KUTAS: SUBCOMPONENTS OF THE CONTINGENT NEGATIVE VARIATION

KUTAS: Oscar-Berman inquired whether one can obtain a CNV without a motor response. I believe the answer is *yes*. For example, on occasion, a CNV comparable to that recorded during a reaction-time task can be obtained when the subjects' task is merely to count silently all or some of the imperative stimuli. The CNV also can be recorded when a person is asked to guess the nature of the imperative stimulus (S2) before the S1-S2 pair is presented (Donchin, Gerbrandt, Leifer, & Tucker, 1972). These findings have in the past been used to support the statement that the CNV is not contingent on a motor response. However, over the last 5 years it has been argued that because short interstimulus intervals (e.g., 1 sec) were used, the results and interpretations of these earlier studies were misleading (Gaillard, 1977; Kok, 1978; Loveless & Sanford, 1974; Rohrbaugh, Syndulko, & Lindsley, 1976; and Weerts & Lang, 1973). Proponents of this view claim that with the employment of longer interstimulus intervals (4-8 sec) it becomes clear that the CNV is comprised of two overlapping components. In the strongest version of this two-component theory (discussed by Ritter in his presentation), an identity is assumed between the late component of the CNV and the readiness potential (RP). The implication is that there is no such entity as the "classic CNV" but merely a waveform caused by the superimposition of the warning-stimulus evoked potential and an RP (Kok, 1978; Rohrbaugh et al., 1976). By inference, then, the late CNV is in fact contingent on a motor response.

Before presenting data that are not consistent with this two component theory, I want to examine the logic of the argument for employing a long foreperiod. The argument assumes that the processes associated with short warning periods are identical, or at least similar, to the processes associated with long foreperiods. But this is a questionable assumption. There is no question that a warning stimulus facilitates the speed of reaction. Furthermore, there is an abundance of data demonstrating that the amount of facilitation is influenced by the interval between the warning and the imperative stimulus. One of the earliest problems faced by CNV investigators was that the maximum RT facilitation provided by the warning stimulus occurred earlier than 1 sec (around 400 msec); yet the CNV did not even begin until around that time. Most of those studies used 1000- to 1500-msec foreperiods, as that interval seemed necessary for the CNV to reach its maximum.

It may be true that when the warning and imperative stimuli are separated by 4 to 8 sec, the CNV appears to decompose into two separate components and does not appear to be sustained throughout the interval. However, this may also be true for the underlying psychological process(es). Thus, the CNV may not be evident because the preparation is not maintained during the foreperiod and not because there is no such entity as the CNV. The behavioral consequences of the contingency between the warning and imperative stimuli cannot be denied. Whether this contingency is also manifest in the components of the CNV is one of the questions we're trying to resolve.

Now, I shall show a series of CNVs from different experiments that I feel will underscore the inadequacies of this two-component theory. As I mentioned previously, a motor response is not always necessary to generate a CNV. I have already mentioned a CNV that can be elicited during a counting task. That CNV was recorded over a 1-sec interval. However, in the examples shown in Fig. 3.7 (Chapter 3, this book), CNVs were recorded over much longer intervals. The first waveform is from a study by David Woods (Woods, Hillyard, Courchesne, & Galambos, 1980), in which subjects had to report verbally or by pushing a button how many tones (one, two, or three) were presented during an interval slightly longer than 3 sec. A response was required, but this response came quite a bit after the trial. The R in the figure represents the cue after which a response could be given. Notice the waveform in the far left corner. No tones were presented in the interval and yet a CNV was maintained for over 3 sec. This CNV had a frontocentral distribution throughout. It is not easily explained by the superimposition of the O wave (the early negative shift) and an RP.

RITTER: I find these rather convincing data, although Rohrbaugh contends that a later slow negativity, which follows the O wave but is also associated with S1, can persist for 3 and even 4 sec.

McCARTHY: Marta, what electrode position is that coming from?

KUTAS: From Cz. The second example appears in Fig. 8.5. This waveform represents an 8-sec interval during which a person silently read a seven-word sentence presented one word at a time. No motor response was required. As is usually the case, all movements were discouraged although of course there were some eye movements. Despite the absence of a consistent motor response, a fairly large CNV is generated and maintained throughout the 8-sec interval. I find these data difficult to explain in terms of the two-component theory.

ALLISON: Marta, would you explain why you think these data are hard to explain by the two-component theory? You can think of this as a series of separate stimuli to which a cognitive response is to be made and a series of seven or eight 1-sec CNVs.

RITTER: It might be claimed that one of the reasons there is a longer CNV is because you're getting early slow negative waves to each of the stimuli.

KUTAS: It's quite possible that the 8-sec CNV is comprised of a series of 1-sec CNVs. I should clarify my position. I am not arguing that all versions of the two-component theory are insufficient to account for the CNV. I am questioning the proposal that all short foreperiod CNVs are produced by the superimposition of a negative wave reflecting the processing of the warning stimulus and a readiness potential. When a motor response is required, there is no question that the late part of the CNV is partially comprised of a readiness potential. However, when a movement is not required, then some other component must be invoked to account for the CNV or negativity sustained for longer than 1-sec intervals.

The data in Fig. 8.6 were again obtained during a 1-sec foreperiod. The important comparisons for our purposes are those between the waveshapes and distributions of the CNVs in the WARNED and CHOICE WARNED conditions. The three waveforms in each case represent the potentials recorded at the frontal, central, and parietal locations on the hemisphere contralateral to the responding hand. In each of the warned conditions the subjects' task was

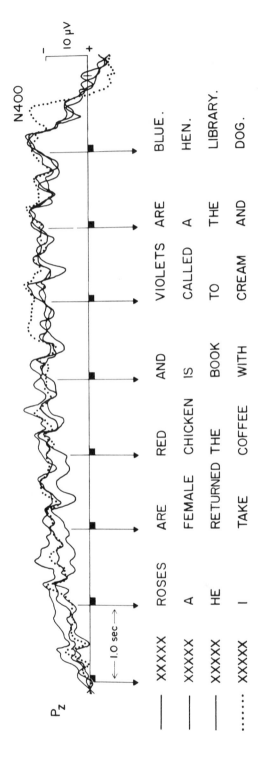

FIG. 8.5 ERPs recorded throughout the presentation of complete seven-word sentences, with the words flashed at one per second. Each tracing is the averaged ERP across 40 sentences in which the last word was either appropriate for the context (solid lines) or semantically inappropriate (dotted line). Samples of the 160 different sentences that were presented to this subject are shown below the waveforms. D.C. recordings from the Pz electrode. (Data from Kutas & Hillyard, 1980.)

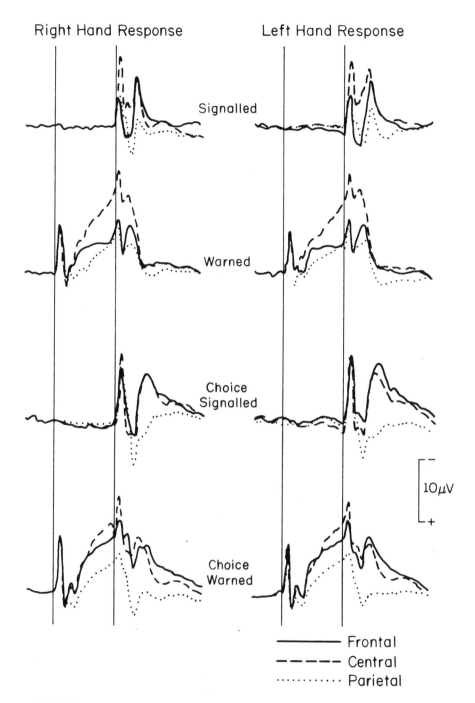

Right Hand Response   Left Hand Response

Signalled

Warned

Choice
Signalled

10μV

Choice
Warned

——————— Frontal
— — — — — Central
·············· Parietal

FIG. 8.6 Superimpositions of the stimulus-locked grand mean ERPs from the contralateral frontal, central, and parietal locations for right- and left-hand responses in four different experimental conditions. The vertical line separates presqueeze from postsqueeze activity. Calibrations: 250 msec, 10μV.

to squeeze a dynamometer as quickly as possible after the occurrence of the imperative stimulus, which was, in all cases, preceded by a warning stimulus. The two conditions differed in that the same hand was used for responding in the WARNED conditions whereas the right or the left hand as cued by the frequency of the imperative stimulus was used in the CHOICE WARNED conditions.

First, note that there is a sharp rise in the negativity immediately preceding the imperative stimulus in the central leads. At least part if not all of this increase is probably a reflection of the superimposition of the RP associated with the movement. However, the most interesting and perplexing aspect of these data is evident in the waveforms recorded at the frontal locations. The frontal waveforms from these two CNV-eliciting paradigms are remarkably dissimilar; there is appreciably more negativity associated with the CHOICE than the simple WARNED conditions. The warning stimulus for both conditions was physically the same and provided the same information. Likewise, the physical parameters of the response in both conditions were quite similar. The reaction times were, of course, different. I find it difficult to argue that the additional negativity in the CHOICE WARNED condition is either a reflection of warning stimulus processing or an RP. If it is an RP, why does it influence the frontal and not the central location waveforms? Furthermore, given that the RTs in the CHOICE WARNED condition were significantly slower than in the WARNED condition, the prediction of waveshape predicated on the superimposition of the RP would have been opposite to the data actually obtained. I believe that these data, even with a 1-sec ISI, indicate that there must be still another negative component to be accounted for.

Figure 8.7 is from McCarthy and Donchin (1978). Again the CNV was recorded over a 1-sec interval. The warning stimulus was a tone. The imperative stimulus was a slide of three line drawings. The subjects were asked to make either a structural or a functional match between items on the slide. The details of the study are unimportant for present purposes. The waveform on the top is the grand average of all the evoked responses that were recorded; that is, the ERPs collapsed over conditions, electrodes, and subjects. The PCA of these data yielded the component loadings presented in the bottom half of the figure. Notice that there are two components during the foreperiod. However, the second component does not seem to be related to an RP. It is not influenced by response variables. The RTs in this experiment were quite slow, occurring 1 to 1.5 sec after the imperative stimulus. Furthermore, there is a post-S2 component that is related to the response. The early component loading probably is related to information provided by the warning stimulus. However, the question remains as to what the second component loading in the S1-S2 interval reflects. It is not the readiness potential and it is not the negative afterwave to the warning stimulus. I don't know what ERP component or psychological process it manifests, but these data indicate to me that some other component must exist.

GRAND MEAN WAVEFORM

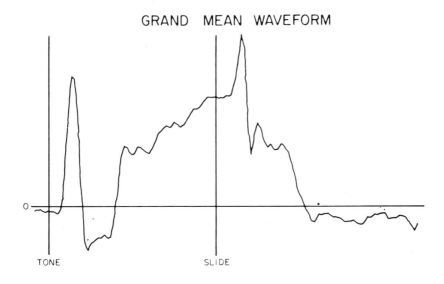

COMPONENT LOADINGS

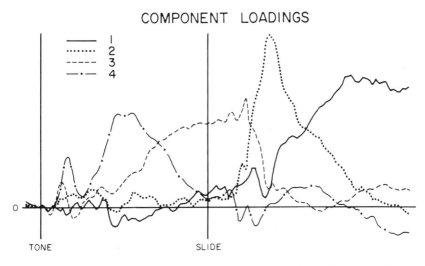

FIG. 8.7 The grand mean waveform (averaged across subjects, electrode positions, and experimental conditions) is shown at the top. Below are displayed the component loadings for the first four components derived from the principal components analysis (using the covariance matrix) of the waveform data.

ZAIDEL: Were any components associated with the functional versus structural matches?

McCARTHY: No.

POSNER: Marta, would you know how the factor loadings would change in that kind of paradigm if you switched from a visual warning signal? Would you get rid of, or reduce, the factor loading that seems to be closely related to the stimulus?

KUTAS: No, I think it would probably still be there.

DONCHIN: That factor was related to whether the stimulus did or did not provide information.

POSNER: Oh, I'm sorry. I didn't realize—it was not just a warning signal.

DONCHIN: There were two conditions. One in which S1 did and one in which S1 did not provide information. The variance accounting for that component was related to this variable.

KUTAS: It is important to remember that a tone or a stimulus rarely occurs in isolation, even in a so-called passive task. The subject may always be anticipating a future event, regardless of experimenter instructions.

POSNER: That's certainly true. There is intersensory facilitation that seems to be very closely related to these effects. For example, if you present an auditory event that's not a warning signal but just an event, even if it doesn't carry any information with respect to the occurrence of other events, it will improve reaction time to a visual event that occurs in close proximity to it (Nickerson, 1973). It has been suggested that the auditory signal produces an automatic alerting effect that improves processing of stimuli that follow it. This effect might be sustained if the stimulus is a warning for some new event. Thus, this would predict a component associated with the alerting produced by the auditory event and another component associated with a voluntary sustaining alertness. Visual events don't seem to produce this automatic facilitatory effect. Hence, you might expect that the visual signal would produce only a sustained component, not an automatic one. The data you present seem consistent with this prediction. The evoked potential ought to be related to the kinds of results that have been obtained behaviorally (Posner, 1978, Chap. 5).

PICTON: Marta, there appears to be a frontal component in the example you've shown. Is that component different from the other components that are related to the processing of S1 or the preparation for S2?

KUTAS: I don't know. It may be related to nonmotor preparation for the imperative stimulus. I assume that a variety of cognitive processes are activated during the foreperiod interval, one of which might be influenced by the S1-S2 contingency and some of which might be reflected in components of the foreperiod negativity. We need to determine the functional role of this nonwarning and nonmotor potential or at the least to define the psychological factors with which it covaries. However, the position taken in the controversy about the structure of the CNV may influence the design of experiments that address the "CNV phenomenon." For example, those who claim that the CNV consists of the superimposition of an "O wave" and the RP deny the presence of an additional negative component. In this view there is not much point in searching for the psychological process underlying the CNV.

PICTON: There is a frontal CNV when the subject is uncertain about which hand will have to make the response. During your sentences there is also a long CNV. Does this also have a frontal distribution?

KUTAS: I don't know. Its distribution varies considerably across subjects.

PICTON: Perhaps there is a third component of the CNV that is frontal and related to uncertainty.

DONCHIN: Well, it seems to me that the idea that there are two components has not been too helpful. There is too much emphasis on the idea that long intervals somehow tease apart the CNV. But the statement that you need a 3-sec interval to bring out multiple components is just not true. As McCarthy and Donchin (1976) have shown, the two components can be observed with 1-sec intervals if the S1 is informative. But that does not mean that there is *no* CNV.

RITTER: Figure 8.3 also shows 1 sec can suffice to reveal two components.

KUTAS: I don't agree with Donchin. We have come closer to explaining two aspects of the CNV.

DONCHIN: I don't see what has been explained. Rohrbaugh et al. (1976) suggested that the CNV is constructed of an early negativity (which is supposedly an orienting reflex) and a late negativity (which is a readiness potential). But, this is just not supported by the literature. The late negativity is *not* a readiness potential as Kutas has shown .

KUTAS: No. I have not just shown that. In fact, I have shown that in some situations the late negativity might well be a readiness potential.

DONCHIN: Yes, it sometimes is and sometimes is not. The important point is that the data demonstrate clearly that it is possible to get a CNV without requiring any motor response. This has been reported by Grey Walter (1965) and by Low, Borda, Frost, and Kellaway (1966) and by Donchin et al. (1972). In short, there are very strong data showing that one can obtain a CNV without a motor response. The "only-readiness-potential" advocates ignore these data and simply fail to cite them. But that doesn't make the data go away. I don't think there is any strong evidence to suggest that the late CNV is entirely a readiness potential. As for the early CNV, it appears whenever the S1 is informative. That an informative stimulus elicits a slow wave is quite well-known.

RITTER: But of course the circumstances where the CNV has been reported to occur without a motor response have generally employed a one second ISI, and the early slow negativity that I was describing can last up to 1500 msec.

KUTAS: That's why I didn't use those data. Rather, I presented waveforms from experiments in which the foreperiod intervals were longer than 1 1/2 sec.

RITTER: That's not entirely true. Only in the data from David Woods was the interval between stimuli longer than 1 1/2 sec. It has been argued that the "CNV" observed when there was no motor response for short intervals was the early slow negativity.

DONCHIN: But that early negativity appears if, and only if, the S1 is informative. In the Donchin et al. study (1972), both an informative and an uninformative S1 were used. This didn't make any difference. We still recorded CNV in the absence of a motor response. If the subject had to perform some task, such as modifying a running product at S2, we always found a CNV. If I'm right and the early negativity appears only if the S1 is informative, then you cannot claim that early negativity accounts for all the CNVs we had without a motor response.

RITTER: But in our studies an early negativity was recorded even though the S1 was only a warning stimulus and did not provide any information specific to S2.

McCARTHY: The information in S1 seems to enhance the positive aspect of the early component. I think there is probably one there frontally regardless, but Marta was showing data from centrals with very large CNVs from Woods et al. (1980) that was from the central and my data also were from Cz. There is no motor response and there is no slow potential as you described at Cz that could account for that.

RITTER: Let me emphasize, my mind is still not made up on the issue. When you don't have a motor response, you still can have the slow negativity that persists for quite a long time and could be mistaken for the classical CNV.

KUTAS: That persistent slow negativity related to the processing of the warning stimulus has been reported to be largest at frontal electrodes. All the waveforms exhibiting features that cannot be explained by the two-component theory that I presented were recorded from the vertex.

RITTER: The early negative waves in Fig. 8.4 have their maximum at the vertex, not at the frontal lead, for both auditory and visual stimuli.

DONCHIN: Let me raise another issue. A panel on the CNV was included in this program not to determine if there is one or two components to the CNV. What is more puzzling is this: the CNV was discovered in 1964. It is a very robust component of the ERP. It is one of the more robust phenomena in the ERP field. It is very easy to record CNVs. They are large and apparently interesting. It appeared to be of great utility. Yet, I submit not a single useful insight about physiology or behavior can be credited to CNV studies done in the past 15 years. I want to know why. What is it about the CNV that makes it so refractive to interpretation? It's easy to talk about "preparation." Grey Walter said the CNV reflects priming for the motor response. Preparation has been studied, behaviorally, in enormous detail. We know a lot about choice reaction times and the response to preparatory stimuli; yet no one seems to find out anything useful from the CNV. Perhaps I am wrong. I will be delighted. But, if I am right, then we should try to understand why this has been the case.

RITTER: One of the reasons for the little progress is that the motor responses used in almost all experiments have been meaningless, isolated movements. Yet the motor system is quite capable of more complex, meaningful activities. Perhaps if more complicated motor performances were required of subjects, more could be learned about the ERP components associated with preparation for movement. In fact, this issue is developed in Scott Kelso's presentation.

[Footnote: The following presents Dr. Kelso's revision of the remarks he made at the conference. The floor discussion of his views has, therefore, been omitted from the transcript.]

8.3 KELSO: CONSIDERATIONS FROM A THEORY OF MOVEMENT

KELSO: Let me first express a concern about the approaches that I have heard thus far to problems of identifying neurophysiological counterparts to behavior. It is one that is not by any means unique to event-related potential work, but rather may be addressed to much of psychology and neurophysiology (see, for example, Gyr, Willey, & Henry, 1979). I refer to the classical Cartesian distinction between sensory and motor function. While such a dichotomy may have served a useful purpose at one time, it is quite clear that modern neurophysiology can no longer support such a view. Sperry (1952) alerted us to this fact many years ago, and it has recently been reiterated by Diamond (1979) as well as in an excellent monograph of Evarts, Bizzi, Burke, DeLong, and Thach (1971). To distinguish between afferent systems on the one hand and efferent systems on the other makes little sense, and it would be a mistake for this relatively new field to adopt such a style of inquiry.

Indeed the whole area of "preparation" rejects a view (common to cybernetic and information-processing approaches) that input and output stages are fundamentally separable. What I wish to do here is discuss ways of thinking about preparation (specifically for activity) in reference to newly developing insights on coordination and motor control. I then wish to point to paradigms that may be useful in identifying more clearly the neural counterparts of movement preparation. As Walter Ritter has already remarked, much of the work on readiness potentials has involved relatively "aimless" tasks. Thus we know little about what aspects of behavior (in terms of the motor tasks employed) relate to the "preparatory waves" that we observe when we record from the brain.

The typical information-processing models about which we have heard much thus far—and which appear to provide the theoretical backdrop for much of the event-related potential work—run into some problems when we raise the issue of preparation. Like its counterpart, attention, preparation is not easily tied to any particular structural stage but rather may be more appropriately viewed as a functional process that manifests itself throughout the system. In this perspective preparation is that process that modifies the functional state of the system in advance arising as an output from some earlier processing stage. Preparation is often tied to the response side of the system and presumably bears a close tie, the related notion of preprogramming. I wish to diverge from this view for principally two reasons: First, the foregoing view perpetuates the sensorimotor distinction that as I have emphasized here and elsewhere is no longer a viable one; second, this view of preparation ignores certain fundamental problems of movement organization that must be considered if we are to understand what preparation really involves.

Recently Requin (1980) has made a strong claim that we can usefully proceed in studying preparation with stage models of information processing and neurophysiological models of the CNS that are isomorphically related. Requin views preparation not only as an intrinsic facilitory aspect of the "building" of motor programs but also as playing a modulatory role in the execution process. In an isomorphic model, however, the structures and pathways involved in programming are distinct from those involved in execution (Requin, 1980). This is an example of the sensorimotor, input-output dichotomy in a more refined guise. Instead of considering simply a response stage as a single entity (which is the case in many information-processing models), the suggestion is to break it up to include response determination (i.e., which stimulus goes with which response), response programming (selection and preparation of the appropriate response), and response execution. Although partialling out the motor system enables experimenters to use chronometric methods to distinguish hypothetical stages experimentally, it does not provide much insight into the organization of movement. At best such experiments have a questionable motivation because there is no neurophysiological support for a view that separates programming and execution. When an animal makes an active movement, for example, afferent information transmitted in ascending spinal tracts is modulated at the level of the second-order neuron (Ghez & Lenzi, 1971; Coulter, 1974). There is therefore centrifugal control of incoming information prior to and during the execution of an activity that renders the programming-execution distinction virtually untenable. Furthermore, there is no clear relationship between neural activity in precentral cortex and movement parameters such as extent or velocity. To view preparation as having selective effects at various serially ordered stages is a conceptual luxury, for such stages overlap considerably, as indeed they must if they are to be consonant with a neurophysiology indicating interaction at all levels of the neuraxis (Evarts et al., 1971).

How then—given a dissatisfaction with serial-order models—should we conceptualize preparation and what should be our direction for an adequate analysis? I believe a more realistic view of movement preparation will come only when we appreciate some of the problems facing a theory of movement coordination and control. Let me briefly discuss motor control theories as they are currently delineated in most corners of neurophysiology and psychology. I should point out that it is not at all clear what the role of preparation may be in these theories. In contrast a viable alternative that I shall suggest includes preparation (feedforward) as an intrinsic aspect of its style of organization.

The currently dominant theories of motor control are essentially offshoots of the past. Peripheralist theory is best expressed in closed-loop, cybernetic models where sensory feedback from the periphery is compared against an internally stored referent value (or setpoint) so that errors in production may be detected and corrected (Adams, 1977; Schmidt, 1975). Centralist theory is exemplified in the motor program viewpoint where the details of the movement are structured prior to initiation. Thus the various dimensions or components of the movement (e.g., amplitude, direction [see later discussion]) are selected in advance and then translated into some muscle-usable code. Although preparation may be seen as a process involved in constructing the motor program, little is known about how this process works. Motor programs are assumed as a priori facts; few have questioned their status as controllers.

In my opinion neither of these models (or their hybrid versions) provides a principled basis for understanding the control and coordination of movement. The arguments for this position have been laid out in detail elsewhere (Fowler,

1977; Kelso, Holt, Kugler, & Turvey, 1980; Kugler, Kelso, & Turvey, 1980; Turvey, 1977) and can only be briefly drawn here. First, the theories previously referred to ignore the problem of what Bernstein (1967) called functional nonunivocality or context-conditioned variability (Turvey, Shaw, & Mace, 1978); second, they ignore the fundamental problem of perception-production systems, namely the regulation of a potentially large number of degrees of freedom. Functional nonunivocality refers to the fact that centrally generated signals are not mapped invariantly to movement outcomes. *Movements cannot be direct reflections of neural events because muscular and nonmuscular (reactive) forces have to be taken into account.* In fact, a notable characteristic of skilled individuals is that of providing only those changes in force during a particular movement that are not given reactively. But the effect of movement context is manifested at a neurophysiological level as well. Monosynaptic control of alphamotoneurons is the exception rather than the rule in the neural regulation of movement. Instead, whether a motoneuron fires or not is ultimately contingent on the influences of suprasegmental, intersegmental, and intrasegmental interneurons whose status varies from one instant to the next (Evarts et al., 1971). The point is that the effects of descending commands are continually modulated by virtue of the continuously active state of the spinal machinery. Thus we can't prepare a program and assume that it will be faithfully executed by the peripheral musculature. That would be to ignore the contextual background against which cortical influences are realized. Indeed, because there can be no isomorphic relationship between muscle commands and the effects observed in the periphery, it seems more appropriate to consider supraspinal influences as organizational rather than executive (Fowler, 1977). This view has significant implications for the concept of preparation and how we might approach it. Although it might be argued that a closed-loop model could solve the problem of context by making available detailed information about the current states of muscles and joints, closed-loop and motor programming models both fail to account for the degrees of freedom problem.

A step toward resolving this dilemma—following the insights of the Soviet school and their supporters (Bernstein, 1967; Gelfand, Gurfinkel, Fomin, & Tsetlin, 1971; Greene, 1972; Turvey, 1977)—is to claim that the skeletomuscular variables are partitioned into collectives where the variables within a collective change related and autonomously. Control and coordination are defined over autonomous muscle collectives rather than potentially freely varying individual muscles. We have referred to these synergistic groups as coordinative structures (Fowler, 1977; Kelso, Southard, & Goodman, 1979; Turvey et al., 1978) defined as functional groupings of muscles often spanning several joints that are constrained to act as a single unit. Evidence for a coordinative structure style of organization comes from research on activities as varied as locomotion, mastication, postural control, and respiration, and extends to volitional two-handed mastication, postural control, and respiration, and extends to volitional two-

movements, handwriting, and speech (Fowler, 1977; Kelso et al., 1980; Kugler et al., 1980).

According to this perspective, coordinative structures are created when the interneuronal pools in the various low-level structures (e.g., brainstem, spinal cord) are selectively facilitated and inhibited (Greene, 1972; Gurfinkel, Kotz, Krinskiy, Pal'tsev, Feldman, Tsetlin, & Shik, 1971). As a consequence of these tunings or biasings—which I wish to refer to as preparation—an aggregate of neuromuscular variables is constrained to act as a functional unit. Well-known examples of this style of control come from work on postural reflexes in the cat (Roberts, 1967). On seeing a mouse, neck flexion reactions as well as the tilt of the head will tune lower spinal centers such that a simple signal for "jump" will be sufficient to initiate the act in the correct direction. As Greene (1972) points out, these feedforward, preparatory adjustments must be set as the act begins; for without them, accurate performance would be impossible. The onset of any active movement then, as Bernstein (1967) theorized, is preceded by a preliminary tuning of sensorimotor elements in accordance with the intended act. Planning and preparing a movement might be best considered as a progressive linking of variables specific to the upcoming action.

I have reviewed a good deal of the evidence for preparatory adjustments elsewhere (i.e., efference as a feedforward mode of organization rather than as a central set of commands to muscles) both in relation to normal animal and human movement (Kelso, 1979) and in pathological conditions such as apraxia (Kelso & Tuller, 1981). A principal source of experimental support for this view comes from findings that show progressive changes in spinal and brain-stem reflex organization before and during voluntary movements (Coquery, 1978; McClean, 1978). The complex of preparatory adjustments can be broken down into three phases (Kots, 1977). The first, *pretuning*, occurs prior to the signal to move and extends throughout the latency period of the movement. It involves a "background" increase in the reflex excitability of all motoneuron pools (as measured by H-reflex techniques, Desmedt, 1973) and is the same regardless of the function of the muscles in the upcoming movement (see Fig. 8.8). Pretuning appears to be associated with a state of expectancy rather than a *muscle-specific* readiness for movement; it is absent during the latent period of elicited reflex or involuntary movements.

Changes in the spinal apparatus specific to the future movement are described by the processes of *tuning* and *triggering*. Approximately 50 to 60 msec prior to the onset of EMG activity in the agonist of the impending movement, there is a smooth and progressive increase in the reflex excitability of the motoneuronal pool of the agonist ("tuning"). During the last 25 to 30 msec of the latency period, the "fast" motoneurons of the agonist show a sharp increase in reflex excitability—as a result of pyramidal "triggering"—and this is accompanied by depression of the inhibitory interneuronal system acting on the motoneuronal pool of the future agonist. In effect, production of the upcom-

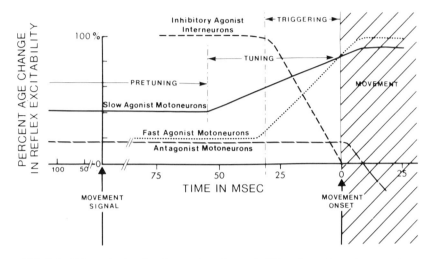

FIG. 8.8   Schematic showing changes in reflex excitability of agonist and antagonist motoneuronal pools during the preparation of voluntary movement. Adapted from Kots (1977).

ing movement is facilitated, whereas movements in the direction opposite to the intended movement are inhibited. Thus, when the functional state of the motor system has been modified, the performer is constrained to produce one of a limited class of acts, reducing the number of control decisions necessary to perform an extended sequence of movements. Preparation then involves the progressive linking of variables specific to the upcoming movement; it is an adaptive functional organization of the motor system that facilitates a specific class of motor activity. The main point is that this view of preparation does not assign priority to any one stage or level of the system but rather is a process that is manifest throughout the system.

   Although tuning and triggering may be best reflected by changes in spinal organization, pretuning may be explored (and enlightened upon) via ERP techniques. What types of behavioral paradigms might be most significant as aids to advancing our knowledge of preparatory events in the brain? From our previous discussion (see Donchin and Ritter comments), there seems to be a general dissatisfaction with the behaviors examined thus far: Waving the hand for several hours has not afforded much insight into brain-behavior relationships. In this case the event may be so boring and aimless as to preclude the possibility of finding significant neural correlates. Let me suggest some alternative approaches that are not so complicated that they negate the tight experimental control necessary in brain potential work. Consider the finding that the time to initiate a movement increases as the number of elements in the response increases (Henry & Rogers, 1960). No one, to my knowledge, has pursued this result (which has been replicated on numerous occasions; see Kerr, 1978 for review) with a view to systematically identifying possible neurophysiological counterparts of the preparation involved. More recently, Sternberg, Monsell, Knoll, & Wright (1978) have shown, in a task that required subjects to recite a list of words following a reaction signal, that initiation time increases as a linear function of the number of elements (specifically stressed syllables). Incidentally, this datum speaks against a view that assigns response preparation to a single stage. If the subject were allowed to plan the movement sequence well in advance of the reaction signal, then the latency to initiate production after completion of a programming stage should not change as the number of elements in the planned response changes. The fact that it does suggests that preparatory biasing adjustments are a function of the entire act and not simply the initial segment. But even more interesting for present purposes is the question of identifying neural events that might be related to the preparation of extended movement sequences. Recently, Grunewald, Grunewald-Zuberbier, Homberg, and Netz (1979) have demonstrated a widespread bilateral potential occurring in both parietal and precentral cortical regions whose negativity is influenced by the accuracy demands of the task. These experiments are among the first to explore brain correlates of goal-directed movements, even though the latter were of the single, discrete type. The Sternberg et al. (1978) paradigm provides a potentially enlightening method for establishing relationships between preparatory brain events and movements of a much more complex kind within an easily controlled experimental setting.

Are event related potentials correlated to specific movement parameters or is preparation at supraspinal levels a more generalized phenomenon? The analysis of pretuning presented earlier suggests the latter. Very recently however, Rosenbaum (1980) has argued that the various parameters of movement tend to be prepared in advance in a serial, invariant order. Consider a situation in which there is uncertainty about which of the two arms is to produce a forward or a backward movement of a short or a long extent. Suppose now that we precue the subject by telling him that the upcoming movement is to be made by the left arm in a forward direction, thus leaving only extent of movement uncertain. Does the subject use this prior, precue information to prepare only those parameters that are known (arm and direction), leaving only extent to be prepared at signal onset, or does the subject use the prior information to simply reduce the number of response alternatives from eight to two? Rosenbaum (1980) found the choice reaction time was shortest when only extent was left to be selected, longer when a directional decision was required, and longer still when arm remained to be selected. Furthermore, when two of three parameters (arm, direction, or extent) had to be selected, reaction times were further elevated and followed a pattern consonant with singly precued conditions. On the basis of this result, Rosenbaum concluded that the parameters were ordered such that first arm, then direction, and finally extent were selected in the movement initiation process.

Our own experiments (Goodman & Kelso, 1980) have failed to support Rosenbaum's selective preparation model, at least when precues and stimuli are mapped compatibly with responses. Using procedures designed to maximize differential parameter selection, we found, like Rosenbaum, that reaction time did decrease systematically as a function of the *number* of precued parameters, but there were no systematic effects of precuing a particular parameter.

Our experimental setup is shown in Figure 8.9. The subject ($N = 10$ in this study) sat with his fingers resting on the home keys of a precuing display that was mounted in an identical configuration to the response board illustrated in Fig. 8.9. To precue a subject on a single parameter, four light-emitting diodes (LEDs) were turned on. For example, to precue left arm, the four lights on the left (1, 3, 5, and 7) appeared. Similarly, to precue a long extent, the outermost lights were activated (1, 2, 7, and 8). A trial sequence consisted of a precue lasting 3 sec followed after a variable foreperiod by the stimulus to move. Subjects were instructed as to the meaning of the precues and to respond as quickly as possible without making errors. Practice was given to familiarize subjects with the response key configuration that was not open to view.

The results of one of our experiments are shown in Fig. 8.10. Each data point under the eight precue conditions consists of 384 trials averaged over

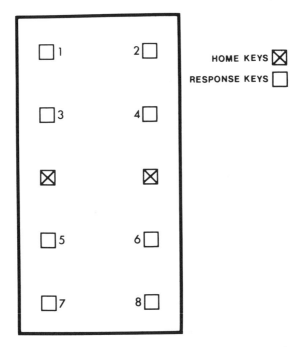

FIG. 8.9   Response configuration for the Goodman and Kelso study. An identical configuration of LEDs was used for precue and initiation signals.

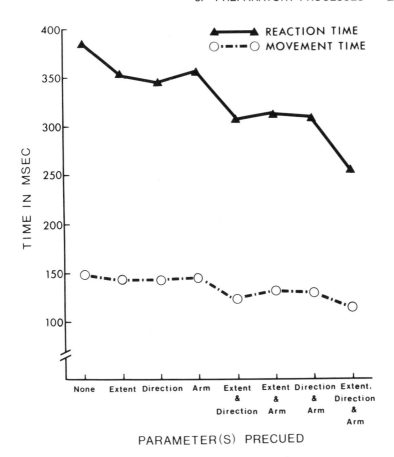

FIG. 8.10   Mean reaction time and movement time (in milliseconds) as a function of
various precue conditions in Goodman and Kelso study.

subjects. Initiation times revealed the following pattern: Completely precued
initiation times (i.e., a simple reaction time situation) were less than two
parameters precued which in turn were less than singly precued conditions.
Significantly, however, the latency function *within* a given precue condition is
essentially flat; there are no differential effects of specific parameters. This
finding, as well as those of additional experiments (Goodman & Kelso, 1980)
suggests that subjects use prior information to reduce the number of possible
alternatives but not to prepare response components partially. Indeed there
does not appear to be any prioritized ordering at least among the parameters
that we have manipulated.

Obviously it would be very elegant indeed to examine event-related brain potentials in this type of paradigm; the fact that subjects effectively use prior information to speed response initiation suggests strongly that there should be

brain correlates of this process and the issue of parameter-specific preparation could be readily examined. Some preliminary evidence (see Kutas' comment, p. 214) favors specificity at least for the limb to be used. When this is known in advance, there is a clearly defined readiness potential that is largest over the hemisphere contralateral to the limb about to be moved. Similarly, Grunewald et al. (1979) have demonstrated a negativity prior to and during goal-directed movements that is restricted to precentral cortex and is larger on the side of the brain contralateral to the moving hand in right-hand subjects. The implication of Kutas' finding is that preparation is at least limb-specific in that there is no negativity when the subject knows neither the time at which to initiate a movement or which limb to move. In contrast, Grunewald et al. (1979) point out that the lateralized component they have identified is *not* a preparatory phenomenon but rather corresponds to the execution of the movement itself. Clearly there is a good deal of work to be done to establish whether these potentials are parameter-specific or not. Our behavioral results (Goodman & Kelso, 1980) and theoretical orientation suggest that preparation at cortical levels does not involve specifying particular parameters in a particular order. That is not to say that brain potential may not reflect the *degree* to which the individual is prepared for the occurrence of an event, as Kutas' data seem to show. Indeed I shall argue in the following that we may well expect to see neural counterparts of this process. Unlike Rosenbaum, however, and for reasons delineated earlier, I do not envisage a motor program whose role it is to order response components and prescribe values for them. However, the paradigm introduced by Rosenbaum is a clever one and ERP researchers could usefully employ it to provide some insight into the issue of parameter-specific preparation.

The final issue that I want to address here concerns a behavioral phenomenon that I believe to be related intimately to preparation and that we have termed the *preselection effect* (Kelso, 1975, 1977a, 1977b; Kelso & Stelmach, 1976; Kelso & Wallace, 1978). I refer to the finding that when a subject makes a self-defined movement of the limb to a certain position (with vision excluded), the subject can reproduce the movement much more accurately than under constrained, exploratory conditions where the movement is defined by an experimenter-defined stop. Elsewhere we have reviewed evidence from over 25 studies illustrating the generality of this effect (Kelso & Wallace, 1978, for a review). Importantly, preselected performance is not dependent on the presence of proprioceptive information from joint and cutaneous sources, whereas constrained and passively generated movements are (Kelso, 1977a; Roy & Williams, 1979). These data on functionally deafferented human subjects appear to concur with the rather global view espoused by investigators in speech control, namely that the greater the ability of the central nervous system to "predictively determine" a motor response, the less the need for peripheral information from sensory receptors (MacNeilage & MacNeilage, 1973).

Are there identifiable neural counterparts to movement preparation in preselected movements? We have some behavioral data that suggest there might well be. Some investigators have suggested that the superiority of preselected movements over those of an exploratory kind might be due to differential attention demands of the two types of movements. The notion is that more so-called "central capacity" is allocated during a preselected than a nonpreselected movement. However, the studies that have been performed thus far (Roy, 1976; Roy & Diewert, 1975) using the probe reaction-time technique to assess attention demands have produced no differences between preselected and constrained trials. The problem with these experiments is that they examined probe performance *during* the movement itself and not in the period of preparation for the movement. We performed some experiments that measured subjects' reaction time to an auditory tone *prior* to movement initiation (Kelso & Pruitt, unpublished). Subjects ($N = 18$) performed 36 preselected and 36 constrained trials, half of which were probed at four different temporal locations during the preparatory period. On probed trials when the subjects heard a tone, they released a microswitch with the nonpreferred hand. After a 3-sec preparatory period, subjects made a preselected movement of their own choice or a constrained movement to an experimenter-defined stop with their preferred hand. Reproduction of the movements followed 3 sec later when subjects were returned to the starting position. These movements were performed in blocks of 12 trials; constrained movements were yoked to preselected trials to facilitate a valid comparison of reproduction errors for different movement extents. In addition, subjects performed 72 nonmovement probe trials that served as baseline controls.

Figure 8.11 shows the reaction time data as a function or probe position (i.e., at 750, 1500, 2250, and 3000 msec). It is quite clear that movement *per se* is more attention demanding than when no primary task is involved. Moreover, although the latency functions for preselected and exploratory movements are similar, the preselected function is considerably—and significantly—elevated overall. I should mention that there was no effect on the primary movement of the probe task. Preselected errors were significantly smaller than constrained both for absolute and variable error ($p < .01$), and groups did not interact with presence or absence of the probe task.

These results suggest quite strongly that one of the differences between preselected and contrained movements lies in the degree to which the former requires preparation. (I should point out that these effects are not unique to limb movements. Bizzi and Dichgans [see Bizzi, 1974 for review] in their work on eye-head coordination show clear differences between the saccadic velocity and agonist—antagonist control of the neck depending on whether the monkey looks for an expected target versus a target that suddenly appears unexpectedly. The "set" that seems to be manifested in probe RT differences in our studies is a fundamental aspect of the pattern of coordination observed.)

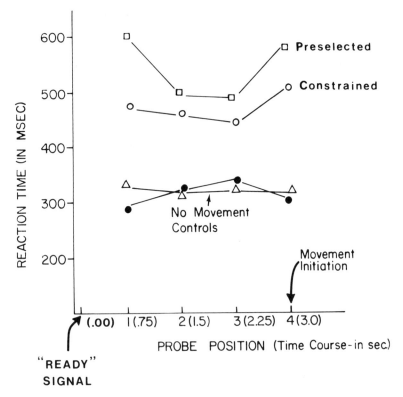

FIG. 8.11   Probe reaction time (in milliseconds) at each of four temporal loci prior to the initiation of preselected and constrained movements.

I am proposing that here we have a significant behavioral effect that appears to reflect varying amounts of movement preparation and that we should be able to identify the same neural processes except to differential degrees. In preselected movements, for example, we might expect to see a well-defined readiness potential, particularly over association areas of cortex. Others have argued that this slowly increasing negativity arising 300-2000 msec before EMG activity represents neural discharges related to preparatory motor set (Vaughan et al., 1968) or motor cortex facilitation (Shibasaki & Kato, 1975). In the foregoing brain-potential studies, however, the tasks employed rather simple stereotyped responses (e.g., thumb flexions, tongue movements) unlike the purposeful and goal-directed movements requiring a high degree of accuracy in the preselection paradigm.

Elsewhere I have argued, after Teuber (1974) and Bernstein (1967), that the preselection effect may be due to a central, feedforward tuning of sensorimotor systems preparing them for the perceptual consequences of the act (Kelso,

1977b). Thus in preselected movements the subject has prior information regarding the terminal position of the limb; constrained, exploratory movements do not have any advance information but must await an externally defined signal to determine the position of the limb. Just as Grunewald et al. (1979) have found "goal-directed movement potential" amplitude differences between tasks requiring low- and high-accuracy demands, so we too might expect to see larger amplitudes of this widespread component in preselected than constrained movements. In sum, my proposal here is one that is consonant with Donchin's (1976) stated "need to examine move complex and skilled tasks . . . so that skilled sequences [may] be compared in terms of electrocortical events synchronous with or related to them [p. 237]." In this case I am presenting the psychophysiologist with a problem that has a good deal of empirical background and asking him to identify possible neural counterparts.

A final cautionary word about the ubiquity of preparation. It now seems to be well-established that events in the brain related to preparation are not at all confined to cortical areas. Neafsey, Hull, and Buchwald (1978a, 1978b), for example, among others have shown the occurrence of single-unit activity in basal ganglia and thalamus long before that of the lateral region of the feline pericruciate motor cortex. There is some reason to believe that this early activity represents "response set" or the priming of neural mechanisms concerned with integrated movements of the body and limbs. I have presented evidence earlier that this type of tuning also extends to spinal levels.

The point, as embellished by Jung (1974), is that we should not expect to see any simple array of cortical correlates of preparation; rather, preparation is manifested in subcortical, reticular and spinal systems as well. All movements, as Sherrington noted long ago, must have preparatory support mechanisms that identify the postural preconditions for goal-directed activities. Recently Lee (1980) has demonstrated—in a simple reaction-time/movement-time task involving arm raising—the presence of a highly ordered sequence of EMG activity in the axial musculature well before activation of the muscles involved in moving the limb itself (Belen'kii, Gurfinkel, & Pal'tsev, 1967). This result is exactly what we would expect on the realization that supportive mechanisms must be activated to prepare the trunk for subsequent actions of limbs.

To reiterate, we should not expect "simple" cortical correlates of preparation as if all that preparation involves is the construction of motor programs at cortical levels. Rather an elaborate preparation is necessary to provide a context of constraint for supraspinal signals, otherwise aimed movements of the distal linkages would be impossible. It seems to me that it would be very difficult indeed to arrive at the perspective on preparation just outlined from currently extant information-processing models. Although cortical correlates are the obvious bailiwick of the cognitive psychophysiologist, they alone are not going to provide much insight into the nature of preparatory processes. Neural events with rather longer time scales appear to be involved in the "psychic" preparation of voluntary action. Cortical activities—we might venture to guess—are closer to the endpoint of preparation than the beginning.

KUTAS: Two important factors in the preparation for a hand movement might be noted: (1) when the movement is to be made; and (2) which hand is going to be making that movement. What you see in Fig. 8.12 are ERPs recorded during several different conditions in which these two factors were varied. At the top are movement-related potentials obtained in association with self-paced ("voluntary") movements. Under those circumstances a person could choose the hand and the timing of the movement. The associated brain potential is the classic RP or Bereitschaftspotential, largest over the contralateral central hemisphere for right- and left-hand movements.

The ERPs in the second row were obtained during a condition in which the subject had to make a response as quickly as possible to the occurrence of a tone whose exact timing was unknown. The interstimulus interval varied randomly from 6 to 15 sec. Thus the subject did not know when he was going to be making that response; however, he did know which hand he was going to respond with, as that was held constant within an experimental run. Under such conditions, the movement-related potentials over the central areas do not show a slow ramp-shaped negativity but rather only a burst of negativity within the 200 msec immediately preceding movement onset, that is, as if the subject, even though he knew the responding hand, could not really prepare because he did not know when the response would be required.

The ERPs in the third row were elicited in a condition in which each trial consisted of a simple warning tone followed 1 sec later by a second tone to which the subject was asked to respond as quickly as possible. Again, in any given experimental run, the same hand was used. Thus, the subject not only knew which hand would be responding but also could estimate fairly accurately when the movement would be required. The associated ERPs are characterized by a large, centrally dominant, asymmetric, premovement negativity.

The ERPs in the final two rows were elicited by movements made in conditions similar to the second (SIG) and third (WARN) ones; however, in the latter two conditions the imperative stimulus provided the subject with information as to the responding hand on a trial-by-trial basis. When the subject knew neither the hand nor the time of the response, the premovement negativity is limited to the 200 msec immediately preceding movement onset. On the other hand, when the subject knew only when he was going to make the response, but not with which hand until the imperative stimulus occurred (as in the WARN condition), there is a large event-preceding negativity but its asymmetry is not consistently related to the responding hand.

KELSO: You're preparing both in that case.

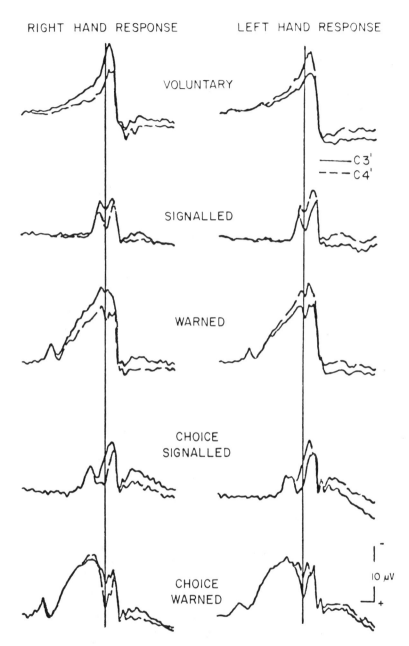

RIGHT HAND RESPONSE   LEFT HAND RESPONSE

VOLUNTARY

———— C 3'
– – – C 4'

SIGNALLED

WARNED

CHOICE
SIGNALLED

CHOICE
WARNED

10 μV

FIG. 8.12   A comparison of the response-locked grand average ERPs recorded at electrodes placed at left central (C3', solid line) and right central (C4', dashed line) loci for right- and left-hand squeezes in five experimental conditions. The vertical line separates presqueeze from postsqueeze activity. Calibrations: 250 msec, 10μV.

KUTAS: Maybe, or alternatively preparing only one or the other hand on different trials based on the preceding sequence of responses, etc. Thus, different parameters of the movement-preceding negativity seem to be indexing the timing and the hand selection aspects of a movement. The presence or absence and onset of the negativity seem to reflect the anticipation or preparation for a movement, and the asymmetry in this component seems to manifest the hand selection process.

ZAIDEL: I'm not sure that I am convinced that the subjects are in fact not expecting intermediate feedback. All you have shown is that when you don't have feedback, you don't need it and you would behave as if it was not there.

KELSO: I accept that wholeheartedly. Nevertheless, these data are supplemented by probe RT effects on preplanned movements. But I'm not saying that feedback is not important here. I'm saying that indeed one can do without it.

TREISMAN: Dr. Kelso said that probes can be interpreted as a demand on general resources, on "conscious attention." Why could it not be a more specific competition between programming and initiating the response to the probe and preparing the preselected movement? One has to prepare one movement and at the same time to make another.

KELSO: Well, then you might expect that there may be some interfering effect of the probe on the movement.

TREISMAN: Well, it would depend on which of the two was more important to the subject. It would be possible to vary that experimentally. Did you look at that?

KELSO: Yes, but there was no interference. That is one of the important features of the probe technique.

TREISMAN: You mean they were giving priority to the preselected movement?

KELSO: Yes. May I ask what the P300 does? Does it change as a function of practice? Have you really looked at that?

DONCHIN: Within the experiments we normally run, using one or two sessions, the subjects have a lot of practice. Subjects receive many hundreds, in fact, thousands, of stimuli and there is no marked reduction in P300 amplitude. We tried to run subjects in an oddball paradigm for 3 months. The subjects and the experimenters did not hold up very well and we could not use the data.

FORD: Tom Roth ran subjects for 3 days and found that the reaction times changed and P300 almost disappeared.

DONCHIN: The P300 seemed to disappear with practice in our long-term study but the data were so poor, and the experiment was so poorly done, that I can't trust it.

SHIFFRIN: Needless to say, I'd like to warn anybody who does this to pay attention to what kind of training sets you're using—whether you are using variable mapping or consistent mapping and so forth.

DONCHIN: Well, we just recruited six people and told them to come in to the lab daily for 3 months. We ran the routine beep/boop study. I wouldn't be surprised if P300 disappears in a beep/boop oddball but will not be reduced when the subject needs to categorize names as male or female, or when they are monitoring complex displays. Very few things are more boring, I think, than an oddball paradigm with tones.

SCHVANEVELDT: Judy, what task was this where you ran subjects for 3 days?

FORD: It was a beep/boop oddball experiment where 80% of the tones were high pitched, 10% were medium pitched, and another 10% were low pitched.

SCHVANEVELDT: The P300s to the rare events disappeared?

FORD: Yes, but the reaction times became slightly shorter with practice.

DONCHIN: One of the longest-duration experiments in our lab was run by Johnson (Johnson & Donchin, 1982). There were many, many conditions and, I think, six sessions per subject with maybe 2000 stimuli. P300 was elicited in all the conditions. The subjects had to detect whether or not the probability in a Bernoulli series changed, so it was a little bit more interesting to the subject.

KUTAS: I've required as many as 800 to 1000 movements from a person in a 3-hr session without an appreciable decline in the amplitude of the associated premovement potentials (RPs).

KELSO: To go back to the issue of whether you might "cue" yourself, as it were, to move a particular extent. This could be more "cognitive" than motor, so you might find the so-called selection process linked to a P300 event rather than a motor event. For example, when I talked about the Rosenbaum paradigm, the notion was that when you prepare movement dimensions you're doing some sort of cognitive operation. Now I'm precued on the limb I have to move and how far to move it. So when you set up this paradigm, do you expect to see some cognitive evoked potentials as well as evidence of general motor preparation?

KUTAS: Yes. There are undoubtedly cognitive as well as motor-related components or potentials elicited prior to preparation for a movement or response. The RP recorded during simple, voluntary movements has a large ipsilateral component that may well manifest cognitive rather than motor processes. It is conceptually and technically difficult to tease apart the various overlapping components whether they represent different aspects of motor or motor and cognitive acts. At present, I view the RP as functionally quite similar to other event-preceding negativities. It seems to differ primarily in its scalp distribution. Much of the emphasis on its motor-relatedness may have to do with the paradigm in which it has generally been recorded.

DONCHIN: I would define operationally as "motor related" that component of the negativity that lateralizes with the responding hand and reverses when you reverse hands. And all other negativity is not necessarily motor.

McCARTHY: Well, you know you can get postural adjustments and synergistic movements on the other side, so that's kind of dangerous to do. Isn't it dangerous to decide that the only thing that is motor is the lateralized portion?

DONCHIN: I did not say necessarily that potentials that do not lateralize are not motor. All I am saying is that I accept as *definitely* motor what is lateralized; the rest is open.

KUTAS: It's been said that my subjects were making simple, relatively inane movements. It's necessary to investigate more complex movements; those may be associated with still other endogenous potentials.

DONCHIN: I am not sure I agree. Squeezing a dynamometer and producing a carefully defined response pattern in an isometric squeeze is not "inanely lifting your hand." It requires a lot of skill for the subject to perform those movements.

KUTAS: True, but we have barely tapped the store of even the most mundane human movements. The few statements about movement-related potential shapes and distributions that we can make, apply with very few exceptions, only to the finger, hand, and arm movements that have been investigated. At this point we cannot generalize to the movement(s) involved in slipping an arm through a shirt sleeve. The area is wide-open for investigation.

DONCHIN: The Grunewalds in Freiburg (1979) have been looking at "goal-directed movements." The subject is required to move a pointer to a target. It turns out that a large, lateralized potential appears as long as the subject is moving the pointer. This lateralized potential disappears if the movement is not goal directed or if the movement is passive.

ZAIDEL: What does "lateralized" mean? Where is the difference?

DONCHIN: Oh, it's always larger contralateral to the responding hand, that's what I mean by lateralized.

9 The Timing of Mental Acts

William Chase
Carnegie-Mellon University, Pittsburgh

9.1 DONDERS AND MENTAL CHRONOMETRY

I want to show you that since Donders' time we have learned a tremendous amount about measuring mental processes from specific tasks. We don't know very much about the so-called control structure, that is, how the system organizes these processes from task to task. I think it is becoming painfully apparent that we need a theory of control structure. In other words, it is not sufficient anymore to do our experimental analysis of isolated mental processes. We need to add a systems analysis.

This emphasis on system analysis raises some issues in the resolution of which electrophysiology, or physiological psychology, can help us. One issue is how control is organized in the brain. I think that this is an empirical question that electrophysiological research can illuminate. Another issue has come up in many different guises, and that is the distinction between controlled and automatic processing, or simple and complex processing, or high-speed versus slow processes, or conscious versus unconscious processes. You can catalog it many different ways, but we seem to think there are some important distinctions here and I think that electrophysiology can potentially tell us something about this. Another issue that was dead at one point is serial versus parallel processing. Of course, now we know better. The brain does both serial and parallel processing at the same time, but we have been batting this issue around for about 10 years.

I think that electrophysiology can tell us more about how processes are organized. Are they serial? Do they cascade? Is an additive stage model a viable approximation to how the brain works? What is an elementary process? I don't know the answers, but I think electrophysiology can potentially give them. We need a physiological model of how reaction time works, at the very least. I am sure electrophysiology can tell us more than we know now. Another issue is analog versus digital, or analog versus symbolic processing. Of course in a general sense we know that the brain does both, but I think we are open to empirical imput from electrophysiology. Those are some issues I thought of as I was organizing my discussion where I think cognitive psychology needs input.

For over 100 years scientists have been attempting to measure the speed of mental processes, and I see historically there have been three periods in this endeavor. There was an early period, beginning with Donders (1868) where analogies were made between mental processes and physiological mechanisms, mainly because a lot of advances were being made in those days toward understanding physiological mechanisms. So there was a long period, starting with Donders, of measuring mental processes, and the theoretical analogies were based on physiological mechanisms. Then there was, for our purposes, a dark age, which we shall label behaviorism. During this period, researchers were actively discouraged from investigating processes intervening between stimulus and response, and very few new insights about the speed of mental processes were achieved. And then, for the past 30 years there has been a resurgence in measuring mental processes. Again there were analogies based on scientific advances in another field. In this case, there were some advances being made in communications theory. So, around World War II, a lot of theorizing was based on analogies to communications systems. Then computers were invented, and there were some rapid strides in understanding how information systems operate with computer types of mechanisms. Now our analogies tend to be couched in computer-like terms and that is the era we are in now.

Let me return to a brief review of the history of the measurement of mental processes. It really started with Donders' (1868) landmark paper. Donders' idea was based on early experiments by Helmholtz who was able, by inference, to measure the speed of nerve conduction.

Helmholtz's experiment is a very simple idea, and Donders based his experiment on it. Donders theorized that processes such as stimulus discrimination and response selection are organized serially in the nervous system and, if one could measure a task that had sensory discrimination in one case and not in the other, then the difference in those times would measure sensory discrimination, by direct analogy to Helmholtz's experiment.

In Table 9.1 I tried to summarize Donders' experiment (Donders, 1868). He assigned subjects three tasks called the A reaction, the B reaction, and the C reaction. Today we would call the A reaction a simple reaction time in which a unique response is required to one stimulus. The B reaction we would call choice reaction, because there were several stimuli each with its distinct response. The C reaction is equivalent to the "information reduction" or

Table 1

Donders' Subtractive Technique

	a reaction	b reaction	c reaction
	$S_1 \longrightarrow R_1$	$S_1 \longrightarrow R_1$	$S_1 \longrightarrow R_1$
S-R mapping:		$S_2 \longrightarrow R_2$	S_2
		$S_3 \longrightarrow R_3$	S_3
		$S_4 \longrightarrow R_4$	S_4
		$S_5 \longrightarrow R_5$	S_5
Stages:		Stimulus discrimination + response selection	Stimulus discrimination
latency:	201 msec	284 msec	237 msec

Sensory discrimination time (c–a) = 36 msec

Response selection time (b–c) = 83 msec

"many-to-one" mapping or search tasks. Many stimuli may be presented but only one response is required. Donders reasoned that the B reaction required stimulus discrimination and response selection because subjects had to decide first which stimulus occurred and then they had to decide which response to emit. The critical task, from Donders point of view, was the C reaction. Because there were many stimuli, subjects had to perform a stimulus discrimination but because only one response was possible, response selection was not required.

Donders served as his own subject and used syllables as stimuli. In Table 9.1 are shown the reaction times of Donders himself. He measured stimulus discrimination time by subtracting A from C because the difference is simply stimulus discrimination. He estimated that time to be 36 msec. Similarly, he subtracted C from B to obtain an estimate of response selection of 83 msec.

Donders was the first to attempt to measure the speed of a mental event, something that was too rapid to measure directly but if it was done by subtraction, it could be measured. In the years that followed, this paradigm appeared increasingly problematic. The first and most obvious problem is that the C reaction does not eliminate response selection. In fact the subject has to decide if the stimulus is or is not a target. Another, more subtle problem, is that the A and the B reactions are organized differently. Subjects approach the task differently; they have different set. They probably even have different patterns of muscle tensions in their hands. The third problem is that researchers just seemed to have 'no luck at measuring things such as cognition time, association time, and attention time.

So in the end the subtraction technique was rejected (Woodworth, 1938, p. 309). I think that the rejection of the subtractive technique was unwarranted even though these are valid objections to Donders' original experiment. There are two primary problems. One is the fallacy of pure insertion. The subtractive technique is based on the premise that it is possible, in some cases, to invent a task, say Task B, that has all the stages of Task A, plus an additional stage whose duration you want to measure. The fallacy of pure insertion is that it is possible to insert a stage leaving the stages of the simpler task untouched. In fact it is often the case that when you invent a task with an additional stage, the other stages change as well.

A second problem is that of parallel processing. Mental processes may overlap in time and many processes obscure each other.

In retrospect, the most serious problem in Donders' paradigm was that it was not based on a good theory. Concepts such as cognition, association, and attention time are based mainly on experimenters' intuitions. There was no independent, converging, theoretical work indicating that these are isolable mental processes with measurable durations. The subtractive technique works a lot better if you have a good cognitive theory.

9.2 STERNBERG AND ADDITIVE FACTORS

The next advance occurred almost 100 years later when Sternberg (1969) presented an important revision of Donders' subtractive technique. Sternberg avoided the fallacy of pure insertion through the invention of the additive factors method. Sternberg's basic experiment is well-known (Sternberg, 1966). Short-term memory is loaded with some material like digits. You then present a probe and ask "is it in memory, or not?" Sternberg's data are shown in Fig. 9.1. The independent variable is the memory load, the size of the "positive set." There is a linear relationship between reaction time and the size of the positive set. The implication is that the technique succeeded in isolating in memory a high-speed serial search process that takes about 38 msec per comparison. At least, that is the slope of the line relating reaction time and memory load.

This procedure avoids the fallacy of pure insertion because the independent variable is the number of times the stage operates, not whether the stage is present or absent. One extrapolates the line to the stage where this comparison with memory stage is missing; that is, one obtains the intercept with zero memory load. The intercept is a measure of all the processes in the memory search when no comparisons are needed.

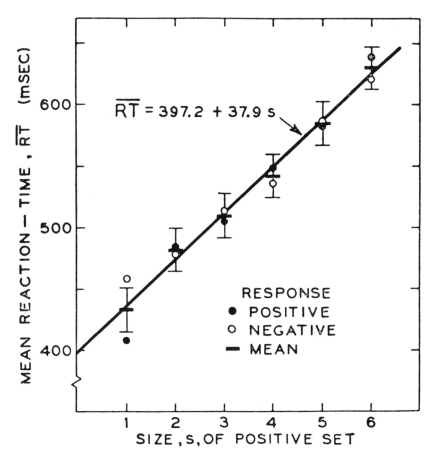

FIG. 9.1   Data from the original Sternberg experiment. Filled circles represent positive responses; open circles represent negative responses; and the bar represents the combined average. The brackets show ± one standard error. The best-fitting straight line is also shown. (Adapted from Sternberg, S. High speed scanning in human memory. *Science,* 1966, 652–654. Copyright 1966 by the American Association for the Advancement of Science. Reprinted by permission.)

The other important finding of Sternberg's was that the slopes were identical for targets and nontargets. This implied the most counter-intuitive part of Sternberg's theory, namely that the search is exhaustive. An exhaustive search means that you scan *completely* through memory before you decide target/nontarget. If you scan until you find a target, then the slope for targets should be half as steep as for nontargets. Sternberg's explanation was that if you stop to make a target/nontarget decision after every comparison it would just be too costly; it would cost a couple hundred milliseconds each time. It is more efficient, according to Sternberg, to do several matches and then at the end stop and ask "was there a match?" Each comparison costs 38 msec, plus at the end there is a 200-msec target/nontarget decision. That is his explanation.

Sternberg conducted a second experiment in which he degraded the stimulus probe (Sternberg, 1967). He loaded memory with a list and then either he presented a very clear probe stimulus or he superimposed a grid on the probe. He found that after some practice the slopes remained parallel. Without practice there is a steeper slope in the degraded condition, meaning that the noise contaminates the comparison process. With practice you can eliminate that noise, and that had an important consequence for his theory: There are two independent stages. There is an encoding stage where the probe is encoded and, if it is degraded, the stage is prolonged. Then, after encoding is completed, memory is scanned.

Sternberg wrote an important theoretical paper in which he developed more fully the additive factors approach (Sternberg, 1969). This approach is a recipe for doing parametric research in which the search is for invariance. In other words, you are looking for additivity rather than interactions, and everytime you find additivity, you claim to have discovered a stage of processing. For example, there must be an encoding stage in memory search that is separate from memory comparison because visual noise affects the intercept but does not affect the memory comparison process (the slope). Similarly, there must be a match/mismatch response decision process that is additive to the memory comparison because response probability affects the intercept but not the slope. It does not affect the speed of that central comparison process. On the other hand, if you make these comparisons more complex, it increases the slope; that is, complexity interacts with memory load and presumably it affects the comparison process, but it does not interact with response probability. This suggests that there is still a third stage involving a match/mismatch decision that is affected by response probability.

That's a fairly straightforward account of Sternberg's work. There are two principles in this approach. One is the subtractive technique with his important revision. The revision is important because it avoids the fallacy of pure insertion. The independent manipulation is the number of times a stage operates, not presence or absence of a stage. In conjunction with this subtractive technique is the additive factors method where you search for invariance. If you can apply the subtractive technique and isolate and measure a mental process, then the next step, according to Sternberg, is to see if that parameter remains invariant when you manipulate variables that theoretically should not affect it. Then if you have another experimental procedure to measure another stage, like stimulus encoding, variables that affect the stimulus should interact but they should not interact with variables that affect other stages, such as the memory comparison.

My evaluation of Sternberg's contribution is this. The work has had a large impact on the field. Yet, additive factors, as a methodology, has its limitations. It is not a substitute for a theory of mental processes; it is proposed as a way of searching for stages. It is a precursor of a theory. We are all aware of the limitations of this serial independent stages approach. The subtractive technique, on the other hand, is much more useful because we can actually measure duration of mental events in some cases. As far as Sternberg's memory search paradigm goes, 10 years later and hundreds of papers later, I don't think we have resolved a lot of the important issues. Most of the papers have been extensions and revisions of Sternberg's original ideas. Most of the theoretical attention has been leveled at the nonintuitive part of the theory, namely the serial exhaustive search process. This has not been resolved. Some of the people I respect claim it is irresolvable, but I don't believe that.

What I find most valuable in Sternberg's approach is that this method can be extended to other processes. I shall describe two extensions in detail: One extension is into verification processes, and the other is in quantification in children.

9.3 THE VERIFICATION PROCESS

In 1972 Clark and I (Clark & Chase, 1972) became interested in how people would verify sentences that describe a picture. We were interested in the mental processes that occur when subjects verify a linguistic structure against a visual structure. We presented people with sentences like "The plus is above the star." To the right of the sentence was a picture that either confirmed or disconfirmed the sentences. They saw either $^+_*$ or $^*_+$, and we manipulated the complexity of the sentence. We would have the word *above* or *below* and the word *is* or *isn't*, and the sentence could either be true or false (Clark & Chase, 1972).

In modeling this task, we faced two theoretical problems. We needed a theory about how the sentences and the pictures were structured. We borrowed the theory, in a straightforward way, from linguistic theory. Second, we needed a theory describing how subjects go about verifying the truth or falsity of a sentence. We derived this theory from Sternberg's ideas on additive stages. We assumed that our subjects look at the sentence and encode it as a sentence. Then they look at the picture and encode it. Then they check the two propositions, and if the propositions matched, they move on. If the propositions didn't match, they change the truth index. We assumed that people were initially set to assume that the sentence was true. But if the proposition underlying the sentence and the picture was mismatched, they flip this index and change it from true to false. Then they looked back to see if there was a negative feature attached to the sentence. If the sentence was negative, they flipped the index again, and then they execute the truth index.

So we had a theory that assumed three, isolable mental processes. Our theory of structure can be presented in relation to the sentence shown in Fig. 9.2. This is an example of a complicated sentence: "The plus isn't below the star." The sentence requires all four of the mental processes we wanted to measure. This is an example of an actual trial, a true case. It turns out that true negative sentences are harder than false negatives, and we think we know why.

Figure 9.2 illustrates the complexities of that sentence. First, you encode the sentence. Clark and I established earlier that lexical marking is associated with costs in processing time. The word *below* costs an extra 100 msec relative to processing the word *above*, and parameter *a* reflects this lexical marking effect in the encoding stage. Second, because the sentence is negative, it requires extra time to generate a negative linguistic structure. There are a variety of ways of representing lexical marking and negation. We assumed that sentences like "A is above B" are represented by a simple relational proposition containing a spatial relation with two arguments. If this is broken down any further, we assumed that *above* is represented by a couple of semantic features. One would be the semantic feature of verticality, and the other would be plus polarity, meaning it is on the positive end of a dimension. *Below* would be represented with an extra semantic feature, or an extra process that flips plus polar to minus polar. If you take these down any further, you are going to have a vector that would be a set of physical features to search for. This is a straightforward application of linguistic theory to represent these sentences. We further assumed that a negative sentence would be encoded as a tag on this whole string, and it takes *b* msec to represent the *false*.

After the sentence is encoded, the subjects inspect and encode the picture. If the sentence says *above*, they look above for the subject of the sentence; if it says *below*, they look below. In this case, it says *below* so we assume that the picture is encoded in a propositional format similar to that of the sentence. All these things cost time, but our subtractive technique would not be able to pull out a parameter for this stage. All the extra time in encoding sentences and encoding pictures, etc., goes into an intercept or base parameter, t.

Next, subjects compare the propositions. If there is a mismatch, that mismatch costs time; then they flip the truth index, and that also costs time. Both of these events cost a total of time c. Then the next thing they do is go back to the semantic structure to see if there is a negation and if there is, they flip the truth index again. This whole mental process costs time d.

When we add all of these up, we obtain an equation for the sentence, as shown in the figure. Our technique in this experiment did not allow us to differentiate parameter b and parameter d, so we just lumped them together. In later experiments we were able to tease them apart and measure them separately (Singer, Chase, Young, & Clark, 1971).

We generate an equation for each sentence like this. For example, the true sentence "The plus is above the star" would not have any extra mental processes in it, and it would simply take time t. The false sentence "The plus is below the star" is lexically marked and it has a mismatch with the picture, and it takes time $t + a + c$, and so on. Well, there are eight combinations

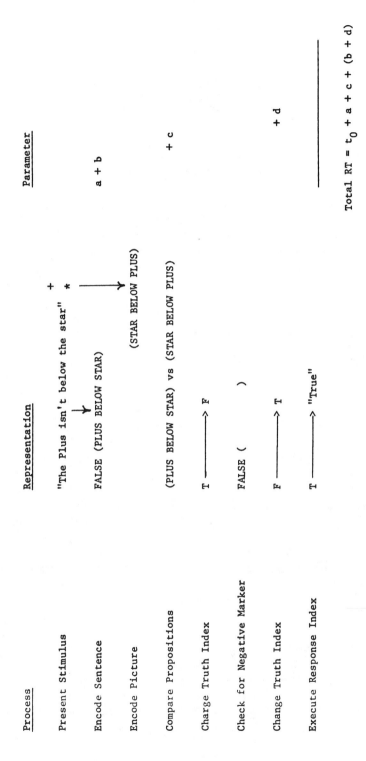

Process	Representation	Parameter
Present Stimulus	"The Plus isn't below the star" + *	
Encode Sentence	FALSE (PLUS BELOW STAR)	a + b
Encode Picture	(STAR BELOW PLUS)	
Compare Propositions	(PLUS BELOW STAR) vs (STAR BELOW PLUS)	+ c
Charge Truth Index	T ⟶ F	
Check for Negative Marker	FALSE ( )	
Change Truth Index	F ⟶ T	+ d
Execute Response Index	T ⟶ "True"	

Total RT = t_0 + a + c + (b + d)

FIG. 9.2   The mental representations, processes, and parameters of the Clark and Chase model for the true sentence, "The plus isn't below the star."

229

like this. Each of the eight combinations has a different equation and each has an average reaction time, so we can just grind out the predictions and apply the method of least squares to fit the data. There are four parameters [t, a, c, and $(b + d)$] and we have four degrees of freedom left over for fitting the data. When we fit the data to our experiment, we obtain the following parameter estimates: It costs about 100 msec to process a lexically marked item. It costs about 150 msec if there is a mismatch on the proposition. Handling a negative sentence costs about 600 msec. Figure 9.3 shows the actual fit of the data. These are the eight combinations of above/below, true/false, and positive/negative.

This is the beginning of a theory, but it is not much of a theory yet unless we can test it again. So the best way to test a theory is to derive some predictions and determine if they work. We instructed our subjects to look at the picture first and then the sentence. This added an extra complication because when you encode the picture, you don't know whether to encode (A *above* B) or (B *below* A). If you look at the sentence first, you simply look above or below depending on the preposition; that is, the sentence dictates how the picture should be coded when you look at the sentence first. But if you code the picture first, you don't know how to code it. Then, when you look at the sentence, you now have an extra thing to check: You have to compare both the subject and the predicate of the sentence. Well, we figured out another parameter to account for that extra mental process. We assumed that people always coded a picture, under normal conditions, as one item *above* another, and they carry that representation into the sentence processing. Now there are two things to check. They have to check the proposition for the spatial relation and then they have to check the subject of that sentence. I won't go into the details but it requires another mental process, and when we make those assumptions, here is what our theory predicts. There is another mental process that costs about 200 msec that we were able to measure, and Fig. 9.4 shows how our theory fared. The figure on the left is the sentence-first case again, which replicates our first experiment, and the figure on the right is the picture-first case. Our theory was able to predict this unlikely pattern extremely well.

In the next experiment we tried to manipulate the picture code. We instructed our subjects to attend to the top picture, attend to the bottom picture, or attend to both the top and bottom of the picture. If they attend to the top of the picture, or to both the top and bottom, we assumed that people would code the picture as (A *above* B). But if they attended to the bottom of the picture, we assumed they would encode it as (B *below* A). So if the subject attended the top, he/she would always carry a structure like (A *above* B) into the sentence comparison. If he attended the bottom, he would always carry (B *below* A) into the sentence processing. This is very straightforward. We just plug those representations into our model and run them through a least-squares fit. Figure 9.5 shows that our predictions worked out very well in every case.

Next, we forced the subjects to break this coding (A *above* B) by experimentally manipulating it rather than by instructing our subjects (Clark & Chase, 1974). In this experiment—a picture-first experiment—we presented subjects with an obvious reference, and we hoped that they would code this picture relative to the reference. In this case, the lines reference was a long line, and the

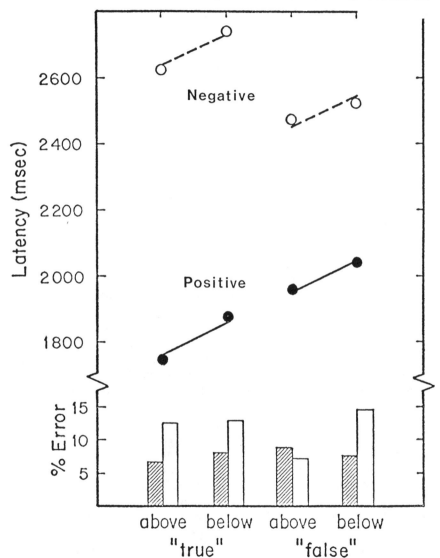

FIG. 9.3   Observed (circles) and predicted (lines) latencies from the Clark and Chase experiment. Error frequencies are also shown at the bottom. (From Clark & Chase, 1972.)

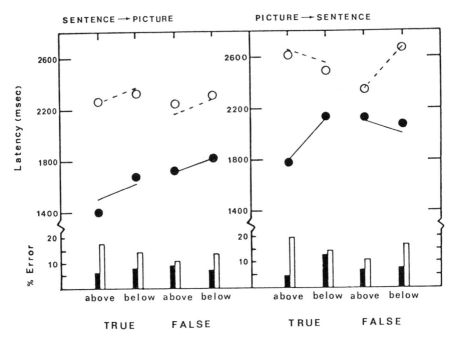

FIG. 9.4   Data from Experiment II of Clark and Chase (1972).

other object was a star either above or below the line. In this experiment, we hoped that people would be perceptually compelled to code these figures as (STAR *above* LINE) and (STAR *below* LINE), respectively. The interesting contrast is whether subjects code the second figure as (STAR *below* LINE) or (LINE *above* STAR). These two types of codes predict very different reaction time patterns. When we examined the data, we found that our subjects very neatly divided themselves into two groups. We found that about half our subjects always coded the star relative to the line, and the other half always coded the top figure relative to the bottom; in each case, the theory fit the data extremely well.

Table 9.2 summarizes all these various manipulations, through all our experiments. The mean lexical marking time (*a*) is about 105 msec, the mismatch time (*c*) averaged out to be 127 msec, negation time (*b* + *d*) averaged out to be about 600 msec, and the translation time (i.e., the parameter for handling that extra comparison in the picture-first condition) turned out to be 171 msec. We think we have done a pretty good experimental analysis of this theory.

In the final experiment we tried to bring the encoding stage under conscious control by instructing our subjects to translate the sentence (Young & Chase, 1971). We had four instructions. There are two ways to get rid of a negative. In one condition, we asked our subjects to convert the sentence from "A isn't above" to "B is above" before verifying it. The other way is to convert "A isn't

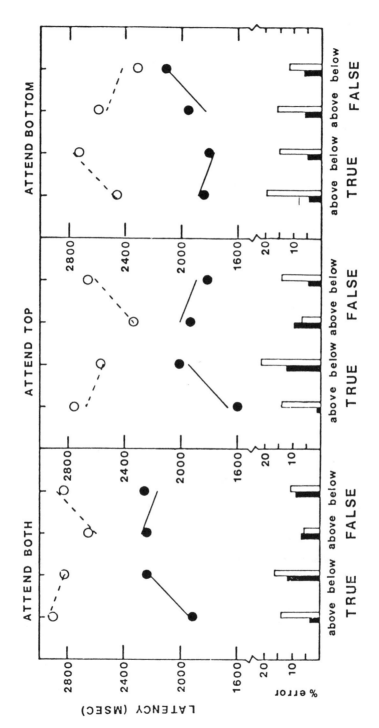

FIG. 9.5 Data from Experiment III of Clark and Chase (1972).

Table 2

Parameter Estimates (msec) from the Clark and Chase Experiments

			Below time $\underline{a}$	Mismatch time $\underline{c}$	Negation time $(\underline{b} + \underline{d})$	Translation time $\underline{e}$
Clark & Chase (1972)						
	Exp. I	Sentence First	93	187	685	-
	Exp. II	Sentence First	106	104	608	-
		Picture First	128	91	504	212
	Exp. III	Attend Both	111	147	643	140
		Attend Top	110	115	743	261
		Attend Bottom	30	173	594	187
Clark & Chase (1974)						
	Exp. II	Attend Star	96	42	531	146
		Attend Top	137	129	748	-
	Exp. III	Sentence First	136	155	671	80
		Mean	105	127	636	171
		Standard Deviation	32.5	44.9	85.6	63.1

above" to "A is below." So we instructed our subjects to convert the sentences before they ever look at the picture. Another transformation we told them to do was to get rid of "below," so, if it said "A is below," make it "A isn't above" and then check the picture. That's Transformation 3. Transformation 4 is if it says "A is below" make it "B is above."

Well, this worked out much better than we expected. Figure 9.6 shows the data for one subject. Our model handled these data extremely well. This transformation—getting rid of a negative or getting rid of "below"—turned out to take about 250 msec.

These studies illustrate the power of the additive factors and of the subtractive technique approach. I am confident that we are measuring the speed of some fundamental operations on propositions. Lexical marking takes about 100 msec. Proposition mismatch takes about 150 msec. That 600 msec on the negative can be broken down into about 250 or 300 msec to set up a negative proposition (*b*) and another 250 to 300 msec to process it during a comparison stage (*d*). Further, people have conscious control over these mental structures, and they can translate those sentences from one form to another. We can measure the time it takes them to do the translation. Under the conditions of our experiment, it took them about 200 msec to get rid of a negative in a sentence or get rid of the word *below* in a sentence.

9.4 THE QUANTIFICATION PROCESS

The next area I would like to talk about is quantification. Figure 9.7 summarizes one experiment. It is representative of a large class of experiments on subitizing (Chi & Klahr, 1975). This task is simply, given N objects, name how many objects are there. Researchers say there are two processes that people

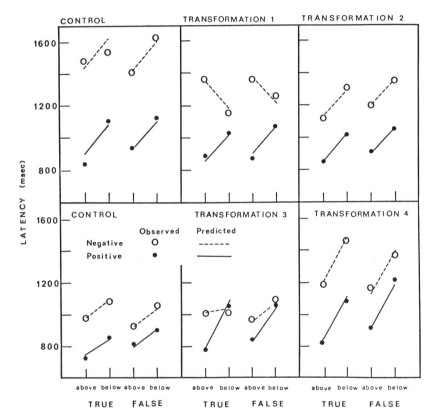

FIG. 9.6   Data of a single subject of the Young and Chase experiment. The top three panels are data from the negative > positive transformations (Experiment I) and the bottom three panels are data from the *below* > above transformations (Experiment II). The two panels on the left are data from a control condition in which subjects were instructed not to perform any conscious transformations. (From Young & Chase, 1971.)

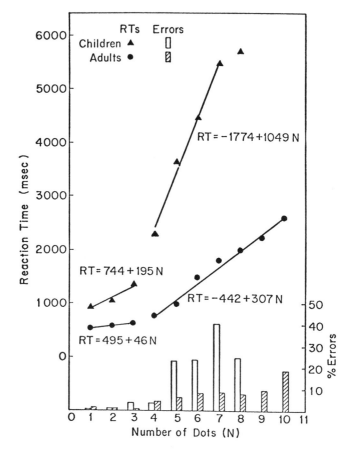

FIG. 9.7   Quantification latencies of 5-year-olds and adults for configurations of random dot patterns. Error percentages are also shown at the bottom. The best-fitting straight lines are shown for the subitizing range ($n = 1 - 3$) and the grouping, subitizing, and adding range ($n > 3$). (From Chi, M. T. H. & Klahr, D., Span and rate of apprehension in children and adults. *Journal of Experimental Child Psychology,* 1975, *19,* 434–439. Copyright 1975 by Academic Press. Reprinted by permission.)

use to quantify. One process is simply to count. However, if the number of objects is small enough, people seem to be able to name that quantity without counting. So there is some unknown process that has been labeled *subitizing* that arrives at the quantity without counting. Researchers have made some speculations about properties of the subitizing process: that it is a high-speed serial search and the slope of that line measures the speed of it. I am not sure that this is true, but there is no question that there is some sort of serial process going on here. The upper curve in the figure presents data on children; the lower curve, data on adults. There is a break somewhere around three or four objects, where people have to resort to another process. Children are counting. This process in adults is obviously some combination of grouping and adding or grouping and enumeration. The steeper slope of the line above three or four objects is the measure of that serial process.

I'll show you some data in which we have been able actually to measure the speed of this iterative process, call it *successive subitizing and adding* (Atkin & Chase, 1978). The subjects are shown some blocks (Fig. 9.8) and have to state the number of blocks. Akin and I tried to measure the speed of the iterative process by which people claim to arrive at the number. So we collected data on quantification latencies as a function of the number of objects. We did it on individual subjects to avoid averaging artifacts. These data in Fig. 9.9 are on individual subjects. The top figures are nine subjects who more or less subitized up to three and then started grouping at four. See how neatly the individual curves break at four items. Off to the right is the group average, which also breaks at four items. Then we had three subjects (shown on the bottom) who were able to subitize up to four items and then above four they were grouping and adding, so we replicated that old finding pretty well.

In addition, we asked our subjects to tell us how they did it. Then we recomputed reaction times contingent on how many groups subjects reported that they used. These data are plotted in Fig. 9.10. We manipulated structural variables like compactness, symmetry, linearity, and planarity. Planarity is how many planes did the blocks lie in. Compactness was measured by how many

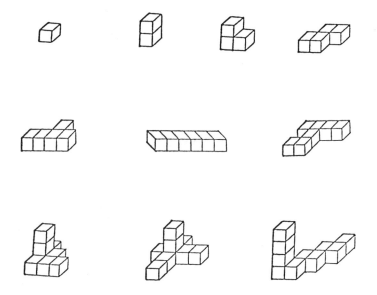

FIG. 9.8   Examples of block configurations from the quantification task of Akin and Chase (1978).

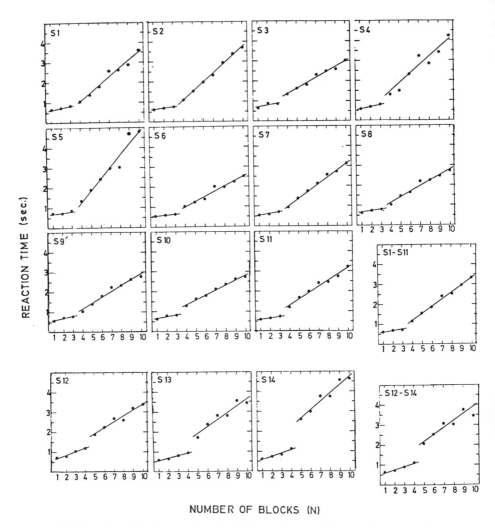

NUMBER OF BLOCKS (N)

FIG. 9.9 Quantification latencies of individual subjects for block configurations. The best-fitting straight lines are shown for the subitizing range separately. The group data are also shown separately for those subjects who subitized over the range $n = 1 - 3$ (S1 to S11) and those who subitized over the range $n = 1 - 4$ (S12 to S14). (From Akin & Chase, 1978.)

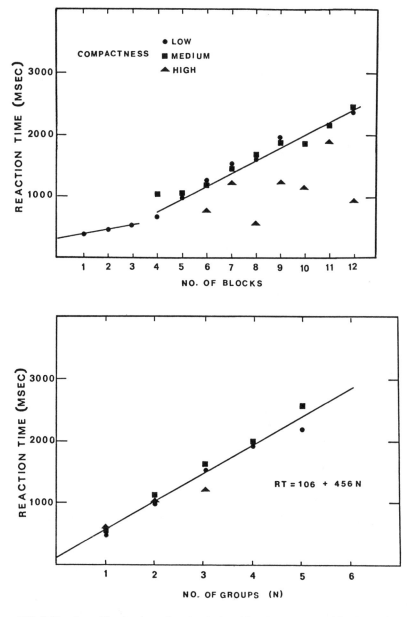

FIG. 9.10   Quantification latencies of a single subject from the quantification task of Akin and Chase (1976). Latencies are plotted both as a function of number of blocks (top) and number of reported groups (bottom). The circles, squares, and triangles refer to block configurations that were high, medium, or low compact, respectively. The best-fitting regression lines in the upper graph do not include the high-compactness configurations.

adjacent faces there are relative to the maximum possible faces. So if you find eight blocks in a cube, that's the highest compactness you can get. You can imagine that processing that configuration would be faster. Compactness was a very powerful variable. Here the data are plotted on top as a function of number of blocks. It is linear, more or less, except for those highly compact blocks. This lowest triangle is the highly compact 2 X 2 X 2 cube that seems to lie on the subitizing function. When we replot the data, not as a function of the number of blocks but as a function of number of reported groups on the bottom, we come out with a much nicer function. The noise caused by compactness goes away, and the slope here is about 500 msec for this one subject. Other subjects were about 1000 msec per group, but the data were every bit as clean as this, or better.

So we were able, by combining the subtractive technique with the use of verbal reports, to isolate and measure a mental process that admittedly has some subprocesses imbedded in it. Now we can study that process.

I now discuss quantification in children. Perhaps you are aware of the Groen and Parkman model (Groen & Parkman, 1972), but even if not you probably know how kids count. When you say "What is 5 plus 3?" at a certain point, sometimes they will go "five," pause, "one, two, three, four, five," pause, "six, seven, eight." But very soon they will go "five," pause, "six, seven, eight." You can sometimes actually see them moving their fingers. After awhile, they will stop counting on their fingers but implicitly they will take the larger number and count upward by the smaller number. That's the so-called "min" model. Reaction time should be a function of the smaller or minimum of two digits.

The data are shown in Fig. 9.11 The lower line is Groen and Parkman's regression line. The upper line is the regression line I find when I recomputed it after taking out the ties. There are two things going on here. Something else is going on with 0 + 0, 1 + 1, 2 + 2, 3 + 3, and 4 + 4. So if you remove the ties, you can fit a regression line through the rest of the points and you come up with a slope of about 400 msec.

In this figure I am plotting the minimum, the smaller of the two digits in the problem. The theory says that if you start counting upward from the larger number with the smaller, then reaction time should be a function of how many counts you do. Let me give you an example. What is 8 plus 1? 8—9. You just do one count. What is 2 plus 1? 2—and 1 is 3. One count again. 5 plus 3 is 5, 6, 7, 8—three counts. And so on. So all I am doing is conditionalizing these reaction times on the smaller digit. This is pretty good evidence in my mind that first-grade children are internally counting.

Now I'll throw this in just to confuse you. In Fig. 9.12 are adult data (Parkman & Groen, 1971). These are problems like "4 plus 3 equals 7, true or false?" We plot reaction time as a function of the smaller digit. Plotted this way, the data show a slope of about 20 msec. I don't seriously believe that

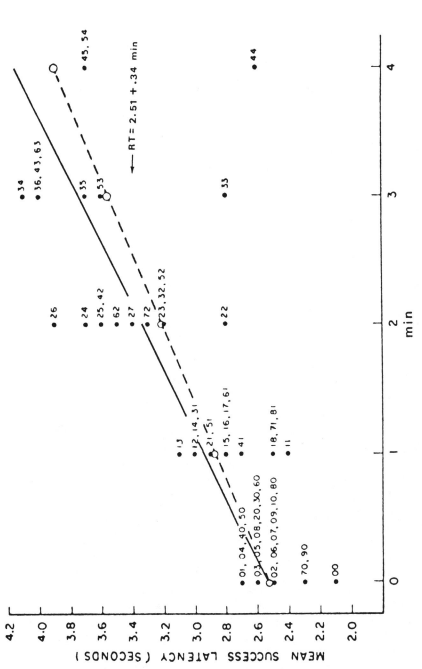

FIG. 9.11 Addition latencies for first-graders as a function of the smaller addend. The pair of numbers adjacent to each point are the two addends for each individual problem. The dotted line is the best-fitting regression line including the ties, and the solid line excludes the ties. (Adapted from Groen, G. J. & Parkman, J. M., A chronometric analysis of simple addition. *Psychological Review*, 1972, *79*, 329–343. Copyright 1972 by the American Psychological Association. Adapted with permission.)

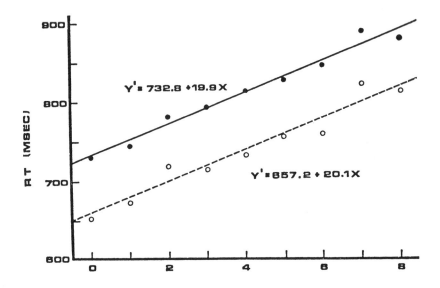

FIG. 9.12   Addition latencies for adults as a function of the smaller addend. Best-fitting regression lines are shown separately for the true responses (for example, 5 + 3 = 9). (From Parkman, J. M. & Groen, G. J., Temporal aspects of simple addition and comparison. *Journal of Experimental Psychology,* 1971, *89,* 335–342. Copyright 1971 by the American Psychological Association. Reprinted by permission.)

adults count at the rate of 20 msec per count. There is other evidence that adults don't implicitly count, but it is an interesting example of how a process like this generative process can affect the structure of semantic memory; that is, when people first learn to add as children, they use this counting mechanism, and this mechanism determines how semantic memory for sums is formed. In other words, I believe that what adults are doing is scanning into some number table and using the smaller digit as an index.

In Fig. 9.13 are data on subtraction, and this is on second-graders (Wood, Resnick, & Groen, 1975). Most 7-year-old kids subtract two ways. The smarter kids will do addition or subtraction, whichever is faster, and the ones that aren't so smart will just do subtraction. There are two ways to do "9 minus 8." One is to do "nine," pause, "eight, seven, six, five, four, three, two, one," to iterate eight times and count down. But there is another way to do this, "9 minus 8, well that's one because if I add 8 to 1, that is 9." So the smarter kids will either decrement or increment, whichever is faster, and the slower kids do brute force decrementing. In Fig. 9.13 are data on these two groups of kids. The top figure is the six kids who did brute force decrementing and the bottom figure is the 30 kids who either decremented or incremented, whichever is faster. There is no doubt in my mind that we are measuring the speed of this iterative process or generative process and that it clicks off at the rate of about 480 msec a count.

I wanted to make another point here in passing. Notice that the slower kids iterate at the same rate as the smart kids: the slopes are 480 msec per count in both cases. In other words, the speed of this basic process is just as fast for slower kids as smarter kids. What do smart kids do? They don't process any faster; they reorganize their processing. You see, this is one of many examples I've seen in the literature where skill or intelligence is reflected not in processing faster but in organizing tasks so that you can save time. These kids are chopping off several seconds worth of processing on problems by very cleverly changing the nature of the task. But again, by means of the subtractive technique, we were able to isolate and measure the speed of mental processing.

I've tried to summarize the literature in Table 9.3 (p. 246). This table illustrates several quantification tasks as a function of age groups so you can observe the developmental trend in these quantification processes. The first three columns are addition, subtraction, and open sentence problems. Open sentence problems, such as "5 + ? = 8" are really not much different than a subtraction problem. These first three columns are measuring pretty much the same generative counting process described earlier. The last two columns are the counting process and the subitizing process from the quantification literature. I think that our understanding of mental arithmetic, at least mental arithmetic in children, has benefitted from an analysis of mental processing.

9.5 DISCUSSION

AUDIENCE: In the subtraction experiment with children, the smart kids apparently have to do one more process first to decide which strategy to use. The slower kids apparently don't have to do anything.

CHASE: Well, Groen and Parkman (1972) had several explanations as to why kids knew which strategy to use without knowing the answer. One is you do both in parallel. You do both decrementing and incrementing at the same time and whichever strategy finishes first yields the answer. That's one explanation. The other is that kids know from past experience when they see a pair which strategy to use, so that knowledge is already in memory.

POSNER: Do you want to comment on Carpenter and Just's (1975) effort to develop a simple mental operation for the sentence-picture verification task?

CHASE: Yes. Maybe I should go back to these data and say that we have three parameters here. We have an above/below parameter, a positive/negative parameter, and a match/mismatch parameter. What Carpenter and Just noticed was that the four points involving true versus false and positive versus negative sentences seem to fall on a straight line, and people seem to be doing the same thing when they do match/mismatch as they do

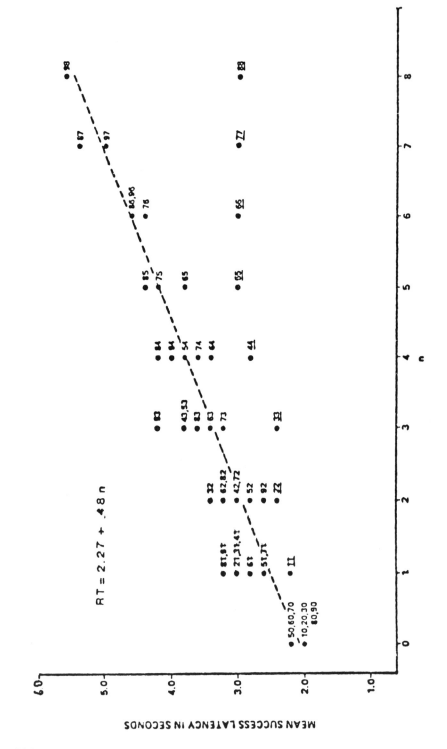

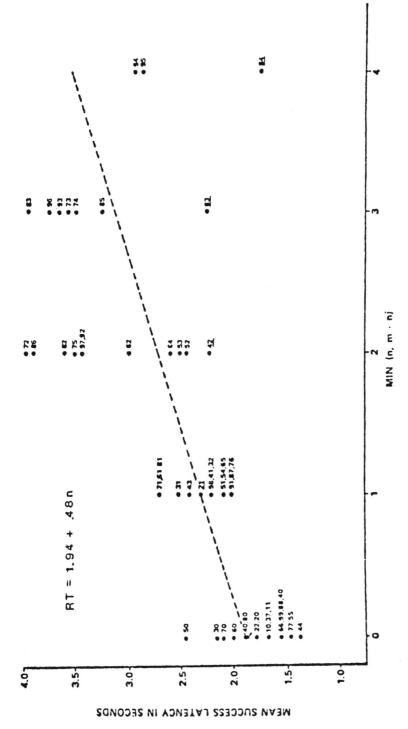

FIG. 9.13 Subtraction latencies of second graders as a function of the smaller addend (top) for six children who used the inefficient strategy and as a function of the *min* for 30 children who used the efficient strategy. The numbers (m, n) to the right of each point identify each problem $(m - n = ?)$. The best-fitting regression lines are shown for each group. (From Woods, S. S., Resnick, L. B., & Groen, G. J., An experimental test of five process models for subtraction. *Journal of Educational Psychology*, 1975, *67*, 17–21. Copyright 1975 by the American Psychological Association. Adapted by permission.)

245

Table 3

Parameters from Quantification and Mental Arithmetic[*]

	Addition	Subtraction	Open Sentence Problems	Counting	Subitizing
			(msec/count)		
Kindergarten				1049	195
Beginning First Grade	710		1400		
Late First Grade	400				
Second Grade		480	410	600	
Third Grade	355				
Fourth Grade		270			
Adults	20			300	25-100

[*]Parameter values are taken from:

   Column 1

     Suppes & Groen (1967)

     Groen & Parkman (1972)

     Svenson (1975)

     Parkman & Groen (1971)

   Column 2

     Woods, Resnick & Groen (1975)

   Column 3

     Groen & Poll (1973)

   Column 4

     Chi & Klahr (1975)

     Beckweth & Restle (1966)

   Column 5

     Chi & Klahr (1975)

with positive/negative comparisons. They were able to devise a different theory of how people represent pictures and a different comparison process. They had to invent a different comparison process and they were able to account for these data with one less parameter. I think that is a beautiful example of how science should go, but I think they are wrong in principle. In their model, there is just the one comparison process, and no matter what you compare, it takes the same time. That has to be wrong.

Let me make another comment. It points out a fundamental problem with this research. We have nice theories of the processing in a particular task, but we don't have a theory of control structure that says how the process should be organized. If we had a general theory like ACT or LNR theory that could tell us how a person organizes his mental processes when he attacks this task, then we wouldn't face these problems. The theory about how a sentence is represented and how the corresponding processing is organized seems to rely mostly on the ingenuity of the experimenters.

DONCHIN: I'm wondering what would happen—I'm sure this must have been done—but if you forced the subject to perform the task in 1000 msec, what would happen to the data? How would the variables interact, and would you get all these individual factors also? The reaction times appear very long.

CHASE: If you forced them to respond in 1000 msec? Well, let's say 2000, so we would get half the data, but drop off half the data. In other words, they wouldn't have time to process negative sentences. What would happen? Statistically some of the time they would be able to do it and some of the time they wouldn't. So you would have a mixture of a couple of processes, one where they would be doing the task quickly, and others when they just press a button at random and that produces statistical mixtures.

DONCHIN: You are assuming they have to do it this way. And if you don't give them enough time, they will have no other way of doing it?

CHASE: Another interesting question is what if you didn't make it a reaction-time task.

DONCHIN: But suppose you force them to do it very rapidly and they don't have 2600 msec. Do you think there is no strategy by which the subjects can perform the task? Perhaps your structure is the one used when subjects have no time restrictions.

CHASE: Well, when you have all the time in the world, you convert the negative sentences to positive. That is something very pervasive. In other words, when I say "plus isn't above star," that means that the plus must be below the star. And they will leisurely convert negative sentences into a positive form. There is lots of that stuff in the literature.

What would they do under speeded condition? You would see the errors going up to 100% and this model would just break down.

You have raised a side issue that I have something to say about, and that issue is if there is indeed evidence that errors and latencies are under the control of different mechanisms. That occurred to me earlier when you were discussing dissociations of latencies and ERPs. Sternberg had some data on this issue. In a memory-search paradigm, if you give subjects the list twice, or three times rather than once, the errors are systematically reduced but it has no effect whatsoever on the latencies. It's as if there is a process that scans memory, but the speed of that process does not depend on the quality of information in memory, but the probability of making an error does. There is other evidence in these memory-scanning types of tasks that suggests that errors and latencies are not perfectly correlated.

10 Report of Panel IV: Mental Chronometry

Panel chair: W. Chase

Panel members: G. McCarthy
K. Squires
R. Schvaneveldt

10.1 INTRODUCTION

CHASE: Cognitive psychologists attend a conference like this because they are interested in finding out what physiological psychology can offer psychology. Without a doubt, the two "physiological" research programs that had the greatest impact on concepts in psychology are the single-unit recordings of Hubel and Wiesel (1962) and the split-brain studies of Sperry and Gazzaniga (Sperry, 1961). For better or worse, cognitive theory has been influenced greatly by these physiological investigations. The question that is at the core of this panel's assignment is, how can ERP research contribute to our understanding of physiological mechanisms and cognitive processes? It's quite obvious by now that electrophysiological research does have a lot to say about cognitive processes. For example, before coming to this conference I thought that filter theory was a dead issue. But it is clear from Hillyard's work that the N100 does have something to do with attention. From Donchin's work it is clear that something interesting is happening with respect to expectancy and P300.

So on what issues will electrophysiological research have an impact? As Shiffrin said, from a chronometric point of view we definitely need a physiological model of reaction time. Research on the ERP can tell us what the physiological mechanisms of reaction time are. There is no question that ERP research can help in changing our ideas about attention. There are ideas about limited capacity mechanisms. I think that as cognitive psychologists we believe that we are measuring limited capacity mechanisms, and I am sure that ERP research can tell us more about that. I personally think that the propositional versus analog issue is not irresolvable even though some of my best friends, whom I respect greatly, say it's irresolvable. Are there measurable central nervous system events that underlie mental imagery, for example? A very nebulous issue, what's the nature of the engram; that is, how is memory organized? What's the system's architecture? What are the physiological correlates of short-term memory and long-term memory? And, last but not least, surely physiological research can tell us something about all these mental processes that we've been measuring for the past few years.

One puzzling aspect of the ERP data is that so little is known about events that correspond in time to the complex processes in which cognitive psychologists are interested. When we talk about complex processes, we generally mean postperceptual processes. But there is only a beginning of work on endogenous components that appear at about the right time. Something may be happening at P165. Ritter's data suggest that the N200 component is involved in some of the early cognitive processing. The bulk of the work is centered around the P300. But the P300 has too short a latency to serve in the interpretation of complex processing. What do we see beyond P300? Well, there are some slow waves, but the relation to cognitive activity is not clear. No one has started from the data on complex processing and looked for corresponding ERP components that have a latency longer than the P300. I'm sure that they will be found if searched for in the right way. As a cognitive psychologist I do wonder. How come electrophysiologists have not looked beyond P300? Well, I believe that the data base will expand and keep growing. The status of ERP research reminds me of the status of mental chronometry 15 years ago. When Sternberg's (1966) paper came out, everybody was excited because it provided an objective way of measuring mental events and the area just exploded, and the data swamped our capabilities and the theory is just now catching up. Well I think the ERP area is another area like this. Here is a methodology for measuring mental events. And the reason we ask how come we haven't discovered anything is because there just isn't much done here.

Our panel reviewed the data base and the first two presentations, by Squires and McCarthy, will introduce these data.

In passing we'll take a look at some of the substantial methodological issues. There is a danger of getting bogged down in them; yet I think that most of the cognitive people in the group would like to take a look at some of these issues. We have a roomful of cognitive people who are experts in reaction time and the corresponding methodological traps, but when you go into ERPs, you have a brand new area. The first thing you want to know is how to measure latencies from trial to trial when you can't get a nice waveform unless you do averaging. When do you decide if a peak is the P300? What do you measure from? If you believe that the P300 is an important cognitive event, where do you measure? Do you measure the amplitude, the onset of the deepest part of the slope? Does the hidden peak in other slow waves distort the P300?

Following that we'll look at some issues in cognitive psychology that have a bearing on ERP research. I'll review this area, then I'll turn it over to Roger Schvaneveldt, who will comment on inferences that can be made from the data base. We'll look at the idea of additive factors as alternative ways of looking at latencies.

10.2 THE LATENCY OF P300

K. SQUIRES: In one of the early studies of the P300 component, Sutton, Braren, Zubin, and John (1967) noted that the latency of that component varied as a function of the timing of an informative cue. Since then a number of studies have been conducted to investigate the relationships between the timing of mental processes and the electrophysiological and behavioral manifestations of such processes. In this presentation I review some of the approaches taken in the electrophysiological study of mental chronometry. I have arbitrarily limited myself, for the most part, to studies conducted outside of Champaign, Illinois. Dr. McCarthy will then discuss the approach taken in the Cognitive Psychophysiology Laboratory at the University of Illinois.

One approach to the study of evoked potentials in relation to cognitive processing utilizes feedback stimuli that provide information regarding the correctness of a preceding decision. In such a procedure, a stimulus that is fixed in its physical characteristics can provide widely varying amounts of information depending on the prior decision. For instance, in one such study subjects performed an intensity discrimination with a six-point confidence rating as to which of two equiprobable stimuli was presented (Squires, K.C., Hillyard, & Lindsay, 1973a). A red feedback light informed the subject that the louder of the two signals had occurred and a green light informed that the softer of the two signals had occurred. Thus, in some instances the red light indicated to the subjects that they were correct, and in other, it indicated that they were wrong.

A highly systematic pattern of P300 latencies was obtained: A highly confirming feedback elicited a short-latency P300 component, whereas highly disconfirming feedback elicited a long-latency P300 component.

Campbell, Courchesne, Picton, and Squires, K.C. (1979) studied this phenomenon in more detail and noted that although the P300 latency was not a function of the specific nature of the feedback (confirming or disconfirming), it was highly correlated with probability that a given feedback stimulus would occur giving the subjects confidence in the prior decision. They suggested that the P300 latency variation might represent the differing amounts of time required to process stimuli carrying various degrees of information. Alternatively, the latency variation might reflect a sequential perceptual process that considers more probable possibilities before less probable ones.

KAHNEMAN: If this is latency to peak, is it correlated with P300 amplitude? That is, is the order of the conditions by P300 latency and by P300 magnitude the same?

K. SQUIRES: Yes, it is. In this paradigm longer latencies are associated with larger amplitudes. This is not always the case, however. For instance, if one were to examine evoked potentials elicited by threshold-level auditory stimuli in a signal-detection task, the shortest-latency P300 components, which are associated with highest confidence decisions, are also the largest in amplitude (Kerkhof, 1978; Squires, K.C., Hillyard, & Lindsay, 1973b). Thus, there is not a fixed relationship between P300 amplitude and latency. In terms of mental chronometry, however, the results obtained from signal-detection studies are consistent because it is likely that distinctly heard signals are processed more rapidly than those perceived less distinctly.

Picton, Hillyard, and Galambos (1976, A & B) also noted in an omitted-stimulus paradigm that P300 latency increased with increasing interstimulus interval in concert with increasing reaction times. Yet, when latency variability was taken into account by measuring the "area" of the P300 component rather than peak amplitude, there was no change in the size of the P300 component. Thus, although the timing of the cognitive process indexed by the P300 component varied with interstimulus interval, the nature of the process apparently did not.

As a final example, Posner and associates (Posner, Klein, Summers, & Buggie, 1973) reported that in a letter-matching task the P300 component for matching letters was both larger and earlier than for mismatching letters.

Manipulation of task difficulty is a second approach to the study of mental chronometry. Ritter, Simson, and Vaughan (1972) required subjects to detect an occasional pitch change in an auditory vigilance task. Two levels of task difficulty were tested: one in which the pitch change was easy to detect, and one in which the pitch change was much more difficult to discriminate. The P300 latency was found to increase with increasing task difficulty, as was the latency of the N200 component preceding it. Reaction times also increased with increased task difficulty, with the reation time preceding the P300 peak latency by approximately 20 msec at both levels of task difficulty. Perhaps more important, a single-trial analysis of the data revealed a high correlation between P300 latency and spontaneous changes in reaction time. A reanalysis of the data (Ritter, Simson, & Vaughan, 1979) further revealed that the N200 latency possibly correlated with reaction time better than did the P300 latency. They suggested that the reason P300 latency "can be used to assess the temporal occurrence of stimulus evaluation is because it is related in time to N2(00)."

Ford, Roth, and Kopell (1976) also noted that N200 as well as P300 latency increased with increasing task difficulty. They further noted that P300 latency was less affected by task difficulty than was reaction time.

In a second study by this group (Roth, Ford, & Kopell, 1978), spontaneous changes in reaction times were classified by quartiles and evoked potentials were averaged on the basis of those quartiles. The P300 latency was found to increase as a function of increasing reaction time. In this study, as in the previous one, the P300 peak always preceded the reaction time and the increase in P300 latency.

N. Squires, Donchin, K. Squires, and Grossberg (1977) studied the effects of task difficulty in both the auditory and visual modality. As expected, both P300 latency and reaction time increased with increasing task difficulty. Interestingly, when the auditory and visual tasks were matched in difficulty, as measured by reaction times, approximately equal P300 latencies were obtained for the two modalities.

The memory-matching paradigm of Sternberg (1969) has also been effectively used to investigate the timing of evoked potential latencies in relation to cognitive events. Marsh (1975) tested groups of young and old subjects in a Sternberg paradigm with set sizes of one, three, and five items. The latency of the P300 component increased by approximately 80 to 100 msec going from a set size of one to a set size of five. The reaction times also increased with increasing set size, by approximately 200 and 160 msec for the young subjects and old subjects, respectively.

Ford, Roth, Mohs, Hopkins, and Kopell (1979) also used a Sternberg paradigm to study young and old subjects. Their results indicated that although the P300 latency increase with set size was the same for young and old subjects (27 msec per item), the reaction time increase, which was greater than the P300 increase, varied with age, being 43 msec and 81 msec per item for young and old subjects, respectively.

Adam and Collins (1978) described two positive peaks, P270 and P350, both of which increased in latency with increasing set size in the Sternberg paradigm. For small set sizes the two components overlapped such that P350 dominated the waveform. However, the latency change with set size was slightly greater for P350 than for P270, so that they became separated at larger set sizes. Up to a set size of seven, the increase in P270 latency was 20.5 msec per item, and for P350 it was 22 msec per item. The slope of the reaction-time function, in contrast, was 38 msec per item. They suggest both components are related to the memory-search process, although alternatively only P270 may be involved, with the P350 component reflecting cognitive processes triggered by the termination of memory search.

In a similar memory-scanning task, Gomer, Spicuzza, and O'Donnell (1976) reported that the P300 latency increased at a rate of 5.5 and 6.3 msec per item for negative and positive instances. The corresponding reaction-time increases were 13.3 and 14.4 msec per item.

The preceding studies are consistent in reporting a correlation between the latency of the P300 (or similar) component and the behavioral reaction-time measure of processing speed. Yet it is clear that reaction times are affected by variables in addition to those affecting the P300 component, because reaction-time changes are uniformly greater than those for P300. Several other studies have also demonstrated marked dissociations between reaction times and P300 latency. Karlin, Martz, Brauth, and Mordkoff (1971), for instance, found little or no difference in P300 latencies when sorted according to reaction times.

Recently N. Squires et al. (1977) reported a study of evoked potentials elicited by bisensory stimuli. In that study each stimulus presentation consisted of a simultaneous auditory and visual stimulus from a quasirandom sequence of rare and frequent tones and flashes. The subjects' task was to attend to one or the other modality and count the rare stimuli in that modality. The result was that the P300 latency for each of the four types of stimulus pairs did not change as a function of changing the relevant modality; yet the reaction times did. There is, thus, a degree of dissociation between the two measures, suggesting that the P300 component is associated with a relatively early stage in processing leading up to the motor act. On the basis of this study, N. Squires et al. suggested that the P300 was correlated with a stage of stimulus evaluation, because it was fixed for each individual stimulus. The reaction time then depended on further processing that varied as a function of the task requirement.

10.3 STIMULUS EVALUATION TIME AND P300 LATENCY

McCARTHY: As a point of departure, I will argue that the studies that we and others have done suggest that the latency of P300 is labile to experimental manipulations that affect stimulus evaluation time but is relatively insensitive to manipulations that affect response selection and execution time. That's a very sweeping statement. I will review in this discussion some of the data that lead me to believe that the statement may be true.

I will describe the studies in the order in which they were conducted. In this way, some of the reasons for our actions may become evident. I will begin by describing an experiment performed at Illinois several years ago (Kutas, McCarthy, & Donchin, 1977; see also Kutas & Donchin, 1977).

The subjects viewed words presented on a visual display. There were several stimulus conditions: In one condition (called the *fixed-names condition*), two names, Nancy and David, were presented with unequal probabilities. In this case, the name David was presented on 20% of the trials and Nancy was presented on 80% of the trials. There was also a variable-names condition in which different males' and females' names were used, but the probability of seeing *any* male's name was still 20% and seeing any female's name was 80%; that is, the probabilities associated with the categories "male" and "female" names were still .20/.80. In another condition, 20% of the words were synonyms of the word *prod* (words like push, nudge, and shove), and the remaining 80% of the words were unrelated to prod, or to themselves.

There were several response conditions, all of which required the subjects to ascertain the category of the stimulus. In the counting condition, subjects were required to keep a mental count of the number of rare category items (i.e., how many Davids were presented, or males' names, or synonyms of prod) and report that count at the end of a block of trials. There were also two choice reaction-time conditions in which one hand was used to indicate the frequent category items and the other hand was used in response to the rare category items. In both RT conditions, subjects were asked to respond "as quickly as possible"—but they were also given instructions intended to manipulate their relative speed and accuracy. Under the accuracy regime, subjects were asked to try to avoid making errors; whereas, in the speed regime, subjects were asked to be very quick and to be relatively unconcerned about errors.

As you might expect, the fastest RTs were obtained in the fixed-names conditions, intermediate RTs were obtained for the variable names, and the synonym condition had the longest RTs. In both regimes the responses to the frequently presented category items were faster than those to the rare category items by an average of nearly 100 msec. Responses in the 'speed' regime were about 90 msec faster than responses in the 'accuracy' regime. This increase in speed, however, was obtained at a cost—more errors were committed. These errors were almost entirely committed by responding to the rare category items as if they were from the frequent category. The percentage of errors was 3% under the accuracy regime and 9% in the speed regime. The subjects were aware that they erred on these trials.

Large-amplitude P300 potentials were elicited by the rare category items (and to a lesser extent by the frequent category items). The latencies of the P300s in the averaged waveforms were ordered in the same way as the RTs. This relationship can be seen in Fig. 10.1 where the ERPs associated with the fixed names, variable names, and synonyms conditions for the rare and frequent items as a function of the three response conditions are shown. The latency of P300 is shortest in the fixed-names condition, intermediate in the variable-names condition. This is true for all three response conditions. P300 latency is longest in the synonyms condition when subjects count more events and when they respond under the accuracy regime. This relationship is not observed in the speed RT regime. Measurement of P300 latencies in the averaged waveform is complicated by the changes in the amplitude and duration or period of P300 that also occur in these waveforms. For example, in the count condition waveforms, P300 amplitude decreases as its latency increases. We were worried by these amplitude changes and wondered whether these amplitude changes were real or the result of increasing trial-by-trial variability in P300 latency for the variable names and synonym conditions. We therefore

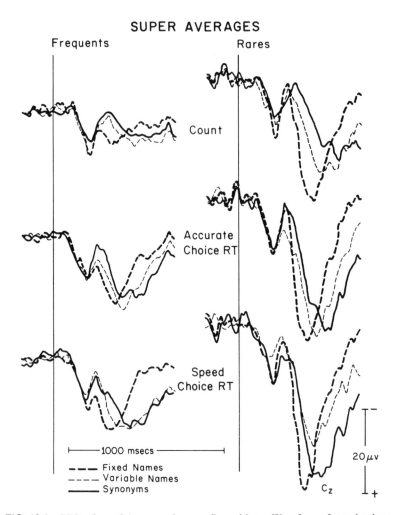

SUPER AVERAGES

FIG. 10.1   ERPs (from C_z) averaged across five subjects. Waveforms from the three categorization tasks (Fixed Names, Variable Names, and Synonyms) are superimposed for the Court, Accurate-RT, and Speed-RT response conditions. From Kutas and Donchin, 1977.

started experimenting with different techniques that adjust the data and eliminate trial to trial variability in latency.

At this point I digress to a brief discussion of the techniques we have used to this end. Keep in mind, however, our motives for engaging in these analyses, as I shall return to a fuller discussion of these data afterward. To determine if the amplitude differences were real or the result of differential latency "jitter," we attempted to identify the peak of P300 for each single trial and then time-shift each epoch so that all were aligned on P300. The resulting average is, to one approximation or another, latency-adjusted. This technique referred to by Donchin in Chapter 5 of this volume is a variant of the technique first described by Charles Woody (1967).

A cross-correlation (or cross-covariance) function is computed between each single-ERP epoch and a template of the component of interest. Usually the average of the single epochs is used as the initial template. The cross correlation function is usually obtained over a restricted region of the epoch (the "search subepoch"). This range must be large enough to contain the time-varying component of interest while it must be narrow enough to exclude other components. The time shift at which the template best matches the single-trial record (i.e., the maximum of the cross-correlation or covariance function) is used as an estimate of the latency to peak of the component in the trial in question. After estimates are obtained for each trial, the data are aligned by the latency estimates and reaveraged. This new average is used as another approximation to the template. Another iteration through the trials is conducted, from which another adjusted average will result. We keep iterating until a stopping rule is met (we monitor the average of the best fit cross-correlations until a plateau is reached; that usually happens within 2-3 iterations).

This is the structure of the latency adjustment technique. To make the discussion more concrete I've prepared an example using simulated data. My intention here is to clarify problems and assumptions so that the resolution of the technique can be assessed. To create my data I used a third-order autoregressive process to make "EEG" with a spectrum as shown in Fig. 10.2. This spectrum is reasonable for EEG with a lot of low-frequency power, a peak at about 10 Hz, and a fairly swift drop in power down to about 20 Hz. I took 100 epochs from this EEG and added a simulated P300 to each. This ersatz P300 was a half sine wave with a 400-msec duration (1.25 Hz). The peak amplitude of this "P300" was about half the peak-to-peak amplitude of the background EEG, which is a pretty favorable signal-to-noise ratio. The P300 latencies were randomly distributed over a 900-msec range. In Fig. 10.3, we see the raw average of these 100 epochs. The average P300 is smeared across the epoch by latency variability. In Fig. 10.4 are some of the individual epochs that are really quite nasty looking. There is a quite large P300 in each epoch but you would be hard-pressed to find it in some of these "trials." In part, this is due to the high-frequency activity—say in the 10-Hz or alpha range—and this was my plan. Large-amplitude rhythmic activity is deadly for techniques based upon cross-correlation. You may end up just aligning peaks of alpha activity. So the first thing to do is to filter the data digitally to remove such activity. One can filter out alpha waves when looking for P300s because P300 is much slower than alpha. This is not the case for other components like N100, which is closer in frequency to alpha. In Fig. 10.5 I show the same epochs as before but now filtered to remove the 10-Hz activity. The picture is considerably im-

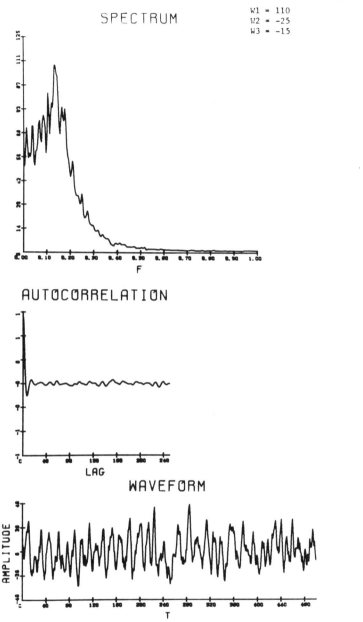

FIG. 10.2 The power spectrum and autocorrelation function for a segment of a time series created by a third order autoregressive process used to stimulate EEG noise. The frequence scale (F) for the power spectrum should be multiplied by 50 for the time base used in the example.

258

FILTERED AVERAGE

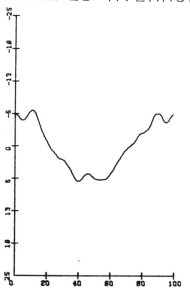

-3dB at 6.28 Hz

UNFILTERED AVERAGE

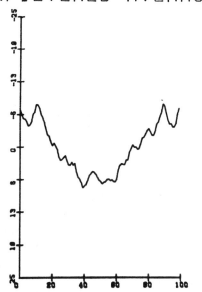

FIG. 10.3   Average of 100 epochs of stimulated EEG noise and P300 signal before application of latency adjustment technique. In the upper figure, the waveform has been low pass filtered to 6.28 Hz (− 3dB).

Woody Simulation Run - Unfiltered "Single trials"

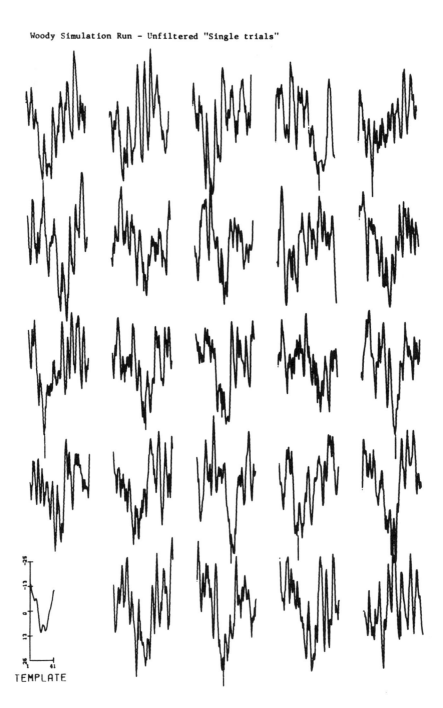

TEMPLATE

FIG. 10.4   A sample of unfiltered simulated EEG noise epochs with the P300 signal added.

260

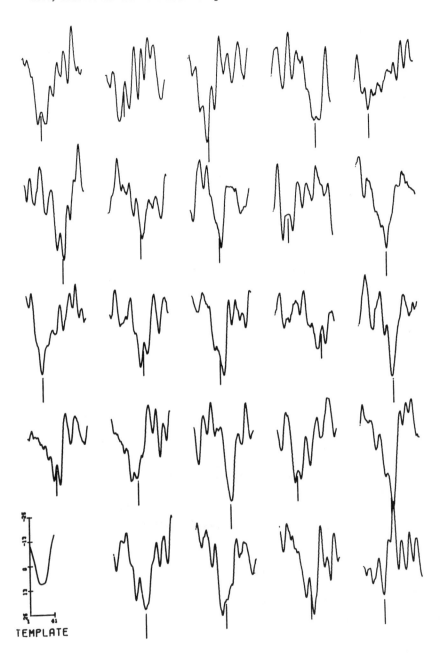

TEMPLATE

FIG. 10.5   The same epochs as in Fig. 10.4, but low pass filtered to 6.28 Hz (− 3dB). The vertical lines for each waveform indicate where the latency adjustment technique 'found' the simulated P300 signal.

proved and some P300s are now evident to the eye. Just to show you how similar these phony data look to real data, I have filtered epochs from a real experiment in Fig. 10.6. These data are from one subject. On the left of the figure are waveforms elicited by rare [P(20)] males' names stimuli, whereas on the right are waveforms elicited by frequent [P(80)] females' names stimuli. Many of the waveforms elicited by the males' names are marked by P300-looking components, and the waveforms elicited by the females' names are not.

In Fig. 10.7 is the result of the analysis performed on the simulated data. What you see is exactly what I put into the waveforms and the resulting latency distribution is almost exactly that which I used in creating the data. This is not surprising, given the favorable signal-to-noise ratio. The correlation between the estimated and the actual latencies is high (.97). However, in Fig. 10.8 is the result of the analysis performed on data in which the 10-Hz activity was not filtered out. As you can see, we now have an N1, P2, N2, P3, and P4 in the latency-adjusted average. These are spurious, of course, the result of locking peaks together.

HILLYARD: What would a final average waveform look like if you had not salted the EEG with the phony P300s, and just applied the Woody technique to the EEG itself?

McCARTHY: I didn't do that with these data but I have done it in the past. You will find an enhanced peak. The latency histogram will look rectangular over the search subepoch because the peaks will be distributed randomly in time. The P300 investigator using this technique must realize that there is no automatic way to verify that the results are valid. You verify your results experimentally. One possibility is to examine the resulting latency histogram. If the latency estimates are randomly distributed over your search subepoch, one should doubt the results. You can (as we do) examine the signal-to-noise ratio with each iteration. If it does not improve, you are probably measuring spurious peaks. You can also examine the mean correlation of the single epochs with the template.

SHIFFRIN: How do you deal with the cases when, say, half the trials have P300s in them and half don't?

McCARTHY: The latency analysis procedure is based on several assumptions. One is that a P300 is present on every trial elicited by the rare, relevant stimuli. Another assumption is that the waveform of P300 is consistent across trials—its onset slope doesn't vary, for example. I've looked at hundreds of single trials to get some feel if these assumptions are tenable, but you cannot know with certainty because the P300s are summate with the EEG, and there

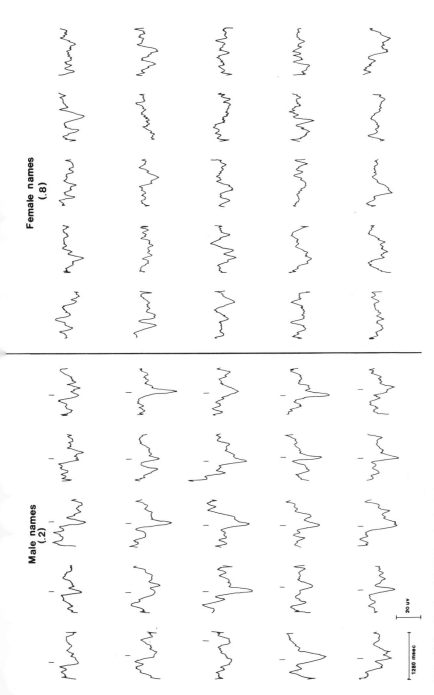

FIG. 10.6 Single trial ERPs obtained from one subject. The waveforms on the left were elicited by the presentations of low probability (p = 0.2) males' names, while the waveforms on the right were elicited by high probability (p = 0.8) females' names. The vertical lines above the waveforms on the left indicate the latency of P300 as determined by the latency adjustment algorith. From Donchin and McCarthy, 1980.

Woody Simulation, Solution for filtered data

LATENCY ADJUSTED

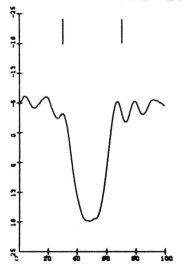

LATENCY HISTOGRAM

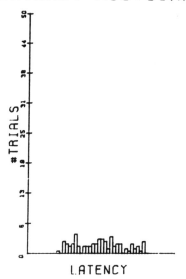

LATENCY

MEAN LATENCY (MSEC FROM ISTIM)= 500.1
MEAN LATENCY (ABS PT)= 50.0
MEAN CORRELATION= 0.656

FIG. 10.7   The latency corrected average and latency histogram produced by the latency adjustment procedure applied to the filtered signal plus noise epochs.

Woody Simulation, Solution for unfiltered **data**

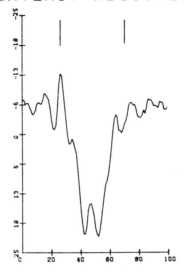

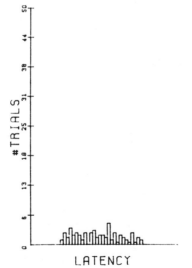

FIG. 10.8.   The latency corrected average and latency histogram produced by the latency adjustment procedure applied to signal plus noise epochs.

MEAN LATENCY (MSEC FROM ISTIM) = 460.3
MEAN LATENCY (ABS PT) = 46.0
MEAN CORRELATION= 0.609

is much low-frequency power in the EEG. One hope is that intracranial recordings of P300 will give us a much better signal-to-noise ratio and we shall have a good idea of its actual waveshape on single trials. Right now, however, we have latency estimates and distributions. We can look for components of the latency distributions or in the distribution of correlations between single epochs and templates. Woody suggested rank-ordering the epochs on the basis of correlation with the template and averaging high- and low-correlation epochs to search for systematic differences among trials. It is important to remember that this technique is not perfect, and demands caution in interpreting what comes out in the end.

HILLYARD: Isn't there an inherent confound between the mean latency of the peak that the Woody filter technique identifies and the signal-to-noise ratio? With a lower signal-to-noise ratio, you will be picking up more noise and hence the mean peak latency will tend toward the mean of the total epoch.

McCARTHY: Absolutely, a good signal-to-noise ratio is prerequisite. We routinely calculate the S-N ratio for each iteration. We've also experimented with ways of eliminating single trials that match the template poorly so as to make the template independent of them. You can try some sort of cluster analysis of the single trials to find those that are quite dissimilar.

KUTAS: Greg, on the whole, is it true that if you could plot all the trials, if you had that time and you wanted to look at all of them, most of the ones that would be well-picked by the technique are also ones that you can see with the eye? If you can't see it with the eye, then the technique isn't really helping you all that much either.

McCARTHY: Yes, but we are dealing with thousands of trials.

KUTAS: The point was more in terms of just checking— knowing that you can take samples of the data and see what percentage of the trials are chosen accurately. A large percentage of the trials don't seem to have any sort of evoked response to them at all.

McCARTHY: That is true, and is why the studies I will describe have taken much time. You have to look at hundreds of trials to determine if we are measuring the signal of interest.

DONCHIN: Well, one of the fortunate aspects of the situation is that the bandwidth of the noise does not overlap by much the bandwidth of the P300. You can filter most of the noise activity and still the P300 remains. The signal has most of its energy below 1 Hz, as compared with most EEG which has most of its activity over 4, between 4 and 12 maybe. So you can filter quite tightly.

McCARTHY: You want to get rid of large amplitude, rhythmic activity which will result in high correlation or covariance when matched in the template and the single epoch.

One unexpected bonus, though, is that by aligning single trials by P300 you may enhance other components which are temporally synchronized to P300 and not to the stimulus. Sometimes it seems as if we are enhancng N200 when latency-adjusting for P300.

SHIFFRIN: I think I missed something here. If you've got two components—an N200 and a P300—and you apply this Woody technique, how can either one enhance the other?

McCARTHY: No, the nice thing about P300 and N200 is that they have different polarities. N200 would be negatively correlated with the peak of a P300 template. Two components of similar latency and period would be a problem of course. You don't look over the entire waveform.

RITTER: Greg, I think I can answer it. The technique is averaging on the P300, but if N200 and P300 have a fairly constant time relationship between them then the N200 will be enhanced along with the P300.

McCARTHY: Two factors operate in our favor. We can specify the period of the component. The other is that we can restrict the search to a sub-epoch of the single trial to the segment where it is likely that the component will be in isolation from others. This is easiest for P300 which can occur at the end of an epoch. You can begin your search epoch just after the end of P200.

SHIFFRIN: Just one question. How far off can the initial template be?

McCARTHY: I have not studied this systematically but I feel that anything reasonable of the correct polarity will work if you iterate long enough.

FORD: Greg, does it change the results if you filter down to about 2 Hz?

McCARTHY: I don't filter to 2 Hz because it hasn't been necessary. I usually stop at about 5 or 6 Hz (-3 DB). What is missing is a well done study of the critical filtering parameters and the acceptable signal-to-noise ratios.

RITTER: Greg, is it not the case that if you just analyze the trials in which you could see the P300 with the eye you will get the same results? It may be faster than what you do "by hand," yet visual inspection may be more accurate.

McCARTHY: I just showed you a hundred trials and it was hard to pick out P300.

RITTER: Well, both Picton and I felt we could see P300 very easily in your data.

DONCHIN: It is not that easy to select the peak even when you've seen the P300. In visual analysis there is too much room for shifting by a few msec back and forth to suit your predilections.

McCARTHY: If a negative wave interrupts the peak of P300 on a single trial, it would be difficult to select the peak by eye.

PICTON: But you filter before your Woody analysis. You're going to have to give the eye the same breaks.

McCARTHY: I will now return to the data and to the question under consideration—that is, were there significant P300 amplitude effects in the categorization experiment? After latency adjustment for P300, no significant amplitude effects remained among the different categories of stimuli (fixed names, variable names, and synonyms). This result can be seen in the next figure where the filtered, latency-adjusted averages are displayed (Fig. 10.9).

When we undertook these analyses, we were interested in the amplitude of P300 and hadn't realized that a bonus would be that we will have an estimate of P300 latency on each trial. Having obtained these estimates, we examined the covariation of reaction times and P300 latencies on the single epoch basis, as Walter Ritter and his colleagues had done previously (Ritter et al., 1972). In Fig. 10.10 we see the mean P300 latencies determined from the single trials plotted against the type of stimulus category (on the left) and the required response (on the right). As you can see, P300 latency is labile for all of these manipulations. But what happens when we correlate P300 latency with RT? These relationships are shown in Fig. 10.11. First let's examine the accurate-RT condition. This plot includes all of the rare category trials from the experiment taken from all stimulus categories. We see a positive correlation between P300 latency (measured at the parietal Pz electrode) and reaction time. The correlation is .66 with a 3% error rate. These errors (where subjects responded with a response appropriate for the frequent category stimuli) are marked by X's and were not included in the regression analysis.

"RAW" AVERAGES   LATENCY-ADJUSTED

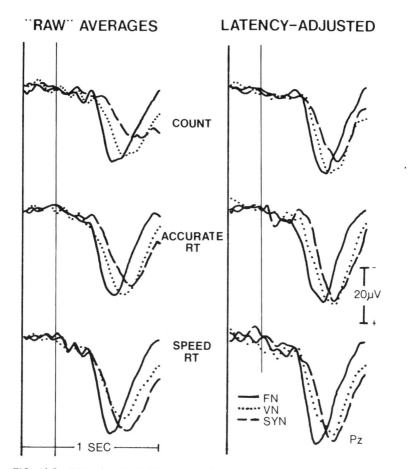

FIG. 10.9 ERPs for the three categorization tasks are superimposed for the three response conditions before and after latency adjustment. From Kutas, McCarthy, and Donchin, 1977, *Science,* Vol. 197, pp. 792–795, reprinted with permission. Copyright 1977 by the American Association for the Advancement of Science.

In the speed-RT condition we see a lot more X's as the error rate was now 9% for the rare trials. The correlation between P300 latency and RT for the correct trials is lower than in the accurate-RT regime. From this change in the correlation of RT and P300 latency due to speed-accuracy tradeoff, we concluded that P300 latency and RT were showing us different things. When we ask the subjects to be accurate, P300 latency and RT are reasonably well coupled, but when asked to respond very fast (as in the speed regime), this relationship begins to break down. One other point before I move on, you might notice that the error trials (marked by X's) tend to cluster on the graph (Fig. 10.11). We will return to this peculiar relationship later.

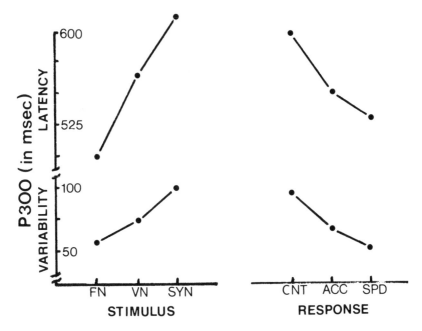

FIG. 10.10   Mean latency and standard deviation of P300 latency (as determined from single trial measurement) for the three categorization tasks (fixed names—FN, variable names—Vn, synonyms—SYN) and three response conditions (count—CNT, accurate-RT—ACC, speed-RT—SPD). From Donchin and McCarthy, 1980.

SHIFFRIN: It may be that if the supposedly correct responses are "guesses," then you wouldn't expect them to correlate with P300 latency.

McCARTHY: Yes, some of the correct responses to the rare stimuli are probably guesses.

SHIFFRIN: But then the correlation should decrease. Yet you seem to be implying that the correlation drops for some other reason.

McCARTHY: I haven't shown all of my cards yet. I just want to point out before I get to the next study that the probabilities for presenting the categories were very unbalanced. The data I have been discussing here are the ERPs elicited by items from the rare category. Almost all of the errors occur when the subjects respond, very quickly, with the response appropriate for the frequent stimulus to a rare stimulus. These trials generate large amplitude P300s but with a somewhat later latency. If the frequent response was correctly made to a frequent stimulus, no such large amplitude P300s were elicited. Let me now describe the next study, in which the error trials were examined in more detail.

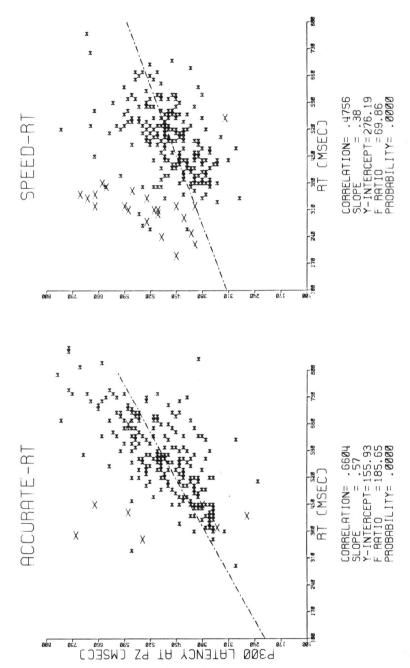

FIG. 10.11 Scatter plot of single trial P300 latency estimates and RTs for the accurate-RT and speed-RT response conditions. From Kutas, McCarthy, and Donchin, 1977, *Science*, Vol. 197, pp. 792–795, reprinted with permission. Copyright 1977 by the American Association for the Advancement of Science.

271

In this next experiment (McCarthy, Kutas, & Donchin, 1978), we took one of the conditions used previously, the variable names, and ran several hundred trials for each subject (ten male university students). We had, as before, unbalanced probabilities: males' names occured on 20% of the trials while females' names occurred on 80% of the trials. There were also three response conditions: count males' names, choice-RT under an accuracy regimen, and choice-RT under a speed regimen. This time, for the rare, males' names, we got 10% errors in the accuracy regime and 40% errors in the speed regime. Please note that, in this experiment, we had more errors for the accuracy regime than we had in the speed regime of the previous experiment.

In Fig. 10.12 are the mean RTs and mean P300 latencies (derived from the single trial analysis procedure described earlier). We see the same pattern of results as before. The correct responses were faster in the speed than in the accuracy regime. This is true for the frequent category items, where responses were overall faster than for the rare items. P300 latencies for correct responses to rare stimuli were longest for the count condition, and somewhat faster for both choice-RT conditions. (P300 latency is somewhat faster for the speed regime, but this difference is very small.) Our interest here, though, is in the error responses. Recall that these are trials when the subject responds with the "frequent" response to a rare category stimulus. We see that the RTs for the error trials are very fast. They are faster, in fact, than the correct responses to the frequent stimuli. Of course these are not "real" errors in the sense that the

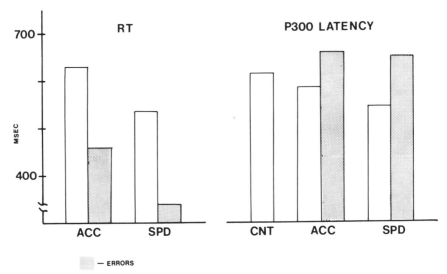

FIG. 10.12   Mean P300 latencies and reaction times (RT) for the count (CNT), accurate-RT (ACC), and speed-RT (SPD) conditions. Shaded bars represent trials in which incorrect responses were made. From McCarthy and Donchin, 1979, reprinted with permission.

subject cannot correctly decide if a male's or a female's name was presented. Rather, we believe that the demand for fast responses induces a response bias in favor of the frequent response. Remarkably, the P300s on these error trials are *longer* than they are in the correct trials. These are the longest latency P300s recorded in the experiment. So, in error trials the RTs are the shortest while the P300 latencies are the longest we record.

If we look at the scatter plots of the single trials for P300 latency and RT we find, again, positive correlations. In Fig. 10.13 we have a scatter plot for subject 1 of this experiment. The triangles represent error trials which cluster as we saw earlier. In Fig. 10.14 we see the averaged data (without latency-adjustment) for all of the subjects comparing waveforms associated with correct and error responses from the speed condition. In most cases it is quite evident that P300 is later for error trials than for correct trials. In Fig. 10.15 we have data from subject 1 again. Here we plotted the distributions of P300 latency and RT for the correct and incorrect trials from the speed condition. For the RTs we see overlapping distributions but with a clear shift to the right in the distribution of the error trials. The opposite relationship is seen in the distribution of P300 latencies. If we examine the distribution of the differences between RT and P300 measured on each single trial, we see a clear separation of the distributions. Also, the means of the distributions are on the opposite sides of a zero difference. If we look at errors, we see the P300-RT difference is mostly positive. For corrects, the difference is close to zero or somewhat negative. This difference was so striking for these ten subjects that we were able to build a discriminant function based on these measures which was able to correctly classify almost all of these error trials when compared to correct trials.

So what do we have? We see that P300 latency is positively associated with RT as a function of the difficulty of categorization. We also see that P300 latency is dissociated from RT for trials in which response-bias errors occur.

KAHNEMAN: Under the speed instruction, when latency to peak went down, did amplitude also go down? Also, did you have the same wave shape displaced in time, or were there indications that your peak was cut short by the onset of a negativity which occurred sooner under the speed instructions?

McCARTHY: The P300s associated with error trials and correct trials look very similar in shape with a difference in latency. This can be seen in Fig. 10.14. The error responses appear, however, to have a later or an enhanced N200.

There is very little difference to the eye between the averaged responses associated with correct responses from the speed and accuracy conditions. That is why I question the small effect found in the single trial analyses of speed condition waveforms having sightly earlier P300s than accuracy condition

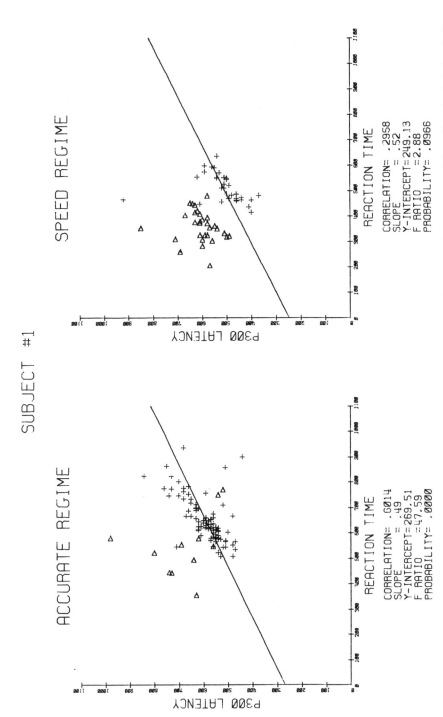

FIG. 10.13 Scatter plot of P300 latency and RT from one subject for the speed-RT and accurate-RT response conditions. The plus (+) signs indicate correct responses, triangles represent errors. Error trials were not included in the regression analysis. From Donchin and McCarthy, 1980.

MALE NAME STIMULUS

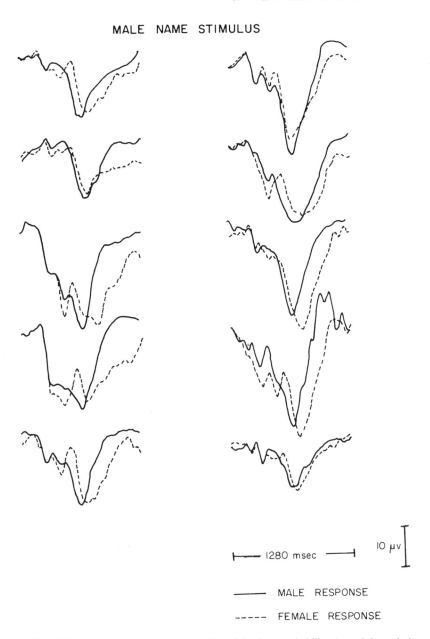

1280 msec — 10 μv

——— MALE RESPONSE

----- FEMALE RESPONSE

FIG. 10.14 ERPs from ten subjects elicited by low probability (p = 0.2) males' names. Waveforms drawn with solid lines are for correct responses in a choice-RT task, while superimposed waveforms drawn with dashed lines are for incorrect responses. From McCarthy and Donchin, 1979, reprinted with permission.

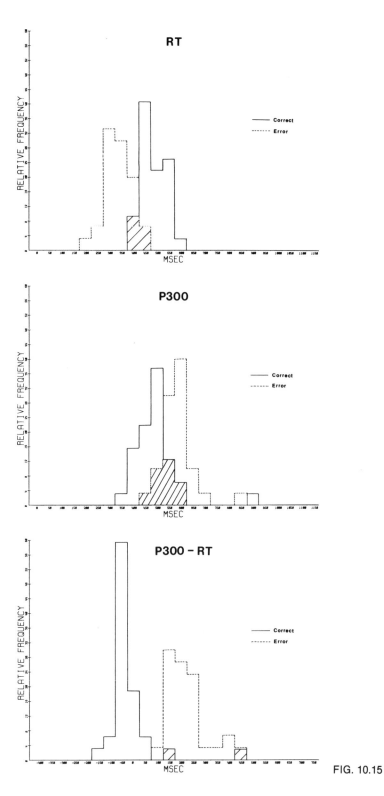

FIG. 10.15

276

waveforms. We have, however, found this small difference in two experiments.

KUTAS: Are the amplitudes of the speed and the accurate P300s the same?

McCARTHY: In these data there is no amplitude difference for P300 when comparing the accuracy and speed conditions. There is an amplitude difference in the raw averages between the count condition and both choice-RT conditions.

SCHVANEVELDT: I want to mention one point that came up about the P300 latency difference between correct responses and errors. This difference is difficult to interpret clearly. For one thing, frequent events don't give peak P300s. And subjects are saying that a female name is a male name or vice versa. On some errors, they identify the stimulus as a common event. It may be that they are not producing a P300 in that case to the stimulus. Rather the P300 may be a response to the noticing of the error.

KAHNEMAN: Yes. It looks very likely.

SCHVANEVELDT: Is it a "whoops response"?

PICTON: The Woody filter analysis is biased against that possibility. It will not pick up two waves. It will align the single trials to give you one wave and one latency. In about half of the subjects there seems to be an early small P300 occurring before the later big P300. This early P300 probably led to the first wrong decision; then, as they realized that they were incorrect, there was a later P300.

KUTAS: Then if you averaged all of the errors you should have, in that average, two P300s; an early P300 and a late P300.

McCARTHY: What is the negativity which follows, if the earlier positivity is P300?

PICTON: It can be just a return to baseline between the two peaks.

McCARTHY: It could be an N200 which is cutting off the P200. I don't see how you can say that the earlier positivity is a P300.

FIG. 10.15 *(Opposite page)* Histograms of reaction times (RT—upper graph), single trial P300 latency (middle graph), and their trial-by-trial differences (lower graph) for correct (solid) and incorrect (dashed) responses. Data were obtained from one subject. From Donchin and McCarthy, 1980.

PICTON: Are you saying that a P2 is occurring at about 300-400 msec?

McCARTHY: The P300s in these waveforms are occurring at about 600 msec.

PICTON: Yes. But does a P2 occur at 300-400 msec? That doesn't make sense. An exogenous component that has a definite latency is now occurring 200 msec later?

McCARTHY: There is obviously a positive potential there, and it is later than we would normally expect to see a P200. We have seen it in several experiments which employ visually presented, word stimuli. I don't know what it is, but don't see any evidence that it is P300.

KUTAS: But, Greg, do you know what the frequents look like? I mean are there any early components in that latency in the response to the frequents?

McCARTHY: I am not sure in that latency range.

KUTAS: That's certainly one way to look at it. If it's a P2, you would expect it to be there in the frequents as well.

SCHVANEVELDT: Well there is a way to test this. You must find out whether subjects are aware of having made an error.

KUTAS: But they do realize they've made an error, and often indicate so with an expletive.

SCHVANEVELDT: Don't you think some brain activity will result from subjects recognizing the error?

DONCHIN: That doesn't mean there is an extra P300. Obviously much is going on in the brain at all times. But it's just activity that is amenable to detection by techniques that can be seen. To me it seems that in 8 out of the 10 subjects the P300 starts descending later in the error ERPs than in the correct ERPs.

McCARTHY: It is clear that a possible hypothesis about this late "P300" is it represents an acknowledgement of an error. But that isn't the only explanation for the data and I don't see how it can be established.

PICTON: But this hypothesis is consistent with what is happening, and what your subjects were telling you. Why do you have to invent something different?

McCARTHY: What have I invented?

PICTON: You invented a dissociation between P300 and reaction time latency that occurs with an error.

McCARTHY: But the data are clearly there.

KAHNEMAN: Not if this is an extra P300. Then, it is not a dissociation.

PICTON: It's an extra P300 generated when the subjects realized they'd made a mistake.

DONCHIN: This is speculation. The data are straightforward, a short reaction time is associated with a long P300 latency. In two subjects out of 8 you see a little wavelet which you interpret as a early P300. But that's not what a complete analysis of the data suggests.

KUTAS: Greg, the earlier positivity that Terry Picton is talking about is there at the same latency for both the correct trials and the error trials.

McCARTHY: I have no objection to Terry's hypothesis. What I don't accept is the intuitive way we are asked to embrace it. We have a hundred msec delay in P300 and they've made an error—but can we simply say that the late P300 is in response to a realization that an error has been made? How about if the subject made a response before he collected enough evidence from that trial to be sure that the response was correct? We may be seeing a P300 which is there as a normal consequence of the evaluation of completed processing, which, for one reason or another, took longer for those trials.

PICTON: The obvious experimental solution is to average trials in which subjects realized that they erred.

McCARTHY: The subjects always realized that they made these errors. In the accuracy condition, most of these names were responded to correctly.

PICTON: Then I think our interpretation is true.

DONCHIN: You don't know that this is an extra P300. You're inventing a step. All we know is that there is a delay. Now you're saying that delay is due to there being an additional P300. But if you examine the data, then in 8 out of 10 subjects the positivity is delayed in the errors.

KUTAS: But Picton is right. That's not the problem. There is a glich there; not in just those two subjects. What is not consistent with Picton's argument is that the same glich appears in the ERPs elicited by the correct responses.

McCARTHY: It is clear from the data that we have a longer latency P300 and a faster RT for the error trials. The notion that p300 on these trials is elicited by a realization that an error has been made is attractive, but I don't think we can definitively say that from the data on hand.

HARTER: So the dissociation is unique to your situation?

McCARTHY: Yes. I have no problem with the interpretation. I just don't think that intuiting the evaluation that the P300 is an acknowledgment of an error is the way you prove it. I mean, we could conceive that this P300 is just occurring when it would have occurred anyway. The reason there is an error is because this is a subset of trials which is particularly hard to discriminate. The subject responds before he has enough information.

DONCHIN: We have to distinguish between two different interpretations of the data. One says that the recognition of the error induces a delay in the process which adds a hundred msec to the latency of P300 elicited by the name. Another interpretation is that there were two distinct P300s, one to the stimulus and then another in response to the error. I tend to accept the first interpretation that a delay is caused by the error. There are behavioral data that show that reaction times after errors are different that is consistent with this interpretation. But—the idea that there are two P300s may have some merit, and I invite empirical evidence in its support.

RITTER: If the N200 moved out in the error trials, and one assumes that in the correct trials N200 was somewhat early, then the reason why the positive peak would get greater in amplitude in the error trials is because the N200 moved away from it and is not cancelling as much.

McCARTHY: I believe that I said that earlier. That we are unmasking the peak, moving N200 later.
   This is a special case. The subject is pressed to be fast. They are responding "female," "female" very quickly, and then along comes a male's name to which they respond "female" again. Their response is very fast, shorter than when responding correctly. A correct "female" response was at about 380 to 400 msec, while an incorrect "female" response took about 330-340 msec.
   I just don't believe we have the data that show the later P300 reflects the realization of an error. You could turn it around. Perhaps the later P300 caused the error! Perhaps the names were less discriminable on the error trials

and the subject didn't wait for the evaluation process to be completed before responding. Maybe they extrapolated from the evidence collected by 300 msec that they were going to be very slow on that trial if they waited for sufficient evidence—so they guessed rather than be slow.

There are several other experiments that I would like to discuss, but in less detail. The next experiment is one from a number of "in progress" studies by John Polich, Emanuel Donchin, Bill Wang, and me, concerned with linguistic processing. Subjects were presented with four types of word pairs. One type consisted of words which were visually, or orthographically, similar and also rhymed. An example would be the pair bake-cake. These pairs were designated Ro (matched by phonology and orthography). Another type consisted of words which were visually similar but did not rhyme, like cough-dough. These pairs were designated WO (matched by orthography). The third pair type rhymed but were orthographically dissimilar, like moose-juice. These were designated R (matched by phonology). As you might expect, the words in the fourth pair type neither rhymed nor looked alike, an example being chair-spoon. These pairs were designated W (unmatched words). In the present experiment, the subjects' task was to indicate with a choice-RT response whether the two members of the pair rhymed or not (i.e., were phonologically similar). There were several different conditions in this experiment distinguished by which pair types were combined. Our interest was how P300 latency (now measured on the average waveform) would compare to these choice-RTs. In Fig. 10.16 we see some of the summary RT data. If we look at condition 2, we see that it takes about 300 msec longer to respond to non-rhyming words when they were orthographically similar (WO) than when they were dissimilar (W). This is not surprising. Most words which look alike also rhyme. So the orthography indicates probable rhyme, but the phonology says non-rhyme. Our interest is in how P300 behaves with respect to this large increase in RT.

I might add parenthetically that this increase in RT to the WO pairs is quite persistent, and even is maintained in conditions such as that in panel 4 where all orthographically similar pairs do not rhyme, while all of the orthographically dissimilar pairs do rhyme. In this condition, subjects were made explicitly aware of this fact. Polich and I have run ourselves for thousands of trials with the same small set of words and still can't eliminate the RT effect, although it attenuates.

The P300 results are tentative, and more experimentation is underway to try to make things more definite. In a nutshell, it seems that P300 latency to the pairs which look alike but don't rhyme (WO) is essentially the same as that to words which do not look alike and don't rhyme (W). If this result holds up it is quite interesting. Here we have a conflict of cues which the words present. We might speculate that the subject has properly categorized the pair (as evidenced by P300 latency), but has not responded because of the conflict engendered by the orthographic cues. Perhaps the delay between P300 latency and

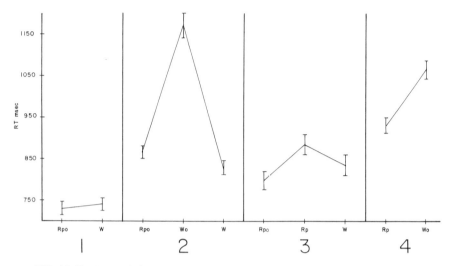

FIG. 10.16   Mean choice reaction times obtained when subjects were asked to decide whether a pair of words rhymed or not. Four experimental conditions are shown, which differ in which kinds of word pairs were presented. Ro pairs rhymed and looked similar, R pairs rhymed but looked dissimilar, Wo pairs did not rhyme but looked similar, while W pairs neither rhymed nor looked similar. See text for examples. From Donchin and McCarthy, 1980.

RT represents some additional processing to resolve the conflict. This experiment is very much like a stroop experiment; there is information from the stimulus which interferes with your response indicating whether or not the words rhyme. The additional processing engendered by this interference does not appear to affect P300 latency.

   The preceding experiment was very complicated, but our tentative interpretation of the results formed the basis for some simpler experiments designed to look at factors which influence P300 latency and RT similarly and dissimilarly. One experiment I am now running is designed to directly test the hypothesis that P300 latency is altered by experimental factors affecting stimulus evaluation, but is relatively unaffected by factors affecting response selection and execution. As Donchin points out in Chapter 5, this hypothesis can explain why P300 and RT can be both associated and disassociated. Factors influencing the durations or processes concerned with stimulus evaluation will similarly alter P300 and RT. Factors influencing the durations of processes concerned with response selection and execution will increase RT only. Of course this is a simplification depending in its strictest sense on a (serial) division of mental processes into those which are stimulus related and those which are response related. Nevertheless, it is a useful start at understanding the phenomena of P300 by understanding upon what mental processes its elicitation depends.

This experiment employed the "additive-factors" design introduced by Sternberg (1969) in which factors found to have additive effects upon composite RT are presumed to affect qualitatively different stages of processing. The task required that a choice-RT response be made to a word presented upon a CRT. On any given trial, either the word "right" or the word "left" was presented. There were two basic experimental factors with two levels each. The first manipulation involved the quality of the stimulus display. The words were either presented alone, or with distractor letters randomly placed about the word. This is the target discriminability condition—targets were presented with "noise" or with "no noise." The second manipulation involved the compatibility between the stimulus and the response. The subject held a response box with two buttons, one placed on the right side of the box, the other on the left. The subject rested his right thumb on the right button, his left thumb on the left button. On half of the trials, the target word and associated distractors (if any) were presented in upper case. On those trials, the right thumb-button was correct for the target "right" and the left thumb-button was correct for "left." These were the S-R compatible trials. On the other half of the trials, the target word and associated distractors (again, if any) were in lower case. For these trials, the left thumb-button was correct for "right" and the right thumb-button was correct for "left." These were the S-R incompatible trials. For half of the subjects, the meaning of upper and lower case were reversed. The discriminability and S-R compatibility manipulations were independently varied across trials. On any given trial, the stimulus might be right or left, with or without distractors, and in upper or lower case. All possibilities were equally probable. Sample stimuli are shown in Fig. 10.17.

	RIGHT	LEFT
	right	left
	TIN Q VA SRIGHTL X UE S N	HQLM S BZLEFTLR CPADI R
	eg k nz d rightb bml pfq	fctu lk amleftqd p ozm

FIG. 10.17 Prototypic stimuli used in the additive factors experiment described in the text. On each trial subjects are presented with either the word 'right' or 'left,' presented in upper or lower case, with or without accompanying 'noise' letters in random surrounding positions. Displays in upper case indicate that subjects are to respond with the hand indicated by the target word (i.e., RIGHT = right hand response). Lower case displays indicate a crossed response mapping (i.e., right-left hand response).

I first ran a test condition in which all of the possible stimulus types were presented, but in which only compatible responses were required to both upper and lower case. The RT data are presented in Fig. 10.18. I found that the presence of "noise" on the screen increased choice-RT by about 100 msec but that there was no difference between upper and lower case, or whether the target was "right" or "left." In the second condition I included the S-R compatibility manipulation. For this condition the compatible responses were performed about 125 msec faster than the incompatible trials. Here we have significant effects for discriminability and for S-R compatibility, but no interaction of these factors—these slopes are parallel. So, given the additive-factors logic, these factors affect different stages of processing—in our interpretation stages concerned with stimulus evaluation and stages concerned with response selection.

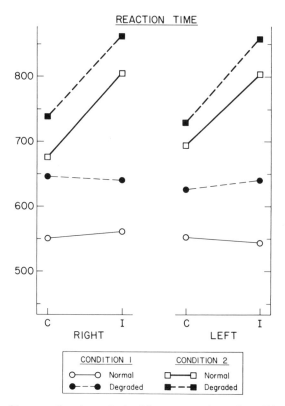

FIG. 10.18   Mean reaction times obtained for two experimental conditions from the additive factors experiment described in the text. In condition 1, subjects always responded with hand indicated by the target word, regardless of case. In condition 2, the case of the stimulus indicated either a compatible (C) or incompatible (I) stimulus-response mapping.

So how did P300 behave? Given our hypothesis, adding noise to the screen should increase the time required to "encode" the target word and since the process manifested by P300 is downstream from encoding, we should see an increase in P300 latency. The response choice depends upon knowing what the stimulus was, therefore this stage should follow categorization and P300 latency should not be affected. A latency analysis of the single trial waveforms from a parietal (Pz) electrode was performed in the manner described earlier. The mean P300 latencies are presented in Fig. 10.19. Here we see an increase in P300 latency as a function of stimulus discriminability for both experimental conditions. There was no significant effect of S-R compatibility, thus confirming our predictions.

KUTAS: Greg, just for information. Amplitudes were the same? You get nice P300s for both compatible and incompatible?

McCARTHY: The P300s for the compatible and incompatible conditions were virtually indentical.

My last figure (Fig. 10.20) I drew last night, inspired by Dr. Treisman's remark on the first day concerning the comparisons of experimental effects upon P300 latency and RT. Here are 5 different manipulations in which RT and P300 latency were compared. The mean RTs and P300s are plotted against the levels of the experimental variables with the same time scale for all. In this way we can compare their slopes, and the RT-P300 difference. Here, for example, is the discriminability manipulation that I discussed earlier. We see that adding "noise" characters to the screen increased RT by about 100 msec, but only increased P300 latency by about 50 msec. Recall also that in Judy Ford's memory search paradigm that while P300 and RT both increased with increasing set size, the RT was much more affected than P300 latency. For the speed-accuracy manipulation, we see a great reduction in RT for the speed regime but only a marginal decrease for P300. This is true for both experiments in which speed-accuracy was manipulated. For the error trials we see a dissociation, P300 latency increases while RT greatly decreases. In every case, the effect of the experimental variables are greater for RT than for P300.

The difference between RT and P300 challenges our simple-minded explanation of our data. This was pointed out by Judy Ford the other day. For example, "noise" characters increases the interval between P300 and RT. If noise affects only early stages of processing, and P300 signifies the end of the categorization process, then we have a problem. Why is there an additional delay imposed by the noise characters which follows the elicitation of P300? I have no ready answer for my question. I think, however, that a profitable approach may be to compare the rate of change of an experimental variable on RT and P300 latency as a means for fractionating information processing.

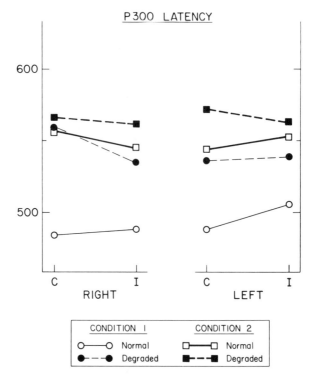

P 300   LATENCY

FIG. 10.19   Mean P300 latencies from single trial estimated from the additive facto
experiment described in the text. Conditions are as described for FIG. 10.18.

TREISMAN: Before coming, I read a paper by McClelland (1979) proposing a Cascade Model of mental processes and I rather think his model might predict just that. The two processes could be in the same sequence, and yet show different effects.

SCHVANEVELDT: I will say something about McClelland's model later.

DONCHIN: One more comment on the relation between P300 latency and errors. Recall the experiment I described in Chapter 5 in which subjects had to learn paired-associates (Horst, Johnson, & Donchin, 1980). The ERPs we studied were elicited by stimuli that indicated to the subject whether he was correct or not. It was the case that the P300 elicited by the stimulus which tells you that you are incorrect has a latency that is about 150-200 msec longer than the P300 elicited by the "correct." The data show that the entire complex (N200-P300-slow wave) is delayed. Thus, it would not be reasonable to suggest that this is a second P300. Rather, additional processing is associated with the incorrect response, as suggested by McCarthy. Note that when the subject was correct, the syllable the subject typed was the same syllable the computer displayed. The subject may recognize that syllable faster. If there is a discrepancy between what the subject typed and what the computer displayed then more processing takes place which delays the P300. It turns out that if two letters are shared between what the computer displays and what the subject types, the latency of the incorrect is shorter by about 70 msec or so. If all the letters are incorrect or one is incorrect then the latency is even longer. If you indicate to the subject that he has made an error it takes him longer to process the stimulus. Now I don't know exactly why. I hope that the cognitive psychologists can tell me why.

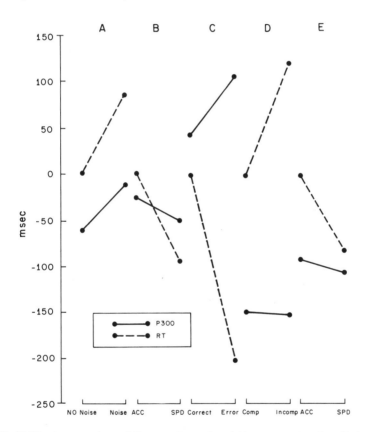

FIG. 10.20 A comparison of five experimental variables on reaction time (dashed) and P300 latency (solid). Panel A represents the noise manipulation and Panel D the S-R compatibility manipulation from the additive factors experiment reported in this volume. Panels B and C represent data from the speed-accuracy experiment of McCarthy, Kutas, and Donchin (1979). Panel E represents data from the speed-accuracy experiment of Kutas, McCarthy, and Donchin (1977). In each panel, the RT from the first level of the experimental variable has been subtracted from all measures.

CHASE: I will now review the data with respect to the issue of the relationship between reaction time and P300. Now before we ever started doing research in the area, a natural question that was asked is, what's the central nervous system correlate of reaction time? I'm sure that's what motivated this research. It was found that there was not a good correlation between reaction time and event-related potentials and the first reaction was "well, by golly, all these ERPs are not all that interesting." Then on second blush they said that because these central nervous system events are not perfectly coupled with motor RT, they're more interesting now. And one point I want to make is that it was an empirical question. Here's a summary of the data. I've listed factors that affect both reaction time and P300 latency. And this is data we went over. Memory set size, word frequency, noise, fixed versus variable names (that's Nancy, David, David, Nancy, David versus a bunch of different names), the number of visual targets that Donchin talked about yesterday, and old versus new items in recognition memory. The next part of the figure lists factors that affect reaction time but not P300 latency; S-R compatibility, the Gasp-Wasp task that Donchin talked about earlier, and I'm not clear on the sequential effects. Sequential dependencies have large effects on reaction time and I'm not sure if there are large sequential effects on ERPs.

DONCHIN: There are no sequential dependencies on the latencies, even though there are such effects in the reaction time data. Now either that's because the experiment is insensitive or because there *is* no effect.

CHASE: Well, I think the people who are doing the ERP research are essentially correct that they have established beyond the shadow of a doubt, as far as I'm concerned, that there is no necessary coupling of reaction time with P300. And one obvious conclusion that they've drawn is that they share early components but that there is some cognitive process underlying P300 that goes on in parallel with later components of the reaction time. They look at the kinds of things that are going on here that have to do more with response organization than they do with memory activation.
   So, then, I can give you some advice. You can stop doing these kinds of experiments. There are some chronometric issues need to be tidied up. There is no question about that. Let me tell you what they are. One obvious thing is that we need to know what the relation is between reaction time and N200, if anything. You guys are telling me that N200 and P300 are very closely coupled. I guess you're right, but that hasn't been demonstrated. If N200 and P300 are coupled then you're not going to expect anything different between reaction time and N200 and reaction time and P300. Well, N200 seems to be an earlier endogenous component and for various reasons earlier components are of interest. It has a different underlying topography, I guess. So that the

fact that you have a different underlying topography in an earlier component that seems to be time-locked to this later P300 component—I think that's unusual. But you have to tidy this up. You have to do the right chronometric research to establish this fact. Does N200 cause P300? Does it generate P300? I suppose you have some good ideas on this.

SHIFFRIN: What kinds of experiments are you suggesting that don't have to be done anymore?

CHASE: You don't have to go and look at correlations between reaction time and P300 anymore.

SHIFFRIN: You'd certainly want to look at it. You mean it is no longer necessary to determine if RT and P300 are coupled. You want to look at it for other reasons.

CHASE: Right. But there are some chronometric issues here. The relationship between N200 and P300. I don't mean go off and correlate them. I mean go off and find out if they are coupled with respect to independent variables. Do they both react the same way when you manipulate various independent variables?

KUTAS: Unless you know what factors generate an N200, though, it's sort of hard to do. I can't design an experiment that would definitely give me an N200. Maybe Walter can, but I can almost always get a P300, if I can set up the conditions right. That's not true for N200.

RITTER: Well sometimes you may have to do subtraction techniques like Russ and I have done. You can get an N200. Russ, would you agree?

HARTER: Always. You may not see it in the raw data but if you use subtraction if will be there.

KUTAS: Well, I'm not always convinced that subtraction is the best procedure.

CHASE: Now we have someone from the Donchin lab saying N200 and P300 are not coupled.

DONCHIN: Nobody says that they are not coupled but that N200 is hard to see because it hides behind P200.

CHASE: You can't use that excuse. Just because it's hard to measure doesn't mean it can't be. You have to do the hard work. That's why we have chronometric issues here. Well, for obvious reasons, an earlier component is interesting. We want to find out what the earliest origins of these components are. Where do, I'll call them control processes, begin and what are their origins? And for that reason alone, we would want to know about N200. Now one obvious brute fact about this research is that there is the giant P300 out there and it has been demonstrated that it is important. It seems coupled with decision-making in cognitive processes. So later on we may want to say the obvious big phenomenon is this P300 thing. We may want to study that more carefully. I'm saying we need to tidy up these chronometric issues and one of them is the N200-P300 thing.

RITTER: Since the N200 is an endogenous component which is earlier in latency, then the kinds of hypotheses originally suggested concerning the functional significance of P300 become rather suspect because most of those can be attributed to N200.

CHASE: If you are saying that if you uncouple then N200 and P300 become independently interesting. If not, then you have this N200-P300 complex and since P300 is the easiest thing to measure . . . .

RITTER: Oh, yes. But I'm not talking about that. I'm talking about what its functional significance in the brain might be.

KUTAS: Walter, how many times do you uncover an N200 in a count paradigm by moving the P300 latency out? Has that been done?

HARTER: In both of our experiments, where we had both paradigms, count and RT, we've gotten N200s using the subtraction procedure from every subject. Certainly enough so you can measure them.

ZAIDEL: Suppose you find that N200 and P300 are not coupled. Then what does that say about the relation between reaction time and P300?

CHASE: It may mean that N200 and reaction time are more closely associated. Then you'd say the earliest stage of the nervous system where you can see information processing related to reaction times is N200. Then you'd want to know how reaction time can be studied with N200.

ZAIDEL: Sure. But I mean if reaction time gives us the same information as P300, then we don't need to look at P300. The fact that N200 behaves differently than reaction time or the same as reaction time, the difference in P300 is not going to be relevant to that issue at all.

CHASE: Right. I say stop doing these experiments because you've demonstrated to my satisfaction that P300 and reaction time are not the same thing.

POSNER: But the argument is that there is a common pathway between the determinants of reaction time and the determinants of P300 up to some point. At some point they split off and Bill is guessing it might be N200.

SQUIRES: A second aspect of that is now we're looking at relationships between P300 and RT. It's a validating exercise. Someday we won't have to look at RT anymore. We can look at the P300 or N200 and say something about cognitive latencies. P300 and RT are just right now just sort of—hard to look at.

CHASE: Well, we have a lot of cognitive theory about mental events and reaction time and we think we know what the reaction time story is, but there is this other thing in the brain called P300, which isn't reaction time, but it seems to be very important. We need to know what it is.

DONCHIN: Well, is that the way to look at it? I am actually a bit surprised to hear that we know what reaction time is. The literature appears more controversial than this. But even if I grant you this, the general idea is that there are multiple components of reaction time. The problem has always been one of breaking apart these components. You want to study them independently. You therefore assume that you have experimental manipulations that work separately on the different components. You do experiments in which you have this single dependent variable and all the manipulations and you infer the components. And I think the implication of the P300 data is that you now have an additional dependent variable with which to test theories about the components of reaction time. And so it would be my inclination to continue doing this sort of experiment and try to test theories about the components of reaction time by using this measure. This assumes that we know what that P300 component represents and that's why the sort of experiments described by Greg are needed.

POSNER: This is a point you have often made, but I do not think you are right. It is true that P300 is another dependent measure, but there are lots of other dependent measures, not just reaction time. You can use speed-accuracy; you can look at intensity-duration functions, etc. There are many different time dependent variables that you can examine. Thus P300 is not the second one, it's one of many.

DONCHIN: Well, even if you are right, with P300 you have one more measure than you had before. Furthermore, all the measures you mention are essentially transformations of the RT.

POSNER: OK. But I think your view was that there are these two things. There are reaction time and P300 latency. I'm saying there are lots of other things.

CHASE: I view it somewhat differently. I don't think you should use P300 as a dependent variable to study any more than you should use reaction time as a dependent variable to understand. I think you should try to understand the process.

One other chronometric issue that I think needs tidying up is, what's the relationship between the amplitude and latency of P300? That's something about which there is just a paucity of data. OK. The first problem we faced in our panel is, we need to know what P300 is. And there is a literature updating expectancy, memory categorization, memory processing. We can say right away it is too slow to be memory activation. Memory activation just does not take 600 msec in a situation where you are deciding between two discriminable stimuli. Now, on the other hand, it's too fast to be complex processing. And our idea, which is not really new but it was said two or three times earlier, is that—it's close to what Norman was saying and it's close to what Picton was saying. Like Norman, we believe that it has something to do with updating memory. And like Picton, we believe it has something to do with onset of a control process. But there are lots of control processes going on all the time. This has to do specifically, we think, with memory control and it has to do with onset because it's fast relative to the kind of mental operations you see in these complex tasks. That is, memory updating can take a lot of time and it would occur subsequently to P300. We'll call the P300 the neural event associated with attention allocation for the memory control processing involved in memory reorganization. I think that's consistent with a lot of the data. It accounts for the sequential effects, I think, because when there is a series of repeated events, there is a shift to automatic processing, whereas when a new stimulus comes along there is attention allocation. To recap some of Posner's results on match-mismatch on physical-identity categorization, it accounts for the old-new business, the fact that you get longer P300s to a new stimulus than to an old stimulus in the recognition paradigm. It accounts for the Sternberg effect because more attention allocation is needed for the controlled search for larger memory probes and the lack of compatibility, we believe, is because there are response organization processes that call for compatibility on memory reorganization. It accounts for the word frequency effect because rare words recruit attention and other kinds of expectancies.

We think it is consistent with all this and now let me very briefly address the issue, "What is a controlled process?" The idea originates several places, but probably more in reference to Shiffrin—the idea that a control process is a mental process which is brought to bear or not at will on a task. And the one they studied is rehearsal. Rehearsal is a control process you can bring to bear to improve memory. And now the Schneider-Shiffrin paper talks about controlled and automatic search in the same way. That is, a highly practiced process can become automated and not be attention-demanding and not a search anymore. Now there are a couple of issues here. Are control processes conscious? Well, I would say not necessarily. Because if you believe the Schneider-Shiffrin idea that Sternberg's search is a controlled search because it is serial, certainly you can't introspect about that in memory search. Very little about that process comes out of a verbal report, and from what I know about conscious processing, it is not necessarily conscious.

KUTAS: Is that synonomous? Are you saying that to be conscious you have to be able to report it? Is a verbal report the equivalent of being conscious?

CHASE: Yes. I would equate consciousness with a verbal report. I'm studying verbal reports now in some of my research. I'm trying to understand what memory processes are available to conscious introspection and what are not. And I would equate consciousness with verbal reports. Are controlled processes conscious? Not necessarily, if you believe Schneider and Shiffrin, because Sternberg's memory search is classified as a controlled process. These are cognitive issues that are unresolved, needless to say.

Well, I don't think we are saying anything really new. Donchin has said it in many papers. But it is a slightly different slant on the issue than the expectancy view and I think it points to a slightly different way of doing experiments. It points toward doing experiments on memory and attention allocation.

Let me just make one final comment. If P300 is an important event (I think, goodness knows, that beyond any doubt it is), it has something very important to do with attention allocation for memory reorganization. It has implications for what follows it. First of all, we need to test that hypothesis on controlled memory processing. And secondly, it seems to me, we need to look downstream from the P300. We need to timelock on the P300 and look downstream for other important neural events. I'm interested to see if we can find mental processes associated with controlled processing of memory reorganization. A lot of these mental processes that we've been measuring chronometrically I think we need to study electrophysiologically. Let me stop here and let Roger Schvaneveldt talk.

SCHVANEVELDT: In view of the late hour, I'm tempted to skip my data, although I would very much like to have your reactions to it (see Schvaneveldt & McDonald, in press). I will comment on the kinds of inferences we want to draw from the chronometric data we've been talking about this evening. Let me briefly review the Cascade Model recently proposed by Jay McClelland

(1979). You ought to be aware of the model as a way of seeing the limits on the inferences we can draw from these latency effects.

If all we knew is that occasionally the overt response preceded P300 in time, there is no reason to believe, on that basis alone, that the process leading to the overt response, occurs earlier in time than the process which is reflected by P300. Let me illustrate this for you with a quick sketch of the function resulting from the cascade type of analysis. The Cascade Model is, in a sense, a descendent of Sternberg's (1969) Additive-Factor Method. Sternberg's conception, following Donders, was that mental processes are organized sequentially in time. Each process is assumed to operate in a discrete stage. When one process operates, it operates to completion and then passes information to the next process, which operates to completion and so on. In the cascade analysis, we can still preserve the series assumption, but each process in a series grows to some asymptotic level of activation (or information, if you want to think of it that way) over time. Also over time, each process continually passes information to the next process in the sequence. These assumptions yield a series of ogive functions like those shown in Fig. 10.21. Each of these functions is characterized by a rate of increase to an asymptotic level. Here I've simplified things somewhat by taking every function to the same asymptote, but that's certainly not necessary. We see that these functions all grow in time. Now suppose, just for the sake of argument, that there is a P300 process that grows in time. The final process leads to the overt response. Given this kind of arrangement, it would be quite easy for the response to precede the peak of the P300 component in time simply by basing the response on less information under some circumstances than you do under other circumstances. So with

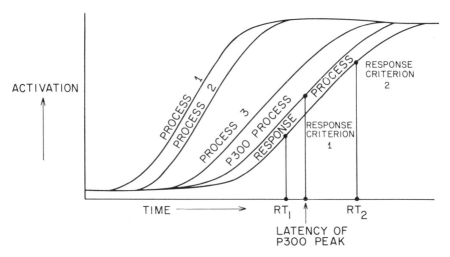

FIG. 10.21   Activation functions for a series of processes in cascade after McClelland (1979).

Response Criterion 1, we have a response that precedes the peak of P300 and with Response Criterion 2, the response occurs after the P300 peak. Thus, both results occur when the P300 process precedes the process leading to the response. The point is that, even when we find that one event precedes another in time, it doesn't necessarily mean that the underlying processes are ordered the same way in time. Other studies show that P300 latency changes with manipulation of independent variables at a faster rate than does reaction time. For some of the very same reasons, such data do not tell you much about whether or not you have processes that are ordered in time as defined by the cascade model, or whether you have independent processes with independent time courses.

Just as many of us working with latency data in cognitive psychology are becoming aware of how different assumptions that we can make about how processes are organized in time lead to different conclusions. Consequently, we are now becoming more careful about the conclusions we can draw from additive and interactive relations among variables. You, too, I think should exercise some of the same caution.

Now, at the same time, I want to say that I think Sternberg's Additive-Factors Method has been a very useful one for us. It certainly has stimulated a lot of information-processing research. Some of this research has come to reflect back on the back on the method, to suggest that there are probably some real inadequacies in the method itself. We often don't get the kind of orderly understanding of a sequence of stages that the method assumes. On the other hand, there may well be processes that are independent in the sense defined by the Additive Factor Method. If we talk about processes that are on an extreme sensory end and processes that are on the extreme response end, they may in fact be independent. There certainly is a fair amount of evidence in the literature supporting that view. When you start investigating processes in the middle, the picture starts to blur. For example with the processes involved in encoding of incoming stimulus information and the processes involved in accessing of information in memory and a process that makes use of that information to generate a response. These processes are probably very interdependent, and it is very difficult to tease them apart with the Additive Factors Method. For these problems, the cascade model may provide a better approximation of the underlying processes.

KUTAS: I don't understand how that's different than saying there is a series of processes going on in parallel.

SCHVANEVELDT: Well, there are a number of labels that could be used for this. I think Turvey (1973) proposed the term, "parallel contingent processes." There is a parallelism here, but there is also a contingency. The contingency is that information is passed from one process to another, in sequence. So that what happens in a process occurring toward the end of the sequence of processes depends on the processes occurring earlier in the sequence.

KUTAS: I don't see that in the figures.

SCHVANEVELDT: No, the figure simply represents the growth of information in each process when we assume the dependency between successive processes. It is hard to see the dependency in this figure, I agree. But, for example, when we have a process (Process 3) that has a slower rate than some of the earlier ones, the slower process will limit the rate of processes that follow it because they are dependent on it in the cascade conception. Clearly there are other possible models of the relation between processes, and this is only one. Now we might ask: What kinds of data do we have that suggest that P300 and RT are dissociated, even in this sense?

RITTER: Doesn't that depend on whether information is going on in both directions?

SCHVANEVELDT: No. The information flows in only one direction.

RITTER: I mean it wouldn't go top down, conceptually driven from right to left?

SCHVANEVELDT: Not in the McClelland (1979) analysis. His paper has a paragraph acknowledging that limitation in the model. If one wants to do formal analyses of this kind, there is only so much you can do at a time. Feedback processes are difficult. Top/down processes present difficulties for formal analyses. So then what evidence do we have that leads us to conclude that P300 and RT are dissociated? I think perhaps we have two things. One thing we have is a lack of variation in P300 when RT varies. An even stronger result would be to show that RT and P300 latency change in opposite directions. If you could show that P300 is sped up by the same variable that slows reaction time, then I think you've got clear evidence of dissociation.

KAHNEMAN: It is possible to have no variation in the P300 process together with a variation in RT. Suppose what happens is that you have an experimental manipulation that has no effect on the rate of all processes up to process K and process K it does alter. It does slow it down. So you have an easy condition and a difficult condition and at process K you alter the slope. Now anything that depends on processes before K are going to—the latencies are going to be independent of that factor and anything that's beyond process K is going to be affected by that factor. So there is no difficulty in presenting in that system a lack of change for one process at an early state for P300 and the dependence on the variable later. This is entirely consistent with the cascade analysis, as I understand it.

SHIFFRIN: Now that's with something you know or something you assume is going to occur.

KAHNEMAN: Anything you can conceive of a variable that begins to operate on a particular state and anything that varies early stages . . . .

SCHVANEVELDT: What about the case of opposite effects on RT and P300? Would you agree with that evidence for dissociation?

KAHNEMAN: You can't have one that slows P300 and not latency.

DONCHIN: That's right.

SCHVANEVELDT: So let's come up with one of those experiments. I have one idea but the chances of its working are about .001. The thought occurred to me that since we already know that stimulus response compatibility does not seem to affect P300, and we also have the Stroop-like effect in the gasp-wasp experiment, we might think about some Stroop-type paradigms where we try to manipulate the amount of interference. Let me take the Stroop paradigm itself. In that paradigm we present a word which names a color printed in ink of some other color. The word interferes with the naming of the color of the ink. Now if you slow down the processing of the word by making the word harder to read, you find a reduction in the stroop interference. Stroop interference decreases and reaction time decreases, but you're slowing down the processing of the word which is probably a faster process than the processing of the color. Slowing the word processing may in fact slow down P300. If so, you would have opposed effects on RT and P300 latency. Are there any comments?

ZAIDEL: It's kind of late and maybe I'm slow. We are discussing examples where reaction time decreases, and P300 latency increases, why isn't this useful?

SCHVANEVELDT: Well because, as Danny Kahneman just pointed out, the lack of change in P300 is not definitive with respect to the sequencing of these processes in the cascade conception. The process that leads to P300 could still precede the response process, supply information to that process in the sense that the later process depended on the P300 process, and yet you could still get no change in P300 and a change in reaction time.

SHIFFRIN: Of course, you might ask why you focus on this particular model as opposed to any other. You always make inferences in the context of certain assumptions.

KAHNEMAN: One of the assumptions of the cascade model is that the output of any early stage can only facilitate subsequent stages, not hinder them. Now you are saying that because of the Stroop situation those stages have two outputs. P300 reflects one of them.

SCHVANEVELDT: I'm not sure what you're saying. You're saying you don't think this is a good model for the Stroop?

KAHNEMAN: Yes. I mean that it is too simple a model for the Stroop. This cascade model assumes that the output of an early stage can only facilitate what happens later, whereas you're building in, because of the conflict, a case where the stronger the output of an early stage, the worse things become later. And that's where you're getting that paradoxical prediction. But that's not a straight application of the cascade model. It just doesn't have that thing in it.

SCHVANEVELDT: I see what you mean, but I'm not trying to model the Stroop. I am trying to find evidence for dissociation between P300 and RT which cannot be accounted for by assuming the cascade relation between the P300 process and the process leading to the response and RT.

The next thing I wanted to talk about was semantic priming. In fact I intended to go through some of our recent research. But time is getting late and I fear that I won't have time to properly set the stage to present what I wanted. So instead, let me just say a couple of things about priming and make one other suggestion for research. The priming paradigm involves presenting one stimulus, following it with a second stimulus, and requiring the subject to perform some task on the second stimulus (see Neely, 1976, 1977; Schvaneveldt, Meyer, & Becker, 1976). We've heard a lot about these kinds of tasks. What we're interested in is the relationship between the first stimulus and the second stimulus in semantic terms. A simple task that I've studied quite a bit over the last several years is called the lexical-decision task. You present a string of letters to subjects and ask them to decide if the string is a word or not. A very consistent finding is a more rapid decision when stimulus 1 (the prime) is a word semantically related to stimulus 2 (the target) compared to an unrelated control. Following Posner and Snyder (1975), we have also used a neutral case where the prime does not supply semantic information. The neutral prime gives you some added analytic power by permitting the analysis of performance in terms of the costs and benefits of priming.

Let me go right from that to an interesting result that not much has been made of in the literature although it's around in two or three places (see Neely, 1977). If you use the name of a category as the prime and a member of the category as the target in a lexical decision task—sure enough, people are better at making the decision when the appropriate category name is presented as the prime. However, the facilitation from having the correct category prime present relative to a neutral prime is not affected by the typicality of the member of the category. By typicality we mean that some members of categories seem to be better members of categories than others. An example of prototypicality is the relationship between bird and robin which we would characterize as prototypical. A robin is a typical bird, as contrasted with something like bird and chicken. A chicken is certainly a bird all right but not nearly as birdy as a robin. Now there is a large literature on this topic, and there are a number of interesting phenomena associated with it. Many studies demonstrate powerful effects of typicality. But the task that shows the typicality effect involves having people make judgments about the category membership of a target item. So, for example, one paradigm is to present the name of the category, present a target item which is either a member of the category or not, and the subject must decide whether it is a member of the category. In that case, you get very large typicality effects. You can decide that a robin is a bird, much faster than you can decide that a chicken is a bird. So here are these two situations. Both show a sort of facilitation, a semantic effect, but in one case (the lexical-decision task) we find the typicality doesn't produce any change in facilitation. Well, typicality, it seems to me, must be a basic process, given what we know about it. I'd be very surprised if typicality does not influence P300. P300 latency, I would expect, would be much longer to an atypical item than to a typical one. Here's a prediction. If you give these two tasks, a category judgment task, and a lexical decision task and manipulate typicality, you will find that reaction time won't be affected by typicality in the lexical decision task. The facilitation that you get from typicality won't be reflected in the lexical decision task, but I would wager that P300 in that task would be. Whereas in the category decision task, you're probably going to find that RT and P300 will vary together. Again, this might be a situation where one memory process is being reflected by P300 and other processes are being reflected by reaction time. Which brings me to the last section.

The discussion we had yesterday on the panel led us to the idea that the P300 has something to do with updating memory. It doesn't seem to have much to do with accessing memory, as Bill Chase suggested. It doesn't appear to have the right characteristics for that. It may well have something to do with storing information in memory and the suggestion that I just made was to begin to do some research on memory. Most of the studies that we've been talking about during the meetings are studies that involve fairly simple memory functions. Within the cognitive literature, people have been examining questions about the structure of memory, and how concepts are related to one another in memory and, of course, there is a very large literature on how we remember things in the first place. Here I'm thinking about the large number of studies of the kind I think Don Norman was talking about when he suggested that you look at problems like correspondence between an event and some schema that one has for an event. Certainly there are a number of studies one could do to examine the relationship between P300 and the difficulty of processing an item for storing it in memory. What are some examples? How about, "The notes were sour because the seams split?" Do you know that one? Bagpipe (Bransford & Johnson, 1972).

Presumably, material that is difficult to comprehend should require more extensive reorganization for storage in memory. We would expect the P300 to reflect this comprehension difficulty. The Bransford and Johnson work may provide a fruitful direction to follow.

There is another literature on levels of processing (Craik & Lockhart, 1972). What you do is give a subject a task that brings the subject's attention to various characteristics of a stimulus. It might be a semantic orienting task where you ask them to categorize the stimulus. It might be some non-semantic orienting task where you ask them to do something like decide whether the word has a double letter in it, or the letter E or something of that sort, which requires processing at some other level. You find that different orienting tasks lead to differences in memory. Semantic orienting tasks generally produce better memory than tasks that orient people to structural characteristics of words. What does the hypothesis about the relationship between P300 and memory storage processes, the allocation of attention for the reorganization of memory, predict about the relationship between P300 and the kind of orienting task one gives a subject in memory experiments? Is it clear? Actually, it's not entirely clear. I imagine we could formulate a position either way because, on the one hand, we're asking people to make a semantic analysis and store that away in memory. A semantic analysis may be something that's fairly simple to perform. On the other hand, non-semantic tasks may be unusual enough to require more effort to store something in memory. At any rate, these kinds of studies, it would seem to me, would give us a little bit more insight into the connection between P300 and some of these other complex memory processes.

RITTER: I thought the reverse is also true, namely that if instead of asking the subjects to recall the words, you give a memory task for the orthographic characteristics, then those subjects who initially were oriented toward the orthographic features have better recall than the subjects who initially attended to the semantic characteristics.

SCHVANEVELDT: Well, you can find that sort of thing in some cuing experiments. But in the typical experiment that simply requires people to process stimuli at different levels and later asks for free recall semantic orienting tasks usually lead to better recall. When you start looking at memory paradigms, you can ask about evoked potentials in at least two different places. You can ask about evoked potentials that occurred in response to the original presentation of the item to be remembered and you can ask about evoked potentials that occur later on, particularly in a cuing paradigm when you provide cues for recall. Now what do we expect if P300 reflects the allocation of attention for the purposes of memory reorganization? If that's what P300 reflects, then I think we ought to see that P300 reflects the difficulty of performing that orienting task. How much does it take to reorganize your memory so that you can perform that task? If the information is readily available, P300 should be smaller. Then what happens later on? You provide a cue, some of these cues lead to easy access of memory. Will the P300 to these cues reflect the ease of access to memory? If so, then the P300 should be larger to the more difficult items to remember. However, P300 may not reflect ease of access. In which case P300 may not differ as a function of orienting task when the P300 is taken at the time of cued recall. Actually we seem to need some data on these issues. My final comment is to reinforce the statement I made earlier. We need to know about the nature of EPs in situations requiring more complex memorial processing. Only then will we be able to evaluate the claim that P300 reflects the allocation of processing capacity for the reorganization of information in memory.

11 ERPs and Psychophysics

David Regan
Dalhousie University, Halifax, Nova Scotia

11.1 INTRODUCTION: SENSORY CHANNELS AND ERPS

My instructions were, as far as I can recollect, to be reasonably critical, and to try to make it reasonably controversial. My own estimate is that ERP recording is a little more scientifically difficult than either psychophysics (auditory or visual) or single-unit recording. Technically I would say that they are all about equally demanding. It therefore, I think, does not make sense to treat evoked potential recording as though it were easy. That is in case you get the impression I'm, from now on, totally pessimistic. That's not the case.

The discussion is entitled "Early Components in Psychophysics." I don't think the concept of early components has a great deal of excitement to it. I like to classify evoked potentials by stimulus manipulation and not by the ERP waveform or the latency.

Having defined a sensory ERP entirely by stimulus manipulations, you might ask, what use is it? I think that an important application is to investigate sensory information-processing "channels" objectively. The appropriate stimulus fits the channel something like the keyhole and the key. The existence of different channels may offer an objective method for the study in children of the functions of the auditory and visual pathways or different parts of the brain or different neural organizations. Different diseases can affect these various neural organizations differently so that testing sensory channels can lead to more discriminating tests of disease processes.

The question of whether the ERP does or the ERP does not correlate with psychophysical data, which one often sees raised, is not such an interesting question, I would say.

That we do not know the site at which the ERPs are generated is considered by many single-unit investigators a damning criticism of ERP recording. But I think one can think of ERPs and psychophysics as being in a similar position here. In a psychophysical experiment the subject might say: "Yes, I see it. No, I don't see it." The critic could well say: "You're studying his vocal cords. That's where the response is coming from. How can you possibly study vision by studying his vocal cords? Do you perhaps listen to the subtle changes in tone?" "No," the psychophysicist says, "we manipulate the stimulus and we take yes or no as a sign of arrival of a signal." Agreed that we are vague as to the sites of ERP generators, but this is irrelevant if, by analogy with the psychophysicist, we regard the evoked potential as merely an objective sign at the scalp that a signal has reached the brain. I think that this formally puts you in at least as good position as the psychophysicist and we know how respectable the psychophysicist is. Having established this fallback position, we can now look at the waveform and argue that the ERP is a more information-rich response than the psychophysicist has available.

I shall not discuss the early components of the auditory ERPs, the so-called brainstem responses. These potentials are in a different category because they can be interpreted fairly well in the light of data recorded, intracranially, from animals. The brainstem auditory ERP is, therefore, quite a success, especially as a clinical tool. Thus my critique of visual ERPs does not apply to the auditory brainstem ERPs.

In vision, several sets of sensory channels have been found whose sensitivities do not much overlap (e.g., sets of channels for spatial frequency, changing-size, stereo motion in depth). In an ideal set of channels only the appropriate stimulus will elicit a response. No other stimulus will be effective. ERPs can be used to define sets of channels, perhaps with the advantage that ERPs have several components.

The visual ERP channels for which there is good evidence include the stereoscopic ERPs, of which there are two different types, one due to motion "toward the head" and one due to motion "away from the head." Another type of evoked potential is a pattern-appearance evoked potential. There is also a pattern-disappearance ERP that again is different from other ERPs and can only be produced by the appropriate stimulus. These pattern ERPs are distinct for long-wavelength, medium-wavelength, and short-wavelength stimuli, which have their own spectral sensitivities. Yet another way of classifying pattern ERPs is into ERPs elicited by local luminance changes and genuine responses to contrast. Flicker ERPs divide into medium-frequency flicker ERPs, high-frequency flicker ERPs, and low-frequence flicker ERPs that have quite different properties and seem to come from different parts of the brain. Clearly there are many ERP potentials that differ from each other in that they are uniquely generated by quite different stimuli. Some of these ERPs might even be generated in the same place. Yet I think they can be defined as different ERPs by "that's how you make them," not by "that's what they look like" (Regan, 1977).

That's an outline of what I hope to illustrate with a few examples.

KAHNEMAN: Could you explain what you mean by saying that the two evoked potentials are different if they are elicited by different stimuli? Do you mean that it is nonsense to say that two different stimuli can evoke the same ERP?

REGAN: No.

KAHNEMAN: Then I've lost you right there.

REGAN: How do you say one ERP is different from another ERP? You can use the strategy used in psychophysics. How do you know that when the subject says *yes* one time, it's totally different from when he said *yes* some other time? You prove that by manipulating your stimulus and showing that in case A the only possible stimulus that could have provoked the response yes (or the ERP) is binocular correlation and in case B is the change in spatial contrast. If a change occurs, for example—something changes its size, many things covary—the total light flux varies, the contrast varies, the position varies. In your experiments you must manipulate the stimulus so that all things that normally covary do not and then you can prove that the response is locked to this aspect. That is the strategy I am using to demonstrate that one ERP is due to one stimulus and is different from another ERP that is due to this other thing.

If the brain is processing different stimulus features independently, then an ERP defined in this way can only be elicited by one stimulus. To the extent that the brain does not process different stimulus features independently, two or more stimuli can produce the same ERP. This can be discovered experimentally, and I think the elucidation of this organization is an important role of research.

11.2 EXPERIMENTAL DEMONSTRATIONS

First, I need to explain the difference between time-domain (*transient*) and frequency-domain (steady-state) ERP analyses. In transient analysis, you investigate a system by giving it a "tap." The tap can be any type of abrupt stimulus change (e.g., changing color or changing position), and you obtain a transient ERP as shown in Fig. 11.1a. In steady-state analysis you "shake" the system, wait awhile for the system to settle into its stereotyped mode of response, and then measure the amplitude or the phase of the ERP and plot it against the frequency of the shake. In this way you describe the system's behavior either in the time domain or in the frequency domain. If it is a linear system, the two methods yield equivalent data. If the system is nonlinear (which the brain certainly is), the two descriptions can give you totally different insights. As we are discussing information-processing channels, either of these two descriptions can be used, and probably both should be used, because they are not redundant.

The first example is stereoscopic ERPs, shown in Fig. 11.1 (Regan & Spekreijse, 1970). These are records that Henk Spekreijse and I made in 1969. Our aim was to record ERPs that were definitely determined at cortical level and not at retinal level. The experiment was that the left eye saw a Julesz pattern of dots and the right eye saw a different pattern of Julesz dots. Either eye, by itself, just saw a pattern of dots. However, in binocular vision the brain correlated these two random dot arrays and you saw a central square floating in depth very vividly.

We arranged that the central square appeared to move backward and forward in depth. When it came forward, we recorded the ERP labeled x ; when it went back, we also recorded another ERP. When we occluded one eye so that there was no depth sensation, only motion, we recorded a very small ERP (z). So we argue that the deflections were an electrical correlate of neural processing, reflecting the processing that takes place when neurons compare the signals from the two eyes. The site of this processing was central to binocular convergence. This result cannot be attributed to monocular cues, because we repeated the experiment, for vertical movement, when no depth sensation was produced and these ERPs were a lot smaller. So we suggested that when you perceived movement in depth, you have a special stereo ERP.

A little later, Beverley and I (Regan & Beverley, 1973) recorded stereo ERPs elicited by four separate movements, namely backward and forward for a target located nearer than the fixation point and backward and forward for a target located beyond the fixation point. Each depth movement gave a different ERP. This ERP data suggested that you have different systems responding to backward and forward motion, and the response also depends on the location of the target relative to the fixation point. We conducted the experiment in 1970, but we did not publish because we dare not base such a conclusion solely on ERP data. So we did psychophysics and we also recorded single cells from cats. All this work supported the story we derived for the ERP data (Regan, Beverley, & Cynader, 1979). It seems it does pay to believe your own ERP data now

---

FIG. 11.1 *(Opposite page)* Evoked potentials to stereoscopic stimuli and control stimuli. The right eye viewed a static random pattern of small black and white squares. The left eye alternately viewed a pattern identical to that viewed by the right eye and a pattern in which the central region had been bodily shifted a short distance to one side (the dotted line at top of figure). The alternation frequency was 0.45 per sec. In these conditions, the central dotted area appeared to jump rhythmically forward out of the plane of the paper and then return. A—EP evoked when retinal disparity of central area changed horizontally and gave rise to depth perception. 1 and 2 are two separate sessions of 200 counts. A shows 1 + 2, B shows difference 1 − 2 indicating noise level. F—Same as A except that the retinal disparity now changed vertically and no stereoscopic perception resulted. From Regan and Spekreijse, *Nature, 255,* 93, 1970.

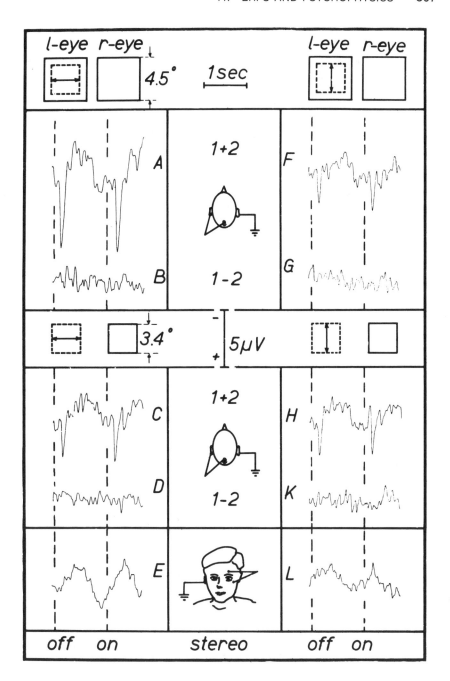

FIG. 11.1

and then. This is an illustration of a case where the stimulus manipulation defines the stereo ERP.

Another example is provided by a series of experiments that we and the Amsterdam group carried out independently between about 1960 and 1966 (Regan, 1972; Regan, 1975A & B). They deal with evoked potentials elicited by flicker and by reversing patterns. The amplitude of the brain response depends on the frequency of reversal. If you look at several electrode positions (Fig. 11.2), you discern three rather sharp resonance regions in many people's evoked potentials. You find a bigger response near the alpha frequency, but this has not proved to be very interesting. There is a fairly sharp resonance in certain circumstances near 16 cps and another at about 40 to 60 cps. These are flicker ERPs produced by unpatterned patches of light. The pattern responses are quite different; ERPs to small checks (or high spatial frequencies) are largest at about 5 Hz.

The flicker ERPs have different distributions over the scalp in the three frequency regions, so they presumably come from different parts of the brain. High-frequency ERPs have about half the latency of medium-frequency ERPs.

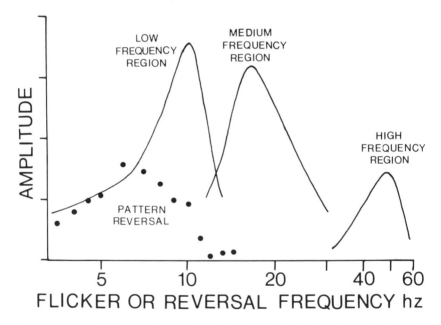

FIG. 11.2   Temporal tuning of flicker and pattern evoked potentials. Ordinates plot the FHz frequency component of EPs elicited by flickering an unpatterned stimulus at FHz (continuous line) and by FHz pattern reversal (filled circles). Flicker EPs show resonant-like peaks in three frequency regions. The flicker EP data are for a large stimulus field (greater than 10' diameter), while the pattern EP data are for small (15 min arc) checks of small field subtense (about 4' diameter). Modified from Regan, *Nature, 253,* 401–407, 1975.

High-frequency ERPs correlate with the brightness of the stimulus. Medium-frequency ERPs do not. They correlate with the wavelength. Medium-frequency ERPs are delayed in multiple sclerosis. High-frequency ERPs are not.

A further point: There is no unequivocal answer to the question whether ERPs correlate with perception. Flicker ERP amplitude does not correlate with perception. You can get a flicker ERP even when you can't see flicker. All you need is a better averager, or average for a longer time, and this will record still smaller ERPs. Nevertheless, high-frequency-flicker evoked potentials can be used to measure the spectral sensitivity of the eye more precisely and rapidly than can be done psychophysically. This measurement can be made when you don't see flicker at all (Regan, 1970).

Some aspects of psychophysics correlate very closely with ERPs. Others (like flicker perception) don't. To give a dramatic example of how much they don't, Fig. 11.3 is a recording we took in about 1969—as part of a study we made in 1967 to 1970 on patients with stroke and brain injury (Milner, Regan, & Heron, 1972). We used the simultaneous stimulation method with two flickering patches of light or two patterns. The subject fixates between two patches of light that are flickering at slightly different rates. The responses from the two hemispheres are recorded, simultaneously. We were using these ERPs to look at stroke patients and also migraine patients during attacks. The occipital pole in the patient, whose data are shown in his figure, had been removed. The patient was therefore cortically blind in the corresponding half-field of each eye. You'll note that at 9-Hz stimulation frequency, her good half-field gave a clear response and also the blind half-field gave a good response. So your conclusion would be even though this patient can't see, she has clear visual ERPs. It's curious, though, that the ERPs on the blind half-field look different to the ones from the side that can see. The ERP is an almost pure 9-Hz sine wave from the blind side. From the good side, however, the 9-Hz flicker produced a 9-Hz sine wave with an 18-Hz sine wave mixed with it. What happens if you stimulate at 18 Hz? The blind side gives you nothing and the seeing side gives you a good 18-Hz response. One possible explanation is as follows. Very early on in the visual system, visual signals are distorted so that a 9-Hz flicker will generate 18-Hz and 9-Hz responses. Those two signals travel up rather independently. What's happening is that the 18 Hz fails to generate 18-Hz ERPs on the blind side although the 9 Hz does generate 9-Hz ERPs. We say that this is because the 9-Hz and the 18-Hz ERPs are generated in different cortical regions.

Although patients who had lost the 9-Hz ERPs while retaining the 18-Hz ERPs were rare, we found this in somebody with very extensive cortical injury. The 9-Hz seems to come from a wide area of the cortex.

The fact that an individual cannot see because of cortical damage doesn't mean he won't produce a visual ERP; visual signals project to several areas of

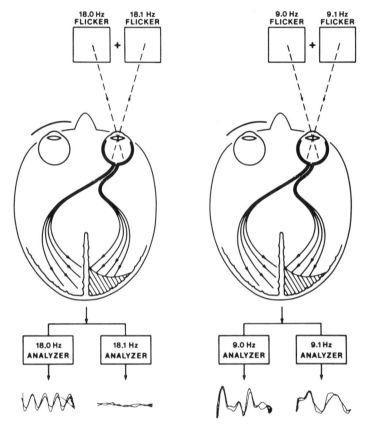

FIG. 11.3   Visual evoked potentials were recorded from a patient whose right primary visual cortex had been surgically removed, leaving her blind in the left visual field of each eye. Stimulating the blind visual field with a light flickering 18 times per sec gave no EPs from the blind brain hemisphere. Surprisingly, stimulating the left visual field with a light flickering 9 times per sec gave EPs of similar amplitude in both the blink and the normal hemispheres. Slower flicker apparently activated the region of the cortex that receives visual information but does not, by itself, give rise to conscious visual perception.

the cortex all of which are presumably necessary for vision. A good deal of visual information circulating in the brain does not reach the level of conscious perception but nevertheless may generate ERPs.

At the very simple level of flicker perception, in Fig. 11.4 is a Stevens plot of the flicker magnitude versus the modulation depth. The relation is a power function. But the relation between ERP amplitude and sensory magnitude is not a power function. Of course, the prime function of the neurons that generate flicker ERPs may not be concerned with flicker perception—after all, flicker perception is not of major importance in everyday life. The graph shows one reason why flicker perception does not ever correlate with ERP amplitude.

It plots the amplitude of ERPs to 20-cps flicker. The amplitude of the 20-Hz ERP component is plotted against the modulation depth of the flicker (i.e., the percentage flicker) of a red light alternating with a yellow light. The 20-Hz response goes up continuously as the flicker modulation depth rises but the second harmonic (40-Hz ERP component) saturates. On the other hand, for the yellow light, the 20-Hz ERP component saturates and so does the second harmonic. So if you have a correlation between ERP and flicker (at one modulation depth), it need not hold at another.

Consider evoked potential amplitude versus the contrast of a grating. In suitable coordinates over a suitable range you obtain a good straight line that extrapolates back to the point of threshold. You can use it to measure the

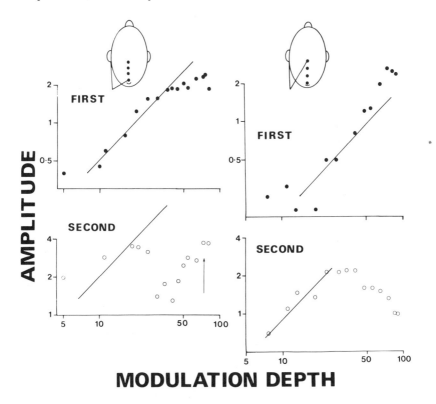

MODULATION DEPTH

FIG. 11.4   Comparison of EP amplitude and sensory magnitude estimates of flicker perception. The upper half of the figure shows first harmonic (22.7 Hz) and the lower half shows the second harmonic (45.4 Hz) evoked potential components elicited by flickering the stimulus light at 22.7 Hz. The left and right halves of the figure show EPs recorded from two electrode sites. The straight lines are power functions plotting estimates of the sensory magnitude of flicker versus log stimulus modulation depth. The stimulus was a 15' diameter white light of mean retinal illumination 540 trolands with a steady adapting white surround of 540 trolands extending to a diameter of 30°. From Regan and Beverley, *Perception, 2,* 61–65, 1972.

modulation transfer function in humans and even in cats, and it looks like a good bridge between single cells and behavior (Campbell, Maffei, & Piccolino, 1973). It certainly can be used in the right hands, providing that you stay within that certain particular format. Indeed, grating evoked potentials show orientation-specific adaptation, just like psychophysics.

Pattern ERPs have been used to measure the visual acuity of children from early age, some using pattern appearance; some using flash patterns; some using pattern reversal. There is a problem in that spatial and temporal tuning of pattern ERPs can be confounded, and both can change with age (Moskowitz-Cook & Sokol, 1980; Regan, 1978). I'm not trying to be pessimistic here. As you know, these experiments are very difficult. They are difficult behaviorally and a lot of effort is needed. ERPs have to be regarded, I think, as a very awkward tool and you are not going to find good reliable results too easily.

Finally, I shall draw attention to the possibility of using the nonlinear systems approach to say quite definitely "this is happening in the retina, but that's happening in the cortex" (van der Tweel & Spekreijse, 1968).

I'd like to finish with a horror story. We stimulated a goldfish's eye with a flickering light, continuously changing the brightness so the mean light intensity was going slowly down then up, down then up. The ERG of the goldfish corresponded closely to mean light intensity. The tectal evoked response (which is the goldfish's nearest equivalent to an ERP), however, did not correlate with light intensity at all. One value of ERP amplitude corresponded with up to five different intensities. It turned out that it has identically the same dynamic nonlinearities with red, green and blue light. So although each of those channels is behaving nonlinearly as light intensity changes, the ratios among red, green, and blue are constant. That means that if you try to use the ordinary way of approaching color vision in goldfish by varying the intensity of each color, you find an incredible story that suggests that the goldfish has no basis for stable color vision. If you use *heterochromatic flickerphotometry*, which is fairly close to everyday conditions, you have a very different story (Regan, Schellart, Spekreijse, & van den Berg, 1975).

As it happens, that doesn't occur with humans at all, but I think the story sounds a warning that very nasty things can occur with ERPs that appear to be almost designed to confuse your experiments. Possibly, the closer you are to the everyday visual situation, the less likely you are to be tripped up over this. So I'll finish by saying that I think one can find decent results in ERPs just as one can in psychophysics, but that more caution is needed as there is less background knowledge of ERPs than there is of psychophysics.

11.3 DISCUSSION

CALLAWAY: Martin, can you elaborate on the study in which you varied pattern and intensity?

REGAN: It's described in a recent paper (Regan, 1981) and was devised by the Amsterdam group. The test is shown in Fig. 11.5.

CALLAWAY: And there is no intensity ERP at all?

REGAN: Yes, you've deliberately introduced an intensity change.

CALLAWAY: I guess what was bothering me was if you take the right part of A and subtract it from the left-hand part of B and vice versa, you'd have nothing that would indicate that there is no intensity ERP, wouldn't it?

REGAN: Right, if you have that extreme case, you have no intensity ERP, it's all pattern ERP. In fact, we often find that.

CALLAWAY: But in reality there is both?

REGAN: Not in that case.

ALLISON: Martin, when you talk about local luminance changes in the pattern situation, do you mean that the black square now becomes a light square? Is that all you mean by local luminance change? Or do you mean something more subtle by that?

REGAN: Yes, "local luminance" does imply something more subtle. Suppose you have nonlinear distortion peripherally and nonlinear distortion is of the rectifier type such that if you have a fairly low spike-firing frequency in the resting conditions; the rate can't go *less* than nothing but it can always increase. So increases of light intensity in that case will always give you more spikes than decreases of light intensity. Let's consider that. You have this square that goes bright and that square that goes dim. Suppose you have nonlinear distortion followed by spatial summation. In that case, essentially the result is that this square going bright produces a bigger signal than that square going dim. So you end up with something that in fact has exactly the same temporal frequency as a genuine pattern response. If you use a much smaller check size there is less contamination due to local luminance EPs because of the finite size of the control fields. What that means is as the check size increases, you find more and more of this local luminance contribution. Another good clue is if you look at the temporal tuning and you find that your pattern ERPs are larger at, say, 17 Hz or 10 Hz. Since flicker EPs are larger at 10 Hz and 17 Hz, pattern responses at these frequencies may include a lot of local luminance contamination.

ALLISON: Can I ask another question about pattern ERPs? Then you obviously have contour changes but you also have motion changes, that is, cells that are selectively fired off by motion in the visual field, so could you not think of a pattern ERP as actually consisting of three different things: contrast, the local lumlinance changes, and a motion change? Can you separate contrast and luminance out and look at the effects of motion, per se?

REGAN: There have been some attempts, particularly by Clarke (1972), and we've tried it too; it really is difficult.

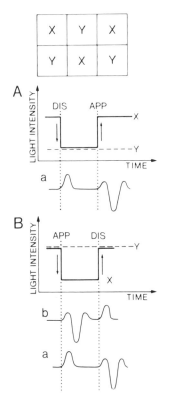

FIG. 11.5 Pattern stimulation does not necessarily give pattern EPs. Presenting a patterned stimulus to the eye does not necessarily give an EP that is entirely (or even partly) specific to pattern, even when there is no change in total stimulus light flux. Flashed-pattern stimulation may, of course, produce responses to luminance change as well as to pattern. In addition there may be EP components related to nonlinear interactions between luminance and pattern responses, but we do not discuss this form of stimulation here. For example, in pattern-reversal stimulation the bright and dim checks abruptly exchange places so that there is no change in total light flux. How, then, can there be any luminance stimulation? Indeed, if the receptive-field size for the luminance mechanism is very much larger than the check size, then there will be no luminance stimulation because each receptive field will "see" zero change in total light flux.

However, if the receptive field for the luminance mechanism is about the same size as a check (or smaller) *and* there is some nonlinear distortion before spatial summation, then there can be a luminance response. Imagine that one receptive field is stimulated by repetitive changes of intensity at a frequency F Hz. Imagine that the neighboring receptive field is similarly stimulated but in the opposite phase, so that the first receptive field is brightest when its neighbor is darkest. (Thus, the two receptive fields are on opposite sides of the contrast border whose contrast reverses at a frequency of 2F Hz.) The point of all this is as follows: it is known that, due to a rectifier-like nonlinearity, local luminance changes at F Hz will generate distorted signals containing a component at 2F Hz, so that after spatial summation (whose effect is to cancel the F Hz signals) there will be a residual 2F Hz signal due to *local luminance flicker*; this residual signal has exactly the same frequency as genuine responses to contrast reversals. The important point is that this net response could occur in the absence of any pattern response (where a true pattern response is generated by a change in spatial contrast across a contrast border). In general, an EP to pattern stimulation contains both a pattern-specific contribution and a local-luminance contribution. Note that the two contributions have identical temporal repetition frequencies. As check size rises (or spatial frequency falls), the local-luminance contribution will grow relatively larger. A procedure for disentangling the two contributions has been described for pattern appearance/disappearance EPs (Tweel & Spekreijse, 1968). (Note that blurring does not distinguish them.) For pattern reversal EPs Bodis-Wollner and Hendley (1977) have discussed a way of distinguishing the two contributions. The Amsterdam group's test is illustrated in Figure 11.5. The essential point is that in A, contrast decreases when total light flux decreases, whereas in B, contrast increases when total light flux decreases. Thus, changes of light flux are dissociated from contrast changes. The uppermost panel shows a check pattern with alternate checks marked "X" and "Y". The intensities of the X checks are modulated as shown in A (continuous line), and the averager is triggered by the modulating waveform. The other checks (Y) are held at a constant intensity, carefully preset to the level illustrated (dashed line). The EP in A is clearly asymmetric, but note that it is not possible to say that the right hand section is characteristic of "pattern appearance" rather than "light flux increase." In B the stimulating squares (X) are the same as in A, but the constant intensity of the Y squares has been present to a different level. One possible outcome is illustrated by the EP waveform b. Here the EP asymmetry has reversed, showing that the first part of the waveform is a response to pattern appearance rather than to light flux increase. A second possible outcome is illustrated by the EP waveform a. The EP asymmetry has not been reversed by the stimulus manipulation. Thus, the second part of the waveform a is a response to light flux increase, and this test has given no evidence for a true response to contrast change. A third possible outcome is intermediate between the waveforms a and b. This would mean that the waveform contained responses to both contrast change and light flux change. By way of illustration, one application of this test has been to show that electroretinograms (ERGs) elicited by pattern stimulation are most probably responses to local changes of luminance rather than genuine contrast responses (Spekreijse et al., 1973). Clearly, this test cannot be used when the EP is symmetric, as in the case of responses to pattern reversal.

12 Report of Panel V: Perceptual Processes

Panel Chair: D. Regan
Panel Members: T. Allison
                 L. Cooper
                 S. Palmer

12.1 CONFLICTS BETWEEN VISUAL PSYCHOPHYSICS AND ERPS

REGAN: We can begin with the data base. We shall discuss types of ERPs that seem to have something to do with perception (though we have not been able to find a clear and consistent distinction between *perception* and *cognition*). I shall discuss visual ERPs; Truett Allison will comment on somatic sensation; and, following that, Lynn Cooper and Steve Palmer will discuss cognition and perception.

The ERPs associated with perception discussed in Chapter 11 do not require the conscious processing of information, whereas cognitive EP components are associated with conscious information processing. One problem in cognitive ERP experiments is possible contamination with perceptual ERP components. The other side of this coin is that if you have an experiment involving a perceptual aspect and a cognitive aspect, then evoked potentials might help you to distinguish the two brain activities. If you factor this element out of a cognitive experiment, you might then be able to see what is processed at a lower level and what you must attribute to cognition.

To take another example, Wheatstone (1838) described the stereoviewer. Looking through it at a stereo pair of drawings or photographs, you saw the scene in three-dimensional depth. Wheatstone then optically reversed the right and left eyes. The two eyes' retinal images were virtually as before, but the depth was reversed. If he looked at a cube, he saw the cube in reversed depth. When he looked at something familiar like a coin, he saw the embossing recessed. But when he looked through a window, the result was different because the trees are outside the window, and obviously the window occludes bits of the trees. But, his stereoscopic mechanism told him that the tree was inside the window. On the other hand, he *knew* that trees are not cut off by windows that are behind them. What Wheatstone saw in this situation was sometimes decidedly peculiar. When he looked at faces with reversed depth, he saw them in correct depth. Presumably, this is a problem in cognition because this stereo system would have transmitted the information that the face had a negative nose. Evidently the visual system can accept a lack of realism with the window and trees but not with faces.

Now if you did an experiment like that with ERPs, you might be able to recognize that part of the ERP that was due to the stereo computation. If so, you could distinguish between two hypotheses. Suppose that the stereo cues in the picture that you are looking at indicate one thing (e.g., a negative nose) but you see something else (e.g., a normal nose). It might be that the stereo-scopic computation is normal and the visual system modifies the output of the stereo stage. On the other hand, it might be that centrally you do something that alters the way in which the stereoscopic computation is carried out so as to give a result that is more in line with your prior expectations. That's the sort of cognitive question that might be feasible to approach via ERP recording. Wheatstone himself didn't approach that question psychophysically but, returning to the question now, you might decide to attack it with an ERP experiment. For example, you might stimulate with a reversed stereo picture, asking the subjects what they see and, at the same time, using ERPs to explore what's happening at two levels of the central nervous system.

Turning to another point, the data base for visual ERPs is very rich indeed. There is a great deal of psychophysics on the topic of "channels." The psycho-logical concept of channel dates at least from 1801 (Young, 1802) in color vi-sion and has a very specific meaning. The existence of a set of psychophysical channels *might* imply the existence of a distinct neuronal population. It does not necessarily follow, of course, that a set of psychophysical channels means that there is a corresponding neural mechanism. So the existence of a psycho-physical set of channels is only a hint, not a guideline. But if there is a neural mechanism behind a particular channel, then ERP recording might enable you to find some information on that neural mechanism in humans, both adults and babies.

To summarize what is known about ERPs and sensory channels, there are stereo ERPs that can only be produced by stereo inputs. Julesz has shown that stereo ERPs can be produced by dynamic random noise, and this means that the ERPs really are cyclopean. For pattern ERPs there are long-wavelength, medium-wavelength, and short-wavelength channels. With flicker ERPs, there are medium-frequency, low-frequency, and high-frequency ERPs that come from different parts of the brain. If you stimulate different parts of the retina, you obtain responses from different areas of cortex.

Now what I want briefly to do is to show a small amount of data to illustrate how this can affect one's experimental approach. Dr. Treisman suggested an experiment that, depending on how it turned out, might cast some light on a cognitive question. The experiment involves using visual stimuli constructed from small line segments, or small elements, and rearranging them so the meaning of the array changes. This would indeed be a very powerful method of getting at certain questions. The warning I would give would be that if you take small line segments, even if the arrangement doesn't mean anything and you rearrange them in different ways that still have no meaning, nevertheless you may obtain totally different ERPs. This can be understood on the basis of Jeffreys' data (Jeffreys & Axford, 1972). As you know, there are different types of neurons in visual cortex, and some respond best to short bars and others to longer bars. Jeffreys' idea was to associate his pattern ERPs with these neurons and their rather complicated spatial properties. In other words, his findings do not have a simple explanation. You can expect complicated ERP effects from rearranging patterns of lines segments without invoking any cognitive elements.

There are three different components (C1, C2, and C3) in the pattern-appearance ERP, and each is affected differently by the physical features of the stimulus. Jeffreys analyzes the stimuli into corners and length of contour, plus amount of contour. He attributes some effects to simple cells and other effects to complex cells. These effects are concurrent and, in order to disentangle these ERP components, it is necessary to use local retinal stimulation. My point here is that if you wish to explore visual ERPs associated with cognitive activities, you must assure that you are not confounding pattern effects on the ERP with the effects of your independent variables.

Jeffreys stimulates either the lower half or the upper half of the retina. He does so for a simple reason. The parts of the brain to which these areas of the retina project have different orientations. Then if you stimulate the entire visual field, the ERPs elicited from different parts of the brain may cancel each other. The same consideration applies to the left and right half field and all four quadrants of the visual field. This may not be a major problem if we all had brains of the same shape. But human brains vary considerably in their geometry. This presents two problems: (1) Unknown visual features of the stimulus affect the different components C1, C2, and C3; and (2) your own personal brain has its own personal formula for how these activities interact and cancel on the scalp. So you have to deliver, as Jeffereys does, stimuli to small parts of the retina. Of course most cognitive psychophysiologists bear this in mind and do not vary the physical stimulus but if you did, you could be in trouble.

In a study by Spekreijse, van der Tweel, and Regan (1972), the subject was presented with a jumping checkerboard to the left eye. The right eye was occluded. You can see in Fig. 12.1 a pattern-appearance ERP and a disappear-

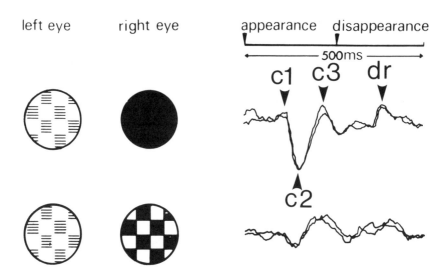

FIG. 12.1   The appearance and subsequent disappearance of a stimulus pattern produce two quite distinguishable responses that have different cortical origins, different
dynamics, different binocular summation and are differently affected by spatial frequency or check size. The pattern appearance response consists of three components
(C1, C2, and C3) of which only C1 originates in striate cortex. Modified from
Spekreijse, Van der Tweel, and Regan, *Vision Research,* 1972, *12,* 521.

ance ERP. If the subject's right eye is presented with a high-contrast static
checkerboard, pattern perception is totally suppressed, and the ERP elicited at
the left eye is much attenuated. The residual ERP is the "local luminance"
ERP that is not suppressed by the right-eye stimulus. So in this type of experiment, in fact, psychophysics and ERPs correlate. The use of the static patterns
suppresses pattern perception but not flicker perception. You perceive faint
flicker in the background. Correspondingly, the ERP that remains is the flicker
ERP. The pattern ERP is abolished. These, and other data, suggest that there
are two totally different constituents to the ERP. One has therefore to be alert
to the level of detail that is required in stimulus specification.

Now I would like to comment on a point that has come up several times,
namely can ERP recording tell you anything that psychophysics doesn't? The
following illustrates that, in principle, it can. We investigated the color coding
of pattern ERPs (Regan, 1977). Our hypothesis was that you have two, or
perhaps three, color-coded channels for pattern. As accommodation fluctuates,
whichever is most effective (red or green) at any instant gets through. What
could be the function of this arrangement? We proposed that it is to counter
the effect of ocular chromatic aberration. You throw away color information
and you improve your acuity. Hence you have a wide depth of focus in white
light and yet you see as well in white light as you do in monochromatic light,

etc. The "switching" arrangement is operating at the front end of the visual system and you're not consciously aware of it.

We measured spectral sensitivity of these channels by means of the "evoked potential feedback" method (Regan, 1975; Regan, 1979). Subjects viewed a very fine pattern of checks on the fovea jumping up and down at 6Hz. A continuous ERP record was taken from the brain. Moment-to-moment values of ERP amplitude controlled the visual stimulus. So your brain was in a feedback loop and the instantaneous values of the evoked potential controlled what you saw. We superimposed on the pattern of checks a patch of light to desensitize the retina and the brain response controlled the brightness of the patch. When we changed the superimposed yellow light to blue, feedback had to keep itself at 6 μV (microvolts). What happened was the brain switched up the brightness of the light 40 times and hunted about for a new value. So then when we continually changed wavelength, the brain feedback loop kept the amplitude of the pattern ERP the same and adjusted the brightness of the desensitized light to ensure this. Hence the apparatus plotted a spectral sensitivity curve. The spectral sensitivities of the pattern ERP channels turned out to resemble the R minus G, R plus G channels of Sperling in the monkey. This held only for pattern ERPs. If you use an unpatterned stimulus field, you have different results. You get the eye's luminance sensitivity curve instead (Regan, 1970).

12.2 THE SOMESTHETIC ERP AND
THE PERCEPTION OF STIMULUS INTENSITY

ALLISON: Many investigators (e.g., Franzen & Offenloch, 1969; Rosner & Goff, 1967) have studied the relation among psychophysics, perception, and ERPs, using somesthetic stimuli. I have the time to discuss, briefly, the perception of stimulus intensity and its relation to ERP recordings. One of a psychophysicist's first steps when assaying a new stimulus is to study its intensity function. This is relatively easy. You just turn the knob, and subjects find it fairly easy to report the subjective intensity of stimuli. In the 1960s, change in somatosensory ERPs as a function of intensity was studied by a number of researchers. In those days everyone was enthusiastic about Stevens' power functions (Rosner & Goff, 1967) so they plotted their results in log-log form. If you plot the psychophysical estimate (i.e., the magnitude estimations), you typically find a straight line over a range of intensities. Now if you look at the ERP—and in the best studies in this area the ERP and the subject's subjective responses were obtained simultaneously—you also find something that looks more or less like a straight line. Usually the electrophysiological slope is less than the psychophysical slope but that's another problem. After the intensity reaches a certain level, the relation breaks down and in a surprising way. The ERP intensity function may flatten out and it may even come back down. Perceptually, the same thing can happen. Investigators with a psychiatric bent call a person who does this a "reducer," and that's a whole different story (Buchsbaum, 1971). But the fact is that it does happen. So first of all, how would one go about explaining this kind of curious leveling-off effect? Although I don't know how to do this, one possibility is that at increasing levels of activity the amount of inhibition in a sensory system (or in any neuronal system) increases relatively faster than excitation. So that, for example, if we think of the evoked potential at any given moment in time as being composed of some mixture of excitation and inhibition, that is of summed EPSPs and IPSPs, then inhibition is going to increase relatively more rapidly at high levels of intensity than is excitation. That may be all we need to account for these results. Certainly we know this happens at the single-cell level. If you record intracellularly, you find a large EPSP with some spikes superimposed but not much IPSP. Then if you increase the intensity, the EPSP increases. Now IPSP starts to come in and at even higher levels you find a much larger, long duration IPSP. And this can happen within a few milliseconds of the excitatory discharge. So at the single-cell level there is no doubt this happens and its function is obvious. It's a negative feedback system. You don't want the cell to become so excited at high levels of intensity that it goes off and starts producing seizures. Whether that can account for the psychophysical results is another matter, because we don't have the foggiest notion what inhibition does at the perceptual level. We know that normal brain function depends on a balance between excitation and inhibition and we know, or we think we know, that discrimination is sharpened by inhibitory processes so that, for example, we say that surround inhibition increases the discrimination of events separated in space. The point is that we cannot interpret these strange curves though we do know that things can be very nonlinear at the neuronal level. Yet, we have no idea how excitation and inhibition actually interact in the brain to affect things like the perception of stimulus intensity.

Let me illustrate another problem by describing an experiment done some years ago by John Swett (Swett & Bourassa, 1967). He implanted a cuff electrode around a peripheral nerve of a cat and placed electrodes over somatosensory cortex. He then trained the cat to press a lever when the cat felt the shock delivered to the nerve. At low levels of stimulation he was only stimulating muscle spindle afferents. These are very large fibers and so they have lower thresholds for stimulation than smaller fibers. Well, the cat never pressed the bar to these stimuli. It never perceived them, and yet Swett recorded a lovely evoked potential from somatosensory cortex. Now it's not somatosensory cortex per se. It's actually a little transitional area, cytoarchitecturally, between somatosensory cortex and motor cortex. In Broadman's terminology, it's area 3A, so that discrete area of cortex receives input from muscle spindle afferants. Yet the cat is not perceiving it. Why not? Well, because it wouldn't do him any good, it would only be confusing, because, as you probably know, if the muscle is passively stretched, the spindles are stretched and they discharge. But if the intrafusal fibers are activated, the muscle spindles are unloaded and the discharge is reduced, so that system provides ambiguous information about what the muscle is doing, how much it is stretched, and therefore about where the arm is in space or anything else that the cat, or the human for that matter, could use. So it just does not enter consciousness although it produces a lovely evoked potential in a region very near primary somatosensory cortex.

KELSO: There has been a recent paper (Roland, 1978) and there has been work from Peter Matthews' laboratory for some time saying quite the opposite to what you're saying. I think in all fairness it should be said that the issue is open.

ALLISON: Well, for the purposes of my argument, let us assume that the classical story is correct, that there is no conscious perception of spindle afferent information wherever it's going to in the brain. Now obviously the cerebellum needs to know a lot about what is going on in the muscles and this transitional region of somatosensory cortex needs to know what is going on. But the sensorium doesn't need to know because that information is not relevant. If we increase the stimulus intensity and stimulate some joint afferents as well, now the cat perceives the stimulus and presses the bar. Let's assume in that situation we were doing an intensity function. What we would find is a combination of evoked potentials generated in primary somatosensory cortex that *may* be involved in neural mechanisms of perception of intensity, combined with some evoked potential activity that is useful to the animal in some other context but has nothing to do with perception of that stimulus. Any conclusion we come to about neural mechanisms in relation to perceived intensity would be incorrect because we're mixing apples and oranges in our evoked potentials. (I should say there is no direct evidence that activity in area 3A is recorded in the human sensory evoked potential. It may well be that in a human somatosensory ERP we are seeing some activity from that region. I don't know, but it is a possibility.) So how can we find a truer measure of neural activity in relation to the judgment of intensity?

Well, obviously we can't go in and ablate area 3A in people but maybe we could find a peripheral nerve in which there were no muscle afferents, a purely cutaneous nerve. Assume we could do that. In fact, Swett also did that experiment in cats, stimulating a purely cutaneous nerve. In that case the evoked potential and perceptual thresholds were about the same. We stimulate the nerve and we record the evoked potential from the somatosensory cortex. Are we going to be any better off? Maybe, but not necessarily. Not necessarily, I think, because it may very well be that primary somatosensory cortex really doesn't care what the intensity of the stimulus is; that is, it may care for other properties of the stimulus, but it may not be the place, if indeed there is any one place, where perception of intensity is carried out. I say that because what primary somatosensory cortex really likes to do is deal with information that is a combination of somatic sensation and active movement. It is a *sensorimotor* area, as Woolsey said many years ago (Woolsey, 1958). It involves an active collaboration of motor output and sensory input. If you remove this cortical area in a monkey, the animal will be very poor at making discriminations based on palpation of an object. Now I can't prove this because there is no direct evidence that I know of, but I would be willing to bet that a monkey could discriminate intensity of a median nerve shock (the stimulus most often used in human SEP studies) perfectly well without his primary somatosensory cortex.

ZAIDEL: Just as animals can perform a brightness discrimination without the visual cortex (Spear, 1979).

ALLISON: That's right. So the point is we placed our electrode, in a sense, in the wrong place. Any inferences we make concerning the neural mechanisms of intensity, based on what we've recorded from primary somatosensory cortex, may be wrong because we just don't have our electrode in an area that really codes intensity. Now the activity in that area may be highly correlated, if we are lucky, with activity in those populations of neurons that do have something more directly to do with intensity. But the moral of the story is that simply putting our electrodes in certain regions and measuring the amplitude of all the bumps that we can measure as we manipulate our independent variables doesn't necessarily have anything to do with what is really going on in the brain. For purposes of argument, let me say it straight out: I don't think we've learned anything about the neural mechanisms by which the brain processes information related to intensity from human ERP studies. Obviously, for practical reasons we need intensity function data. For example, in the somatosensory system high-intensity stimuli—particularly at high rates of stimulation—tend to be unpleasant if not downright painful. In a clinical testing situation we want to stimulate as rapidly as possible so that we can be done in some reasonable amount of time, so one of our objectives is to pull the maximum microvolts per minute out of that patient. To do that we need to know some optimum tradeoff between response amplitude and intensity so that we can pick the lowest possible intensity and still obtain the highest-amplitude response. I'm not suggesting at all that it's silly to do intensity functions, but let's not kid ourselves that we've really learned very much about how the somatosensory system codes intensity. There are lots of things going on in the brain that have nothing to do with conscious sensation. In this particular case, if the story holds up that activity in muscle spindle afferents never enters conscious perception, you will have evoked activity that is generated quite close to neural activity that does indeed have a lot to do with somatic sensation and perception. We need to know these things so we can at least try to record only the activity that might, at least in principle, give us some handle on what we're looking at. But that's pretty hard to do.

12.3 REPRESENTATIONS: IDEAS FOR EXPERIMENTS

COOPER: You can imagine in the face of all this unbridled optimism that our panel was stimulated to develop cognitive experiments using ERPs. We did not, but we do have a few suggestions. We do not find terribly useful, as others do, the distinction between perception and cognition because we take a rather positive view of perceptual activity. We assume that our perceptual experience of the world is determined both by the sensory information and its organization and also by how that information is adapted, selected, and processed by internal mechanisms. It is the internal mechanisms and structure that we would like to know about. Some of the concepts from previous panels like memory, expectations, and knowledge about the world are important in determining how we perceive. I'm going to give a brief overview of what we take to be some important issues in cognitive, or information-processing, approaches to perception. For some of those issues we tried to frame our thinking in terms of categories of experiments that might be useful. For each problem we asked the following questions: First, is it the case that evoked potentials could tell us anything at all? Second, is it the case that evoked potentials could tell us anything different from, or perhaps additional to, behavioral data that we already have? Finally, is it possible that evoked potentials might provide an easier method than behavioral experiments to obtain certain answers? All the experiments I shall discuss are fantasy-land experiments. The P300 is going to be notably absent from most of them. They all have the following property. A positive outcome would be useful and would tell us a lot, but negative results really wouldn't basically change our minds at all about what we believe to be the underlying mechanisms or explanations. What this means is that we feel rather reluctant to couch our cognitive models in terms of specific predictions about brain activity. But, were we to find some useful measure of brain activity underlying a cognitive process, then I think we'd know something more than we would by simply observing the process behaviorally.

What are the current issues in information-processing approaches to perception? We've divided them into issues concerned with representation of perceptual information and issues that are concerned with aspects of processing perceptual information. Steve Palmer will discuss in detail issues of representation, but, briefly, one current issue concerns whether an internal representation of a visual object is best thought of as a combination of features or whether something like a spatial-frequency model is a more appropriate way of describing the stimulus. Another issue that has already been alluded to here is the "analog versus propositional representation" issue; that is, is information represented in some kind of symbolic, discrete, qualitative form or, in some cases anyway, is it in a form that preserves more quantitative information about the external objects to which it corresponds? In terms of processing issues, one aspect of the analog/propositional debate is the question of the extent to which imaginal processes and perceptual processes share the same sort of underlying mechanism. There have been a lot of experimental demonstrations recently of functional equivalences between imaginal and perceptual tasks. I have in mind, for example, experiments that have been done by Steve Kosslyn (Kosslyn, 1973) on scanning visual images, where the time course of that scanning seems to be very much like the time course of actually scanning a visual object. Also, there are the experiments of Ron Finke's (Finke & Schmidt, 1977) where he shows that one can obtain certain kinds of adaptation effects like the McCollough aftereffects using purely imaginal conditions. So the question is, is there any way to demonstrate that more than just a functional equivalence is involved—that similar mechanisms perception and imagination? Other processing issues, ones that are familiar by now, concerns data-driven versus conceptually driven processes. That is, to what extent do expectations and knowledge about the world influence selection and the activity of lower-level, perceptual mechanisms? Still other processing issues have to do with the operation of processing mechanisms. For example, there is the sequential-serial versus parallel processing issue. Also, there is the issue of whether perceptual information is analyzed in an analytic or a feature-dimensional way or in a more holistic or integral fashion, and some of the data that we've discussed in the attention session were, I think, relevant to this— for example, some of Harter's data. Another issue is the global to local processing issue. Don Norman talked about this briefly in his tutorial, giving an example from some of Steve Palmer's work. This issue is this: If we perceive some kind of complex stimulus, do we first extract global, configural information and then extract information concerning more local features? Or, do these operations go on simultaneously? I think these are the main representational and processing issues that we want to address now.

DONCHIN: May I ask you something, Lynn? It struck me, as you were talking, that you are constructing a series of dichotomies in which a choice must always be made between one of two options. But it may be the case that all of those things you described are going on simultaneously all the time. There will not be a simple answer. Sometimes one and sometimes the other option is used. Do you really feel that a choice has to be made on all these dichotomies? That one choice would be incorrect and the other will always turn out to be correct?

COOPER: No, certainly not. However, it is sometimes useful to phrase problems in this dichotomous way. It is conceptually easier to deal with. It also
has been the case that, in terms of experimental operations, for different purposes and for different types of stimulus materials and tasks, processing can be
fundamentally different. So, these dichotomies may be psychologically real—
not just convenient conceptual tools.

PALMER: I'm going to assume that P300 is the end of the line perceptually
and we're going to talk about other sorts of measures and experiments. I have
argued that you can talk about two aspects of representation (Palmer, 1978).
One is the nature of the information that is represented. That concerns the
correlates of perception of the real world and psychophysical relationships
between the world and the internal representation. It seems to me that you
can do evoked poential studies, but they are not going to tell you much of anything that is new or different from what you can learn behaviorally through
psychophysical tasks. The second aspect of representation concerns the physical realization of the internal representation, and here it seems to me that
evoked potentials may be of some use. Some examples were given by Regan.
One concerned evoked potentials to flickering spatial-frequency gratings (see
Chapter 10). It turns out that if you flicker a grating on and off at a certain
rate, the ERP response depends on both the flicker rate and the frequency of
the grating. High flicker rate emphasizes the low spatial frequencies and the
low flicker rate emphasizes the high spatial frequencies. This is an example of
what is psychologically and, in many or most respects, psychophysically a continuum. Spatial-frequency gratings do not seem to be qualitatively different at
low and high frequencies; yet the evoked potential results suggest that at some
brain level two different populations of neurons are responding differently. As
I see it, this is fairly similar to the auditory domain where there is a
frequency-sensitive pitch perception mechanism that seems psychologically to
be a completely smooth, continuous process. But from everything that we now
know about auditory mechanisms, there is a difference between the mechanisms that code low- and high-frequency information in terms of neural structure and process (Green, 1976). So this is an example of how one might be
able to find more detailed information about perceptual representation through
the use of evoked poentials than one could behaviorally.
   Now the issue of propositional versus analog representation is messy for all
kinds of reasons (Palmer, 1978). I briefly mention an idea I had for a relevant
ERP study, which I now believe to have been naive. You might be able to sort
out some issues like the quantitative/qualitative distinction, that is, the extent
to which representation for different values of a dimension is symbolic and
qualitative as opposed to quantitative. The notion is that you could look at the
ERPs to various different perceptual dimensions to see how they vary. Now

there are a number of different ways in which they might do so; for example, they could vary in the amplitude of the response, the latency of the peak response, the shape of the waveform, the scalp distribution of the waveform, and the polarity of response. It seems to me that certain of these measures are at least more consistent with and more suggestive of qualitative or quantitative mechanisms underlying them. There are all kinds of problems, however. You can always make up stories where a qualitative mechanism would result in nothing but a change in amplitude. But the most straightforward explanation for an increase in amplitude is either that the same neurons are more active or that a larger population of the same sort of neurons are active. If you get a change in the shape of the waveform or in the polarity of the waveform or in its spatial distribution, one suspects that different populations of neurons are working and that there might be some qualitative changes in the underlying representation. Again, none of these distinctions is hard and fast, because you can make up all kinds of alternative explanations.

Finally I shall discuss the relations of perception and imagination. It has been suggested that the imaginal representation shares at least some, or maybe all, of the mechanisms that underlie the corresponding perceptual events (Cooper & Shepard, 1973; Shepard, 1975). Lynn Cooper will present some experiments bearing on this hypothesis. The technique is due to Martin Regan who proposed a very clever method for studying orientation perception using ERPs. It was up to Lynn and myself to try to come up with some ERP studies that might yield useful evidence about whether the same neural mechanisms underlie perception and imagination.

The technique is different from the others described at this meeting. It is based upon the flicker experiments that Regan discusses in Chapter 10. Suppose a person is looking at a pattern that consists of three differently oriented gratings, each flickering at a different rate (Fig. 12.2). For example, the stimulus might consist of a low-intensity, vertical, sinusoidal grating that is flickering at a frequency of say 8 Hz, a second grating at a different orientation

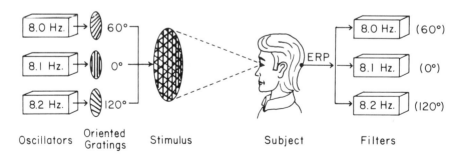

FIG. 12.2   A proposed experiment using event-related potentials to study perception, attention, and imagery. (See text for details.)

that is flickering at 8.1 Hz, and still a third grating at another orientation that is flickering at 8.2 Hz. In other words, there would be a stimulus pattern that would probably look like a kind of mottled, gyrating, jellylike sort of grayish thing. Now Regan assures me that the magnitude of the ERPs associated with different populations of cells can be sorted out by using either spectral analysis or narrow-band filters. The outputs of each of the three filters (at 8, 8.1, and 8.2 Hz) will reflect the response of the cell populations to the stimulus. In other words, the power in these three portions of the spectrum presumably represents the current activity levels of the population of neurons activated by each flickering component.

Before I reach the imagination experiment, I want to suggest a perceptual-attention experiment that could be done using this technique. It is, in fact, fairly similar to the experiments that Russ Harter has done (Harter & Previc, 1978; Harter, Previc, & Towle, 1979). Although these three gratings are simultaneously flickering at different rates, one could present tones to subjects to cue them to attend to different orientations. The highest tone might indicate attending to the vertical grating, the lowest tone to the left oblique, and the middle one to the other oblique grating. The idea is to instruct the subject to attend differentially to the three oriented components at different times so that the ERP response can be measured at the output of the filters to see whether changes occur when attention is switched.

SHIFFRIN: I missed something. I thought you told us it was going to look like vibrating, muddy jelly, or something. What is the subject going to attend to?

PALMER: Well, I don't know. I've never seen one of these things. My guess is that you should be able to pick out the vertically oriented stripes attentionally when the appropriate cue is presented and that there should then be some change in the relative output of the three filters. I don't know whether it would be slow or fast or even whether it would increase or decrease. Another question of some interest is whether the other two ERP responses would increase, decrease, or stay the same. These are some issues the experiment is designed to investigate. But the basic idea of the experiment, I think, is fairly clear: If, in fact, attention does something at a low perceptual level (I'm assuming it's a fairly low level, say area 17 of visual cortex), then one should find changes in the aggregate ERP responses for populations of cells sensitive to different orientations as a function of attentional set. Various sorts of controls would be necessary to make sure people aren't attending to the flicker rate rather than the orientation, but I think that those things are all fairly straightforward and could be done with some ingenuity. And, if it turned out that people could do this task, then we could answer some of the same kinds of questions that Russ Harter has investigated (Harter & Previc, 1978; Harter,

Previc, & Towle, 1979). This technique might be easier or it might be harder, but it would be interesting and important to have some converging evidence.

Now let's move on to the perception versus imagery experiment. The basic idea is fairly similar. For the perceptual conditions, high-contrast, steady-state stimuli can be presented on top of this mottled background while measuring ERPs. It would be best to use patterns that have a lot of power at one of the three orientations and minimal power at the other two when analyzed spectrally. For example, if you presented an H over the flickering gratings (where the H has a large component in the vertical orientation), something ought to happen in the corresponding filter output. The ERP response might be enhanced or reduced, but something should change in the relative output of the orientation channels when the H is presented. Now the obvious question is whether the same changes occur when the subject imagines an H on top of that grating. Subjects would have to be pretrained about the size and orientation of the H, of course. The question is whether the imagined H would produce the same ERP pattern as the perceived H.

SHIFFRIN: Is the H flickering or is the background pattern of gratings flickering?

PALMER: The background pattern flickers to stimulate these presumed orientation channels—these populations of neurons that are orientation-specific—and to drive them at a rate so that their output can be picked up by the filters. The H is constant in intensity over time. The idea is that the perceptual response to the H should interact with the orientation channels differentially. If it isn't flickering, it should be driving those neurons that respond to its main orientational information. If so, there are not going to be as many neurons from the orientation channel that are free to flicker, and, therefore, the ERP output at the corresponding flicker frequency should decrease. But the only important thing is that the relative outputs for the different orientational channels change systematically with the orientational characteristics of the figure.

HARTER: I see some similarity between the instructional set for imagery and for selective attention. If you say imagine an "H", aren't you saying attend an "H"? This is particularly true in our grating experiments since the attended grating was not physically present prior to the presentation of the evoking flash—the subject had to remember what this specific grating was. Our size and orientation specific tuning functions may, in fact, reflect the specificity of the image represented in memory. These were not sensory tuning functions, which were reflected by the effects of check size *per se.*

PALMER: I agree. I guess you could do two things to decouple the image from the flickering gratings. One would be to choose the stimuli appropriately where the power of the pattern wouldn't align with the gratings that are presented. A checkerboard, for example, has its main power along the diagonals rather than along the edges of the squares. Another possibility would be to have people imagine the H in a different place than the flickering pattern. If you still found the same interaction between what people were imagining (or perceiving) and the output these flickering channels, it would suggest it wasn't just an attentional response.

POSNER: Don't the evoked potentials to these gratings show an adaptation from staring at a grating for a long time? One test of this imagery hypothesis would be to ask the person to imagine a grating for some length of time and then to look at the evoked potential to a weak threshold grating for adaptation. Maybe that's already been done.

REGAN: After the first few seconds, there is no contrast adaptation of the ERP response to flicker. We once investigated that using a running average with a 7 min continuous record. It was less than plus or minus 5%, moment to moment, over the whole 7 min.

PALMER: From here it's fairly straightforward to see how one might be able to do an ERP study of mental rotation. People could imagine rotating a letter or some other well-oriented stimulus that is quite different from the three components in the background. The transformations from one orientation to another should be reflected in changes in the output of the filters. If you just told somebody to imagine rotation clockwise or counterclockwise, you should be able to tell the direction by looking at the ERP. I don't know what the sensitivity of this technique might be, but in theory it could give us a handle on what orientation a person was thinking about as they were performing mental rotation.

COOPER: The interesting thing about that experiment would be as a test of the claim that Shepard and I have wanted to make; that is, what is really rotating in mental rotation is some kind of anticipation for perceiving a particular object in a particular orientation. To the extent that you might be able to show that in the perceptual and mental cases similar patterns in evoked potential data emerge, one might take this kind of evidence as an indication of similar underlying brain mechanisms.

PALMER: I left out the condition where you show the nonflickering figure physically rotating in front of the flickering background, but it was probably straightforward enough that everybody imagined that I had said it.

DONCHIN: One of the problems in this design is that the information that is picked up by the filter may have nothing to do with the processing of the stimuli. It may be information about the frequency of the input where all the contour and figural information has been filtered out by the brain. All that is retained is the fact that the stimulus has a dominant frequency because you are averaging over a lot of time and a lot of space. This whole technique is built on the assumption that you pick out of the EEG a frequency component that is analogous to the frequency component of the input.

REGAN: Not really. The frequency is pretty arbitrary. The idea is that you have those three low-contrast, orthogonal gratings that you are just using as probes.

DONCHIN: But your ERP is not really an ERP in the sense that we've been talking about it. It is the amount of power in the frequency of the EEG that corresponds to the frequency of your input.

PALMER: It is in this sense that Regan has been talking about ERPs.

DONCHIN: That is what he calls a "steady-state" ERP.

REGAN: That's right. We're talking about a very narrow bandwidth. But you know that the only power at that temporal frequency is due to that particular grating or that orientation. You set a grating at $45°$ with a signature, and that signature is 8.2 Hz. This is one probe. If something hits that orientation and spatial frequency, you are going to see it straightaway via the ERP. The actual temporal frequency really isn't material to this; it's merely the signature you attach to that orientation and spatial frequency.

DONCHIN: In other words, the component that you are looking at in the activity may end up having nothing to do with any cognitive process; that is, you are assessing the response to primary sensory activity that even in Regan's scheme contains neurons that are sensitive to certain gratings, and as long as you stimulate them, you will obtain a response. If so, it doesn't really matter if the subject is processing the stimulus or not.

PALMER: But if you can modulate that output as a function of what you tell the subject to do or by what you tell him to attend to or by what you tell him to imagine, then that would be evidence that the subject was processing the stimulus.

DONCHIN: Well, it would be interesting if somebody could show that this works.

REGAN: We had hypothesized that the mental processes share the same neural mechanisms and physical ones. Here is the spatial-frequency-analyzing physical process. We are now tapping onto the stimulus and it doesn't matter whether it is time-synchronized or it isn't, or whether it takes half a minute to happen. The hypothesis here is whether orientation-tuned mechanisms are affeted by cognition. The technique taps those neural mechanisms. If you don't see it in the ERP, well then mental rotation is *not* doing something that happens in the real rotation situation at that level.

DONCHIN: You're assuming that perception is a subroutine.

PALMER: We're not assuming that; it is part of our hypothesis. Assuming that these detectors, these cells, are in area 17 of visual cortex, then we are testing the hypothesis that attention and mental rotation and so forth have some affect on that level. Of course, if we find a negative result, we don't know that there isn't some other mechanism shared by cognitive and sensory activities.

DONCHIN: Well, I thought Regan said that negative results would mean something.

REGAN: Yes. The hypothesis is that mental rotation is mediated by the same physical mechanisms that mediate real rotation. Now if you really rotate something, it changes its orientation. If we do *not* see ERP evidence of rotation during mental rotation, the orientation-timed cortical neurons that respond to gratings are *not* responding during mental rotation.

DONCHIN: It is not clear to me if the idea that the imaginal mechanism is identical to the perceptual mechanism—is it assumed that when I imagine a rotating light, somehow my world model (or homonculus) has grabbed a hypercomplex diagonal cell in area 17 and activates it? That is, are you assuming that the images are produced by activating the initial sensory processing areas? It does seem not like a very sensible thing to do because if area 17 is my detector for rotation, and it feeds upward in the homunculus to indicate rotation, then the image may operate by activating the subsequent stations rather than area 17.

PALMER: This whole argument has developed in cognitive psychology as an argument about images and the extent to which they are really like pictures, but the discussion is in terms of processing without a necessary translation to neuronal processes.

REGAN: Well, if you are going to test a hypothesis, the hypothesis has to make some sort of prediction. When you make a prediction and stick your neck out, you may have it chopped off.

DONCHIN: There is no question this would be an interesting experiment. I think if the results are positive, I would be amazed and convinced—very surprised, but convinced.

HARTER: The results will be positive. Because if you compel somebody to attend, and we've done it with orientations, it influences the response—now maybe not these same ones—these 8 cps ones, because they could be coming from a different place in the brain, but it wouldn't be surprising.

REGAN: Attention does not seem to affect steady-state pattern ERPs.

HARTER: You mean you've done this already?

REGAN: We have never tried this rotation experiment, but we did look at the affect of attention many years ago. I had thought that if you want to do cognitive experiments, you should not use the steady-state ERP, but I have modified this opinion during discussions in this meeting. If someone proposes that certain cognitive variables influence low-level mechanisms then steady-state ERPs could perhaps be used to study cognitive processes.

PALMER: Perhaps you're talking in terms of ambiguous triangle experiments where the triangles are ambiguous in the sense that you can see them point in any one of three directions at once but only one at a time. You put fields of these together in various configurations and bias people toward seeing them one way or the other. Anyway I was explaining this as a kind of experiment that I do and Martin came up with this technique for studying them, the idea being that you could look at the differential sensitivity of different systems by probing with the flicker—steady-state flicker ERPs. I'm less optimistic that it would work if it doesn't work with attention.

REGAN: As to the triangle illusion, Ginsburg has argued that because there are different orientation channels, whichever channel is most effective at any moment will determine the way the triangle seems to be pointing. If the relative sensitivity of these channels fluctuates from moment to moment, those triangles will appear to change directions as indeed they do and as indeed they do all at once just like a flock of birds, which is what you'd expect. Now there are two possible hypotheses here. (1) Channel outputs are affected by a cognitive stage of processing; (2) it's no more than variation of relative channel sensitivity. If you carried out our proposed ERP experiment, and you superimpose on those gratings a lot of triangles, now those triangles are going to switch every now and then. Hypothesis 2 is that that's because the spatial-frequency channels at a low level change their relative sensitivity. In this case, where you see those three ERPs switch at the same instant, you expect that the triangles will switch. In this case, the person could push a button or you'd get a P300 or whatever you feel like. On the other hand, it may be that those channels are switching their relative sensitivities and the triangles are switching, but they are not linked at all, so now we go to hypothesis 1. You've really shown that it's cognitive in this sense, but you can't explain it. There is a third possibility, namely that the relative sensitivity of the channel switches and a little bit later than the perception switches, and sometimes perception switches but the channels do not, in which case you have both a cognitive process and a low-level process and you don't know which is which. I think that is at least what we're trying to get at. Here we have a cognitive model that gives predictions testable by ERP recording. Also, you can use the ERP to tell you which event is determined by cognitive and which by low-level processing.

COOPER: I have two more points. One is an idea of a type of experiment that one could do to show that something like expectation or world knowledge could influence lower-level stages of processing. Again, given a positive outcome, we could make some statement about similarity between perceptual and other kinds of mechanisms. Are most of you familiar with the adaptation experiments that Naomi Weisstein (Weisstein, 1973) has done?

Consider the displays in Figure 12.3. What we have here is a grating, the same grating interrupted by a hexagon and the same grating interrupted by drawing a cube in the middle of it. Those of you who know Weisstein's (1973) experiment know that the effects are small, but you can obtain bigger effects. (We recently replicated it using different displays from her cubes and hexagons with much bigger effects.) Anyway, what she showed was that in an adaptation situation you find adaptation as you normally would to just a regular grating like A. The test patch that she used in all her experiments was a circle of the

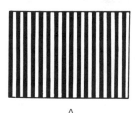 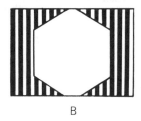 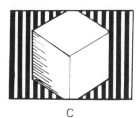

A   B   C

FIG. 12.3   Examples of the displays used in Weisstein's experiments (adapted from Weisstein, 1973).

same spatial frequency and orientation as the grating itself in the middle of this display. So in the case of the regular grating it would be someplace where the subject had actually been exposed to a grating. In the case of B and C no grating had been experienced during adaptation. She found substantial adaptation in case A. Let's pretend it's a perfect world now. She didn't find adaptation in case B and found some adaptation in case C. The question here is why you find adaptation in case C. The subject has never actually experienced a grating in the particular location where she is testing, and her notion is that you find adaptation because the visual system has rules about the way objects in a three-dimensional world are organized. These rules are such that our perceptual systems know that three-dimensional objects in front of surfaces have those surfaces continue behind them. The adaptation in this case with a cube interrupting a grating presumably was due to some population of neurons responding as though the grating had actually been perceived. The idea for an evoked potential experiment is sort of a simple one. Say you could find that you could get something in the evoked response that was similar in cases A and C and was not present in case B. There you could sort of meet Martin's objection. If you could rig your displays B and C correctly, you could have two identical stimulus conditions that lead to differences in evoked response data; in case C and A, two nonidentical stimulus conditions that lead to similar patterns of evoked potential data. In the perceptual world we would want to believe that gratings continue behind the cube and that this leads to similarities in the evoked response. That would be another type of rather powerful demonstration that in fact there were real brain mechanisms that were affected by higher-level rules and expectations about the relationships among objects in three dimensions. This is another class of experiments that we though might be a useful one.

HARTER: If I remember, wasn't it Cambell and Maffei (1970) who showed that adaptation to gratings was not restricted very well to the exact location of the adapting stimulus? They showed with evoked potentials that the adaptation effects were not restricted to just the area of the adapting field but extended to adjacent parts of the visual field. Couldn't this explain the effect you just mentioned?

COOPER: Even if it were true, Russ, the real dramatic feature of this experiment as idealized in the psychophysical data is that you don't have adaptation to B (hexagon interrupting grating). That's the powerful thing. Any eye-movement or "spread of effort" hypothesis would have to predict similar results in cases B and C.

ZAIDEL: An interesting manipulation would seem to me to be if you can create adaptation in a place that would continue the lines without the top space so that you would imagine that the lines should continue because the top space is different. Even though there are no lines you have adaptation. Did anybody find that?

COOPER: The point of this sort of demonstration, too, is that, as Martin Regan noted earlier, you really can present your hypothesis in terms of similarities in underlying brain mechanisms. If you could find similarities in these two cases, then this positive result would really tell you something.

TREISMAN: You said you had replicated it and found better results.

COOPER: Yes. Weisstein's effects were very small but reliable. We used displays in both the two- and three-dimensional cases that were shaded in order to create two- and three-dimensional biases. We had reasonable adaptation effects in the case of the three-dimensional bias and none in the two-dimensional situation. We coupled this condition with just using instructions for two- and three-dimensional sets. The effects are smaller there. They are not so large as in the shaded case, but they are more substantial than the ones that Weisstein originally reported. We're doing the experiment now using stereoscopic displays.

SHIFFRIN: Have you thought about doing this with rotating three-dimensional objects? You would think that would set fire to all sorts of . . .

COOPER: Rotating three-dimensional objects? A good idea. Again, the trick is that you want to make these two conditions—the two- and three-dimensional ones—as comparable as possible. I think that the stereoscopic experiments will probably turn out to be best.
 I don't know that we have any other experiments to propose, but one thing I wanted to mention is the use of evoked potentials in areas of perception where one might argue that evoked potentials could provide an easier method of data collection than behavioral experiments. One such area is the study of the perceptual capabilities of human infants. I don't know exactly how you would go about doing the experiments, but I know I've spent the last 3 years with my laboratory down the hall from an infant laboratory. I've seen how extremely difficult it is to do those behavioral experiments with infants. If you could, for example, find evoked potential correlates to habituation and other paradigms that people are using in infant research now, it might provide an attractive alternative to the behavioral experiments.

HARTER: Unfortunately, we have similar methodological problems in infant ERP studies. It is difficult to keep the baby awake, still, fixating the visual display, etc. The lack of control results in variable data which, in turn, requires more replication. Many mothers lose their patience in the process and do not want to return for replications.

COOPER: Is it really as bad as I think? I mean, when you do some of these preferential looking and habituation experiments, you literally need to have five experimenters in the room, and you need to video-tape everything that is going on.

REGAN: Spekreijse and Khoe, during the last 7 years at Amsterdam, have done what might seem to be a fairly simple experiment (but it isn't). They recorded pattern ERPs using a manipulation that tells you what component is contrast-specific and what component isn't contrast-specific. They monitored ERP development from 1 day of age onward. The technological problem is formidable, but the results of this long-term study are something you couldn't find out behaviorally. Summarizing it very much, you have a pattern ERP that doesn't look like an adult's at first. The different components, some of which are due to contrast-specific processes and some of which are due to local luminance develop differently.

Because, according to Jeffreys and Halliday, component C1 comes from the striate cortex and C2 from extrastriate cortex, eventually when these components become recognizable, you can look backward and see what they used to look like at a very early age and find out which area of the visual cortex develops fastest in human. The conclusion, as I mentioned, is not intuitively obvious. The conclusion is that humans and monkeys are different in that area 17 matures faster than 18 in human (I think) and vice versa in monkey. It is a difficult project but one does appear to come out with something potentially useful, because it could be that those two areas in human are differentially susceptible to trouble during development. So I think there is some mileage in that sort of study and Russ Harter can speak of this from personal experience, having done the first study of this type.

HARTER: Yes. The data are difficult to obtain but the results have been worth it. The data from our work suggest that different components of ERPs are generated from different sources and are associated with different types of cognitive function. The earlier components are particularly sensitive to check size but less sensitive to behavioral measures of visual preference whereas the later components are more sensitive to visual preference and less sensitive to check size. This approach promises to provide insight as to the nature of both sensory and cognitive development.

13 Report of Panel VI: Individual Differences and Clinical Applications

Panel chair: M. Oscar-Berman

Panel members: E. Callaway
N. Squires
E. Zaidel

13.1 INTRODUCTION

OSCAR-BERMAN: We begin this session with a definition of "Neuropsychology" and of "individual differences." Thus this chapter begins with a very short tutorial, introducing the topics of concern to psychophysiologists and to neuropsychologists. Then we shall discuss some of the ERP data in neuropsychology and individual-differences research that we consider to be important. This will be followed by a discussion of issues confronting cognitive psychologists and neuropsychologists to whose solution ERP studies may contribute.

13.2 A TUTORIAL SURVEY: NEUROPSYCHOLOGY

Neuropsychology is concerned with the relationship between the structure and the function of the brain, and neuropsychologists approach this relationship from different perspectives or different training histories. As seen in Table 13.1, I have divided the techniques used by neuropsychologists into two major classes according to whether or not the techniques are biologically invasive. Some techniques are used primarily to study brain functions in humans, and others are used to study brain functions in nonhuman animals (as models for human behavior). In both human and animal work, invasive and noninvasive techniques can be used in conjunction with each other in the study of behavior.

TABLE 13.1

Techniques Commonly Used to Study the Relationship Between Brain

Function and Structure

	INVASIVE TECHNIQUES	NONINVASIVE TECHNIQUES
HUMANS	1. Sodium amytal intracarotid injections	1. Postmortem histology
	2. Cerebral bloodflow inhalation procedures	2. EEGs and ERPs
	3. CT X-ray scans	3. Neuropsychological test batteries used with neurological patients
	4. Naturally occuring lesions, e.g., from stroke, tumor, trauma, disease, malnutrition, toxicity	4. Behavioral procedures borrowed from Experimental, Comparative and Physiological Psychology; used with neurological patients
NONHUMANS	1. Radiological labeling techniques	1. Electrophysiological recording techniques
	2. Selective brain lesions (electrical, radio-frequency, biochemical) combined with tests of behavioral changes and/or histological verification	
	3. Electrical recording techniques (single cell and brain surface)	
	4. Brain stimulation	

13.2.1 Human Neuropsychology

13.2.1.1 Invasive Techniques

One *invasive technique* applied to humans involves a neurosurgeon making lesions that remove already damaged brain tissue (e.g., to treat epilepsy) or are intended to stop pain or to decrease psychotic symptoms. Other lesions occur naturally as a consequence of a stroke, a tumor, or a metabolic disorder. Behavioral consequences of these lesions can frequently be measured by noninvasive behavioral techniques. Another invasive procedure involves injecting sodium amytal into one or the other carotid artery to see which functions are lost first. This procedure, as well as brain stimulation in awake patients, is part of a clinical examination, usually intended to determine side-of-language dominance in patients requiring neurosurgery. Then there are cerebral blood-flow studies in which subjects inhale a radiologically labeled gas (e.g., xenon) that is metabolized in the brain. These techniques have provided considerable information on the distribution of brain activity during the performance of certain tasks. Computerized tomography (CAT or CT scans) and positron emission tomography are procedures that allow relatively good localization; these procedures are much better than angiography and X-ray techniques that were formerly used for localizing lesions in brain-damaged patients. Finally, electroconvulsive shock therapy (ECT) is frequently used for treating disorders like depression and schizophrenia, and results of ECT can be studied experimentally.

13.2.1.2 Noninvasive Techniques

In discussing the noninvasive techniques, I shall be mentioning tests used in cognitive psychology as well as methods used in event-related brain potential research. However, first I shall consider other measures. For example, there are neuroanatomical studies that are not invasive because they are done on people who have had brain damage, who have died, and whose brains are rushed to a laboratory for histochemical analysis. For example, Norman Geschwind's group (Mesulam, 1979), at the Beth Israel Hospital in Boston, is now conducting a study in which silver impregnation staining procedures are used with fresh brains to trace the efferent connections of areas of the cortex known to have been damaged one to five weeks before death. Silver impregnation methods allow axon degeneration to be observed, giving neuroanatomical localization to major pathways of cortical regions with known functions. If the functions are concerned with language, human brains *must* obviously be used.

Other sources of data on the human brain are clinical examination procedures and test batteries. There are hundreds of individual procedures and tests; many are described by Lezak (1983), who reviews various methods for diagnosing and differentiating numerous behavioral anomalies resulting from brain damage. Some tests can only differentiate organic from nonorganic problems; other procedures are good for quantifying symptoms and localizing sites of damage. At the Aphasia Research Unit of the Boston VA Medical Center, we use the Boston Diagnostic Aphasia Examination (Goodglass & Kaplan, 1972), an excellent procedure for studying aphasias and related disorders (e.g., apraxias).

Another technique involves the recording of electrical potentials from the scalp. Callaway and N. Squires will discuss below the application of the ERP technique to "special" populations. Finally, I note that experimental tests also provide information of use to the neuropsychologist. This last approach may have special significance at this conference, especially for the cognitive psychologists here, and I will review it in more detail.

The specific procedures I have chosen to list come from experimental and comparative psychology. I selected a few tasks that I consider to be important for the present discussion, and you can add whatever others you may consider relevant. Here is my selection:

1. Backward-masking paradigms.

2. Various kinds of short-term memory paradigms (e.g., Peterson and Peterson's, 1959).

3. Dichotic listening and visual half-field tasks to look at hemispheric differences.

4. Levels-of-processing tasks that people feel are important in understanding information processing, perception, memory, and learning.

5. The "oddball" paradigm and other types of probability-learning procedures.

6. Tests of strategy formation such as those described by Marvin Levine (1975).

7. Other instrumental learning paradigms.

8. Tests of attention.

9. Classical conditioning paradigms.

Ideally, each of the tests mentioned here can be designed to tap a particular type of function. Given that you know what kind of function it is, the paradigms can be used for tapping the residual functions of various parts of the brain in patients who have lost some brain regions. In that sense, we can depend heavily on the suggestions of cognitive psychologists. We want to use the best paradigms available to give us a handle on normal function so that we can see whether or not a brain region that is destroyed loses the function that we think it should lose.

13.2.2 Animal Physiological Psychology

There is a huge literature from animal psychology that has relied heavily on "lesion" techniques (electrical lesions, knife lesions, chemical lesions [e.g., 6-hydroxy dopamine]). Animal models in physiological psychology were developed to understand the nature and evolution of brain mechanisms in human behavior (Morgan & Stellar, 1950). The typical experimental approach has employed test procedures designed specifically to test behavioral function of animals; from the pattern of deficits observed in brain-damaged animals compared to controls, normal functions of lost structures are inferred. The functions allegedly discovered are usually ones homologous to human behavioral functions. However, the alternative experimental approach has been largely ignored; that is, human neuropathology rarely has been reexamined in the context of experimental paradigms that are known to be valid and reliable tests of nonhuman functional breakdown following brain damage. This approach, which we have called *comparative neuropsychology* (Oscar-Berman, 1980), is especially promising because elementary samples of behavior can be assessed with remarkable accuracy for teasing out subtle differences among brain-damaged groups. In addition, there is a large literature on the immediate and long-term effects of brain lesions on the behavior of nonhuman primates. Hence, by using performance measures on humans that are in common with those used with animals, the behavioral relevance of homologous brain structures would be directly comparable. Finally, physiological recording and brain-stimulation techniques continue to be used and are considered by many as potentially valuable for verification of some of the human ERP phenomena. If our main goal is to understand structural-functional relationships, whatever techniques are going to give us new information can be applied. I feel that, at the present time, we need to use everything that is listed here, and more.

13.2.3 Individual Differences

CALLAWAY: We study individual differences for various reasons, but fundamentally they break down into two sorts. On one hand individual differences give us a way of dissecting systems. Diseases perform an experiment of nature. Maturation lets us see the system developing. Individual differences allow us to test certain theories. Lynn Cooper gives a beautiful example of how you can use global cognitive-style differences to show you something about differences in strategies.

Lots of other things in normal life produce individual differences that dissect systems: Consider sex, sleep and waking, aging, fatigue, and recreational drugs. The other reason is practical. We want to use our understanding of systems to modify or utilize individual differences: treat disease, select candidates for jobs, etc.

COOPER: I would like to add that individual differences research focuses not on the differences, per se. Rather, these differences are used as a tool for examining basic visual and memory processes. By seeing patterns of differences in individual subjects that you can change by manipulating task and stimulus variables, you can learn something about basic processes.

13.3 ERPS AND DIMINISHED MENTAL FUNCTIONING

N. SQUIRES: As Enoch Callaway and M. Oscar-Berman have just pointed out, there are two primary reasons for studying ERPs as a function of individual differences. The first is to use what we know about ERPs to get a handle on the nature of particular brain dysfunctions. The second, and to me the more interesting, is to dissect the system, to determine which sensory and psychological processes are reflected in which ERP components. To illustrate these two uses of clinical ERP data I shall be showing some data of mine on ERPs in the severely and profoundly retarded, and some data of Ken Squires' on ERPs in aging and dementia.

A tremendous variety of dysfunction is represented among mentally retarded persons. For this reason, and because of the difficulty in using conventional assessment tools with this group, the task of sorting out the dysfunctions and correlating them with ERP measures is formidable. On the other hand, because dysfunctions at all levels of information processing occur among these individuals, the potential for dissecting the system and studying interactions among processes is also great.

In one of our projects we have been studying the auditory brainstem potentials (ABRs) in the retarded. In many types of retardation it appears that the auditory system is more likely to be involved than are other sensory systems, and the incidence of hearing impairment increases with the level of dysfunction. One of the diagnostic categories we have been looking at is Down's syndrome, where in addition to the evidence for hearing impairment there is evidence for neuroanatomical abnormalities in the brainstem pathway. A schematic representation of the abnormalities we find in the ABRs of Down's syndrome adults is shown in Fig. 13.1. Except for wave I, all the ABR peaks are of reduced amplitude in the Down's syndrome group. Furthermore, there are characteristic aberrations in the peak latencies; the intervals between waves

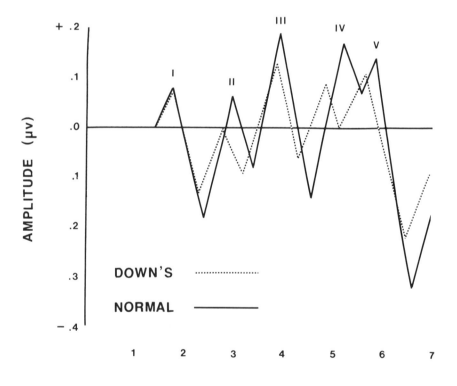

FIG. 13.1 Schematic ABRs representing the mean amplitude and latency of each positive and negative ABR peak for a group of Down's Syndrome retarded and a control group of nonretarded.

I and II and between waves III and IV are significantly shorter for the Down's group than for the nonretarded. This pattern of latency abnormalities does not correspond to any that result from known types of hearing loss (e.g., conductive or sensorineural loss). It is unclear what these data imply about hearing in Down's syndrome. With regard to the role of brainstem auditory structures in the analysis of acoustic information, however, it is interesting that the latencies of waves I and III in the Down's group are essentially normal, whereas waves II and IV have a shorter than normal latency. The conceptualization of the ABRs has been in terms of a serial process, a sequential elaboration of the acoustic information as it transcends the auditory pathway. These data, however, imply some degree of parallel processing at a very early stage, perhaps in the ipsilateral and contralateral pathways, with waves II and IV part of a different system than wave III. In this manner, investigation of the ABRs of Down's syndrome retarded may provide a means for attaching unique functions to the individual waves or subgroups of waves by indentifying the perceptual functions that correlate with these ABR abnormalities.

Figure 13.2 shows wave V latency in the Down's syndrome group compared to that of the nonretarded as a function of increases in the rate of click stimulation. As is typical of most ERP components, increased stimulation rate produces a peak latency increase. However, the meaning of such ERP "recovery cycle" functions for auditory perception has been unclear (Hillyard, Picton, & Regan, 1978); even though in general larger amplitudes and shorter latencies correlate with greater loudness, loudness does not vary with stimulation rate. In this figure we see that wave V latency is much less affected by high stimulation rates for the Down's group than for the nonretarded. Again, the question is how these measures relate to abnormalities in auditory perception in the retarded. At first glance these data might indicate that some aspect of perception is more acute in the Down's group since their ABRs are less degraded at high rates. Alternatively, one might consider that there is some advantage, perceptually, to refractoriness at high rates. One auditory process that requires analysis of rapid streams of acoustic information is speech perception. We therefore thought it would be of interest to correlate the flat recovery functions in Down's subjects with measures of speech perception. Among the 16 Down's syndrome adults tested, the correlation between judgments of the intelligibility of their speech and the slope of the recovery function was .78 (i.e., the more normal the slope, the more intelligible the speech). Neither the recovery functions nor speech intelligibility correlated with IQ ($r = -.04$ and .14, respectively) so that we are not simply making parallel measure of the level of dysfunction. Rather, these data suggest tentatively that abnormal ABR recovery functions may reflect a specific aberration of acoustic processing that interferes with learning to speak clearly.

The late endogenous ERP components, which have been the focus of most of the discussion in this volume, have been studied more intensively as a function of individual differences. The effects of one important variable, age, on

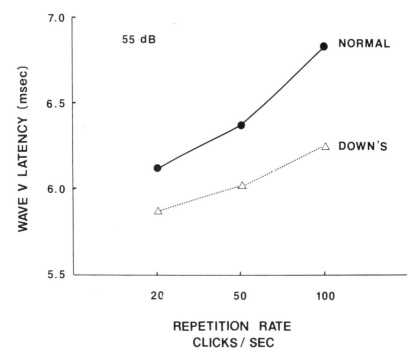

FIG. 13.2   ABR wave V latency as a function of increasing rate of stimulation in Down's Syndrome and nonretarded adults.

the latencies of the late components are shown in Fig. 13.3. These data are taken from an auditory-oddball experiment conducted by K. Squires and his colleagues at UC Irvine (Goodin, Squires, Henderson, & Starr, 1978a). As you can see, there is a sharp drop in the latencies of N200 and P300 up to the age of about 14 years. Of major interest here, however, is the slow but steady increase in the latency of these components with increase in age beyond 14. This increase was significant for the P200, N200, and P300 components but not for N100. Furthermore, it was determined that these changes in latency of the endogenous components were not a function of decreased auditory sensitivity.

Figure 13.4 shows the P300 latencies of two groups of patients with diminished mental status compared to the P300 latencies of the normal controls (Goodin, Squires, & Starr, 1978b). The nondemented subjects, who include patients with depression, schizophrenia, multiple sclerosis, and other disorders had P300 latencies that were normal for their chronological age. The demented patients, on the other hand, had P300 latencies that averaged 3.2 standard deviations longer than normal. This group was also heterogenous, including patients with metabolic encephalopathy, hydrocephalus, Alzheimer's, and other dementing diseases.

DONCHIN: Are those two individuals that are inside the band diagnosed differently?

K. SQUIRES: No, those two were problematic, particularly the younger one, who is about age 30. This person, according to our tests, would be considered demented. The person had essentially a pure amnestic syndrome. The P300 latency is a speed-measure of processing and he was normal in this respect. The P300 latency will not reveal this type of a mental problem.

PICTON: I don't think it's a problem that you have two people within the normal range. I think you now have another dimension of dementia. Those

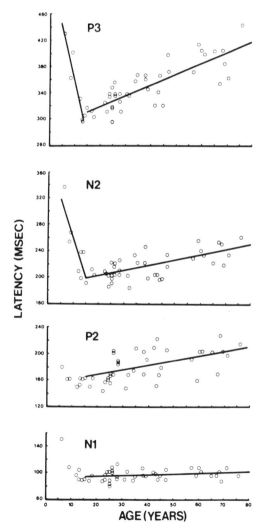

FIG. 13.3 Peak latencies of components N1, P2, N2, and P3 as a function of aging in normal subjects. (From Goodin et al., 1978a).

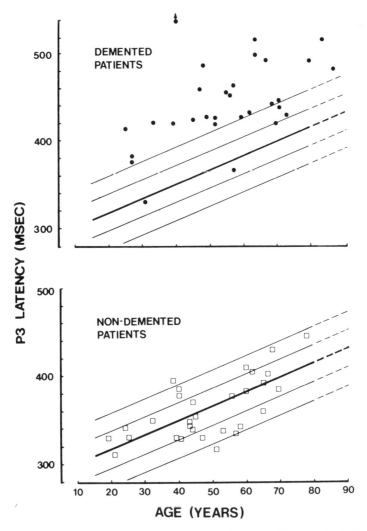

FIG. 13.4   P3 latency in demented and nondemented subjects. The heavy line indicates the mean latency for the control group as a function of age, and the lighter lines represent ± 1 and 2 standard deviations from the normal mean.

two patients have a different dementia than the others. The patient with herpes simplex encephalitis has mainly a memory problem rather than the global processing problem that the other patients (with late P300s) have.

K. SQUIRES: The older person is a confused lady. That's her only obvious problem, and we did not know the reason at the time. There have been instances where people were rediagnosed, not on the basis of this but because of other tests.

POSNER: Are there reaction time data on these demented patients?

K. SQUIRES: No.

N. SQUIRES: Figure 13.5 illustrates the similarity in the alterations that occur in the late ERP components with aging, dementia, and retardation. The data on aging and dementia, which I have just described, were taken from an auditory-oddball paradigm, and the data on the retarded were from a visual-oddball experiment. In each case there were significant differences in the latencies of P200, N200, and P300 between the experimental and control subjects but no significant differences in N100 latency. In the case of the retarded, the small N100 difference shown here is of some interest because it is accounted for by a subgroup of the retarded who had been identified as having visual difficulties. A comparison of N100 latency among these 5 subjects with visual defects and the other 25 retarded subjects showed a significant prolongation of N100. However, the effect of visual impairment was not reflected in P300 latency, which did not differ between the two subgroups of retarded. P300 latency did have a moderate correlation with IQ $(r = -.44)$, supporting the assumption that the earlier components are relatively more sensitive to sensory factors and the later components to general cognitive factors and that these components can vary independently.

The data from the retarded subjects were collected in a variation on the oddball procedure that is illustrated in Fig. 13.6. The alteration in the procedure was necessitated by the fact that the mean IQ of the retarded subjects was 32, and they were not capable of counting the rare events. Therefore, instead of one oddball stimulus we used two, the second being a long-duration, readily identifiable event, a red circle on a white background, to which the subjects had to make a recognition response. The nonretarded subjects pressed a button to the target, and the retarded subjects said "token" if they were verbal or pointed to the stimulus or made some other response if they were nonverbal. Correct responses were rewarded with tokens that could later be exchanged for a record album. This procedure has a number of advantages for use with subjects with reduced mental functioning. First, it requires that the subject attend to and discriminate between the stimuli and provides the experimenter with some information about the subject's attention. Second, any motor contamination of the EEG is confined to the target stimulus and allows for comparison of the uncontaminated rare and frequent, nontarget ERPs. Finally, it allows for variations in the similarity of the rare and frequent nontarget events, unconfounded by the subject's ability to discriminate between them, as would be the case if the subject were required to respond to a rare event that was difficult to discriminate from the frequent. The effect of discriminability on P300 latency is shown in Fig. 13.7. For the nonretarded subjects there was an increase in P300 latency as the difference in the luminance of the rare and frequent stimuli decreased. This dependence of P300 latency on the dissimilarity of the rare

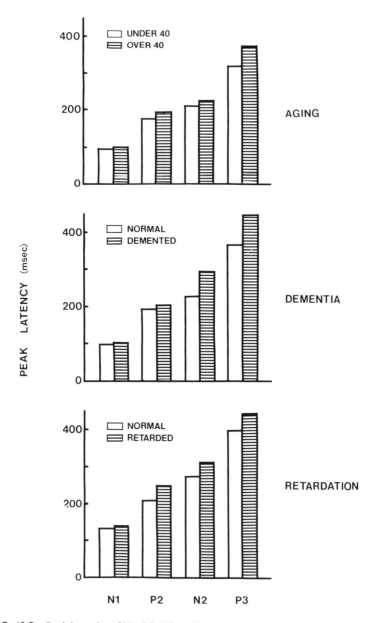

FIG. 13.5   Peak latencies of N1, P2, N2, and P3 in aging, dementia, and mental retardation (hatched bars) compared to their respective control groups (open bars).

350

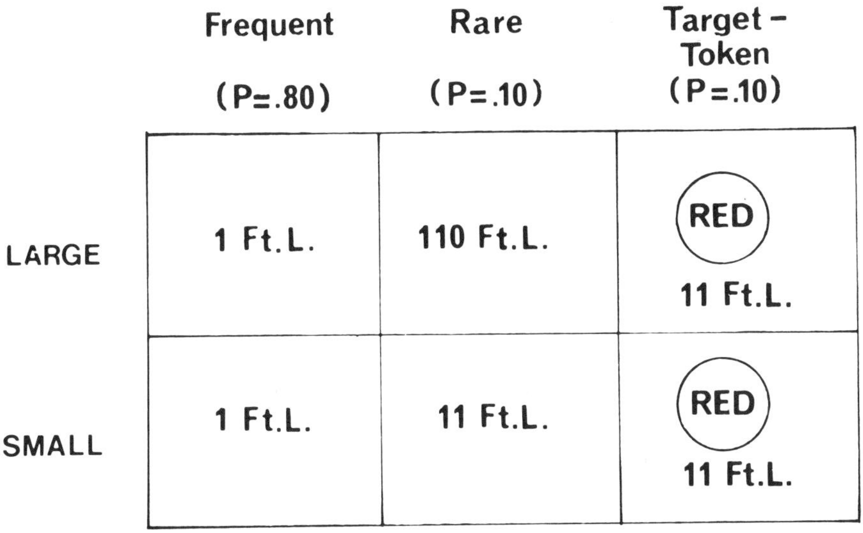

	Frequent (P=.80)	Rare (P=.10)	Target – Token (P=.10)
LARGE	1 Ft.L.	110 Ft.L.	(RED) 11 Ft.L.
SMALL	1 Ft.L.	11 Ft.L.	(RED) 11 Ft.L.

FIG. 13.6 Procedure for studying endogenous ERPs in the retarded. In each experimental condition ("large" or "small" difference in luminance between the nontarget rare and frequent stimuli) three types of visual stimuli were presented. The target stimulus was a red circle on a white surround.

and frequent events has been previously demonstrated by a number of investigators. The data of the retarded subjects show a similar effect, except that the P300 latencies in both conditions are about 50 msec longer than normal. This finding may suggest that the retarded suffer from a diminished ability to recognize that a change has occurred in the environment.

Because all three populations, the aged, the demented, and the retarded, show normal N100 latency but prolongation of the later ERP components, whatever processes are reflected in these later components would be expected to be diminished in a similar fashion in all three groups. More detailed investigations of the similarities and differences in cognitive functioning in these groups might then prove very useful in identifying the unique psychological determinants of these components.

ALLISON: Nancy, were the children with Down's syndrome who showed small wave V amplitudes tested audiometrically? Have they had pure tone audiograms?

N. SQUIRES: No, they haven't. Good audiometric data are almost impossible to get from retarded at this low level of functioning. (The mean IQ of this group was 29.) At our institution the major audiometric tests for this type of individual are in fact the brainstem potentials. However, the data shown here

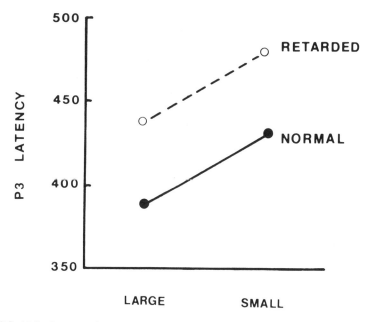

FIG. 13.7   Latency of P3 to non-target rare stimuli in the retarded and nonretarded as a function of the degree of luminance difference (large or small) between the non-target rare and frequent stimuli. (From N. Squires et al., 1977.)

on the Down's subjects, particularly the short-interwave intervals, raise some question in my mind about what the appropriate norms are for conducting ABR audiometry on this group.

HARTER: Why do you think the latency of P300 is delayed in these subjects? Do you think the differences in latency are due to differences in conduction time, differences in arousal level, or what?

N. SQUIRES: I don't think it is arousal level, because I would expect that to influence P300 amplitude rather than latency and also to influence N100 amplitude that was the same in the two groups. Slow conduction is a possibility, but the question is, of course, where in the brain the slowed conduction is taking place. These types of data on the retarded, on the demented, and in aging suggest that in all three cases the prolongations are beyond the level of simple sensory analysis and relate to a diminished capacity to recognize change in the environment.

DONCHIN: Did you have an "ignore" control? That is, did you present the same stimuli while the subjects engaged in some other task?

N. SQUIRES: Not in the sense that the subjects were instructed to ignore all these stimuli and attend to something else, which is difficult in the visual modality anyway. However, with this procedure the subject is never required to make any decisions about the nontarget bright and dim slides—they are irrelevant to the task—yet you still get P300s to the rare nontargets.

13.4 HYPERKINESIS AND ERPS

CALLAWAY: I am rather surprised that, with all our discussions about attention, there has been no mention of arousal. Arousal and attention are intimately bound up and I think their relationships pose some very interesting problems. These are particularly apparent when one considers the management of hyperkinetic children, for these children have problems with attention and they benefit from stimulants, drugs that are presumed to augment arousal.

For purposes of illustration I will discuss some data that came from a rather extensive study designed to see if we could identify those hyperkinetic children who are most likely to benefit from stimulant drugs. I will discuss those aspects of the results that have been on the issue of the relationship between attention and arousal.

First, let me point out that hyperkinetic children are not simply children that teachers don't like because they are noisy. They tend, in addition, to be unhappy, unpopular, and they function academically very poorly despite apparently good potential. I won't say much about the issues of picking those more likely to respond. We can predict success in a statistically significant but clinically trivial way. One reason for this is that very few children selected on proper clinical grounds fail to respond. In fact, normal children also show the same sort of improvement in attention when treated with stimulants (Rapoport, Buchsbaum, Zahn, Weingarten, Ludlow, & Mikkelsen, 1978). Although there are many references in the literature to the hyperactive child's response to stimulants being parodoxical, this appears not to be the case. Let us simply say that, in general, stimulants may improve attention and reduce restless fidgeting.

The details of how stimulant medication affects hyperactive children are, however, interesting. In the laboratory, stimulants improve performance on vigilance tasks and also improve memory. Clinically the immediate results can be quite dramatic. The quality of homework improves and the quality of relationships with their peers and parents improve. In spite of these dramatic immediate effects, the long-term gains from the treatment of these children with stimulants alone is rather meager. Why such dramatic short-term gains do not translate into more substantial long-term gains is an interesting puzzle.

Another phenomenon of note is the diversity of stimulant dose response curves. In general, as the doses increase performance may at first improve and then deteriorate. Of course with any substance that improves performance, an inverted U will occur if the dosage is pushed far enough for toxic levels to be reached. The problem is not so trivial in the case of the hyperkinetic child. For example, as dosages increase, performance on simple tasks may tend to improve while performance on more complex tasks may begin to deteriorate. At high doses teachers may continue to rate classroom performance as improving while parents may report that home performance has begun to decline. In other words, the inverted U dose response function may show different peaks depending on what sort of performance is being looked at. I can illustrate this further with some evoked response data. Before going on with this data, however, I want to emphasize that the most striking finding was the relative paucity of the effects the stimulant methylphenidate on the event related potential. In general, effects of age and of instructions given to the subject had much more dramatic effects on the ERP than did a fairly wide range of doses.

Our procedure has been described in detail elsewhere, but I will briefly outline it here. We recorded visual evoked responses from the vertex electrode referenced to the linked ears. The child was seated in a comfortable chair watching a light that flashed every two to four seconds. Most of the flashes were bright but during the first run, the child was instructed to watch for an occassional dim flash. If, in response, he pressed a switch quickly enough, he was given a reward. At the end of this run he was asked to sit for another run and just watch the bright flashes with no dim flashes. These constituted active and passive attention conditions. The data that we will present, however, are only from the target dim flashes and from children under 10 years of age since the evoked potentials obtained from the older children are not comparable.

The children came to the laboratory four times. On the first time they were given a placebo and on the next three times they were given, in randomized orders, three doses of methylphenidate. The three doses were labeled "low," 0.16 milligrams per kilogram; "medium," 0.3 milligrams per kilogram; and "high," 0.66 milligrams per kilogram. For an 80 lb. youngster this corresponded to 5, 10, and 20 milligrams. As shown in Fig. 13.8, the most dramatic effect is a striking nonlinear dose/response in the N100 component. The N100 is significantly larger at the medium dose than at the high or low dose. Figure 13.8 presents the grand average of nine hyperactive children. You will note that we are only considering active doses since only the active doses were counter-balanced by order. This is because our primary task was to predict response to methylphenidate, so the placebo trial was always run first. There is not a strong linear effect here, although there is a linear trend for the integrated P300 amplitude to drop with increasing dose. One could make a case for an augmented N100 response at the medium dose, with impairment RT the high dose and contrast this with a monotonic impairment of P300 response.

We do not have a good model by which to explain this sort of non-monotonic effect of an arousing medication, either on performance or on

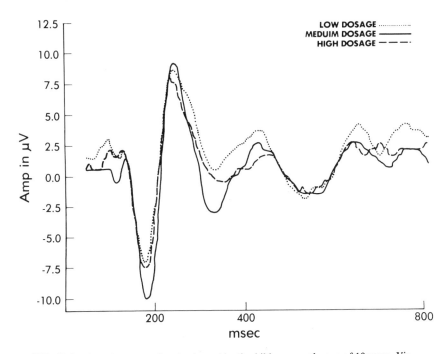

FIG. 13.8   Grand averages for nine hyperkinetic children over the age of 10 years. Visual EP at three doses of methylphenidate as described in Text.

evoked potential but there are two models we can consider. One is the Yerkes-Dodson model and the other is the Broadbent Stepwise Filter model. The Yerkes-Dodson model is little more than a description of the phenomenon. It simply states that there is a level of arousal that is optimum in any particular task and that an optimum level of arousal will be proportional to the difficulty of the task. That is to say, higher arousal is optimum for a simple task and lower arousal is optimum for a more difficult task. This, of course, describes what has been found with the performance measures of the hyperkenetic child and one could make some sort of case like this for the evoked potential data that I have just presented.

We might imagine that the early N100 component of the evoked response represents a simple operation and shows a peak at the medium dose, whereas the later P300 component represents a more complex operation and is already being impaired at the medium dose. The Broadbent model offers a way of thinking about this. It postulates a series of filters with broadband processing ability that preceed the narrower-band high frequency processes. If we try to apply Broadbent's model, we might imagine that an earlier filter operating on simpler principles is reflected in N100. Its functioning is improved up to a medium level of stimulant dose whereas the later more complex filter reflected by P300 is most effective with the lowest dose by stimulants. This would imply that the stimulant produces a kind of narrowed focus of attention. Narrowing the early, broad filter impairs performance only at the greatest narrowing whereas the later filter is already narrower and so impinges on responses at a medium dose.

This is all somewhat far fetched and I present it more for discussion than as a suggested principle. Subsequent analysis of our data has shown that the effects of methylphenidate on the ERP are very sensitive to the age of the child and to the instructions given the child, and are generally trivial compared to the effects that can be directly related to age and instructions.

SHIFFRIN: Do you have the actual reaction-time data for the processes?

CALLAWAY: Yes. Older children show a monotomic speeding of reaction time with an increasing dose of medication up to the medium dose. There is a flattening out with no gain or some slowing from medium to high dose. Incidentally, P300 latency does not shorten when reaction time is speeded by methylphenidate.

SHIFFRIN: You'd want to know something about the speed-accuracy tradeoff, particularly when you use increasing dosages of stimulants. Do you have any data about errors?

CALLAWAY: Yes. These children make, at the most, one error. We were alerted to this problem early and we decided to emphasize accuracy in our instructions. We rewarded correct responses only. Thus there was speed, but it was not traded for accuracy.

ZAIDEL: It doesn't seem that the clinical management of these children is very scientific. If you increase the dose, they improve on reaction-time and their performance then seems to worsen. What do you use to decide what the "right" dose is?

CALLAWAY: Clinically, one stops increasing the drug when the child is judged by the teachers to be performing "well-enough." That is a vague end-point. Some doctors never go above 15 mgs and say that if the child does not begin to respond at that dose, he will begin to show side effects. Others will go to doses of 45 mgs or more.

ZAIDEL: So all you can rely on is a vague analysis of the children's behavior; you just go with the impressions of parents and teachers. Why are you insisting on doing research with such vague variables?

CALLAWAY: Doctors who are treating children have only their clinical judgment to rely upon. They would be very happy to have a scientific basis for their practice.

ZAIDEL: Wouldn't it be better to determine the proper dose by measuring short-term memory performance?

CALLAWAY: That would be fine if all we are trying to do is to improve short-term memory performance. But there are many other things that go into a child's behavior in school. These children, for example, don't have any friends. If you give them an adequate dose of a stimulant, they start being asked to play baseball with the other children. Is it more important to be able to do well on a Peterson and Peterson short-term memory task than to be invited to play baseball on Saturday?

I think it is very intriguing that we give a child a drug that improves his short-term memory. The important result as far as the teacher, parent, and pediatrician are concerned is that the quality and quantity of his homework increases. Nevertheless, a few years later, the long-term effects seem meager. There is a lot about this that we don't understand.

POSNER: Maybe this kind of experiment would be related to the idea that you were proposing. In cognitive psychology, there has been a belief that to raise arousal level you "funnel in." Most of those experiments involve fairly complicated procedures with a central task (such as tracking) that attracts a person's attention. In procedures that we used, we wanted to see if funneling would occur in a situation where there was no real strong incentive to deal more with one part of the visual field than another. We strung lights across the visual field. We looked at the bias that a person might have for central versus peripheral lights as a function of time after a warning signal. Typically, we give a person a warning signal and, of course, reaction time drops over half a second following the warning signal. Then we look at the bias across the visual field. As a person becomes more alert, presumably more aroused, then you might expect his attention to funnel in. We found no evidence whatsoever of an interaction between the distribution of attention across the visual field and this alerting function.

One other thing I was going to note was that this would be a good place where evoked potential methods would be useful. You obtain a change in arousal so you desynchronize the EEG. However, you could look at the N100 effect at a target position at every level within the alerting function. That should answer the question of whether there is an automatic funneling associated with alerting.

CALLAWAY: One could perhaps use a sustained negative potential paradigm. If an individual is looking for a slightly longer tone burst at a particular frequency, the farther away the actual frequency is, the less the sustained negative potential. There you have an extended field where you don't have to worry about the fact that the eyes may be defocused and so on. Do you think the visual would be better than the auditory for this?

POSNER: No. I don't necessarily think it would. In fact, it really would be quite interesting to see if it worked well in the frequency domain for auditory stimuli. It should be analogous.

CALLAWAY: That's why we would go after it first.

TREISMAN: This might be related. Ken Bowers (Bowers & Drenneman, 1977) was looking at selective listening as a function of changing the instructions. Some subjects were told that it was very important that they not miss anything coming into the right ear. Other subjects were told to relax, that they probably would not miss anything coming into the right ear, and that they could afford to sit passively and let things happen. He found that the group with passive instructions did better over all. The effect of motivating subjects to really attend to one side and then to pick up whatever they could from the other side as well, was to reduce the overall performance.

CALLAWAY: On the unattended side or the attended side?

TREISMAN: They lost more on the unattended side without gaining much on the attended side. The other group was told just to relax, and to feel confident that they would not miss any relevant signals.

CALLAWAY: Someone studied children and their siblings after they had spent 15 min waiting for the dentist. The child who was going to have the dental work done could tell you nothing about what was in the room. The child who was not going to have the dental work done could. Well, that doesn't tell you much about the underlying cognitive model, but it is certainly a common experience we've all had. You can motivate people to dive into foxholes by scaring them, but they don't solve equations very well under those conditions.

TREISMAN: That could be related to controlled versus automatic processing.

13.5 KORSAKOFF'S DISEASE

OSCAR-BERMAN: For the last 10 years, I have been studying alcoholic Korsakoff's disease, and much of this work has been summarized in a recent review paper (Oscar-Berman, 1980). There are two reasons that I am interested in this particular disorder. One is that I want to understand the functions of brain structures that are known to be damaged in these patients. Furthermore, Korsakoff's syndrome is a fascinating syndrome. Korsakoff patients show a defect of recent or short-term memory (STM). They are unable to recall new information beyond a time period of about 45 sec. Digit-span is intact, and IQ is normal, but there appears to be little or no recall of events or new experiences beyond a minute. The STM impairment, also called anterograde amnesia, exists despite an essentially intact long-term store for premorbid experiences, hence the normal IQ. In 1973, I saw a patient who had worked overseas for the United States government during World War I; he had excellent recall for his war experiences. He could name army generals and battle locations. However, this same patient was unable to name the current President of the United States (Richard Nixon) and declared with conviction that it was Harry Truman.

When I first started studying Korsakoff's syndrome at the Boston V.A. Medical Center in 1970, I had come directly from PhD training in a laboratory of animal physiological psychology. I was very interested in understanding the functions of various brain structures, in particular the frontal and temporal lobes and their connections. Because the amnesia of Korsakoff patients resembles the STM deficit characteristic of monkeys with frontal lobe damage, I felt that my background in nonhuman primate cortical functions might be applied directly to understanding human memory impairments.

In the early 1970s, information-processing flow models (Broadbent, 1957) were gaining attention from cognitive psychologists. I had read a chapter by Ervin and Anders (1970) in which amnesic patients were described as having perfectly normal registration capacities, based upon results of a visual metacontrast task that had been given to one patient one day at MIT. That patient was the famous H.M. (Milner, Corkin, and Teuber, 1968) whose amnesia was related to bilateral lesions of the medial temporal lobes for relief from epilepsy. I thought it would be nice to demonstrate that the results obtained from one patient with amnesia resulting from bilateral hippocampal damage would be similar for amnesic Korsakoff patients. It was especially important to demonstrate that perceptual processing is intact in amnesics because abnormalities of processing would almost invariably have deleterious effects upon memory.

We first measured the time it took the alcoholic Korsakoff patients to analyze incoming visual information (Oscar-Berman, Goodglass, & Cherlow, 1973). To do this, we used a tachistoscope (t-scope) that can present visual stimuli for brief durations, as short as a millisecond. First, we measured visual thresholds, the amount of time a stimulus such as a word or a figure must be shown on a t-scope screen before subjects can identify what they have seen. In comparison to normal subjects and to alcoholic patients with no clinical signs of Korsakoff's disease, alcoholic Korsakoffs needed much more viewing time (about 85 msec compared to about 25 msec for the controls). We then used backward visual masking to measure "sensory memory," the time during which the trace of a stimulus that is no longer present "remains" in the central nervous system; this trace, the icon, is held in the brain for some milliseconds while the information is being categorized and converted into a more durable memory trace (short-term memory). In the backward masking paradigm (see Fig. 13.9) two visual stimuli are presented successively on the t-scope. (We used lateral visual half-field presentations, but the reasons need not be noted here.) The first stimulus, called a target, is shown for a short time, but above threshold, to any given subject. Its offset is followed by the brief exposure of a second stimulus, called a mask (usually a pattern not resembling the target). The time interval between target offset and mask onset is the interstimulus interval (ISI), and it is this interval that we varied in the experiment. If the ISI is relatively long (e.g., 2 sec), subjects report having seen both the target and the mask in succession. But, if the ISI is too short (e.g., 10 msec), subjects report seeing only the masking stimulus. It is thought that processing of the visual target is interfered with or blocked in the nervous system by the neuronal activity required to process the mask. The *critical ISI* is the minimum time interval required between target offset and mask onset, at which target recognition returns to premasking levels. We found that the Critical ISIs for Korsakoff patients were nearly twice as long as the control subjects' ISIs (about 90 msec in the patients versus 50 msec in the normals). It was clear that Korsakoff patients do not process incoming visual information as efficiently as do control subjects. This was our first evidence that their memory impairment might be confounded with "other" deficits, in this case a limited processing capacity. If they have a registration impairment and are described as having a short-term memory impairment, it is hard to tell which function influences the other, and the reasoning becomes circular. It is like saying that a deaf person does not have an auditory memory. Well, the deaf will not remember auditory information because they are unable to hear, but you cannot assess the extent of the deaf's memory capabilities by this test. One lesson that we learned for future experiments is that the use of typical short-term memory paradigms

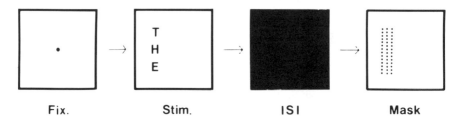

Fix.   Stim.   ISI   Mask

FIG. 13.9   The sequence of events that appears on a tachistoscope viewing screen for visual backward masking. First a fixation point is shown. The fixation point disappears and a target stimulus appears in one of the visual fields. Then follows a variable interstimulus interval, and finally, a masking stimulus. (After Oscar-Berman, 1980.)

with stimulus exposure durations fixed at a couple of seconds puts Korsakoff patients at an initial disadvantage. They are not getting an exposure level that is comparable to controls' yet is likely needed to measure the "same" memory functions as controls. It should be noted at this point that the critical ISIs for alcoholic control patients (hospitalized for psychiatric or medical but not neurological symptoms) were midway between those obtained from Korsakoffs and normal controls. The intermediate ISI values of the alcoholic control subjects suggested that those patients might be approaching a Korsakoff condition not discernible by standard clinical evaluation with less sensitive tests. ERP research could afford a valuable way of checking to see if there are any deficits in the endogenous components in the different sensory systems of Korsakoff (and other types of amnesic) patients. Nancy and Ken Squires said earlier that an amnesic patient with herpes encaphalopathy had a *normal* P300. What about the P300 in alcoholic Korsakoffs (with more diffuse brain damage); is it abnormal? Or the N100; is that abnormal? It would be very interesting to see correlations between ERP components and results from perceptual processing tasks such as the one just described. We might learn more about Korsakoff's disease, and you might learn about the meaning and possible brain foci of certain endogenous components.

We know now that there is some kind of processing deficit in Korsakoff patients. We were also interested in whether or not their arousal level was normal. Anders Gade, a colleague from Copenhagen, was also interested in studying Parkinson patients and their cognitive deficits; he suspected that they might have an abnormality in arousal functions. He set up in our lab a simple skin conductance experiment in which subjects sat relaxed in a chair and were exposed to a series of unpredictably occurring loud noises while we measured their palmar sweat responses (Oscar-Berman & Gade, 1979). There were five different groups of subjects, four of which were brain damaged: Korsakoffs, Parkinsonians, Broca's aphasics, and Huntington choreics. The fifth group consisted of neurologically intact controls. We found by this relatively archaic method of measuring arousal from the periphery, that Korsakoff patients have a much smaller response to the loud stimuli than do normal subjects and brain-damaged (Parkinson and aphasic) patients. We also found no difference between Korsakoffs and patients with Huntington's disease. I am not sure what to attribute that similarity to, perhaps the commonality of frontal lobe damage in both groups. However, the important thing for our present purposes is that Korsakoff patients had an arousal deficit, whatever "arousal" means. In that respect, it would be nice to determine to what extent abnormal endogenous components may accompany hypoarousal. What about the N100? And the N200? It would be fascinating to see what Korsakoffs look like there because it really seems as though they do have arousal deficits. To confirm it with ERP data would have important implications for understanding the STM loss. Furthermore, it might tell us about the anatomy of attention since we know something about the neuropathology accompanying alcoholic Korsakoff's disease (Oscar-Berman, 1980; Horel, 1978).

In another study we measured selective attention (Oscar-Berman & Samuels, 1976). We began with the knowledge of each patient's own individual preference hierarchy among four stimulus dimensions; that knowledge was derived from a previous experiment using a two-choice visual discrimination paradigm (Oscar-Berman, 1973). To test for selective attention in the patients, they were again given two-choice visual discriminations with the stimuli still differing in the same four dimensions: color, size, form, and position. Following this training, several test trials were given in which each dimension was presented alone; this enabled us to determine which stimulus dimensions had been relevant to the patients in their original training experience. As we had anticipated might happen, the Korsakoffs responded to fewer stimulus dimensions than the control subjects (aphasics, alcoholics, and normals). For example, in the process of learning to choose a large, dark X on the left side (rather than a small, light T on the right), the Korsakoffs often used only the color and size differences between the two stimuli to tell them apart and did not seem to notice differences in form or position. Thus, unlike other patients, Korsakoffs seemed to restrict their attention to only one or two features while ignoring the other features. These results suggest that there might be (whatever it means) a selective attention deficit in Korsakoffs. Thus, here again the N100 might be a very important component to look at.

A few points should be emphasized. First, to understand Korsakoff's syndrome, it is essential to know about "other" perceptual/cognitive deficits that are possibly contributing to the anterograde amnesia, or it will be difficult to have a valid measure of the memory impairment. Alternatively, these other deficits may be independent of the STM impairment. A resolution is important for a thorough understanding of Korsakoff's syndrome. Second, the brain structures that are damaged in alcoholic Korsakoff's syndrome are known to some extent; at least there is more "localization" than in senile dementias. Therefore, the lost functions can be linked to the damaged structures. Bill Chase suggested that the P300 is involved somehow in "attention allocation for control-processes needed for improving, updating, and reorganizing memory." My prediction for amnesics before this session would have been that the P300 would be diminished or absent in these patients. However, N. Squires presented data recorded from one patient with herpes encephalitis (a disease that produces "cleaner" pathology than in the Korsakoff patient who has drunk his brain away). That patient showed very clear P300s. What does that say about the function of P300? In other words, we have patients who seem to have attention and memory deficits; yet the ERP component that is hypothesized to reflect "attention" and "memory" is normal. Either the patient with herpes encephalopathy doesn't have an attention/memory deficit or P300 doesn't measure those functions!

SHIFFRIN: Cognitive psychologists usually think of the deficit as affecting either storage (from short-term to long-term memory) or retrieval (getting information out of memory). If so, there still could be quite a bit of normal reorganization of memory going on in these patients (or at least in short-term control memory), even if the information is not being stored properly or is not being stored the way it is retrieved. There could be a lot of reorganization of short-term memory going on even if the information that is so reorganized is not stored further or is not retrievable.

OSCAR-BERMAN: The functions of which you speak are difficult to tease apart with behavioral techniques. That's where ERP data might be helpful, but you must be prepared to redefine the functions of ERPs should that data from brain-damaged patients suggest consistently that their lost functions are what we think they are in the clinic and in behavior laboratories. Many Korsakoff patients have normal digit spans; they can correctly repeat back to you seven digits forward and five digits backward. But that's why I did the backward masking experiment. I wanted to know if registration of information was deficient, despite "normal" digit spans (immediate, as compared to short-term memory).

TREISMAN: If it were a registration deficit, one would have thought all processing would stop there, preventing storage and retrieval.

OSCAR-BERMAN: Well, it can in a way because it is probably not an all-or-none effect. The patients might have processed enough information to hold it for a few seconds, but the deficit begins to manifest itself when greater demands are placed on memory.

McCARTHY: Maybe if you varied the presentation rate so that it is slow enough, the deficit would disappear, but with fast presentation rates, the deficit appears again.

TREISMAN: And then you would expect the long-term memory to improve as well.

OSCAR-BERMAN: That is exactly what happens. Felicia Huppert and Malcolm Piercy from Cambridge, England came to our laboratory and tested our Korsakoff patients on tasks in which exposure duration was varied, and they measured subsequent retrieval. It was much, much improved, but it still was not what we call "normal" (Huppert & Piercy, 1977). From all the experiments I have done, it seems to me that there *is* a short-term memory defect in Korsakoff patients; there is no question about that. But there are other deficits as well, including a slowness in visual processing, hypoarousal levels and restricted selective attention, all of which probably exacerbate the STM deficit. That is what most of my research has been about. My colleagues and I have been trying to define the "other" deficits and to determine the extent of their contribution to the memory impairment, if there is any interaction at all.

To continue, let's look at another factor that might be feeding into the short-term memory defect. At the time that we were exploring perceptual and attentional abnormalities in Korsakoff patients, it became apparent that we should also consider their motivation levels. This was especially important because the regions of the brain that are known to be damaged include a neuroanatomical substrate traditionally regarded to have control over normal motivational processes: the limbic system. Major brain structures in the limbic system include the hippocampus, the mammillary bodies of the hypothalamus, anterior nuclei of the thalamus, and cingulate cortex. Alcoholic Korsakoff's disease is known to involve widespread damage of: (1) the mammillary bodies of the hypothalamus, a major recipient of hippocampal output; and (2) the medial and anterior portions of the thalamus, most notable the dorsomedial nucleus (an area important in linking the limbic system with prefrontal cortex). In addition, motivational changes had been noted frequently in Talland's Korsakoff patients (Talland, 1965), but these symptoms had not been observed in a systematic way. Therefore, my colleagues and I used two experimental paradigms to assess the sensitivity of Korsakoff patients to changes in reinforcement contingencies (Oscar-Berman, Heyman, Bonner, & Ryder, 1980; Oscar-Berman, Sahakian, & Wikmark, 1976). The first of these paradigms is called a spatial probability-learning test (PL) and the second is called a concurrent variable-interval variable-interval test (*conc* VI VI).

The spatial PL paradigm resembles the "oddball" paradigm used with P300. Reinforcement (a penny) is made available differentially on the right and left sides of a board placed on a table directly in front of the subject, but the subject never knows in advance on which side the penny will appear. As such, the task resembles a game of chance where the stakes on each bet are unknown to the player, but the overall payoffs become obvious as the game is played. In this particular situation, we changed the stakes each day to see if the changes would be noted equally well by Korsakoff and by control subjects. A patient faced the experimenter seated on the opposite side of a small table, and the two people were separated by a curtain that could be raised and lowered. Two identical black, square, wood plaques (about 4 X 4 in.) were placed over two cloth-covered wells, about 1 ft apart, on a movable tray. The patients were instructed to find, as often as possible, a penny hidden under one of the black plaques. Only one of the plaques could be lifted each time the curtain was raised, and only one plaque hid a penny. If the penny was found under one of the plaques, the patient could keep it. However, if no penny was found (an error) the curtain was lowered and the patient had another chance to respond with the reward contingency unchanged (i.e., the penny remained where it had been). The subjects were tested for 300 trials on each of three consecutive days, and the side of reward was random, given our constraints on the reward contingencies that were changed each day. On the first day, the penny was hidden equally often on the right and left sides (50-50 reinforcement ratio). On the second day, the reinforcement ratio was 70-30, with the right side being rewarded on the majority of the trials. On the third day, the ratio was 30-70 (left majority). Also on the third day, in order to allow for more training to the poorer subjects, a maximum of 200 additional trials was permitted.

Results of the first day of testing showed that when the Korsakoff patients made an initial error, they persisted in going to the wrong side over and over again. However, once they corrected an error on any particular trial, they were as able as control subjects (see Fig. 13.10) to distribute each subsequent initial response (on new trials) equally between the left and right sides. On the second and third days of testing their tendency to perseverate erroneous responses decreased, but they seemed to be very slow at adjusting to the changes in the reward contingencies; that is, although on the first day the Kor-

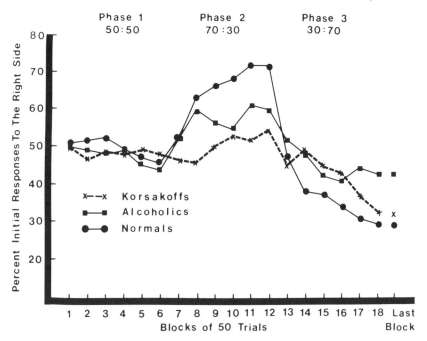

FIG. 13.10   Mean percentage of choice as a function of reinforcement ratio on left-right spatial probability learning problems. (From Oscar-Berman et al., 1976.)

sakoff patients had distributed their initial responses in accordance with the 50-50 reinforcement ratio (showing that they knew how to play the game), they did *not switch* to 70-30 on the second day, and only began to show a 30-70 ratio of responding by the last block of trials on the third day. The Korsakoffs appeared not to notice the changes in payoffs and continued to respond for nearly 3 days according to the payoff they had received on the first day. A similar result was obtained in the next experiment.

In the "*conc* VI VI" experiment, a subject faces an automatic apparatus containing translucent response keys (onto which different colored lights can be projected) and a reinforcement well (into which pennies can be dropped from behind). Reinforcement is made available by two independent timers, and each timer is associated with its own discriminative stimulus (a red or a green light) and manipulandum for responses (the keys onto which the lights are projected). Although inter-reinforcement times are random, the average inter-reinforcement time for one timer is shorter than for the other. When an interval is completed at a timer, it stops; a reinforcer is made available at the appropriate manipulandum; and the next response on that manipulandum is reinforced. The reinforced response resets the primed timer for a new (random) interval, and the process repeats itself. Because the two timers run independently, a reinforcer may be available at any moment from both, either, or neither of the two sources. Consequently, subjects switch back and forth from one alternative to the other, dividing their time between the two schedules. Normal subjects will perform in the *conc* VI VI situation much like they perform with the spatial task: They distribute their responses in accordance with the two different payoffs available to them. However, we found that the Korsakoff patients showed a relative insensitivity to the different payoffs, just as they had on the task described above (see Fig. 13.11). Sometimes they even preferred to respond most often to the schedule with the lower stakes. In neither the PL task nor the *conc* VI VI task did the Korsakoffs seem to have a *generalized* motivational deficit; they cooperated fully and wanted to earn as much money as they could. Rather, they seemed to have an abnormally low sensitivity to the existing reward contingencies.

The P300 component has been associated with "expectancy" or "probability estimation." Here again, Korsakoff patients are a good group for studying P300s. In the beginning of a PL task, when they "match" responses with reinforcement payoffs, the P300 should be normal on initial responses but perhaps abnormal on the errors. As perseverative errors decrease but initial responses are wrong (i.e., when the reinforcement ratio changes), the opposite trend should be obtained. In the *conc* VI VI situation, perhaps P300 would change as a function of the difference between the payoffs.

There are other experimental paradigms that tell the same kind of story (Oscar-Berman, 1980). The main point I want to make is the one I made at the Airlie House Conference (Oscar-Berman, 1978). There are patients who

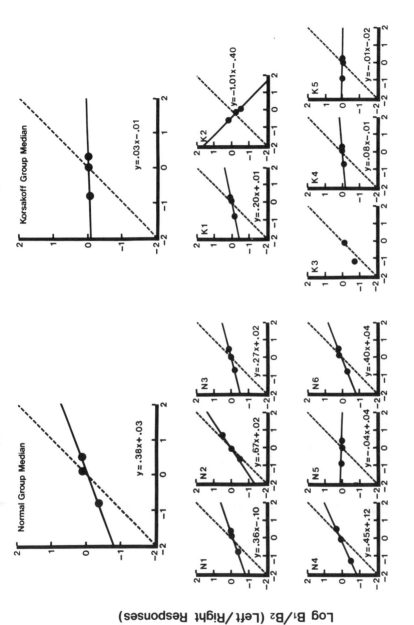

Log R₁/R₂ (Left / Right Reinforcements)

FIG. 13.11   The ratio of left to right responding on concurrent VI VI schedules as a function of left to right reinforcement rates in logarithmic coordinates. The dashed lines represent perfect matching. The solid lines were fit to data points of normal and Korsakoff participants (except K3) and the equation for each regression line is given. (From Oscar-Berman et al., 1980.)

have specific, sometimes focal lesions and who show behavioral deficits that can be measured precisely if you take the time to do it. You can put electrodes on these patients and you can test your hypotheses about the functional significance of ERP components. I am stressing this approach because I think it is extremely important.

In a previous session, someone suggested another method to get a handle on the P300: Condition it. Use operant techniques or classical conditioning techniques to vary the conditions that produce it. Maybe that will help you understand it. The top of Figure 13.12 is a schematic of how we might find out what P300 does. Neuropsychologists are on the right and cognitive psychologists are on the left. How does P300 change as experimental variables (e.g., CS-USC) are changed? What functions are absent when the P300 is knocked out? On the bottom of Figure 13.12 is a list of human neurological groups that might be used to study the relationship between ERP components and their functions on one hand, and clinical symptoms and loci of CNS damage on the other. I do not know what will be found. I have offered just a few suggestions. Maybe Korsakoffs are not the best patients to study for understanding all ERP components. They seem to be appropriate for trying to understand P300, because

WAYS TO UNDERSTAND P300

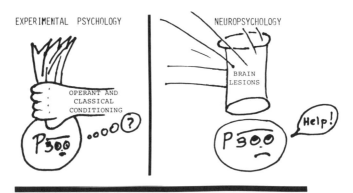

SOME POSSIBLE GROUPS TO BE STUDIED FOR INSIGHT INTO THE FUNCTIONAL SIGNIFICANCE OF THE ENDOGENOUS COMPONENTS

BILATERAL FRONTAL LOBOTOMY PATIENTS: SEQUENCING

PARKINSON PATIENTS: PREPARATORY RESPONSES (MOVEMENT?)

KORSAKOFF PATIENTS: ATTENTION

ECT PATIENTS: ETC.

NONHUMAN PRIMATES WITH CIRCUMSCRIBED BRAIN LESIONS: ALL OF THE
    ABOVE PLUS MUCH MORE

FIG. 13.12   Methods for understanding the functional significance of the endogenous components of ERPs.

there are situations in which they show normal sequencing (if sequencing is measured in terms of initial response probability), but there are other situations in which they show abnormal sequencing (e.g., perseverative responding). I do not think that anybody has run the same kinds of tests on bilateral frontal lobe patients. I think those types of patients also would show an abnormal P300.

As far as preparatory responses are concerned, it occurred to me when listening to Marta Kutas that it may be worth studying Parkinson patients because they have CNS-produced motoric rigidity. Do they have abnormal preparatory-response components? If their rigidity is decreased during high CNS arousal, do their RPs return to normal? How about the effects of l-dopa on the RP in successfully treated Parkinson patients?

As far as attention is concerned, I think there is good evidence of an attentional deficit in Korsakoff's patients, so maybe they are a population of choice for the N100 studies. Al Mirsky might stress the need to use patients with petit mal.

Finally, patients with language disorders also might be good patients to study. Some aphasic groups have phonological deficits. Others have semantic deficits. If there are ERP components that are supposedly measuring some of these functions, then they should show up to be abnormal in patients with a lesion at a particular region and who have specific behavioral deficits.

FORD: Dolf Pfefferbaum (Pfefferbaum, Horvath, Roth, & Kopell, 1979) in our laboratory has some data that might be interesting to you. He recorded from chronic alcoholics with no manifest CNS pathology. Based on the relation between P300 latency and RT, and the single-trial correlations of P300 latency and RT, he suggested that alcoholics did not respond to the stimulus probabilities in the same way that normals did. It appears that the P300s and RTs were useful in adding to the information about performance of alcoholics in a simple perceptual discrimination task.

OSCAR-BERMAN: That is what would have been predicted, and it is encouraging that ERPs do correlate well with performance measures. I wonder whether or not patients with herpes encephalopathy would have normal expectancies in comparison to alcoholic Korsakoff patients. Other data suggest that the two amnesias are different (Butters & Cermak, 1980; Lhermitte & Signoret, 1976).

Since the heuristic value of combining electrophysiology with cognitive psychology is becoming manifest, I should also mention that if you do find confirmation of predictions about ERPs based upon patient populations with lesions that are fairly well defined, you can test animals in whom you have made precise lesions in those regions and look for exactly the same kinds of disappearances of ERP components. If the results are similar with both species, then you have some very good reasons for suspecting that that absent structure is involved in the altered function. There is a pervasive feeling in cognitive psychology, in physiological psychology, and in neuropsychology that one way to study brain function in humans is first to have animals do "human tasks," then to take out the brain region that is thought to be necessary for performing the task, and finally to retest the animals for evidence of lost functions. It is assumed that it is not useful to employ animal tests with human subjects because the use of language by humans makes the task different. Another assumption is that the tests are too easy and lead to ceiling effects. I have used simple paradigms from animal experimental and physiological psychology to test clinical populations, and I have had excellent results (Oscar-Berman, 1980; Oscar-Berman, Zola-Morgan, Oberg, & Bonner, 1982; Oscar-Berman & Zola-Morgan, 1980a, 1980b). Because the animal paradigms were developed in the first place to measure structural-functional relationships, why not use them with humans? Combine such an approach with neuroanatomical methods, precise lesion techniques, ERP technological sophistication, etc., and we might someday understand how the brain works.

13.6   SOME PLANS AND PARADOXES IN THE INTERFACE OF BEHAVIORAL AND ERP INDICES OF HEMISPHERIC ASYMMETRIES

13.6.1 Introduction

ZAIDEL: Let me begin by telling you something about what I believe in. For example, I believe that the earth is round. I believe that the mind is the brain. These are not controversial statements, I suppose. To be more controversial, I also assert a third belief, namely, that hemispheric specialization exists. That last belief is what I'm going to talk about. Earlier, Mike Posner described the cutting edge for an interface among ERP work, cognitive psychology, and neuropsychology. He felt that the choice topic was selective attention. This sounds very good, but I would like to suggest another way to approach the interface that is quite different and, I think, at least equally promising. The approach focuses on the access to long-term memory and deals with the representation of verbal and nonverbal materials in the brain. This topic already serves as an interface between cognitive psychology and neuropsychology. We know that highly selective long-term memory disorders can be produced by focal lesions to either side of the brain. These lesions seem to impair certain aspects of the access to, or representation in, long-term memory. Let me just list a few of those. Lesions to diverse parts of the left cerebral hemisphere (in right-handed adults) commonly result in specific aphasic disorders, called "anomias," that involve the inability of patients to name certain objects when confronted with them but in the presence of correct naming of the same when the patient happens to talk about them spontaneously. A second example is jargon aphasia, where phonological and semantic errors that occur with regularity tell us about the way lexical information is structured. To take a third example, we have something called deep dyslexia where a patient will not be able to read a word letter by letter or phoneme by phoneme. He may not be able to identify individual letters in a word but he may nonetheless be able to read the word as a whole. In fact, the kinds of errors he makes show that in some sense he is seeing the word because sometimes he will read the word "fox" as "rabbit." Those are called semantic paralexic errors and again they tell us something about semantic organization or representation. There are other, converse disorders such as word blindness where the whole word cannot be read but its components are recognizable. This suggests that one needs to distinguish between processes involving words as units and those operating on sublexical units; the distinction is neurologically justified. So I think it is easy to see the profitable interface between neuropsychology and cognitive psychology, especially psycholinguistics, at the level of lexical analysis.

Research along the interface consists of attempts to simulate the cognitive deficit that appears in the damaged brain by using behavioral techniques in a normal person. An example is the attempt to split the brain using reaction-time paradigms or threshold detection experiments. This has been a fairly successful endeavour (Kinsbourne, 1978). Second, there is a set of experiments by Marcel and Patterson (1978) that claims to show that it is possible to simulate in a normal subject under certain experimental conditions the deficits I described previously as deep dyslexia. Using brief presentations of printed words and appropriate prestimulus and poststimulus maskings and interstimulus intervals, it is presumably possible to have the subject be unaware that she has seen a word and yet demonstrate objectively that she has nonetheless actually seen the word and retained its semantic meaning, in some sense, by showing the effect of its exposure on some subsequent task, such as lexical decision or a list search. By manipulating the interstimulus interval it is allegedly possible to show that the subject can lose the "word value" (i.e., conscious judgment of lexicality) while retaining separately visual and auditory components. In particular, he can be made to read a word as a deep dyslexia would—without being able to tell what it was but retaining its meaning and thus likely making a semantic error.

There are many other ways of simulating specific or general cognitive deficit in a normal subject (Kinsbourne, 1971). Experimentally induced tip-of-the-tongue may well approximate certain forms of aphasic anomia, and, more generally, fatigue or cognitive overload may well approximate the cognitive consequences of certain forms of brain damage. These, then, are illustrations of a possible interface between neuropsychology and cognitive psychology. But how should we proceed to investigate the interface between evoked responses and neuropsychology? That's a bit more difficult because the processes described in this volume all have very short latencies and are yoked to precise stimulus and response onsets. These paradigms are not particularly suited for the study of long-term memory because they don't tell you about strategies in ongoing processing of information. So let me now suggest how this problem can be approached in a programmatic way.

Presently I shall refer to so-called disconnection syndromes, disorders that are due to cerebral lesions and result in some kind of disconnection or separation of one part of the brain from another and thus in very obvious behavioral deficits. The point is that such disconnection syndromes can be associated with very precise and prominent anatomical facts. The processing reaches up to a certain level in the nervous system but will not go any further. It seems to me natural to ask in which components of the ERP, or the ongoing EEG, will the disconnection express itself? This presupposes merely that later components of the ERP refer to later stages in the information-processing sequence. In other words, we are assuming that the time line in the ERP represents the sequence of information-processing stages and that specific stages of information processing correspond to particular cerebral loci. So the correlation between the ERP and behavior will tell us "what" is happening and then the ERP will also yield the "where" and "when."

I shall now illustrate this research plan more explicitly. My own work concerns only one aspect of this plan. I do not have the facilities for investigating its electrophysiological component. I study the *behavioral* consequences of laterality, or hemispheric specialization. Our first task is to find behavioral effects of lateral asymmetry in cases where they are very obvious, where they are magnified. A classical source of such data has been patients with dramatic cognitive deficits following unilateral cerebral disease. Another useful starting place is the split brain patient. In these patients you can stimulate each hemisphere separately in order to assess directly and positively what the hemisphere can do. If one disconnected hemisphere is far superior to the other and if this is also true of the normal brain, then you would hope to find a laterality effect in a properly designed experiment with normal subjects, but the laterality effect in the split brain should be much larger. This is because in the normal brain, although the better hemisphere takes charge, the corpus callosum is present, allows for interhemispheric interaction, and makes the data noisier (callosal relay models). But in situations where the split-brain data show substantial competence by both hemispheres and thus only small laterality effects, you would expect the same effects in the normal brain (direct-access models). In this way, from a similar laterality effect in the split and normal brains, we can infer that the task is processed by direct access; whereas if the split effect is much larger, we can infer a callosal relay stage in processing the task when presented to the weaker hemisphere. These speculative and always indirect inferences can be put to a direct test using ERP methodology. It would be exciting to find ERP correlates of callosal transfer itself.

If you have an idea about the differences that exist between the hemispheres, you can try to identify ERP correlates, or EEG correlates, of these behavioral differences. Once you identify these, you want to determine if they can serve as indices of hemispheric specialization in normal subjects. This provides, first of all, a further index of lateral asymmetry that can be checked against the existing indices based, say, on reaction time and accuracy measures. Finally, if the ERP index turns out to be more sensitive than others, one can use it as an index for abnormal states of cerebral dominance in people who appear otherwise normal, as in latent cases of "learning disability." Let me illustrate this plan and begin with an introduction to split-brain work.

13.6.2 Hemispheric Specialization in Lexical Analysis by Split-Brain Patients

I'm summarizing 100 to 150 years of "natural" experiments when I say that only lesions in the left hemisphere (LH) of the brain of a right-handed adult can result in gross deficits of language. Lesions in the right hemisphere (RH), on the other hand, seem to lead to gross visual-spatial deficits. Now, there appears to occur a paradox when we follow my proposed research program and consider ERPs from a neuropsychological viewpoint. Neuropsychology leads to certain predictions about laterality effects in normals. But when we try using the ERP techniques to verify these predictions, the results are weak or negative, as Donchin's and McCarthy's review shows (Donchin & McCarthy, 1978). In fact, conversely, laterality effects in ERPs are typically found in tasks where no behavioral laterality effects occur. Why? Well, let me give you the data first. These data are offered as a base for generating experiments in the interface of research on hemispheric specialization and ERP.

13.6.2.1 Patients

I shall describe a very short series of experiments with split-brain patients from the Bogen-Sperry series. The surgery is radical—used for treating otherwise intractable epileptic disorders. The massive fiber system that connects the hemispheres, the corpus callosum including the anterior and hippocampal commissures, is all cut at the same time, usually by retraction of the right hemisphere. The patients seem to improve considerably in terms of epileptic management (Bogen & Vogel, 1975). Now behaviorally, if you do not conduct special tests, the split-brain patients appear quite normal. You can't easily detect anything unusual about them. They have well-coordinated movements; they can ride bicycles; they can write; they speak quite fluently. There is no obvious deficit. But when you provide sensory data to one side, the other side is not aware of these data. It is as if there are two independent persons who ignore each other. For example, if you present an object to the left hand, out of view, the patient may or may not tell you that he has felt an object, but he will generally not be able to name it. But if now you mix this object with others on a table and ask the patient to retrieve the target object by touch with the left hand, he will do so very reliably. This is because the left hand is controlled by the right hemisphere that has no speech. The speaking, left hemisphere controls the right hand and does not know which object was palpated by the left hand. In the visual modality, you can restrict information to one hemisphere by projecting it into one-half of the visual field. The common way to restrict visual projection is to control presentation time during central fixation—for less than 150 msec so that no saccadic eye movements toward the stimulus can be initiated. In case of auditory information it is even more complicated because both ears project to both hemispheres and the only way to provide information selectively or predominantly to a contralateral hemisphere is to use dichotic, synchronous stimuli.that are acoustically similar and are addressed to both ears at exactly the same time. Under these conditions, it appears that the ipsilateral projection is more or less suppressed and each ear projects to the contralateral hemisphere. Of course in the normal brain the left ear stimulus will eventually reach the left hemisphere through the corpus callosum and so on.

13.6.2.2 Technique

My own interest is in fairly complex linguistic processes and I was unhappy with a technique that required me to flash stimuli very quickly for up to about 100 msec. The tachistoscopic paradigm seems especially useful and appropriate for ERP research, however, because it provides discrete stimuli and discrete responses that occur in sequence. The stimuli are simple; otherwise they could not be presented quickly. So, also, does the dichotic listening paradigm. But for my interest in complex linguistic and cognitive processes these were not adequate paradigms. I developed, therefore, another technique that did not prevent subjects from visual scanning and yet restricted input to one visual half-field at a time (Zaidel, 1975). The technique requires placing a contact lens on one eye and covering the other. The stimulus source is on the subject's lap. It is reflected by a mirror and reduced by a lens system to a very small image projected very close to the eye; about 12 in. from the cornea. The subject wears a very large contact lens, a stable triple-curvature scleral lens of the type that some football players used to wear. And it is very stable indeed. On the lens we mount a little aluminum tube that has a powerful lens in its base so that it is possible to focus on the stationary aerial image 1 cm away from the eye and observe an enlarged virtual image of the reduced stimulus. Without the lens, you can't accommodate the eye that much. Further, the subject has an occluding screen hanging at the focal plane of the collimator that is therefore stabilized on the retina. Again, it is not the scanned image that is stabilized on the retina, it is the half-field occluding screen. The system can really be used to create an arbitrary scotoma, but I'm using only a hemianopic scotoma, and it works. So now we can engage each hemisphere separately for 12 hour or an hour and we can see what it can do in a myriad of complex processes. In fact, with this set up, we can have the patient visually guide himself to construct or draw something on the stimulus board but do it only with one hemisphere. In using that kind of paradigm I was first interested in the relationship of language to thought. The right hemisphere seemed a good model for cognition without language, so my first task was to find out how much language there is in the right hemisphere. It turned out that there is so much of it and of such an interesting kind that I wanted to look closer at right-hemisphere language before going on to look at other cognitive processes.

13.6.2.3 Auditory Comprehension

So, if I want to look at language comprehension, how do I lateralize the stimulus? Well, I don't. I say the auditory message aloud. Both hemispheres can then hear it. But I make the response conditional on multiple choices presented to one-half of the visual field. Now if I project an array of picture choices to the left visual half-field, as I have done in the experiments reported here, and I say a word, whereupon the patient points with the left hand to the one of four pictures corresponding to the word, then the patient must both have understood the word, scanned the picture, and interpreted it correctly with the right hemisphere. Because otherwise how could the patient point to the correct picture without being able to describe it verbally? So although both hemispheres heard the word, only the right hemisphere is responding in this case.

KELSO: What is the nature of tactile exploration in these tasks?

ZAIDEL: In these tasks it is minimal. There is hardly any. All the patient has to do is to look at the multiple choices and point to one of them. So perhaps there is some visual-kinesthetic feedback and perhaps some tactile exploration to find where you are on the response page relative to the edge. But this is probably irrelevant even if there is some ipsilateral (uncrossed) projections in the tactile/kinesthetic system from the left hand to the left hemisphere. Now you don't find hemispheric specialization for simple stereognostic tasks in the commissurotomy patients (Zaidel, 1978b).

To continue, first, I want to see if the right hemisphere has auditory language comprehension. If you show four pictures to the right hemisphere and ask the right hemisphere to tell you what these pictures are, it cannot. It has no speech. But then if you say a word like "emerge" (Fig. 13.13, top), the left hand can point to the correct picture. In fact, the right hemisphere has an

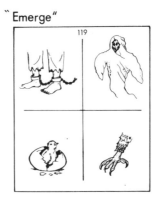

"Emerge"

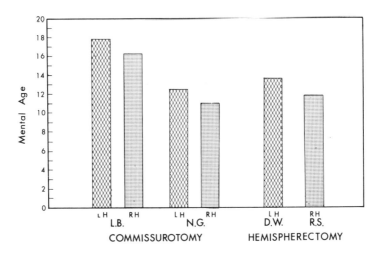

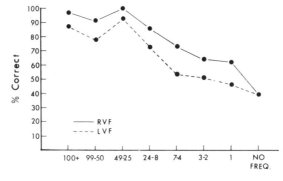

FREQUENCY (per million)

FIG. 13.13   Results of the Peabody Vocabulary Test. Top: a sample item from PPVT reproduced with the special permission of the author, Lloyd M. Dunn, American Guidance Service, Inc. Middle: unilateral equivalent mental ages. Bottom: hemispheric scores (RVF = right visual field = left hemisphere = LH) as a function of word-frequency category (per million printed words) on PPVT. Chance guessing is 25% correct.

amazingly rich auditory vocabulary. I was very surprised when I saw how large it is. The right hemisphere of one of the patients on which I tried this had a vocabulary of something like a normal 18 year old. Another one had something like a normal 12 year old (Fig. 13.17, middle). (For a brief description of the patients please see 13.6.2.5.1.)

TREISMAN: Do you worry about the possibility that one hemisphere may be cuing the other?

ZAIDEL: We have run many control tests showing that the left hemisphere has no access to the visual multiple choices shown to the left visual field. For example, we may ask the patient to point with his left hand to the picture (of an arrow) that goes with "swift" and he does it correctly. But when you ask him which picture he had pointed to, he will ask hesitantly "was it a jet?" His "left hemisphere" heard the word but did not see the picture. So you can run some controls and show that the left hemisphere is not helping in an obvious way. Of course, the left hemisphere could still provide the right with some help in orientation, selective attention, or even the auditory analysis of the linguistic stimulus itself. The real control for that would be to take the left hemisphere out and see how well the right does without it. But we can't do that.

TREISMAN: Or present the word visually to the right hemisphere.

ZAIDEL: Oh, yes, we can do that, but of course then we would be assessing reading, not auditory comprehension. I shall soon describe some reading experiments and compare the results to auditory comprehension.

RITTER: Do you find differences between nouns and adjectives and things of that sort?

ZAIDEL: No. Now the only thing that does seem to make a difference is word frequency. So when you test words from various categories, such as nouns, verbs, adjectives, and adverbs, you find the same dependency on word frequency in both hemispheres. The curves for the two hemispheres are fairly parallel, and it is as if the right hemisphere has a higher threshold for retrieving the meanings of words (Fig. 13.13, bottom). No. I did not find those differences.

13.6.2.4 Reading

So we know now that the right hemisphere has auditory lexical comprehension (i.e., connection 1c in Fig. 13.16). The next question is, how good is its reading? First, you can administer a reading version of the previous test. Instead of saying the word out loud, you just present it visually; print it in the middle of the page. Otherwise, the task is exactly the same. Well, it turns out that the scores go down for both patients (Fig. 13.14). The interesting thing here is that it seems as if the visual vocabulary is a proper subset of the auditory vocabulary. In other words, I found many cases where the right hemisphere could understand a word but not read it, but I never found the converse. That suggests to me that the right hemisphere has no grapheme-phoneme translation. If it did, all it had to do when it saw the printed word was to sound it out (subvocally) in its "mind's" ear and then "hear" it. Because the right hemisphere knows what the word is when spoken, it should then be able to know what it is when printed. The frequent failure of the RH to do so suggests to me that it doesn't have phonetic encoding. In other words, the RH reads ideographically.

POSNER: Are we to assume that the left hemisphere would be right at the top of this graph?

ZAIDEL: Theoretically, at the top in both patients and at exactly the same level on all of these three tests. But, as you get higher and higher up in age, the differences in scores in these standardized tests (such as between a 19 and an 18 year old) become minor and some tests show ceiling effects at younger ages.

Now in Fig. 13.14 (top, right), I show a second version of a reading test. Instead of showing pictures, you say the word out loud and have the patients pick the correct spelling. Both patients do just as well in this version as on the previous reading test. I also tried a lexical decision version of the spelling test where instead of telling the patients "point to the correct spelling of emerge" I said "point to the one that spells a real word." The RHs were just as good at that. We denote this reading ability of the right hemisphere by connection 2c in Fig. 13.16.

CHASE: Would an alternative interpretation be that the right hemisphere does have these orthographic performing rules but it can only read as well as a 10 year old?

ZAIDEL: You see, if the RH had those rules, it should be able to read anything that it understands.

CHASE: Then why can't 10 year olds read anything?

ZAIDEL: Oh, unless they have exclusively sight vocabularies, they can read just about any word out loud—pronounce it, even if not understand it. In fact, if they understand a word, they can usually read it. Of course, English orthography has so many exceptions that it takes awhile to master them all. At any rate, I am not claiming that the RH reads without some visual parsing, only that the process does not involve an intermediate auditory representation.

SCHVANEVELDT: I'm also not clear on this. It sounds as if you are saying that if the spoken word is understood, the understanding mediates the visual recognition. Is that what you are saying?

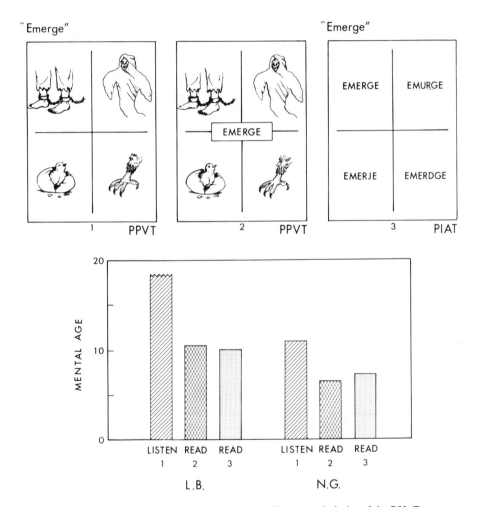

FIG. 13.14   A comparison of the reading and auditory vocabularies of the RH. Top: Sample items from three tests. 1. The Peabody Picture Vocabulary Test (PPVT) where the subject has to point to a picture in response to a spoken word, reproduced by special permission of the author, Lloyd M. Dunn, American Guidance Service, Inc. 2. A reading version of the PPVT where the stimulus word is printed in the middle of the response plate. 3. The spelling subtest of the Peabody Individual Achievement Test. Bottom: RH mental-age scores of two commissurotomy patients on the three tests.

ZAIDEL: I am suggesting that covert auditory comprehension *could* mediate reading if one had access to grapheme-to-phoneme correspondence rules. I am saying that when you pronounce the printed word out loud, even without immediately understanding it, you can then interpret it and associate it with what it stands for.

SCHVANEVELDT: And what it stands for is in turn associated with appearance?

ZAIDEL: With a picture of the referent, not the orthography of the word. In other words, there is some deep semantic representation accessible to the right hemisphere and associated with the picture and with the spoken word, and the picture will mediate the two. In any case, I contend that the RH does *not* mediate reading by auditory comprehension.

DONCHIN: If you give the orthographic—if the word is visually presented to the *left* hemisphere—it would be the same thing as speaking it out loud?

ZAIDEL: Yes, just about. The LH knows grapheme-to-phoneme correspondence and its visual vocabulary is similar to its auditory vocabulary.

KAHNEMAN: Can it read handwriting?

ZAIDEL: Yes, certainly the LH can. Now what about the RH? Until recently I believed that lowercase words were much less frequent, as they in fact are in Hebrew, and so I reasoned that I shouldn't try them first. Israeli newspapers and books are all printed in uppercase. But it turns out that in English, of course, lowercase is what you see most often. Well, the RHs studied here can read in lowercase as well as uppercase, as well as diverse type fonts and handwriting styles. That means that the internal visual lexicon must be stored as a fairly abstract representation that generalizes across handwriting styles, across typefaces, etc.

POSNER: Do you have any data on whether the left hemisphere has any trouble with the lexical decision task because they are all correct phonetic interpretations?

ZAIDEL: No. I found perfect performance there. I did find another interesting aspect of lexical analysis in the RH, however. The right hemisphere may have a funny sort of semantics reference. Suppose you show it four pictures all of which are related to a spoken word but do not *quite* depict the word, like "sewing." In one case you see a needle and thread; in another case you see a sewn patch; in yet another case you see someone actually sewing. The right hemisphere is not going to be very good at picking the correct picture, so its semantic representation is fairly loose in some sense, as if it has a wider range but not so much sensitivity in discrimination. But this remains to be clarified experimentally. Now, in order to show you in some detail why I say that the RH cannot phonetically encode printed words, let me present more formally a small series of experiments. These were conducted at Caltech by Dr. Ann Peters of the University of Hawaii and myself during 1977-1978 (Zaidel & Peters, 1981).

13.6.2.5 Phonetic Recoding

To recapitulate first, clinical neurology traditionally viewed the right cerebral hemisphere in most normal right-handed adults as having no role in the processing of natural language. However, as I have outlined previously, early experiments with the surgically disconnected RHs of split-brain patients have demonstrated that, though mute, the RH can read simple words and has well-developed auditory language comprehension (Sperry & Gazzaniga, 1967; Zaidel, 1978). We have also seen (Fig. 13.14) that with newer techniques, it was found that the RH has a substantial reading lexicon but that its ability to read words as well as sentences was consistently below its auditory comprehension (Zaidel, 1978). This suggested that the RH does not infer the sound of a word from its orthography, i.e., that it does not use grapheme-to-phoneme correspondence rules as does every beginning English reader. Does then the RH read ideographically, retrieving the meaning of the word directly from its visual gestalt without going through an intermediate auditory representation or phonetic recoding? This hypothesis is consistent with data from the present experimenter.

13.6.2.5.1 Subjects.
As I have already mentioned, two patients, N.G. and L.B., who had complete cerebral commissurotomy for relief of intractable epilepsy, were each equipped with a scleral contact-lens system for free scanning of visual stimuli in only one visual field at a time. L.B., a male, was 3 when seizures started, 13 when complete cerebral commissurotomy was performed, and 25 when tested. N.G., a female, was 18 when epilepsy started, 30 when surgery was performed, and 44 when tested (Bogen & Vogel, 1975).

13.6.2.5.2 Tests.
Three tests that use pictures, words, or combinations of pictures and words were administered first to the RHs and then to the LHs, at 1-week intervals. Answers were signaled without speech by pointing with one hand to multiple-choice arrays shown in the homolateral visual half-field (VHF) so that each hemisphere could respond separately. Previous reading tests had already shown that the equivalent reading mental ages of N.G.'s and L.B.'s RHs were 6.5 and 10, respectively (Fig. 13.14; Zaidel, 1978) but that their corresponding age estimates for auditory vocabularies were higher, 12 and

18 years, respectively (Fig. 13.13). The three rhyming tests used for the present study, a "picture-picture test" (see also Levy & Trevarthen, 1977), a "picture-spelling test," and a "spelling-spelling test," all employed a common subset of written words and pictures of their referents. These words had been shown in control tests to be within the RH picture-vocabulary repertoires of both patients.

The picture-picture rhyming (and alliteration) test required the subjects to scan three line drawings and point to the two pictures representing words that start (or end) with the same sound (see example, test 1, in Fig. 13.15). In this way the ability of each hemisphere to "evoke the sound images" of the names of pictures was tested without speech. The test consisted of three training cards and 32 test cards presented in two sets of 16 cards each, a rhyming set, and an alliteration set. Each card contained three line drawings: a target word, either its rhyme (ending with same sound) or alliteration (beginning with the same sound), and its semantic associate. For each of the 16 target words in the rhyming set there was a homonymous target word in the alliteration set (e.g., a !flying bat and a !baseball' bat). If the phonological associate to the target word of a pair in the rhyming set was a rhyme, then the phonological associate to the homonymous target word in the alliteration set was an alliteration, and vice versa. For example,

Rhyming set	Alliteration set
picture of a mitt	picture of flying-*bat*
----------------	----------------
picture of a picture of baseball-*bat* a *hat*	picture of picture of a *back* a sp

Each subject was confronted by one triplet of pictures at a time and requested (task 1) to "find two pictures that start (or end) with the same sound." If a wrong or no answer was forthcoming, the examiner pointed to the target picture and asked the subject (task 2) to "find another picture that starts (or ends) with the same sound as this one." The guessing probability in task 1 is one-third and in task 2 it is one-half so that the total guessing rate is $(13 + 23) \times 12 = 23$. Comparisons between LH and RH scores and between either hemisphere and chance used the $X2$ (chi-squared) test for two matched or independent samples, respectively.

13.6.2.5.3 Results. The results (test 1, Fig. 13.15) showed that the LHs of both patients could perform the task without error. The RHs were significantly inferior ($X2$ = 57.63, 28.85, p < .001, for N.G. and L.B., respectively): L.B.'s RH could recognize both rhyme and alliteration in the absence of ver-

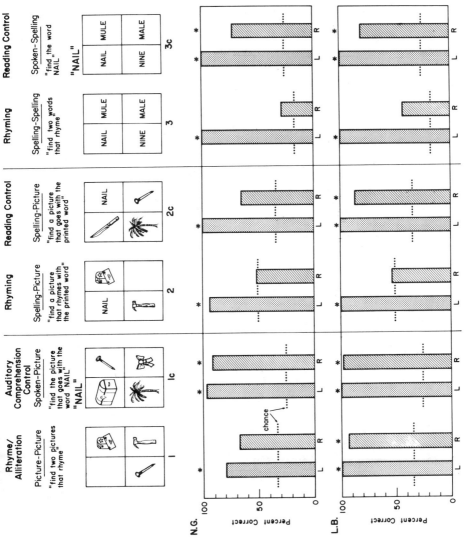

FIG. 13.5 Illustrations of the three tests used in this study and their controls (top) and scores of N.G.'s and L.B.'s disconnected left and right hemispheres on the tests (bottom). * = score is significantly higher than chance.

383

balization above chance ($X2 = 71$, p<.001) at the rate of 93% correct responses (60% on task 1, mean chance = 44%), whereas N.G.'s RH could not recognize rhymes better than chance (Fig. 13.15). Thus, it is possible for a disconnected RH to detect rhymes although this is apparently difficult. The LHs could immediately name any picture on request and often they spontaneously named the pictures systematically, one by one, either overtly or covertly, in order to find the matching pair. In contrast, as expected, the RHs could never readily verbalize the names of any of the pictures. Some 15 years postoperatively, this was still dramatic and often the patient (really his LH) expressed surprise and even irritation at his own (RH) ability to match pictures for sound without being able to verbalize these same sounds, "How could I tell which words sound alike when I don't know what that sound is?"

It may be objected that the RH could match two rhymes by evoking the visual orthographic representation of their names and matching those instead of their "sound images." However, 8 out of 16 rhymes and 4 out of 16 alliterations used in the test matched in sound but not in spelling (e.g., blue—blew, stare—chair, and red—wrench. It turned out that orthographic similarity did not improve the ability of the disconnected RHs to match pictures with rhyming or alliterative names in this experiment, nor is visual similarity necessary for above-chance performance of this task by the RH (patient L.B.).

Control tests showed that both N.G. and L.B. had the names of the target rhyming pictures in their auditory comprehension repertoires. Thus, they could match the spoken name with the picture of its referent (test 1c, Fig. 13.15). L.B.'s RH then could both transform sound → picture (test 1 for rhyming) and picture → sound (test 1c for auditory comprehension control), whereas N.G.'s RH could transform sound → picture but not picture → sound. These observations are summarized schematically as connection 1c in Fig. 13.16 and as possible connection 1 (broken line).

However, the ability of the disconnected RH to match pictures with rhyming names does not mean that it can phonetically recode a printed word. The RH may evoke the sound image of a name directly from the meaning without the intermediate step of retrieving the orthographic representation of that name and then deducing the sound by grapheme-phoneme correspondence rules. To check this, we administered two critical phonetic recoding tests. In the first, picture-spelling test, we replaced one of the rhymes in each of the cards used for the picture-picture rhyming test by its printed name (see test 2 in Fig. 13.15). Now instead of matching two pictures that rhyme with each other, the subject had to find a picture that rhymed with the printed word. In contrast to the picture-picture rhyming test, neither RH could perform this task above chance, even though a control test showed that both RHs could match the printed word with its own pictorial referent (i.e., read it) (see test 2c in Fig. 13.15). Thus, even though the disconnected RH can associate a printed word with its pictorial referent, and, in the sense of the Rhyming test, L.B.'s RH can also often associate the same pictorial referent with the sound image of its name, nevertheless the RH cannot directly associate the printed word with the sound image of its name. In other words, the transformation of lexical representation is not transitive in the RH: we can have SPELLING → MEANING (PICTURE) (connection 2c in Fig. 13.16) and MEANING (PICTURE) → SOUND (connection 1 in Fig. 13.16) but not directly SPELLING → SOUND (disconnection 3, Fig. 13.16).

It may be more difficult for the RH to match a printed word with a picture of its rhyme than to match two printed words directly. In order to control for such "spurious" cross-modal confusions, we also administered a spelling-spelling rhyming test. Each stimulus card had four words printed in uppercase, 12 pt. Helvetica medium lettrasets: The two target words were rhymes, often with very different visual shapes. The original 16-item stimulus set from the picture-picture and picture-spelling phonetic recording tests was extended to 44 cards. An attempt was made to choose rhymes with different orthographies and to include decoys that had a similar visual shape but different sound than

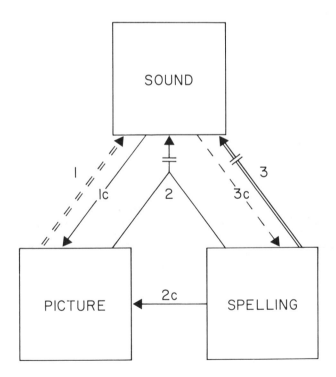

FIG. 13.16 A schematic summary of the three experiments showing the transformations available to the disconnected RH among the spoken word, the printed word, and the picture of the referent named.

the rhymes !e.g., NAIL (target word), MALE (a rhyme), MULE (similar visual frame to MALE), and NINE (similar visual frame to NAIL)

Again, the RHs could not match the rhyming pairs. The results on the spelling-spelling phonetic recoding test were identical to those on the picture-spelling test: errorless performance by the disconnected LHs but chance guessing scores by the RHs (see test 3 in Fig. 13.15). Thus RH failure to recode words phonetically is general and cannot be attributed to the extraneous cognitive load (on a resource-limited RH processor) imposed by the need to analyze two different categories, pictures and written words.

The "sound image" of a word can be evoked in at least two ways, by associating an auditory template with the whole word or by constructing the sound of the word from its phonological components using grapheme-phoneme correspondence rules. Success on our phonetic recoding tests could be achieved by template matching and need not involve grapheme-phoneme rules. L.B.'s RH success on the picture-picture rhyming test (1 Figure 13.16) means that the RH may be able to encode a word phonologically by template (at least from a picture of the referent). However, the failure of the RHs on our phonetic recoding tests suggests that they do not possess phonological encoding by grapheme-phoneme rules for meaningful words. To show specific failure of grapheme-phoneme translation, we would need to show RH inability to do a spelling-spelling rhyming test using nonsense words. This is just what we found (Zaidel & Peters, 1981).

13.6.2.5.4 Discussion. The emerging pattern of linguistic competence in the RH transcends individual differences in clinical histories. The RH cannot speak at all but it can comprehend many spoken words. The RH can also read and it may or may not evoke the sound image of some words, but it cannot under any circumstance translate graphemes into phonemes (see also Levy & Trevarthen, 1977). Its reading is therefore ideographic.

I would like to emphasize again that the claim that the disconnected RHs read ideographically is merely a shorthand for the claim that they read without intermediate phonetic recoding, together with the suggestion that this reading process is based on gestalt pattern matching rather than serial feature detection. The nature of these processes remains vague. Even if the right hemispheres do in fact read ideographically as we hypothesize, the process must be fairly abstract rather than strictly iconic; for it must be invariant over typeface, handwriting style, and case and show size and shape constancies over wide ranges. Thus the fact that the RH reading process accommodates also, say, vertically or backward-printed words is just another example of an invariant and cannot be taken as evidence that the process is not ideographic.

The inability of the RH to recode words phonetically shows that intermediate translation into sound is not necessary for reading single words (Bradshaw, 1975) and suggests that the normal RH may be involved in ideographic reading in the efficient adult reader. Ideographic reading obscures the morphological relationships below the level of the word (i.e., it hides the linguistic structure within a word, such as the relation between "nature" and "natural"). But even if the RH perceived written words as modality-specific templates or visual gestalts, the abstract internal representation may retain certain linguistic structures.

Our findings may have several clinical implications. First, the ideographic, nonphonetic reading of the disconnected RH is reminiscent of what I referred to earlier as acquired deep dyslexia, where patients suffering from posterior LH lesions apparently lack phonetic encoding and can consequently read certain content words but not their components, not even function words that are their nonhomographic homophones (e.g., "bee" but not "be") (Coltheart, Patterson, & Marshall, 1980). Second, our findings explain data from prior studies of Japanese aphasics showing that the ideographically based Kanji are not so susceptible to LH lesions of the classical speech area as are the phonetically-based Kata Kana (Sasanuma & Fujimura, 1971). Third, the pattern of ideographic reading in the disconnected RH also bears resemblance to the reading of so-called congenital "dysphonetic dyslexics," who encounter problems in grapheme-to-phoneme translation but have some gestalt reading and intact visuospatial skills (Boder, 1971). This group of congenital dyslexics may rely on their RHs for reading, can therefore be diagnosed with verbal tachistoscopic tests, and may respond to therapy for developing LH skills and increasing interhemispheric interaction.

Our findings suggest that the normal RH may be involved in ideographic lexical reading, but it is as yet unknown whether this ability is especially important during the initial stages of reading acquisition (in order to facilitate the recognition of new linguistic symbols) or rather during efficient, mature reading (in order to recognize recurring visual patterns quickly) (Zaidel & Peters, 1981).

SCHVANEVELDT: If these other routes (from print to picture and from picture to sound) are intact in the disconnected RH, why can't they get these together?

ZAIDEL: That's my point, they cannot. In other words, cognitive transformations in the mind may not be naturally transitive. The RH may be able to go from print to picture and separately from picture to sound but not directly from print to sound. It remains to be found whether transitivity can be achieved by special training.

DONCHIN: Are you showing us two patients because that's the data base or are those representative of a larger?

ZAIDEL: Those are the two that have contact lenses and I am now designing a universal half-field occluder that will allow me to test more patients. That universal occluder is not finished. It's just difficult to put different contact lenses on different patients. I chose two that are considered fairly representative.

DONCHIN: The thing that I'm worried about is that these patients have a long history of clinical difficulties and who knows what is going on in their two hemispheres? Is it possible that the properties of the right hemisphere of L.B. reflect the fact the L.B. was epileptic for many years before the split surgery? These patients also have had practice for 15 years playing around with this sort of test. Who knows what sort of skills they have developed?

ZAIDEL: These patients have developed linguistically interesting and orderly skills. The extent to which these skills are also present in the normal RH needs to be determined empirically. In fact, we now have data suggesting that the disconnected RH actually underestimates the ability of the normal RH to perform lexical decision task (Zaidel, 1982). Let me next address the issue of generalizability in more detail.

13.6.2.6 Generalizability

Concerning the Clever Hans danger, it turns out that these patients were quite naive on these tasks. I was afraid of that when I went into the field, but that's really not a serious problem. There is, of course, always the issue of how much the left hemisphere helps the right in orientation to task and even in perceptual analysis, especially with nonlateralized auditory stimuli. We carefully and continuously monitor for verbalization of stimuli presented to the left sensory field in order to exclude suspect trials that suggest LH cuing and interference. Now, about the issue of reorganization, I would ask you first of all to compare the pattern of lateralization that is apparent in these patients to that apparent in other patients who have had massive brain damage that causes reorganization. It's just not the same. Compare, for example, the right hemispheres of these patients and the right hemisphere of, say, an infantile right hemiplegic. The left hemisphere in the latter may be removed later in life but it atrophied at infancy. Well, it turns out that the RHs of these infantile hemiplegics are just not the same as the RHs of the commissurotomy patients. The hemiplegic can read and write and speak quite well with the residual right hemisphere. The disconnected RH cannot. What I am interested in is the dissociation of abilities or systems in the disconnected RH, not in the absolute scores on particular tests. Conversely, the adult hemispherectomy patients of Aaron Smith and the amytal patients of Brenda Milner's show rather similr dissociation of abilities to those observed in the commissurotomy patients, when comparable data exist.

Now, I have been trying to distinguish two aspects of the perceptual-cognitive-linguistic profile of these commissurotomy patients: first, those universal constraints on RH abilities that hold for all of them regardless of dramatic differences in clinical history; second, those score patterns that reflect individual differences in extracallosal damage, personal IQ, etc. Thus the contrast between good comprehension and no or very limited speech seems universal; the specific size of the auditory vocabulary seems to be subject to considerable individual differences. I have tried to correlate laterality scores in the commissurotomy patients on a variety of tasks in all modalities and generally did not obtain a correlation with predominant hemisphericity of extracallosal damage. The one case where *individual* laterality effects did correlate with hemispheric extracallosal lesions was in a manual stereognosis task that showed no consistent laterality effects across all patients (Zaidel, 1978b).

But to answer your first question last, there is suggestive converging evidence that the observed pattern of lexical representation in the disconnected right hemisphere is representative of the normal brain. Thus, some "deep alexics" show a left visual half-field (LVF) advantage in their limited reading; the ideographic Japanese ideolect Kanji shows a weaker RVF advantage or even an LVF, whereas the phonotactic Katakana ideolect shows the usual RVF advantage. I am told by a neurosurgeon acquaintance (Robert Iacano, p.c.) that right-hemisphere lesions in Japanese often result in selective Kanji loss. Further, lexical decision tasks in normal subjects sometimes fail to show laterality effects but show better facilitation (priming) effects within rather than across fields (Marcel & Patterson, 1978), as well as showing phonological facilitation in the RVF though not in the LVF (Cohen & Freeman, 1978). This is consistent with the split-brain data in the sense that the right hemisphere can also do lexical decisions but reads nonphonologically. Moreover, a series of lexical decision tasks administered by Allen Radant, Christine Temple, and myself at UCLA, have shown, first, that the normal RH has a greater lexical facilitation effect than either the disconnected RH or the normal LH, and, second, that best performance in lexical decision occurs with interhemispheric interaction: when the prime is flashed to the LVF, and the target to the RVF]

Lexical decision tasks in some forms, then, show laterality effects consistent with a "direct-access model." This says that both hemispheres can process the task, though one may be better than the other, and that the hemisphere that receives the input is the one that will process it. Then, at best, small laterality effects can be expected, no callosal transfer is involved, and the effects obtained with the split brain should be identical to those obtained with the normal brain. The direct-access model lends itself to information-processing analysis and experimental manipulation of laterality effects. For example, hemispheric facilitation or overloading can change the solution strategy and the relative hemispheric contributions to a task if we presuppose a direct-access model and a resource-limited processor in each hemisphere.

As already mentioned, the direct access model contrasts with the callosal-relay model that presupposes that only one hemisphere is specialized to process the task so that stimuli reaching the other hemisphere first will have to be re-layed across the corpus callosum to the competent hemisphere, before they can be processed. This model holds, for example, for the typical dichotic listening procedure with nonsense CV syllables (ba, da, ga, pa, ta, ka) (Zaidel, 1983). Tasks obeying the callosal relay model typically show massive laterality effects in the split brain but only small effects in the normal brain where facile callosal-transfer is almost as effective as direct, crossed sensory field-hemisphere connections.

Consequently, as already mentioned, a comparison between laterality effects on a given task in the split and normal brains can serve as a decision procedure for classifying the task as "direct access" or "callosal relay." Small and similar laterality effects in the split and normal brains signal a direct-access model; large laterality effects in the split brain contrasting with small effects in the normal brain, on the other hand, suggest a callosal-relay model. Unfortunately, the absence of a laterality effect in the normal population alone is insufficient for deciding whether there is no hemispheric specialization on the task or whether effective callosal transfer masks the existing hemispheric asymmetries. One potentially promising solution to this dilemma is to identify temporal ERP correlates of callosal transfer itself.

Of course, even if the pattern of competencies observed in the disconnected RH is quite close to the pattern of the normal RH, as the direct-access model suggests, it still does not follow that the RH is actually *used* in the normal brain for linguistic communication. Conversely, if you take an aphasic who has a massive lesion to the classical speech area, using the sodium amytal technique it is possible to show that sometimes language control transfers to the other side. Why not in the commissurotomy patients? Perhaps because speech real-ly requires a fine, unified motor control system, which precludes bilateral in-teraction.

13.6.3 Theoretical Implications and Paradoxes

We may then discern two applications of the observed cognitive status of the disconnection syndrome: First, as a guide for a research program on RH abili-ties in the normal brain; second, as a unique case study or proving ground for resolving important theoretical issues. In mapping RH abilities, we note (i) the dissociation between rich semantics and poor syntax in its language repertoire; (ii) the continuum of laterality effects from strongest LH specialization for speech to weakest LH superiority for auditory comprehension of single words; (iii) the better RH comprehension of single words than of longer phrases; (iv) the better auditory comprehension than reading in the RH; and (v) the non-phonetic nature of RH reading. Thus, a natural interface for ERP and laterali-ty research would be the lexical analysis of phonetic information, and this pro-cess should show a consistent LH superiority using measures from both fields.

Examples of theoretical issues that can be resolved by neurological data include the motor theory of speech perception that seems logically unnecessary in the view of good RH auditory language comprehension without speech; or the availability to the RH of certain syntactic structures, such as passivization, without necessarily having the alledgedly logically prior Piagetian ability of reversibility. In a sense the disconnected RH illustrates the linguistic limit of a cognitive system that does not include the innate species-specific linguistic mechanism outlined by Chomsky. In particular, the RH pattern shows that natural cognitive transformations of the mind are not necessarily subject to simple logical relations, such as symmetry, reversibility, or transitivity. More generally, perhaps all the superior RH abilities can be characterized as related to a cognitive style of pattern recognition by template and spatial closure, whereas the LH may be specialized for the cognitive style of feature detection and disembedding.

Now, I have reviewed these experiments in order to present a data base for interfacing ERP and laterality research. Yet when the most promising lead is in fact followed, as by Donchin and McCarthy, the ERP fails to show an expected LH specialization for processing lexical phonetic information. Why? Either the statements on LH phonological specialization are not true of the normal brain or ERP methodology is too insensitive, invalid, etc., or do we have a paradoxical result.

DONCHIN: I don't see why you expect us to find it. It's not clear to me why you would expect normals to get this. You're bothered by the rhyming task.

ZAIDEL: One gets consistent laterality effects on this task. In convergent studies with commissurotomy patients, hemisphere-damaged patients, and normal subjects; in visual field studies, in dichotic listening studies; . . .

DONCHIN: What do you mean by "get it"?

ZAIDEL: Here is a robust phenomenon that expresses itself in some behavioral index. Why shouldn't it express itself in an electrophysiological index?

DONCHIN: Well, I think that you have to avoid confusing *products* with *processes.* When you say you're getting an effect, you're describing the product of a large number of complicated processes. Now we happened to look with the ERP at one or two or three of these component processes. It need not be the case that the processes that we happen to study are related in any way, shape, or form to the lateralization of the product.

ZAIDEL: Then I'd like to find something that is so related. I think it will be extremely useful. Then the technique can bootstrap itself. You could start by looking at behavioral differences in special preparations like neurosurgical, brain-damaged, or amytal patients and try to outline the ERP correlates of these. Then, you can find out whether normal subjects show similar differences and next treat the asymmetric ERP components as an index of individual differences. For example, it's known that laterality differences correlate with sex, handedness, and the cognitive style of field dependence. Now you can apply the new ERP technique in a variety of new situations that do not lend themselves to the old type of analysis such as latency and accuracy.

DONCHIN: Well, you are making various assumptions. For example, the experiment I described in Chapter 5 was undertaken because Bill Wang expected we would get lateralities that would reflect the phonetic/orthographic dichotomy. He prepared different lists that were supposed, on intuitive grounds, to lead the subject to use either phonetic or orthographic cues. The prediction was that if you give the subject a list which involved phonological cues, the CNV or the P300 will be larger on the left side of the head. The behavioral data show that people perform both the phonological and the orthographic analysis *all the time in all circumstances*, no matter what you tell them to do. In fact, they cannot avoid making the two analyses and therefore there is no reason to expect lateralization.

ZAIDEL: Did you lateralize the stimuli?

KUTAS: No.

ZAIDEL: There is no question that the hemispheres interact with each other all the time, but that does not tell you what each hemisphere is doing. In any case, I think your last interpretation of the experiment with Wang is very strong] You are not saying that the ERP does not tap a laterality difference but, rather, that a laterality effect does not occur because distinct processes are activated in each hemisphere, the ERP is sensitive to both, and so as a net result there is no laterality effect. In that case, we want an ERP component that is selectively sensitive to one process, say phonetic recoding, and not the other, say orthographic matching.

DONCHIN: Well, I personally have a minimal belief in any study of lateralization that does not include monitoring of EOG with DC recording.

ZAIDEL: I would disagree with you here. I think that's a red herring.

DONCHIN: How do you know where the person is looking?

ZAIDEL: Because if he's looking around he is not going to get the right dissociations. Some tasks are better in the LVF.

DONCHIN: Oh, yes. If you find positive results, you're OK; but if you find negative results, you never know why.

ZAIDEL: Oh, sure. I'll buy that. Bolles of Oregon did show that laterality effects in hemi-field tachistoscopic studies increase with bilateral presentations or with a control fixation stimulus. Correct reporting of such a stimulus can also serve to verify fixation although care should be taken not to bias the laterality effect by including fixation stimuli that themselves evoke strong hemispheric differences in processing.

It seems to me there are two ways to proceed now. One way is to regard the P300 as a meta-cognitive window that you can map everything onto. It expresses some resolution or an identifiable stage of the cognitive process as long as the paradigm includes a stimulus followed very soon by a response. Now if you could design a cognitive task that involves asymmetric hemisphere components and that maps onto the P300 window, you may very well find P300 correlates of that asymmetry. The problem with that is that the paradigm always depends on precisely yoked stimulus-response conditions and is therefore perhaps contaminated by them. In particular, repetitive tasks may well involve systematic shifts in hemispheric processing control from the right to the left hemisphere as the task becomes more familiar and as the strategies used to process it perhaps become more analytic.

When you look at EEG, Enoch tells me that you don't really find lateral asymmetry in the power spectrum unless you include the sensorimotor components. When you control for those by other tasks that don't have the same sensorimotor components but have the same presumed loading on laterality factors, it turns out that the EEG asymmetries disappear (Gevins, Zeitlin, Doyle, Yingling, Schaffer, Callaway, & Yeager, 1979). This is disturbing if true. Perhaps higher-order frequency-time factors in the EEG analysis will give us what we want, but it's clear that we want a continuous, real-time monitor of cerebral processing. Its usefulness? Let me cite just one example. If indeed the RH reads ideographically and if it is true that those patients who read ideographically use their RH to support the process (all I need to determine this is some measure that would tell me that the RH is selectively active during reading), then I may be able to suggest means and strategies for improving language ability in such patients. I know a little bit about the cognitive style of the RH and perhaps can suggest therapies that capitalize on that style.

What nobody has shown me in this discussion is a methodology for using evoked potentials on people with lesions. Truett has mentioned that lesions will have some consequences. The fact that there is a hole in the brain from which you are recording will naturally affect the waveforms. I want to factor this effect out and still be able to track the cognitive processes in the residual brain, and I have heard little about this problem here.

HARTER: One way to do that is look at how whatever is leftover is modulated by task variability. That would be one example of looking at the variance in the data. And, forget about the basic waveform.

KUTAS: What would happen, Eran, if you were to test normals with the same tests? What would the practice effects be?

ZAIDEL: The research literature is conflicting on this. There is considerable interest now in stages of processing and hemispheric involvement (Hellige, 1980; Moscovitch, 1979). My personal belief is that the right hemisphere is especially important in the initial stages of processing, so that you will tend to find an increasing rather than a decreasing right-ear advantage in a dichotic listening task as a function of practice. You will tend to show RH superiority in the beginning of a task or the acquisition of a cognitive skill that eventually shifts to the LH superiority (Goldberg & Costa, 1981; Silverberg, Gordon, Pollack, & Bentin, 1980; Zaidel, 1979).

KUTAS: Do you know how long it takes?

ZAIDEL: Well, that's an important point. You can show it on the scale of 2 hours; you can show it on a scale of several weeks; and you can show it on a scale of 2 years as in the acquisition of musical expertise or reading proficiency, all depending on the complexity of the task or skill involved. One study by Silverberg et al. (1980) involved Israeli children who were learning to read. They administered a Hebrew dichotic listening study that showed the usual right-ear advantage throughout. Then they also administered a visual half-field reading task to first-, second-, and third-graders. The younger children had a left visual-field advantage, whereas in the older group a right visual-field advantage emerged for the same words.

KUTAS: That's part of the problem in designing good evoked potential studies, particularly with hemispheric effects, because, you really have to have a good signal-to-noise ratio and you have to record many, many trials. What seems to happen is that the laterality effect disappears by the time you reach the point you're ready to record, and although you know you have good electrophysiological responses, you don't have the behavioral effects.

ZAIDEL: Well, I would say it would shift in a systematic manner, but it won't disappear unless the task becomes bilateralized or automatized.

REGAN: Our experience is that it is difficult to use EPs as an aid in locating cortical pathology because intersubject control variability is so great. Also, patients with cortical blindness due to removal of cortex may give EPs, though they are abnormal.

ALLISON: No, I don't think so either because, particularly in the later components, there is enough interaction between areas of the brain that you could knock out activity coming presumably from area B, whereas in fact it's area A that has the lesions; so, it's very tough.

ZAIDEL: But if area A is small, it may give rise to such a small bump that it will be unnoticeable or disappear altogether if you look at a normal person; yet it will be clearly seen in a person with a lesion if you know where to look and what to look for. It's that kind of bootstrapping that seems most promising to me.

Bibliography

Adam, N., & Collins, G. I. Late components of the visual evoked potential to search in short-term memory. *Electroencephalography and Clinical Neurophysiology,* 1978, *44,* 147–156.

Adams, J. A. Feedback theory of how joint receptors regulate the timing and positioning of a limb. *Psychological Review,* 1977, *84,* 504–523.

Allison, T., Goff, W. R., Williamson, P. D., & VanGilder, J. C. On the neural origin of early components of the human somatosensory evoked potential. In J. E. Desmedt (Ed.), *Clinical uses of cerebral, brainstem and spinal somatosensory evoked potentials. Progress in Clinical Neurophysiology, Vol. 7.* Basel: Karger, 1980, pp. 51–68.

Arezzo, J., Legatt, A. D., & Vaughan, H. G., Jr. Topography and intracranial sources of somatosensory evoked potentials in the monkey. I. Early components. *Electroencephalography and Clinical Neurophysiology,* 1979, *46,* 155–172.

Arezzo, J., Vaughan, H. G., Jr., & Koss, B. Relationship of neuronal activity to gross movement-related potentials in monkey pre- and postcentral gyrus. *Brain Research,* 1977, *132,* 362–369.

Atkin, O., & Chase, W. Quantification of three dimensional structures. *Journal of Experimental Psychology: Human Perception and Performance,* 1978, *4,* 397–410.

Becker, C. A. Semantic context effects in visual word recognition: An analysis of semantic strategies. *Memory and Cognition,* 1980, *8,* 493–512.

Belen'kii, V. Y., Gurfinkel, V. S., & Pal'tsev, Y. I. Elements of control of voluntary movements. *Biophysics,* 1967, *12,* 154–166.

Bernstein, N. *The coordination and regulation of movement.* New York: Pergamon, 1967.

Bishop, G. H. The relation of nerve polarization to monophasicity of its response. *Journal of Cellular and Comparative Physiology,* 1932, *1,* 371–386.

Bizzi, E. The coordination of eye–head movements. *Scientific American,* 1974, *231,* 100–106.

Blakemore, C., & Campbell, F. W. On the existence of neurones in the human visual system selectively sensitive to the orientation and size of retinal images. *Journal of Physiology* (London), 1969, *203,* 237–360.

Boder, E. Developmental dyslexia: Prevailing diagnostic concepts and a new diagnostic approach. In H. R. Hyklebust (Ed.), *Progress in learning disabilities* (Vol. II). New York: Grune and Stratton, 1971.

Bogen, J. E., & Vogel, P. J. Neurologic status in the long term following complete cerebral commissurotomy. In F. Michel & B. Schott (Eds.), *Les syndromes de disconnexion colleuse chez l'homme*. Lyon: Hopital Neurologique, 1975.

Bolt, B. A. The fine structure of the earth's interior. *Scientific American*, 1973, *228*, 24–33.

Bowers, K. S., & Drenneman, H. A. Doing two things at once: An information approach to hypnosis and hypnotic susceptibility. Presented at the Society of Clinical and Experimental Hypnosis Convention, Los Angeles, October 15, 1977.

Bradshaw, J. L. Three interrelated problems in reading: A review. *Memory and Cognition*, 1975, *3*, 123–134.

Brand, J. Classification without identification in visual search. *Quarterly Journal of Experimental Psychology*, 1971, *23*, 178–186.

Bransford, J. D., & Johnson, M. K. Contextual prerequisites for understanding: Some investigations of comprehension and recall. *Journal of Verbal Learning and Verbal Behavior*, 1972, *11*, 717–726.

Brazier, M. A. B. Evoked responses recorded from the depths of the human brain. *Annals of the New York Academy of Science*, 1964, *112*, 35–59.

Broadbent, D. E. Immediate memory and simultaneous stimuli. *Quarterly Journal of Experimental Psychology*, 1957, *4*, 1–11.

Broadbent, D. E. *Perception and communication*. London: Pergamon, 1958.

Broadbent, D. E. Stimulus set and response set: Two kinds of selective attention. In D. I. Mostofsky (Ed.), *Attention: Contemporary theory and analysis*. New York: Appleton-Century-Crofts, 1970.

Broadbent, D. E. *Decision and stress*. New York: Academic Press, 1971.

Broughton, R. J. Discussion. In E. Donchin & D. B. Lindsley (Eds.), *Average evoked potentials: Methods, results, and evaluations*. NASA SP-191, Washington, D.C.: U.S. Government Printing Office, 1969, 79–84.

Buchsbaum, M. Neural events and psychophysical law. *Science*, 1971, *172*, 502.

Bushnell, M. C., Robinson, D. L., & Goldberg, M. E. Dissociation of movement and attention: Neuronal correlates in posterior parietal cortex. *Neurosciences Abstracts*, 1978, *4*, 621.

Butters, N. & Cermak, L. S. *Alcoholic Korsakoff's Syndrome: An information processing approach to amnesia*. New York: Academic Press, 1980.

Callaway, E., Tueting, P., & Koslow, S. H. (Eds.) *Event-related brain potentials in man*. New York: Academic Press, 1978.

Campbell, F. W., Cooper, G. E., & Enroth-Cugell, C. The spatial selectivity of the visual cells of the cat. *Journal of Physiology* (London), 1969, *203*, 223–235.

Campbell, F. W., & Maffei, L. Electrophysiological evidence for the existence of orientation and size detectors in the human visual system. *Journal of Physiology*, 1970, *207*, 635–652.

Campbell, F. W., Maffei, L., & Piccolino, M. The contrast sensitivity of the cat. *Journal of Physiology*, 1973, *229*, 719–731.

Campbell, K. B., Courchesne, E., Picton, T. W., & Squires, K. C. Evoked potential correlates of human information processing. *Biological Psychology*, 1979, *8*, 45–68.

Carpenter, P. A., & Just, M.A. Sentence comprehension: A psycholinguistic processing model of verification. *Psychological Review*, 1975, *82*, 1–25.

Chapman, R. M., McCrary, J. W., & Chapman, J. A. Short-term memory: The "storage" component of human brain responses predicts recall. *Science*, 1978, *202*, 1211–1214.

Chesney, G. L., Michie, P., & Donchin, E. Selective attention and a slow, negative component of the human event-related potential. Proceedings of the 19th Annual Meeting, Society for Psychophysiological Research. *Psychophysiology*, 1980, *17*, 291–292.

Chi, M. T. H., & Klahr, D. Span and rate of apprehension in children and adults. *Journal of Experimental Child Psychology*, 1975, *19*, 434–439.

Clark, D. L., Butler, R. A., & Rosner, B. S. Dissociation of sensation and evoked responses by a general anesthetic in man. *Journal of Comparative and Physiological Psychology,* 1969, *68,* 315-319.

Clark, H. H., & Chase, W. G. On the process of comparing sentences against pictures. *Cognitive Psychology,* 1972, *3,* 472-517.

Clark, H. H., & Chase, W. G. Perceptual coding strategies in the formation and verification of descriptions. *Memory & Cognition,* 1974, *2,* 101-111.

Clarke, P. G. H. Visual EPs to sudden reversal of the motion of a pattern. *Brain Research,* 1972, *36,* 453-458.

Cohen, G., & Freeman, R. Individual differences in reading strategies in relation to cerebral asymmetry. In J. Requin (Ed.), *Attention and performance VII.* Hillsdale, N.J.: Lawrence Erlbaum Associates, 1978.

Coltheart, M., Patterson, K. E., & Marshall, J. C. (Eds.) *Deep dyslexia.* London: Routledge & Kegan Paul, 1980.

Cooper, L. A., & Shepard, R. N. Chronometric studies of the rotation of mental images. In W. G. Chase (Ed.), *Visual information processing.* New York: Academic Press, 1973.

Coquery, J. M. Selective attention as a motor program. In J. Requin (Ed.), *Attention and performance VII.* Hillsdale, New Jersey: Lawrence Erlbaum Associates, 1978.

Coulter, J. D. Sensory transmission through leminiscal pathway during voluntary movement in the cat. *Journal of Neurophysiology,* 1974, *37,* 831-845.

Courchesne, E., Hillyard, S. A., & Galambos, R. Stimulus novelty, task relevance, and the visual evoked potential in man. *Electroencephalography and Clinical Neurophysiology,* 1975, *39,* 131-143.

Craik, F. I. M., & Lockhart, R. S. Levels of processing: A framework for memory research. *Journal of Verbal Learning and Verbal Behavior,* 1972, *11,* 671-684.

Davis, P. A. Effect of acoustic stimuli on the waking human brain. *Journal of Neurophysiology,* 1939, *2,* 494-499.

Desmedt, J. E. (Ed.) *New developments in electromyography and clinical neurophysiology.* Basel: Karger, 1973.

Desmedt, J. E. Some observations on the methodology of cerebral evoked potentials in man. In J. E. Desmedt (Ed.), *Attention, voluntary contraction and event-related cerebral potentials, Vol. 1.* Basel: Karger, 1977, 12-29.

Desmedt, J. E., Debecker, J., & Robertson, D. Serial perceptual processing and the neural basis of changes in event-related potentials components and slow potential shifts. In J. E. Desmedt (Ed.), *Cognitive components in cerebral event-related potentials and selective attention.* Basel: Karger, 1979, 53-79.

Desmedt, J. E., & Robertson, D. Differential enhancement of early and late components of the cerebral somatosensory evoked potentials during forced-paced cognitive tasks in man. *Journal of Physiology* (London), 1977, *271,* 761-782.

Diamond, I. T. The subdivisions of neocortex: A proposal to revise the traditional view of sensory, motor and association areas. In J. M. Sprague & A. N. Epstein (Eds.), *Progress in psychobiology and physiological psychology, Vol. 8.* New York: Academic Press, 1979.

Dick, A. O. Spatial abilities. In H. Avakian-Whitaker and H. A. Whitaker (Eds.), *Current trends in neurolinguistics.* 1978.

Donchin, E. Event-related brain potentials: A tool in the study of human information processing. In H. Begleiter (Ed.), *Evoked potentials and behavior.* New York: Plenum Press, 1979, 13-75.

Donchin, E. Surprise! . . . Surprise? *Psychophysiology,* 1981, *18,* 493-513.

Donchin, E., Callaway, E., Cooper, R., Desmedt, J. E., Goff, W. R., Hillyard, S. A., & Sutton, S. Publication criteria for studies of evoked potentials in man. In J. E. Desmedt (Ed.), *Progress in clinical neurophysiology, Vol. 1.* Basel: Karger, 1977, 1-11.

Donchin, E., Gerbrandt, L. L., Leifer, L., & Tucker, L. Is the contingent negative variation contingent on a motor response? *Psychophysiology,* 1972, *9,* 178-188.

Donchin, E., & Heffley, E. Multivariate analysis of event-related potential data: A tutorial review. In D. Otto (Ed.), *Multidisciplinary perspectives in event-related brain potential research.* EPA-600/9-77-043, Washington, D.C.: U.S. Government Printing Office, 1979, 555-572.

Donchin, E., Kutas, M., & McCarthy, G. Electrocortical indices of hemispheric utilization. In S. Harnad, R. W. Doty, L. Goldstein, J. Jaynes, & G. Krauthamer (Eds.), *Lateralization in the nervous system.* New York: Academic Press, 1977, 339-384.

Donchin, E., & McCarthy, G. Event-related brain potentials in the study of cognitive processes. In C. Ludlow & M. E. Doran-Quine (Eds.), *Proceedings of the Symposium on Neurological Bases of Language Disorders in Children: Methods and direction for research.* Washington, D.C.: U.S. Government Printing Office, 1980, NINCDS Monograph #22, 109-128.

Donchin, E., Ritter, W., & McCallum, C. Cognitive psychophysiology: The endogenous components of the ERP. In E. Callaway, P. Tueting, & S. Koslow (Eds.), *Brain event-related potentials in man.* New York: Academic Press, 1978, 349-441.

Donchin, E., & Sutton, S. The "psychological significance" of evoked responses: A comment on Clark, Butler, & Rosner. *Communications in Behavioral Biology,* 1970, *5,* 111-114.

Donders, F. C. On the speed of mental processes. *Acta Psychologica,* 1969, *30,* 412-431. (Translated from the original by W. G. Koster from *Onderzoekingen gedaan in het Physiologisch Laboratorium der Utrechtsche Hoogeschool,* 1868, *Tweede reeks, II,* 92-120.)

Duncan, J. The locus of interference in the perception of simultaneous stimuli. *Psychological Review,* 1980, *87,* 272-300.

Duncan-Johnson, C. C. The relation of P300 to reaction time as a function of expectancy. Unpublished doctoral dissertation, University of Illinois, 1979.

Duncan-Johnson, C. C., & Donchin, E. The P300 component of the event-related brain potential as an index of information processing. *Biological Psychology,* 1982, *14,* 1-52.

Eason, R., Harter, M., & White, C. Effects of attention and arousal on visually evoked cortical potentials and reaction time in man. *Physiology and Behavior,* 1969, *4,* 283-289.

Eason, R. G., & Ritchie, G. Effects of stimulus set on early and late components of visually evoked potentials. Paper presented to Psychonomic Society, St. Louis, 1976.

Epstein, W., & Rock, I. Perceptual set as an artifact of recency. *American Journal of Psychology,* 1960, *73,* 214-228.

Ervin, F. R., & Anders, T. R. Normal and pathological memory. In F. O. Schmitt (Ed.), *The neurosciences: Second study program.* New York: Rockefeller University Press, 1970.

Evarts, E. V., Bizzi, E., Burke, R. E., DeLong, M., & Thach, W. T. The central control of movement. *Neurosciences Research Program Bulletin,* 1971, *9,* 1-170.

Finke, R., & Schmidt, M. Orientation-specific color aftereffects following imagination. *Journal of Experimental Psychology: Human Perception and Performance* 1977, *3,* 599-606.

Ford, J. M., Mohs, R. C., Pfefferbaum, A., & Kopell, B. S. On the utility of P3-latency and RT for studying cognitive processes. *Progress in Brain Research,* 1980, *54,* 661-667.

Ford, J. M., Roth, W. T., & Kopell, B. S. Auditory evoked potentials to unpredictable shifts in pitch. *Psychophysiology,* 1976, *13,* 32-39.

Ford, J. M., Roth, W. T., Mohs, R. C., Hopkins, W. F., III, & Kopell, B. S. Event-related potentials recorded from young and old adults during a memory retrieval task. *Electroencephalography and Clinical Neurophysiology,* 1979, *47,* 450-459.

Fowler, C. A. Timing control in speech production. Indiana University, Linguistics Club, Bloomington, Ind., 1977.

Francolini, C. M., & Egeth, H. Perceptual selectivity is task dependent: The pop-out effect poops out. *Perception and Psychophysics,* 1979, *25,* 99-110.

Franzen, O., & Offenloch, K. Evoked response correlates of psychophysical magnitude estimates for tactile stimulation in man. *Experimental Brain Research,* 1969, *8,* 1-18.

Friedman, D., Hakerem, G., Sutton, S., & Fleiss, J. L. Effect of stimulus uncertainty on the pupillary dilation response and the vertex evoked potential. *Electroencephalography and Clinical Neurophysiology,* 1973, *34,* 475–484.

Furedy, J. J., & Scull, J. Orienting-reaction theory and an increase in the human GSR following stimulus change which is unpredictable but not contrary to prediction. *Journal of Experimental Psychology,* 1971, *88,* 292–294.

Gaillard, A. W. K. The late CNV wave: Preparation versus expectancy. *Psychophysiology,* 1977, *14,* 563–568.

Gaillard, A. W. K. *Slow brain potentials preceding task performance.* Amsterdam: Academic Press, 1978.

Gall, F. J. *Anatomie et physiologie du système nerveux en general, et du cerveau en particulier.* Paris: F. Schoell, 4 vols., 1810–1819.

Gelfand, I. M., Gurfinkel, V. S., Fomin, S. V., & Tsetlin, M. L. (Eds.) *Models of the structural-functional organization of certain biological systems.* Cambridge: MIT Press, 1971.

Gevins, A., Zeitlin, G., Doyle, J., Yingling, C., Schaffer, R., Callaway, E., & Yeager, C. Electroencephalogram correlates of higher cortical functions. *Science,* 1979, *203,* 665–668.

Ghez, C., & Lenzi, G. L. Modulation of sensory transmission in cat lemniscal system during voluntary movement. *European Journal of Physiology,* 1971, *323,* 272–278.

Goff, W. R., Allison, T., & Vaughan, H. G., Jr. The functional neuroanatomy of event-related potentials. In E. Callaway, P. Teuting, and S. H. Koslow (Eds.), *Event-related brain potentials in man.* New York: Academic Press, 1978, pp. 1–79.

Goldberg, E., Costa, L. D., & Bilder, R., Jr. Hemispheric differences in relationship to acquisition and use of descriptive systems. Unpublished manuscript, 1980.

Goldberg, M. E., & Wurtz, R. H. Activity of superior colliculus in behaving monkeys. II. Effect on neuronal responses. *Journal of Neurophysiology,* 1972, *35,* 560–574.

Gomer, F. E., Spicuzza, R. J., & O'Donnell, R. D. Evoked potential correlates of visual item recognition during memory-scanning tasks. *Physiological Psychology,* 1976, *4,* 61–65.

Goodglass, H., & Kaplan, E. *The assessment of aphasia and related disorders.* Philadelphia: Lea and Febiger, 1972.

Goodin, D. S., Squires, K. C., Henderson, B. H., & Starr, A. Age-related variations in evoked potentials to auditory stimuli in normal human subjects. *Electroencephalography and Clinical Neurophysiology,* 1978, *44,* 447–458.

Goodin, D. S., Squires, K., & Starr, A. Long latency event-related components of the auditory evoked potential in dementia. *Brain,* 1978, *101,* 635–648.

Goodman, D., & Kelso, J. A. S. Are movements prepared in parts? Not under compatible (naturalized) conditions. *Journal of Experimental Psychology: General,* 1980, *109,* 475–495.

Green, D. M. *Introduction to hearing.* Hillsdale, N.J.: Lawrence Erlbaum Associates, 1976.

Greenberg, G. Z., & Larkin, W. D. Frequency-response characteristic of auditory observers detecting signals of a single frequency in noise: The probe-signal method. *Journal of the Acoustic Society of America,* 1968, *44,* 1513–1523.

Greene, P. H. Problems of organization of motor systems. In R. Rosen and F. Snell (Eds.), *Progress in theoretical biology Vol. 2.* New York: Academic Press, 1972.

Groen, G. J., & Parkman, J. M. A chronometric analysis of simple addition. *Psychological Review,* 1972, *79,* 329–343.

Grunewald, G., Grunewald-Zuberbier, E., Homberg, V., & Netz, J. Cerebral potentials during smooth goal-directed hand movements in right-handed and left-handed movements. *Pflugers Archives,* 1979, *381,* 39–46.

Gurfinkel, V. S., Kotz, Y. M., Krinskiy, V. I., Pal'tsev, E. I., Feldman, A. G., Tsetlin, M. L., & Shik, M. L. Concerning tuning before movement. In I. M. Gelfand (Ed.), *Models of the structural-functional organization of certain biological systems.* Cambridge: MIT Press, 1971.

Gyr, J., Willey, R., & Henry, A. Motor-sensory feedback and geometry of visual space: An attempted replication. *The Behavioral and Brain Sciences,* 1979, *2,* 59–94.

Halliday, R., Callaway, E., Rosenthal, J., & Naylor, H. The effects of methylphenidate dosage on the visual event related potential of hyperkinetic children. In D. Lehman and E. Callaway (Eds.), *Human evoked potentials: Applications and problems.* New York: Plenum Press, 1979.

Hansen, J. C., & Hillyard, S. A. Endogenous brain potentials associated with selective auditory attention. *Electroencephalography and Clinical Neurophysiology,* 1980, *49,* 277–290.

Harter, M. R., & Previc, F. H. Size-specific information channels and selective attention: Visual evoked potential and behavioral measures. *Electroencephalography and Clinical Neurophysiology,* 1978, *45,* 628–640.

Harter, M. R., Previc, F. H., & Towle, V. L. Evoked potential indicants of size and orientation-specific information processing: Feature-specific sensory channels and attention. In D. Lehmann and E. Callaway (Eds.), *Human evoked potentials: Applications and problems.* New York: Plenum Press, 1979, 169–184.

Harter, M. R., Towle, V. L., & Musso, M. F. Size specificity and interocular suppression: Monocular evoked potentials and reaction times. *Vision Research,* 1976, *16,* 1111–1117.

Heffley, E., Wickens, C., & Donchin, E. Intramodality selective attention and P300-reexamination in a visual monitoring task (abstract). *Psychophysiology,* 1978, *15,* 269–270.

Heilman, K. M., & Watson, R. T. Mechanisms underlying the unilateral neglect syndrome. In D. A. Weinstein and R. P. Friedland (Eds.), *Hemi-inattention and hemisphere specialization.* New York: Raven Press, 1977.

Hellige, J. Visual laterality and cerebral hemisphere specialization: Methodological and theoretical considerations. In J. B. Sidowski (Ed.), *Conditioning, cognition, and methodology: Contemporary issues in experimental psychology.* Hillsdale, N.J.: Lawrence Erlbaum Associates, in press.

Henry, F. M., & Rogers, D. E. Increased response latency for complicated movements and a "memory-drum" theory of neuromotor reaction. *Research Quarterly,* 1960, *31,* 448–458.

Hillyard, S. A., Hink, R. F., Schwent, V. L., & Picton, T. W. Electrical signs of selective attention in the human brain. *Science,* 1973, *182,* 177–180.

Hillyard, S. A., & Picton, T. W. Event-related brain potentials and selective information processing in man. In J. Desmedt (Ed.), *Progress in clinical neurophysiology Vol. 6. Cognitive components in cerebral event-related potentials and selective attention.* Basel: Karger, 1979, 1–52.

Hillyard, S. A., Picton, T. W., & Regan, D. M. Sensation, perception and attention: Analysis using ERPs. In E. Callaway, P. Tueting, and S. Koslow (Eds.), *Event-related brain potentials in man.* New York: Academic Press, 1978, 223–322.

Hillyard, S. A., Squires, K. C., & Squires, N. K. The psychophysiology of attention. In D. Sheer (Ed.), *Attention: Theory, brain functions and clinical applications.* Hillsdale, N.J.: Lawrence Erlbaum Associates, in press.

Hillyard, S. A., & Woods, D. L. Electrophysiological analysis of human brain function. In M. S. Gazzaniga (Ed.), *Handbook of behavioral neurobiology. Vol. 2.* New York: Plenum, 1979, 345–378.

Hink, R. F., & Hillyard, S. A. Auditory evoked potentials during selective listening to dichotic speech messages. *Perception and Psychophysiology,* 1976, *20,* 236–242.

Hink, R. F., Hillyard, S. A., & Benson, P. J. Event-related brain potentials and selective attention to acoustic and phonetic cues. *Biological Psychology,* 1978, *6,* 1–16.

Hink, R. F., Van Voorhis, S. T., Hillyard, S. A., & Smith, T. S. The division of attention and the human auditory evoked potential, *Neuropsychologia,* 1977, *15,* 597–605.

Horel, J. A. The neuroanatomy of amnesia. A critique of the hippocampal memory hypothesis. *Brain,* 1978, *101,* 403–445.

Horst, R., Johnson, R., Jr., & Donchin, E. Event-related brain potentials and subjective probability in a learning task. *Memory and Cognition,* 1980, *8,* 476–488.

Huang, C. M., & Buchwald, J. S. Interpretation of the vertex short-latency acoustic response:
A study of single neurons in the brain stem. *Brain Research,* 1977, *137,* 291–303.

Hubel, D. H., & Wiesel, T. N. Receptive fields, binocular interaction and functional architecture in the cat's visual cortex. *Journal of Physiology* (London), 1962, *160,* 106.

Huppert, F. A., & Piercy, M. Recognition memory in amnesic patients: A defect of acquisition?
Neuropsychologia, 1977, *15,* 643–652.

Jeffreys, D. A., & Axford, J. Source locations of pattern specific components of human EPs.
Experimental Brain Research, 1972, *116,* 1–40.

Jewett, D. L., & Williston, J. S. Auditory-evoked far fields averaged from the scalp of humans.
Brain, 1971, *94,* 681–696.

Johnson, R., Jr. Electrophysiological manifestations of decision making in a changing environment. (Doctoral dissertation, University of Illinois, 1979.) Dissertation Abstracts International, 40, 485B. (University Microfilms No. 79-15372.)

Johnson, R., Jr., & Donchin, E. Sequential expectancies and decision making in a changing environment: An electrophysiological approach. *Psychophysiology,* 1982, *19,* 183–200.

Jung, R. Comments on readiness potentials in: Key problems in the programming of movements. *Brain Research,* 1974, *71,* 552–555.

Kahneman, D. *Attention and effort.* Englewood Cliffs, N.J.: Prentice-Hall, 1973.

Karlin, L., & Kestenbaum, R. Effects of number of alternatives on the psychological refractory
period. *Quarterly Journal of Experimental Psychology,* 1968, *20,* 167–178.

Karlin, L., Martz, M., Brauth, S., & Mordkoff, A. Auditory evoked potentials, motor potentials and reaction time. *Electroencephalography and Clinical Neurophysiology,* 1971, *31,*
129–136.

Karlin, L., & Martz, M. Response probability and sensory evoked potentials. In S. Kornblum
(Ed.), *Attention and Performance IV.* New York: Academic Press, 1973, pp. 175–184.

Keele, S. W. *Attention and human performance.* Pacific Palisades, Calif.: Goodyear, 1973.

Keele, S. W., & Neill, W. T. Mechanisms of attention. In E. Carterette (Ed.), *Handbook of perception, Volume 9.* New York: Academic Press, 1978.

Kelso, J. A. S. Central and peripheral information in motor control. In J. King and W. W.
Spirduso (Eds.), *Motor control symposium.* Austin: University of Texas Press, 1975, pp.
101–114.

Kelso, J. A. S. Motor control mechanisms underlying human movement reproduction. *Journal
of Experimental Psychology: Human Perception and Performance,* 1977, *3,* 529–543 (a).

Kelso, J. A. S. Planning and efferent component in the coding of movement. *Journal of Motor
Behavior,* 1977, *9,* 33–47 (b).

Kelso, J. A. S. Motor sensory feedback formulations: Are we asking the right questions? *The
Behavioral and Brain Sciences,* 1979, *2,* 72–73.

Kelso, J. A. S., Holt, K. G., Kugler, P. N., & Turvey, M. T. Coordinative structures as dissipative structures. II. Empirical lines of convergence. In G. E. Stelmach and J. Requin (Eds.), *Tutorials in motor behavior.* Amsterdam: North-Holland, 1980.

Kelso, J. A. S., Southard, D. L., & Goodman, D. On the nature of interlimb coordination. *Science,* 1979, *203,* 1029–1031.

Kelso, J. A. S., & Stelmach, G. E. Central and peripheral mechanisms in motor control. In G.
E. Stelmach (Ed.), *Motor control: Issues and trends.* New York: Academic Press, 1976.

Kelso, J. A. S., & Tuller, B. Toward a theory of apractic syndromes. *Brain and Language,* 1981,
12, 224–245.

Kelso, J. A. S., & Wallace, S. A. Conscious mechanisms in movement. In G. E. Stelmach (Ed.),
Information processing in motor learning and control. New York: Academic Press, 1978.

Keren, G. Some considerations of two alleged kinds of selective attention. *Journal of Experimental Psychology: General,* 1976, *105,* 349–374.

Kerkhof, G. A. Decision latency: The P3 component in auditory signal detection. *Neuroscience Letters,* 1978, *8,* 289–294.

Kerr, B. Evaluating task factors that influence selection and preparation for voluntary movements. In G. E. Stelmach (Ed.), *Information processing in motor control and learning.* New York: Academic Press, 1978.

Kinsbourne, M. Cognitive deficit: Experimental analysis. In J. L. McGaugh (Ed.), *Psychobiology: Behavior from a biological perspective.* New York: Academic Press, 1971.

Kinsbourne, M. (Ed.). *Asymmetrical function of the brain.* Cambridge: Cambridge University Press, 1978.

Kirsner, K. Naming latency facilitation: An analysis of the encoding component in reaction time. *Journal of Experimental Psychology,* 1972, *95,* 171–176.

Kok, A. The effect of warning stimulus novelty on the P300 and components of the contingent negative variation. *Biological Psychology,* 1978, *6,* 219–233.

Kornhuber, H. H., & Deecke, L. Hirnpotentialanderungen be: Wilkurbewegungen und passiven Bewegungen des Menschen: Bereitschaftspotential und reafferente Potentiale. *Pflugers Archives ges. Physiol.,* 1964, *284,* 1–17.

Kosslyn, S. Scanning visual images: Some structural implications. *Perception & Psychophysics,* 1973, *14,* 90–94.

Kots, Y. M. *The organization of voluntary movement.* New York: Plenum, 1977.

Kramer, A., & Donchin, E. A chronometric analysis of the role of orthographic and phonological cues in a non-lexical decision task, *Psychophysiology,* (Abstract), 1982.

Kugler, P. N., Kelso, J. A. S., & Turvey, M. T. On coordinative structures as dissipative structures. I. Theoretical lines of convergence. In G. E. Stelmach and J. Requin (Eds.), *Tutorials in motor behavior.* Amsterdam: North-Holland, 1980.

Kutas, M., & Donchin, E. Studies of squeezing: Handedness, responding hand, response force, and asymmetry of readiness potential. *Science,* 1974, *186,* 545–548.

Kutas, M., & Donchin, E. The effects of handedness, the responding hand, and response force on the contralateral dominance of the readiness potential. In J. Desmedt (Ed.), *Attention, voluntary contraction and event-related cerebral potentials. Progress in clinical neurophysiology Vol. 1.* Basel: Karger, 1977, pp. 189–210.

Kutas, M., & Hillyard, S. A. Reading senseless sentences: Brain potentials reflect semantic incongruity. *Science,* 1980, *207,* 203–205.

Kutas, M., McCarthy, G., & Donchin, E. Augmenting mental chronometry: The P300 as a measure of stimulus evaluation time. *Science,* 1977, *197,* 792–795.

LaBerge, D. H. Acquisition of automatic processing. In P. Rabbitt and S. Dornic (Eds.), *Attention and performance V.* London: Academic Press, 1975.

LaBerge, D. H., & Samuels, J. Toward a theory of automatic information processing in reading. *Cognitive Psychology,* 1974, *6,* 293–323.

Landau, W. N. Evoked potentials. In G. C. Quarton, T. Melnechuk and F. O. Schmitt (Eds.), *The neurosciences.* New York: Rockefeller University Press, 1967, 469–482.

Lappin, J. S. The relativity of choice behavior and the effect of prior knowledge on the speed and accuracy of recognition. In N. J. Castellan, Jr., and F. Restle (Eds.), *Cognitive theory* (Vol. 3). Hillsdale, N.J.: Lawrence Erlbaum Associates, 1978.

Lassen, N. A., Ingvar, D. H., & Skinhoje, E. Brain function and blood flow. *Scientific American,* 1978, *239,* 62–71.

Lee, W. A. Anticipatory control of postural and task muscles during rapid arm flexion. *Journal of Motor Behavior,* 1980, *12,* 185–196.

Levine, M. *A cognitive theory of learning.* Hillsdale, N.J.: Lawrence Erlbaum Associates, 1975.

Levy, J., & Trevarthen, C. Perceptual, semantic, and phonetic aspects of elementary language processes in split-brain patients. *Brain,* 1977, *100,* 105–118.

Lewis, J. Semantic processing of unattended messages during dichotic listening. *Journal of Experimental Psychology*, 1970, *85*, 225–228.

Lezak, M. D. *Neuropsychological assessment*. New York: Oxford University Press, 1983.

Lhermitte, F., & Signoret, J. L. The amnesic syndrome and the hippocampal-mammillary system. In M. R. Rosenzweig and E. L. Bennett (Eds.), *Neural mechanisms of learning and memory*. Cambridge, Mass.: MIT Press, 1976.

Libet, B., Wright, E. W., Jr., Feinstein, B., & Pearl, D. K. Subjective referral of the timing for a conscious sensory experience. A functional role for the somatosensory specific projection system in man. *Brain*, 1979, *102*, 193–224.

Lindsay, P. H., & Norman, D. A. (Eds.) *Human information processing: An introduction to psychology*. New York: Academic Press, 1972.

Lorente de No, R. *A study of nerve physiology (Part 2), 132*. New York: Rockefeller Institute, 1947.

Loveless, N. E., & Sanford, A. J. Slow potential correlates of preparatory set. *Biological Psychology*, 1974, *1*, 303–314.

Loveless, N. E., & Sanford, A. J. The impact of warning signal intensity on reaction time and components of the contingent negative variation. *Biological Psychology*, 1975, *2*, 217–226.

Low, M. D., Borda, R. P., Frost, J. D., Jr., & Kellaway, P. Surface-negative slow potential shift associated with conditioning in man. *Neurology*, 1966, *16*, 771–782.

MacKay, D. G. Aspects of the theory of comprehension, memory and attention. *Quarterly Journal of Experimental Psychology*, 1973, *25*, 22–40.

MacNeilage, P. F., & MacNeilage, L. A. Central processes controlling speech production in sleep and waking. In F. J. McGuigan (Ed.), *The psychophysiology of thinking*. New York: Academic Press, 1973.

Maltzman, I., Harris, L., Ingram, E., & Wolff, F. F. A primacy effect in the orienting reflex to stimulus change. *Journal of Experimental Psychology*, 1971, *87*, 202–206.

Marcel, A. J., & Patterson, K. E. Word recognition and production: Reciprocity in clinical and normal studies. In J. Requin (Ed.), *Attention and performance VII*. Hillsdale, N.J.: Lawrence Erlbaum Associates, 1978.

Marsh, G. R. Age differences in evoked potential correlates of a memory scanning process. *Experimental Aging Research*, 1975, *1*, 3–16.

Marshall, J. C., & Newcombe, F. Patterns of paralexia: A psycholingustic approach. *Journal of Psycholinguistic Research*, 1973, *2*, 175–198.

McCarthy, G. The P300 and stages of human information processing: An additive factors study. Unpublished doctoral dissertation, University of Illinois, 1980.

McCarthy, G., & Donchin, E. The effects of temporal and event uncertainty in determining the waveforms of the auditory event related potential (ERP). *Psychophysiology*, 1976, *13*, 581–590.

McCarthy, G., & Donchin, E. Brain potentials associated with structural and functional visual matching. *Neuropsychologia*, 1978, *16*, 571–585.

McCarthy, G., & Donchin, E. Event-related potentials — Manifestations of cognitive activity. In F. Hoffmeister and C. Muller (Eds.), *Bayer-Symposium VII, Brain function in old age*. New York: Springer, 1979, 318–335.

McCarthy, G., & Donchin, E. A metric for thought: A comparison of P300 latency and reaction time. *Science*, 1981, *211*, 22–80.

McCarthy, G., Kutas, M., & Donchin, E. Detecting errors with P300 latency. Paper presented at the 18th Annual Meeting of the Society for Psychophysiological Research, Madison, Wisconsin, September 1978.

McClean, M. Variation in perioral reflex amplitude prior to lip muscle contraction for speech. *Journal of Speech and Hearing Research*, 1978, *21*, 276–284.

McClelland, J. L. On the time relations of mental processes: An examination of systems of processes in cascade. *Psychological Review,* 1979, *86,* 287–330.

McClelland, J. L., & Rumelhart, D. E. An interactive activation model of the effect of context in perception: Part I. *Psychological Review,* 1981, *88,* 375–407.

McLean, J. P., & Shulman, G. L. On the construction and maintenance of expectancies. *Quarterly Journal of Experimental Psychology,* 1978, *30,* 441–454.

McSherry, J. W., & Borda, R. P. The intracortical distribution of the CNV in rhesus monkey. *Electroencephalography and Clinical Neurophysiology,* 1973, *Suppl. 33,* 69–74.

Messick, D. M., & Rapoport, A. A comparison of two payoff functions on multiple-choice decision behavior. *Journal of Experimental Psychology,* 1965, *69,* 75–83.

Mesulam, M.-M. Tracing neural connections of human brain with selective silver impregnation. *Archives of Neurology,* 1979, *36,* 814–818.

Milner, B., Corkin, S., & Teuber, H.-L. Further analysis of the hippocampal amnesic syndrome: 14-year follow-up study of H. M. *Neuropsychologia,* 1968, *6,* 215–234.

Milner, B. A., Regan, D., & Heron, J. R. Theoretical models of the generation of steady state evoked potentials, their relation to neuroanatomy and their relevance to certain clinical problems. *Advances in Medicine and Biology,* 1972, *24,* 157–169.

Moray, N. A data base for theories of selective listening. In P. Rabbitt & S. Dornic (Eds.), *Attention and performance V.* New York: Academic Press, 1975, 119–136.

Morgan, C. T., & Stellar, E. *Physiological psychology.* New York: McGraw–Hill, 1950.

Moscovitch, M. Information processing and the cerebral hemispheres. In M. S. Gazzaniga (Ed.), *Handbook of behavioral neurobiology* (Vol. 2). New York: Plenum, 1979.

Moskowitz–Cook, A., & Sokol, S. Spatial and temporal interactions of pattern evoked potentials. *Vision Research,* 1980, *20,* 699–707.

Naatanen, R. Selective attention and evoked potentials in humans: A critical review. *Biological Psychology,* 1975, *2,* 237–307.

Naatanen, R., & Michie, P. T. Early selective attention effects on the evoked potential: A critical review and reinterpretation. *Biological Psychology,* 1979, *8,* 81–136.

Navon, D., & Gopher, D. On the economy of the human processing system: A model of multiple capacity. *Psychological Review,* 1979, *86,* 214–255.

Neafsey, E. J., Hull, C. D., & Buchwald, N. A. Preparation for movement in the cat. I. Unit activity in the cerebral cortex. *Electroencephalography and Clinical Neurophysiology,* 1978 (A and B),*44,* 706–713.

Neely, J. H. Semantic priming and retrieval from lexical memory: Evidence for facilitory and inhibitory processes. *Memory and Cognition,* 1976, *4,* 648–654.

Neely, J. H. Semantic priming and retrieval from lexical memory: The roles of inhibitionless spreading activation and limited capacity attention. *Journal of Experimental Psychology: General,* 1977, *106,* 226–254.

Nickerson, R. Intersensory facilitation of reaction time: Energy summation or preparatory enhancement? *Psychological Review,* 1973, *80,* 489–509.

Norman, D. A., & Bobrow, D. G. On data-limited and resource-limited processes. *Cognitive Psychology,* 1976, *7,* 44–64. (a)

Norman, D. A., & Bobrow, D. G. On the role of active memory processes in perception and cognition. In C. N. Cofer (Ed.), *The structure of human memory.* San Francisco: Freeman, 1976. (b)

Oscar-Berman, M. Hypothesis testing and focusing behavior during concept formation by amnesic Korsakoff patients. *Neuropsychologia,* 1973, *11,* 191–198.

Oscar-Berman, M. Commentary. In E. Callaway, P. Tueting, & S. H. Koslow (Eds.), *Event related brain potentials in man.* New York: Academic Press, 1978.

Oscar-Berman, M. Neuropsychological consequences of long-term chronic alcoholism. *American Scientist,* 1980, *68,* 410–419.

Oscar-Berman, M., & Gade, A. Electrodermal measures of arousal in humans with cortical or subcortical brain damage. In H. D. Kimmel, E. H. van Olst, and J. F. Orlebeke (Eds.), *The orienting reflex in humans.* Hillsdale, N.J.: Lawrence Erlbaum Associates, 1979.

Oscar-Berman, M., Goodglass, H., & Cherlow, D. G. Perceptual laterality and iconic recognition of visual materials by Korsakoff patients and normal adults. *Journal of Comparative and Physiological Psychology,* 1973, *82,* 316-321.

Oscar-Berman, M., Heyman, G. M., Bonner, R. T., & Ryder, J. Human neuropsychology: Some differences between Korsakoff and normal operant performance. *Psychology Research,* 1980, *41,* 235-247.

Oscar-Berman, M., Oberg, R. G. E., Zola-Morgan, S. M., & Bonner, R. T. Comparative neuropsychology and Korsakoff's syndrome. III. Delayed response, delayed alternation and DRL performance. *Neuropsychologia,* 1982, *20,* 187-201.

Oscar-Berman, M., Sahakian, B. J., & Wikmark, G. Spatial probability learning by alcoholic Korsakoff patients. *Journal of Experimental Psychology: Human Learning and Memory,* 1976, *2,* 215-222.

Oscar-Berman, M., & Samuels, I. Stimulus-preference and memory factors in Korsakoff's syndrome. *Neuropsychologia,* 1976, *15,* 99-106.

Oscar-Berman, M., & Zola-Morgan, S. M. Comparative neuropsychology and Korsakoff's syndrome. I. Spatial and visual reversal learning. *Neuropsychologia,* 1980, *18,* 499-512. (a)

Oscar-Berman, M., & Zola-Morgan, S. M. Comparative neuropsychology and Korsakoff's syndrome. II. Two-choice visual discrimination learning. *Neuropsychologia,* 1980, *18,* 513-526. (b)

Ostry, D., Moray, N., & Mark, G. Tension practice and semantic targets. *Journal of Experimental Psychology: Human Perception and Performance,* 1976, *2,* 326-336.

Palmer, S. E. Visual perception and world knowledge: Notes on model of sensory-cognitive interaction. In D. A. Norman, D. E. Rumelhart, & the LNR Research Group (Eds.), *Explorations in cognition.* San Francisco: Freeman, 1975.

Palmer, S. E. Fundamental aspects of cognitive representation. In E. Rosch & B. Lloyd (Eds.), *Cognition and categorization.* Hillsdale, N.J.: Lawrence Erlbaum Associates, 1978.

Parasuraman, R. Auditory evoked potentials and divided attention. *Psychophysiology,* 1978, *15,* 460-465.

Parkman, J. M., & Groen, G. J. Temporal aspects of simple addition and comparison. *Journal of Experimental Psychology,* 1971, *89,* 333-342.

Peterson, L. R., & Peterson, M. J. Short-term retention of individual verbal items. *Journal of Experimental Psychology,* 1959, *58,* 193-198.

Pfefferbaum, A., Horvath, T. B., Roth, W. T., & Kopell, B. S. Event-related potential changes in chronic alcoholics. *Electroencephalography and Clinical Neurophysiology,* 1979, *47,* 637-647.

Picton, T. W., Campbell, K. B., Baribeau-Braun, J., & Proulx, G. B. The neurophysiology of human attention: A tutorial review. In J. Requin (Ed.), *Attention and performance VII.* Hillsdale, N.J.: Lawrence Erlbaum Associates, 1978, 429-467.

Picton, T. W., & Hillyard, S. A. Human auditory evoked potentials. II. Effects of attention. *Electroencephalography and Clinical Neurophysiology,* 1974, *36,* 191-200.

Picton, T. W., Hillyard, S. A., & Galambos, R. Habituation and attention in the auditory system. In W. D. Keidel & W. D. Neff (Eds.), *Handbook of sensory physiology, Vol. 3: Auditory system; clinical and special topics.* New York: Springer, 1976, 343-390. (a)

Picton, T. W., Hillyard, S. A., & Galambos, R. Habituation and attention in the auditory system. In W. D. Keidel & W. D. Neff (Eds.), *Handbook of sensory physiology, Vol. 5: Auditory system, Part 3; clinical and special topics.* Berlin: Springer, 1976, 345-389. (b)

Polich, J. M., McCarthy, G., Wang, W. S., & Donchin, E. When words collide: Orthographic and phonological interference during word processing. *Biological Psychology,* 1983, *16,* 155-180.

Posner, M. I. *Chronometric exploration of mind.* Hillsdale, N.J.: Lawrence Erlbaum Associates, 1978.

Posner, M. I. Orienting of attention. *Quarterly Journal of Experimental Psychology,* 1980, *32,* 3–25.

Posner, M. I., & Boies, S. J. Components of attention. *Psychological Review,* 1971, *78,* 391–408.

Posner, M. I., Klein, R., Summers, J., & Buggie, S. On the selection of signals. *Memory and Cognition,* 1973, *1,* 2–12.

Posner, M. I., Nissen, M. J., & Ogden, W. C. Attended and unattended processing modes: The role of set for spatial location. In H. L. Pick and I. J. Saltzman (Eds.), *Modes of perceiving and processing information.* Hillsdale, N.J.: Lawrence Erlbaum Associates, 1978.

Posner, M. I., & Snyder, C. R. R. Attention and cognitive control. In R. Solso (Ed.), *Information processing and cognition: The Loyola symposium.* Potomac, Md.: Lawrence Erlbaum Associates, 1975.

Rabbitt, P. Some experiments and a model for changes in attentional selectivity with old age. In F. Hoffmeister & C. Muller (Eds.), *Brain function in old age.* Berlin: Springer, 1979, 82–94.

Ransom, B. R., & Goldring, S. Slow hyperpolarization in cells presumed to be glia in cerebral cortex of cat. *Journal of Neurophysiology,* 1973, *36,* 879–892.

Rapoport, J. L., Buchsbaum, M. S., Zahn, T. P., Weingarten, H., Ludlow, C., & Mikkelsen, E. J. Dextroamphetamine: Cognitive and behavioral effects in normal prepubertal boys. *Science,* 1978, *199,* 560–563.

Regan, D. Objective method of measuring the relative spectral luminosity curve in man. *Journal of the Optical Society of America,* 1970, *60,* 856–859.

Regan, D. *Evoked potentials in psychology, sensory physiology and clinical medicine.* London: Chapman & Hall; New York: Wiley, 1972.

Regan, D. Colour coding of pattern responses in man investigated by evoked potential feedback and direct plot techniques. *Vision Research,* 1975, *15,* 175–183. (a)

Regan, D. Recent advances in electrical recording from the human brain. *Nature,* 1975, *253,* 401–407. (b)

Regan, D. Steady state evoked potentials. Proc. Symp. Electrophysiol. Techniques in Man. *Journal of Optical Society of America,* 1977, *67,* 1475–1489.

Regan, D. Assessment of visual acuity by evoked potential recording: Ambiguity caused by temporal dependence of spatial frequency selectivity. *Vision Research,* 1978, *18,* 439–443.

Regan, D. Electrical responses evoked from the human brain. *Scientific American,* 1979, *241,* 134–146.

Regan, D. Evoked potential studies of visual perception. *Canadian Journal of Psychology,* 1981, *35,* 77–112.

Regan, D., & Beverley, K. I. Electrophysiological evidence for the existence of neurones sensitive to the direction of depth movement. *Nature,* 1973, *246,* 504–506.

Regan, D., Beverley, K. I., & Cynader, M. The visual perception of motion in depth. *Scientific American,* 1979, *241,* 136–151.

Regan, D., Schellart, N. A. M., Spekreijse, H., & van den Berg, T. J. T. P. Photometry in goldfish by electrophysiological recording. *Vision Research,* 1975, *15,* 799–807.

Regan, D., & Spekreijse, H. Electrophysiological correlate of binocular depth perception in man. *Nature,* 1970, *255,* 92–94.

Requin, J. Toward a psychobiology of preparation for action. In G. E. Stelmach & J. Requin (Eds.), *Tutorial in motor behavior.* Amsterdam: North-Holland, 1980.

Ritter, W., Rotkin, L., & Vaughan, H. G., Jr. The modality specificity of the slow negative wave. *Psychophysiology,* 1980, *17,* 222–227.

Ritter, W., Simson, R., & Vaughan, H. G., Jr. Association cortex potentials and reaction time in auditory discrimination. *Electroencephalography and Clinical Neurophysiology,* 1972, *33,* 547–555.

Ritter, W., Simson, R., Vaughan, H. G., & Friedman, D. A brain event related to the making of a sensory discrimination. *Science,* 1979, *203,* 1358–1361.

Roberts, T. D. M. *Neurophysiology of postural mechanisms.* New York: Plenum, 1967.

Rohrbaugh, J. W., Syndulko, K., & Lindsley, D. B. Brain wave components of the contingent negative variation in humans. *Science,* 1976, *191,* 1055-1057.

Rohrbaugh, J. W., Syndulko, K., & Lindsley, D. B. Cortical slow negative waves following non-paired stimuli: Effects of task factors. *Electroencephalography and Clinical Neurophysiology,* 1978, *45,* 551-567.

Rohrbaugh, J. W., Syndulko, K., & Lindsley, D. B. Cortical slow negative waves following non-paired stimuli: Effects of modality, intensity and rate of stimulation. *Electroencephalography and Clinical Neurophysiology,* 1979, *46,* 416-427.

Roland, P. E. Sensory feedback to the cerebral cortex during voluntary movement in man. With commentary. *Behavioral Brain Science,* 1978, *1,* 129-171.

Rosenbaum, D. A. Human movement initiation: Selection of arm, direction and extent. *Journal of Experimental Psychology: General,* 1980, *109,* 444-474.

Rosner, B. S., & Goff, W. R. Electrical responses of the nervous system and subjective scales of intensity. In W. D. Neff (Ed.), *Contributions to sensory physiology, Vol. 2.* New York: Academic Press, 1967, 169-221.

Roth, W. T., Ford, J. M., & Kopell, B. S. Long-latency evoked potentials and reaction time. *Psychophysiology,* 1978, *15,* 17-23.

Rowland, V., & Anderson, R. Brain steady potential shifts. *Progress in Physiological Psychology,* 1971, *5,* 37-51.

Roy, E. A. An assessment of the role of preselection in memory for movement extent. Ph.D. Dissertation, University of Waterloo, 1976.

Roy, E. A., & Diewert, G. L. Encoding of kinesthetic extent information. *Perception and Psychophysics,* 1975, *17,* 559-564.

Roy, E. A., & Williams, I. D. Memory for location and extent: The influence of reduction of joint feedback information. In K. M. Newell and G. C. Roberts (Eds.), *Psychology of motor behavior and sport.* Champaign, Ill.: Human Kinetics, 1979.

Ruchkin, D. S., & Sutton, S. Equivocation and P300 amplitude. In D. Otto (Ed.), *Multidisciplinary perspectives in event-related brain potential research.* U.S. Environmental Protection Agency EPA-600/9-77-043.

Rumelhart, D. E., & McClelland, J. L. An interactive activation model of the effect of context in perception: Part II. *Psychological Review,* 1982, *89,* 60-94.

Sasanuma, S., & Fujimura, O. Selective impairment of phonetic and nonphonetic transcription of words in Japanese aphasic patients: Kana vs. Kanji in visual recognition and writing. *Cortex,* 1971, *7,* 1-18.

Schlag, J. Generation of brain evoked potentials. In R. F. Thompson and M. M. Patterson (Eds.), *Bioelectric recording techniques. Part A. Cellular processes and brain potentials.* New York: Academic Press, 1973, 273-316.

Schmidt, R. A. A schema theory of discrete motor skill learning. *Psychological Review,* 1975, *82,* 225-260.

Schvaneveldt, R. W., & McDonald, J. E. Semantic context and the encoding of words: Evidence for two modes of encoding. *Journal of Experimental Psychology: Human Perception and Performance,* 1981, *7,* 673-687.

Schvaneveldt, R. W., Meyer, D. E., & Becker, C. A. Lexical ambiguity, semantic context, and visual word recognition. *Journal of Experimental Psychology: Human Perception and Performance,* 1976, *2,* 243-256.

Schwent, V. L., Hillyard, S. A., & Galambos, R. Selective attention and the auditory vertex potential. Effects of stimulus delivery rate. *Electroencephalography and Clinical Neurophysiology,* 1976, *40,* 604-614.

Schwent, V. L., Snyder, E., & Hillyard, S. A. Auditory evoked potentials during multichannel selective listening: Role of pitch and localization cues. *Journal of Experimental Psychology: Human Perception and Performance,* 1976, *2,* 313-325.

Shafer, G. *A mathematical theory of evidence*. Princeton, N.J.: Princeton University Press, 1976.

Shepard, R. N. Form, formation, and transformation of internal representations. In R. L. Solso (Ed.), *Information processing and cognition: The Loyola symposium*. Potomac, Md.: Lawrence Erlbaum Associates, 1975.

Shibasaki, H., & Kato, M. Movement-associated control potentials with unilateral and bilateral simultaneous hand movement. *Journal of Neurology*, 1975, *208*, 191–199.

Shiffrin, R. M., & Gardner, G. T. Visual processing capacity and attentional control. *Journal of Experimental Psychology*, 1972, *93*, 73–82.

Shiffrin, R. M., McKay, D. P., & Shaffer, W. O. Attending to forty-nine spatial positions at once. *Journal of Experimental Psychology: Human Perception and Performance*, 1976, *2:1*, 14–22.

Shiffrin, R. M., & Schneider, W. Controlled and automatic human information processing: II. Perceptual learning, automatic attending, and a general theory. *Psychological Review*, 1977, *86*, 127–190.

Shulman, G. L., Remington, R. W., & McLean, J. P. Moving attention through space. *Journal of Experimental Psychology: Human Perception and Performance*, 1979, *5*, 522–526.

Silverberg, R., Gordon, H. W., Pollack, S., & Bentin, S. Shift of visual field preference for Hebrew words in native speakers learning to read. *Brain and Language*, 1980, *11*, 99–105.

Simson, R., Vaughan, H. G., & Ritter, W. The scalp topography of potentials in auditory and visual discrimination tasks. *Electroencephalography and Clinical Neurophysiology*, 1977, *42*, 528–535. (a)

Simson, R., Vaughan, H. G., & Ritter, W. The scalp topography of potentials in auditory and visual Go/No Go tasks. *Electroencephalography and Clinical Neurophysiology*, 1977, *43*, 864–875. (b)

Singer, M., Chase, W. G., Young, R. M., & Clark, H. H. Practice effects in the comparison of sentences and pictures. Paper presented at the meeting of the Midwestern Psychological Association, Detroit, May 1971.

Snyder, E., Hillyard, S. A., & Galambos, R. Similarities and differences among the P3 waves to detected signals in three modalities. *Psychophysiology*, 1980, *17*, 112–122.

Somjen, G. G. Electrogenesis of sustained potentials. *Progress in Neurobiology*, 1973, *1*, 199–237.

Spear, P. D. Behavioral and neurophysiological consequences of visual cortex damage: Mechanisms of recovery. In J. M. Sprague and A. N. Epstein (Eds.), *Progress in psychobiology and physiological psychology*, Vol. 8. New York: Academic Press, 1979, 45–89.

Spekreijse, H., van der Tweel, L., & Regan, D. Interocular sustained suppression: Correlations with evoked potential amplitude and distribution. *Vision Research*, 1972, *12*, 521.

Spekreijse, H., van der Tweel, L. H., & Zuidema, T. Contrast evoked responses in man. *Vision Research*, 1973, *13*, 1577–1601.

Sperry, R. W. Neurology and the mind–brain problem. *American Scientist*, 1952, *40*, 291–312.

Sperry, R. W. Cerebral organization and behavior. *Science*, 1961, *133*, 1749–1756.

Sperry, R. W., & Gazzaniga, M. S. Language following surgical disconnection of the hemispheres. In F. L. Darley (Ed.), *Brain mechanisms underlying speech and language*. New York: Grune and Stratton, 1967.

Squires, K. C., Donchin, E., Herning, R. I., & McCarthy, G. On the influence of task relevance and stimulus probability on event-related potential components. *Electroencephalography and Clinical Neurophysiology*, 1977, *42*, 1–14.

Squires, K. C., Hillyard, S. A., & Lindsay, P. H. Cortical potentials evoked by feedback confirming and disconfirming an auditory discrimination. *Perception and Psychophysics*, 1973, *13*, 25–31. (a)

Squires, K. C., Hillyard, S. A., & Lindsay, P. H. Vertex potentials evoked during auditory signal detection: Relation to decision criteria. *Perception and Psychophysics,* 1973, *14,* 265-272. (b)

Squires, K. C., Squires, N. K., & Hillyard, S. A. Decision-related cortical potentials during an auditory signal detection task with cued observation intervals. *Journal of Experimental Psychology: Human Perception and Performance,* 1975, *104,* 268-279.

Squires, K. C., Wickens, C., Squires, N. K., & Donchin, E. The effect of stimulus sequence on the waveform of the cortical event-related potential. *Science,* 1976, *193,* 1142-1146.

Squires, N. K., Donchin, E., Squires, K. C., & Grossberg, S. Bisensory stimulation: Inferring decision-related processes from P300 component. *Journal of Experimental Psychology: Human Perception and Performance,* 1977, *3,* 299-315.

Starr, A. & Achor, L. J. Anatomical and physiological origins of auditory brain stem responses (ABR). In D. Lehmann and E. Callaway (Eds.), *Human evoked potentials: Applications and problems.* New York: Plenum, 1979, 415-429.

Sternberg, S. High-speed scanning in human memory. *Science,* 1966, *153,* 652-654.

Sternberg, S. Two operations in character-recognition: Some evidence from reaction-time measurements. *Perception and Psychophysics,* 1967, *2,* 45-53.

Sternberg, S. The discovery of processing stages: Extensions of Donders' method. In W. G. Koster (Ed.), *Attention and performance II.* Amsterdam: North-Holland, 1969.

Sternberg, S., Monsell, S., Knoll, R. L., & Wright, C. E. The latency and duration of rapid movement sequences: Comparisons of speech and typewriting. In G. E. Stelmach (Ed.), *Information processing in motor control and learning.* New York: Academic Press, 1978.

Stuss, D. T., & Picton, T. W. Neurophysiological correlates of human concept formation. *Behavioral Biology,* 1978, *23,* 135-162.

Sutton, S., Braren, J., Zubin, J., & John, E. R. Information delivery and the sensory evoked potential. *Science,* 1967, *155,* 14-36.

Swett, J. E., & Bourassa, C. M. Comparison of sensory discrimination thresholds with muscle and cutaneous nerve volleys in the cat. *Journal of Neurophysiology,* 1967, *30,* 530-545.

Talland, G. A. *Deranged memory.* New York: Academic Press, 1965.

Teuber, H. L. Key problems in the programming of movements. *Brain Research,* 1974, *71,* 533-568.

Timsit-Berthier, M., Dehaunoy, J., & Gerono, A. Morphological analyses of the CNV in psychiatry. Comparison of resolution, mode and cumulative curve methods. In D. A. Otto (Ed.), *Multidisciplinary perspectives in event related brain potential research.* (EPA-600/9-77-043), U.S. Environmental Protection Agency, Washington, D.C., December 1978, pp. 389-591.

Treisman, A. Strategies and models of selective attention. *Psychological Review,* 1969, *76,* 282-299.

Treisman, A. The psychological reality of levels of processing. In L. S. Cermak & F. I. M. Craik (Eds.), *Levels of processing and human memory.* Hillsdale, N.J.: Lawrence Erlbaum Associates, 1979.

Treisman, A., & Gelade, G. A feature-integration theory of attention. *Cognitive Psychology,* 1980, *12,* 97-136.

Treisman, A., Squire, R., & Green, J. Semantic processing in dichotic listening. *Memory and Cognition,* 1974, *2,* 641-649.

Treisman, A., Sykes, M., & Gelade, G. Selelctive attention and stimulus integration. In S. Dornic (Ed.), *Attention and performance VI.* Hillsdale, N.J.: Lawrence Erlbaum Associates, 1977.

Tueting, P., Sutton, S., & Zubin, J. Quantitative evoked potential correlates of the probability of events. *Psychophysiology,* 1971, *7,* 385-394.

Tukey, J. W. A data analyst's comments on a variety of points and issues. In E. Callaway, P. Tueting, and S. H. Koslow (Eds.), *Event-related brain potentials in man.* New York: Academic Press, 1978, 139-151.

Turvey, M. T. On peripheral and central processes in vision: Inferences from an information-processing analysis of masking with patterned stimuli. *Psychological Review,* 1973, *80,* 1–52.

Turvey, M. T. Preliminaries to a theory of action with reference to vision. In R. Shaw and J. Bransford (Eds.), *Perceiving, acting, and knowing.* Hillsdale, N.J.: Lawrence Erlbaum Associates, 1977.

Turvey, M. T., Shaw, R. E., & Mace, W. Issues in the theory of action. In J. Requin (Ed.), *Attention and performance VII.* Hillsdale, N.J.: Lawrence Erlbaum Associates, 1978.

van der Tweel, L. H., & Spekreijse, H. Signal transport and rectification in the human evoked response system. *Annals of the N.Y. Academy of Sciences,* 1968, *156,* 678–695.

Van Voorhis, S., & Hillyard, S. A. Visual evoked potentials and selective attention to points in space. *Perception and Psychophysics,* 1977, *22,* 54–62.

Vaughan, H. G., Jr., Costa, L. D., & Ritter, W. Topography of the human motor potential. *Electroencephalography and Clinical Neurophysiology,* 1968, *25,* 1–10.

Walter, W. G. Slow potential waves in the human brain associated with expectancy, attention, and decision. *Archives fur Psychiatrie und Nervenkrankheiten,* 1964, *206,* 309–322.

Walter, W. G. Brain responses to semantic stimuli. *Journal of Psychosomatic Research,* 1965, *9,* 51–61.

Walter, W. G., Cooper, R., Aldridge, V. J., McCallum, W. C., & Winter, A. L. Contingent negative variation: An electric sign of sensori-motor association and expectancy in the human brain. *Nature,* 1964, *203,* 380–384.

Weerts, T. C., & Lang, P. J. The effects of eye fixation and stimulus and response location on the contingent negative variation (CNV). *Biological Psychology,* 1973, *1,* 1–19.

Weiskrantz, L. Trying to bridge some neurophysiological gaps between monkey and man. *British Journal of Psychology,* 1977, *68,* 431–445.

Weisstein, N. Beyond the yellow volkswagon detector and the grandmother cell: A general strategy for the exploration of operations in human pattern recognition. In R. Solso (Ed.), *Contemporary issues in cognitive psychology: The Loyola symposium.* Washington, D.C.: W.H. Winston & Sons, 1973.

Welford, A. The "psychological refractory period" and the timing of high-speed performance: A review and a theory. *British Journal of Psychology,* 1952, *43,* 2–19.

Wheatstone, C. Contributions to the physiology of vision. I. *Philosophical Transactions of the Royal Society,* 1838, *128,* 371–394.

Wheatstone, C. Contributions to the psychology of vision. II. *Philosophical Transactions of the Royal Society,* 1852, *142,* 1–18.

Wood, C. C., Allison, T., Goff, W. R., Williamson, P. D., & Spencer, D. D. On the neural origin of P300 in man. Presented at the 5th International Symposium on Electrical Potentials Related to Motivation, Motor, and Sensory Processes of the Brain, Ulm, West Germany, May 1979.

Wood, S. S., Resnick, L. B., & Groen, G. J. An experimental test of five process models for subtraction. *Journal of Educational Psychology,* 1975, *67,* 17–21.

Woods, D. L., Hillyard, S. A., Courchesne, E., & Galambos, R. Electrophysiological signs of split-second decision-making. *Science,* 1980, *25,* 655–657.

Woodworth, R. S. *Experimental psychology.* New York: Holt, 1938.

Woody, C. D. Characterization of an adaptive filter for the analysis of variable latency neuroelectric signals. *Medical and Biological Engineering,* 1967, *5,* 539–553.

Woolsey, C. N. Organization of somatic sensory and motor areas of the cerebral cortex. In H. F. Harlow and C. N. Woolsey (Eds.), *Biological and biochemical bases of behavior.* Madison: University of Wisconsin Press, 1958, 63–81.

Wurtz, R. H., & Mohler, C. W. Organization of monkey superior colliculus: Enhanced visual response of superficial layer cells. *Journal of Neurophysiology,* 1976, *39,* 745–765.

Young, R., & Chase, W. G. Additive stages in the comparison of sentences and pictures. Paper presented at the meeting of the Midwestern Psychological Association, Detroit, April 1971.

Young, T. An account of some cases of the production of colours. *Philosophical Transactions of the Royal Society,* 1802, *92,* 387–397.

Zaidel, E. A technique for presenting lateralized visual input with prolonged exposure. *Vision Research,* 1975, *15,* 283–289.

Zaidel, E. Concepts of cerebral dominance in the split brain. In P. Buser and A. Rougeul-Buser (Eds.), *Cerebral correlates of conscious experience.* Amsterdam: Elsevier, 1978. (a)

Zaidel, E. Lexical organization in the right hemisphere. In P. Buser & A. Rougeul-Buser (Eds.), *Cerebral correlates of conscious experience.* Amsterdam: Elsevier, 1978. (b)

Zaidel, E. On measuring hemispheric specialization in man. In B. Rybak (Ed.), *Advanced technobiology.* Proceedings of the NATO-ASI, Paris, June 27–July 13, 1978. Sijthoff Noordhoff Alphen Aan Ben Rejn, 1979, 365–404.

Zaidel, E. Reading by the disconnected right hemisphere: An aphasiological perspective. In Y. Zotterman (Ed.), *Dyslexia: Neuronal, cognitive and linguistic aspects.* Wenner-Gren Symposium Series, Vol. 35. Oxford: Hurdleman Press, 1982, 67–91.

Zaidel, E., & Peters, A. M. Phonological encoding and ideographic reading by the disconnected right hemispheres: Two case studies. *Brain and Language,* 1981, *14,* 205–234.

Author Index

415

Subject Index

421